Theories
Of
Personality

RICHARD M. RYCKMAN
University of Maine

D. VAN NOSTRAND COMPANY
New York   Cincinnati   Toronto   London   Melbourne

DVN Series In Psychology
Series Advisor: Stephen Worchel

D. Van Nostrand Company Regional Offices:
New York   Cincinnati

D. Van Nostrand Company International Offices:
London   Toronto   Melbourne

Copyright © 1978 by Litton Educational Publishing, Inc.

Library of Congress Catalog Card Number 77-81475
ISBN: 0-442-27107-7

Published by D. Van Nostrand Company
135 West 50th Street, New York, N. Y. 10020

10 9 8 7 6 5 4 3 2

To Leona, Bobby, and Mark

Preface

THEORIES OF PERSONALITY has the primary purposes of reviewing basic concepts and principles of the major theories of personality and of assessing how well they meet criteria for judging the scientific worth of a theory. The material is presented in a clear and accessible manner for undergraduates who have had little or no exposure to the field of personality psychology.

The text is written with minimal use of technical terminology. I have included examples from everyday life, an extensive glossary at the end of each chapter, and unusual topics to attract student interest.

Each major theoretical position is introduced by an objective overview, on the assumption that students should focus first on the theorist's basic concepts and propositions. Comparisons of the theorists follow more easily from this foundation.

I would like to express my appreciation to the many people who played a role in the preparation of the book. My thanks to my publisher, Judith R. Joseph, for her guidance, patience, and consideration, to my editor, Harriet Serenkin, for her skillful processing of the text material, and to Bernard Gorman and Stephen Worchel for their insights and detailed comments on the chapters. I owe a debt to my colleagues Joel Gold, Gordon Kulberg, and Alan Stubbs for their constructive comments on specific chapters and to my students Denise M. C. Carrier, Michael Robbins, Gayle Surrette, and John Sutton, for their help. I also want to express my appreciation to the many students enrolled in my courses during the past ten years. They have helped me tremendously by their provocative questioning and substantive comments on many of the theories. The chairman of the psychology department, Roger B. Frey, generously provided the financial assistance and secretarial help necessary to complete the book.

Lastly, I thank my parents, my brothers and sister, and my relatives, most notably, my Uncle Lawrence, for their continual encouragement. To my wife, Leona, I am especially grateful. She not only provided me with a healthy writing environment but also contributed many ideas that were incorporated into the text.

Organization of
The Book

THEORIES OF PERSONALITY is divided into eight parts. Part 1, An Introduction to the Discipline, addresses itself to the problem of establishing an acceptable definition of personality and to the reasons for studying individual differences from a scientific stance. It provides the reader with basic information concering the scientific process and the interrelatedness of theory and research. It also lists the criteria by which scientists judge the worth of a theory so that the student will be able to evaluate the theoretical perspectives reviewed in succeeding chapters. Evaluation of each theory in terms of how well it meets these standards is provided near the end of each chapter in a Critical Comments section.

Part 2, Psychoanlytic and Neo-analytic Perspectives, reviews the seminal contributions of Freud and his psychoanalytic theory and the personality theories of neo-analytic theorists Jung, Adler, and Fromm. The decision to include only Jung, Adler, and Fromm was a difficult one. Jung and Adler are included because their views of personality represent, in many respects, significant and original departures from Freud's position. Fromm is included because his view of personality, with its strong elements of existentialism and humanistic psychology, also moves considerably beyond the Freudian viewpoint.

My choices in this and other chapters may be at variance with the views of some instructors. I have therefore included a suggested readings list at the end of each chapter so that instructors may substitute or add other materials.

Part 3, Trait Perspectives, covers the major trait theories of Allport and Cattell. The Allport chapter includes a discussion of the contemporary humanistic psychology movement and his devotion to the construction of a psychology of personality which focuses on the uniqueness of the individual.

The chapter on Cattell's factor analytic position shows that theorist's commitment to the establishment of a personality theory based upon sound measurement principles and procedures. It provides students with an introduction to factor analysis so that they can appreciate Cattell's use of the technique in his discovery of the major source traits of personality.

Part 4, Cognitive Perspectives, reviews the fundamental philosophical assumption underlying Kelly's theory. It then deals with the basic concepts, postulates, and corollaries of the theory. The chapter also describes Kelly's Role Construct Repertory Test, as assessment procedure designed to measure the personal construct systems of individuals, and discusses its use in therapy to appraise client experience.

Part 5, Social-Behavioristic Perspectives, discusses the theories of Skinner, Rotter, and Bandura. The chapter on Skinner stresses recent changes in his thinking about the role of cognition and his willingness to incorporate cognitive constructs into his system. The Rotter chapter discusses his neo-Hullian model and shows how cognitive processes are involved in the study of personality. The basic concepts of the theory are examined and their usage for the understanding of adjusted and maladjusted behavior is considered. Some of the recent research evidence for Rotter's locus of control construct is reviewed.

The chapter on Bandura discusses the basic assumptions underlying his social learning theory and the reasons for his reliance on observational learning to account for individual differences. The highlight of the chapter is the presentation of research studies that show how modeling principles can be used to help us understand the acquisition, maintenance, and modification of aggressive behavior.

Part 6, Humanistic-Existential Perspectives, covers the positions of Rogers, Maslow, and Rollo May. The first point of emphasis in the Rogers chapter is the emergence of a theory of personality development from his clinical experiences. This discussion leads to an analysis of his organismic wisdom hypothesis, a central conception in his theory as well as in Maslow's. The second focus is on the application of Rogers' ideas to education.

For Maslow, I have presented his hierarcy of needs scheme and a discussion of the possible dangers of B-cognizing in order to make the important point that, as Maslow conceptualized it, the self-actualizing process involves the integration of both D- and B-needs. Many students tend to think of the process as a progressive overcoming and elimination of the basic needs as one moves toward actualization. This chapter also includes a discussion of the characteristics of self-actualizing people, along with comments about their imperfections. As Maslow pointed cut, all too often people have the misconception that self-actualizers are godlike individuals with no flaws. The text discussion of their limitations will, I hope, remedy this misconception.

The chapter on May begins with a definition of existentialism and a survey of its roots in European philosophy. It shows that the existentialists were and are disenchanted with our present views of science and how they hope to revise it in order to study issues more closely related to major concerns of human existence. In order that the reader understand May's position, some of the similarities and dissimilarities between existentialism and psychoanalysis are examined, and the major concepts and principles in May's approach are given.

Part 7, Constitutional Perspectives, reviews a Sheldon's classic work on somatotyping. The review highlights his concern with the liberal-environmentalist bias in contemporary psychology and his attempts to correct it by developing a biological theory of personality. Although contemporary personality psychologists pay homage to the role played by biology in determining behavior, in practice they have tended to ignore its contribution. As a result, we know very little about the ways in which genetic factors influence individual behavior. I hope these materials will make students aware of the fact that concern with the biological determinants of personality is by no means a dead issue.

Part 8, The Future of Personality Psychology, reviews some of the basic issues confronting personality investigators in their attempts to create a new and unified image of the person. Chapter 16, "New Directions in the Discipline: Mischel's Proposal," describes a tentative model of personality which Mischel hopes will contribute to our understanding of personality functioning and will point out new directions for the field. The strengths of his model are reviewed, and criticisms of it by leading personality psychologists are presented.

Contents

PART $\mathcal{I}$

AN INTRODUCTION TO THE DISCIPLINE

D espite the universal and eternal appeal of studying and understanding human personality, there is as yet no single, integrated, and systematic theory of personality that provides a set of valid explanations to account for individual differences in behavior. Instead, there are almost as many definitions of personality as there are investigators in the discipline; there is also a large number of different, and often conflicting, theoretical perspectives. This state of affairs exists despite the fact that personality psychology has been blessed with an array of highly creative and original thinkers whose insights and theories are of immense value in helping us to understand personality functioning. But because the subject matter covered by these theorists is incredibly complicated and difficult to study, differences of opinion concerning how the discipline should be defined and studied inevitably emerged.

It is clear that the time has come for investigators to stop smiling indiscriminately on these positions and to begin making tentative judgments concerning their scientific worth and utility. There are some rumblings in this direction currently in personality psychology. The discipline is in a state of flux. A few investigators continue to make attempts to consolidate the contributions of the various theorists and to eliminate some of the weaknesses in their positions. These investigators are also making efforts to point out new directions for investigation to develop more adequate theory and research.

On what bases can these evaluative decisions be made? The answer to that question is relatively straightforward. Since all the theories reviewed here claim to be scientific in nature, they can all be judged in terms of how well they meet the standards ordinarily used by investigators to judge the worth of scientific theories and research. The materials in Chapter 1 involve a review and discussion of these criteria. They also include a discussion of the major concepts used in the construction of scientific theories and the major kinds of research strategies used to test them. Exposure to this basic information should enable the reader to evaluate the scientific utility of the theoretical positions presented in succeeding chapters.

Personality and the Scientific Outlook

HOW IS PERSONALITY DEFINED?

Virtually all of us are fascinated by and interested in knowing more about ourselves and other people. In our attempts at making sense of our experiences, we tend to engage in naive analyses of our own behavior and the actions of others many times each day. We wonder, for example, why one of our friends refuses to date a young man or woman we find particularly attractive. We are puzzled by the fellow student who is interested in learning all he can about physics, while we find it difficult to listen attentively to more than ten minutes of the professor's lecture on the topic. We are curious about the actions of a presidential assassin, and at a loss to explain why he and not countless others with similar or perhaps even greater frustrations and personal problems did not act. In a related way, we are sometimes frustrated in our attempts to explain why a quiet, unassuming person who is well-liked by neighbors and relatives suddenly decides to buy a high-powered rifle and snipe at unsuspecting and innocent passengers on a passing commuter train. Almost inevitably, his friends and relatives are quoted in the media as having expected such violence from any number of boys his own age in the neighborhood, but not from him.

In each of these instances, we are concerned with generating explanations for our observations. We want to know *why* these people behaved as they did. The answers to that general question are also sought by psychologists who work in the discipline of personality. In seeking explanations for individual differences in behavior, they construct theoretical systems that will account for a wide variety of behavior differences in many different situations. Their efforts are aimed at understanding human motivation and behavior throughout the entire developmental process. They range from attempts to gather information about individual differences in activity level at birth to the study of the attitudes of young and elderly people toward dying. It should be clear from this statement that the behavior under consideration is so vast and complex that no investigator, no matter how knowledgeable or creative, can study every aspect of it.

Each investigator therefore brings to the discipline his or her own particular perspective on the subject matter. In other words, investigators' own unique theoretical orientations guide their efforts. These perspectives range from Sheldon's almost total emphasis on the biological or inherited determinants of personality to Rotter's stress on the ways in which social learning experiences affect behavior. The upshot is that each investigator generates his or her own particular definition of personality, as well as working assumptions of the manner in which personality operates.

For the ordinary person, personality is often defined in terms of social attractiveness. The person with a "good" personality is one who impresses others with his or her ability to get along well with people. Beauty pageant contestants are typically judged on their physical attractiveness, talent, and "personality." Here the judgment of a good personality is based upon their popularity with judges and other contestants and upon their social poise and sophistication. Some students also talk about each other in these terms. Laura is said to have a "great" personality, which usually means that Laura behaves in ways that the perceivers find acceptable; Henry is said to have "no personality," which means that they find Henry's behavior highly objectionable. Personality is sometimes also treated as a consolation prize by students: Bob encourages Joe to date a "real dog" because she has a "great" personality or Jane encourages Linda to date an ugly male because he has a "really dynamite personality."

This definition of personality is inadequate in two major and unique respects. First, it limits the number and kinds of behavior considered worthy of incorporation into the investigation of personality. Second, it makes the absurd point that some individuals, who obviously have unique learning histories, are devoid of personality. There are also a number of other deficiencies in the definition, including its inattention to the unique ways an individual's experiences are organized and its neglect of biological contributions to behavior. Of course, these criticisms also apply to many of the definitions of personality offered by investigators in the area.

Despite the plethora of definitions, there is some basic agreement among investigators that personality is a hypothetical construct; that is, it is an abstraction which refers to an internal, *mediating* state of the individual. This state includes the person's unique learning history and biological propensities and the ways in which these organized complexes of events influence his or her responses to certain stimuli in the environment. Thus, personality is seen by many investigators as the scientific study of individual differences in thought and behavior that occur under given situational circumstances. It also involves the similarities between individuals in thought and behavior that occur under different situational circumstances. Thus, providing explanations, buttressed eventually by *empirical evidence*, for each individual's unique ways of responding to his environment is the primary focus of interest in the discipline.

WHY A SCIENTIFIC STUDY OF PERSONALITY?

An important outgrowth of the current student "spirit of the times" seems to be disenchantment with almost any endeavor associated with science and technology. Students often seem to harbor the belief that these enterprises are to blame for many of the social problems that confront us, from the menace of industrial pollution to the terrifying possibility of world destruction by nuclear weapons. Although this viewpoint has considerable validity, it sometimes overlooks the fact that science and technology are primarily tools or instruments controlled and guided by *people*. These sophisticated and powerful techniques can be used by men and women either to further or to hinder human development. Psychologists use the scientific approach to study individual differences because they believe it is the most effective way to gather accurate information. There is also the hope that such knowledge can be used to benefit people. In the final analysis, they are convinced that this orientation will lead us more directly and surely to these goals than those which rely almost exclusively on rational speculation, mysticism, intuition or "common sense." This conviction, however, should not be interpreted as meaning that these alternative ways of knowing have no value and can never be used to help us understand human behavior. Insights stemming from the work of philosophers, novelists, poets, and theologians have always indicated otherwise.

SCIENCE AND COMMON SENSE

According to some students, psychology, including personality psychology, is a discipline that only mirrors the observations of common sense. They argue that, since this is the case, it really cannot contribute much to our understanding of people beyond what we all already know. Thus, there is not much point in devoting our energies to it. The major flaw in this argument is that although many of the findings in psychology confirm our commonsense impressions, there are also countless instances when research results reveal our knowledge to be incomplete or inaccurate. We are, of course, never certain of the validity of these beliefs until we test them empirically.

A study by Darley and Latané illustrates this point by showing that reliance on common sense could even spell physical disaster for any one of us (Darley and Latané, 1968, pp. 377–383). They investigated the conditions under which it was more or less likely that a victim in an emergency situation would receive help from bystanders. Their interest in this problem had been aroused by a dramatic incident in the spring of 1964 in which a young woman named Kitty Genovese had been stabbed to death in the middle of a street in a residential area of New York City while thirty-eight people watched. Although news commentators, clergy, and professors offered a variety of explanations for the nonintervention behavior, including calling it an indication of "moral decay," "existential despair," and "alienation," Darley and Latane focused on a more prosaic, but eventually more compelling, reason. Their explanation involved the number of witnesses to the event. In contrast to the commonsense belief that the more observers to an emergency, the more likely the victim will be to receive aid, they argued that the more bystanders there are in such a situation, the less likely it is that a victim will receive help. Their conjecture was based upon the argument that the more bystanders there are to an emergency, the more the responsibility for intervention would be seen by any individual to be shared among them. If there is only one observer, the burden for intervention rests squarely with him or her. As the number of bystanders increases, the less responsible any one will feel about his or her failure to act. Consequently, the more observers, the less likely the victim will receive aid.

To test their hypothesis, Darley and Latané created an "emergency" situation in the laboratory by leading study participants to believe that another individual was undergoing an epileptic seizure during a discussion about personal problems of college students in a high-pressure academic environment. In one condition, the person perceived that only he and one other person, the "victim," were present. In another condition, the person believed he, the victim, and one other subject were present; in the final condition, he perceived that there were six people present, himself, the victim, and four others. The results were in accord with the investigators' expectation and are shown in Table 1.1. The larger the group, the lower the percentage of subjects who came to the aid of the victim and the more slowly they reacted. This hypothesis has been retested in a variety of contexts with essentially the same results and does not therefore appear to be a finding that can easily be dismissed as a fluke occurrence.

TABLE 1.1 Effects of Variation in Group Size on Likelihood and Speed of Intervention

Group Size	Sample Size	Percentage of Ss Responding to "Seizure"	Time in Seconds
2 (person and victim)	13	85%	52
3 (person, victim and one other)	26	62%	93
6 (person, victim and four others)	13	31%	166

Adapted from Darley and Latané, 1968, p. 380.

An even more convincing example of the inaccuracy of some commonsense beliefs can be seen in Milgram's classic work on obedience to authority (Milgram, 1963, pp. 371–378). In his study, an experimenter ordered a naive subject to administer varying levels of electric shock to a "victim" as part of a learning experiment to study the effects of punishment on memory. The subject, as "teacher," was ordered to apply greater levels of shock to the "learner" every time he made an error on a paired-associates task. The shock levels varied in intensity from 15 to 450 volts. Milgram was concerned with the extent to which subjects would comply with the commands of the experimenter and administer the highest degree of shock. He asked a group of psychiatrists and other mental health professionals how many subjects in a group of a thousand would administer the highest level. Their estimate was that only one in a thousand would do so. A sample of senior psychology majors predicted that out of one hundred persons, only 1 percent would comply to the fullest degree. In actuality, twenty-six out of forty subjects, or 65 percent, administered maximum shock, a finding in dramatic opposition to commonsense beliefs.

Thus, it would appear that scientific effort can provide knowledge that may have important implications for each of us, knowledge that builds upon and often corrects the assumptions of common sense. At the very least, these findings suggest that we should be cautious in making indiscriminate statements about the obviousness of findings compiled by scientific psychology.

THE SCIENTIFIC ORIENTATION: THEORY AND RESEARCH METHODOLOGY

Our next concern is with the nature of science, including the manner in which *theories* are constructed and tested through empirical research. Such information will prove useful in critically evaluating the positions presented in this book, with the aim of relating them in a meaningful way to our own lives and experiences.

What Is Science?

In general terms, science is an enterprise concerned with the description, explanation, prediction, and control of events. The outcome of all the efforts by countless investigators is the accumulation of systematized knowledge based upon the observation of phenomena. Science is grounded in human values and concerns, from which investigators select certain problems for study. At its best, it is a process which excites their imagination and taxes their ingenuity. Often, it is frustrating—for example, when one's hypotheses are disconfirmed—but it is rarely dull. For each investigator, it is definitely not the passionless, automatic, and impersonal activity imagined by the uninitiated. In its essence, it involves an inevitable intertwining between two major processes, theory and method. There are, of course, a wide variety of research techniques available to investigators. We will focus on only three of them, the experimental method, correlational techniques, and case studies. At this point, let us briefly examine the nature of these processes.

Interrelatedness of Theory and Research

Scientific theories are conceptual systems constructed by researchers to help them make sense of existing information and, more important, to aid in the prediction of as yet unobserved relationships between events. Ideally, they consist of a set of interrelated and internally consistent assumptions or *propositions* from which hypotheses are derived and made testable by the use of operational definitions. Thus, the concepts in the hypotheses are defined in terms of the specific procedures or operations used to measure them. For example, a person's characteristic level of self-esteem may be measured by scoring his answers to a series of items on a questionnaire. Such definitions are important because they allow other investigators to know precisely how the characteristics were measured, thus providing an objective basis for communication among investigators who are using the concepts in their own theorizing or who want to replicate the results of another investigator's efforts. Although sometimes considered a trivial aspect of science, replication is critical and necessary, since the outcomes of any research effort are considered not as facts in any absolute sense, but as probability statements. Through replication, investigators begin to base more or less confidence in any one hypothesis. Successful replication tends to increase confidence in the findings; failure causes them to question the empirical validity of the relationship. One of the outcomes of persistent failures to replicate is that investigators may be forced to revise their theories and perhaps make new predictions.

In a theory of *cognitive dissonance* created by psychologist Leon Festinger, for example, the major propositions are that people tend to strive for consistency in their beliefs and behavior and that inconsistent or "nonfitting" cognitions about ourselves or other people, inanimate objects, or events in the environment give rise to an aversive psychological state called dissonance (Festinger, 1957). Cognitions refer generally to opinions, beliefs, attitudes, behaviors, or feelings about one's environment or oneself. Once a dissonant state is generated, it is assumed there will be pressures to reduce it by various means and to avoid its increase. For example, a heavy coffee drinker should experience dissonance when he learns, while drinking his fourth cup of coffee at the breakfast table and reading the morning paper, that medical research has shown people who consume large quantities of coffee daily are ten times as likely to have major heart attacks as nondrinkers. The fact that he likes to drink coffee is dissonant with the report that such behavior is likely to be harmful to his health.

He can reduce the dissonance in a variety of ways: (1) by telling himself that coffee drinking is so enjoyable it is clearly worth the risk; (2) by arguing that the results in the report are correlational in nature, thereby merely implying that some coffee drinkers will never experience heart attacks—after all, his father consumed even more coffee and lived until 102; (3) by arguing that coffee helps calm his nerves and that without it he would turn to other potentially self-destructive activities like overeating or smoking; (4) by maintaining that the dangers of excessive coffee drinking have been exaggerated; or (5) by reducing or stopping his coffee drinking. Although there are a number of other alternatives available to him, the general point is that the dissonance-reducing behaviors are ways of rationalizing or justifying one's actions to oneself *after* the behavior in question has occurred. We will see how Festinger's theory has been tested by use of the *experimental method* in the following section.

Experimental Method

In order to test hypotheses based on theory in a precise and rigorous manner, investigators study problems in laboratory experiments. In these situations, the experimenter actively manipulates or systematically varies certain *variables* and checks their effects on other variables. The variables actively varied are called *independent* variables; the others are called *dependent* variables. In the traditional and strictest sense, such experiments demand the use of *control groups* in which the independent variable is manipulated in one group, but not in the other. In this way, a more accurate assessment of the effects of independent variable manipulation on the dependent variable is possible. It should be recognized, however, that the basic function of control groups is to allow investigators to make comparisons between the ways in which their manipulations affect dependent outcomes. Thus, in the broadest sense, experimental studies that allow such comparisons, even though they do not use a control group in the traditional sense, are considered to have utilized control (Kerlinger, 1967).

You might bear these points in mind as we discuss a classic example of laboratory research conducted by psychologists Aronson and Carlsmith and based on Festinger's dissonance formulations (Aronson and Carlsmith, 1962, pp. 178–182). These researchers were concerned with the relationship between individual differences in ability and task performance. They argued that once a person's ability level on a task was clearly established, future performances on the same task which are consistent with this ability level would be pleasant and sought out, whereas performances which were inconsistent would be unpleasant and thus avoided or minimized. Specifically, they maintained that people who expect to do well on a task and who instead do poorly will experience dissonance and will attempt to reduce it by minimizing the performance. We do not really need dissonance theory to help us make this rather uninteresting prediction, however, since people in our culture are usually rewarded for good performances and punished for poor ones. But dissonance theory did allow Aronson and Carlsmith to generate an interesting and nonobvious prediction regarding the behavior of people who are incompetent at a task and who suddenly perform superbly. In such an obviously dissonant situation, they hypothesized that individuals would, if given the opportunity, change a superior performance to an inferior one in order to make it consistent with their poor task ability.

To test the prediction, a large sample of college students viewed 100 cards, each of which had three individual photographs of young men pasted on them. They were asked to judge which of the three on each card was schizophrenic. Some of them were led to believe they were incompetent at the task over the first 80 cards; others were led to believe that they had considerable skill at making such judgments. Once their ability levels were clearly established, they viewed the remaining 20 cards and then scored their own performances, noting for each of the 20 cards the number of correct selections. A short time later, all the participants were told by the experimenter that she had forgotten to record the speed of the performance for the last 20 trials. It would be necessary for the subjects to reexamine these cards and make their judgments as if they had never seen the cards before. The key question was: How many previously correct decisions would the low- and high-ability participants change to incorrect ones? As predicted, the low-ability participants made significantly more changes than the high-ability ones. Thus, there may be circumstances under which people with particular personality characteristics perform in unexpected and self-defeating ways.

Correlational Method

Much of the research in personality is *correlational* in nature; that is, it is concerned with establishing relationships between variables. For example: Is the need for achievement related to students' performance? Is need for achievement related to a person's chronic anxiety level? Is there a relationship between prejudice and self-esteem? The direction and size of the relationship is expressed by a statistical device called the *correlation coefficient*. The direction of the correlation coefficient tells us whether high scores on one variable are associated with low or high scores on the other. Positive correlations indicate that low scores on one variable are associated with low scores on the other or that high scores tend to be associated with high scores. For example, research indicates that high scores on the dogmatism scale, a test designed to measure a person's general intolerance of the beliefs of others, are associated with high scores on *self-report* anxiety scales (Vacchiano, Strauss, and Schiffman, 1968, pp. 83–85). So, intolerant people (high dogmatics) tend to be be high in anxiety, whereas tolerant people (low dogmatics) tend to be low in anxiety. Negative correlations indicate that high scores on one variable are associated with low scores on another, or that low scores tend to be associated with high scores. An example of a negative correlation is the research finding that high dogmatics tend to have lower self-esteem. Conversely, low dogmatics would tend to have higher self-esteem.

The size of a correlation indicates the degree of the relationship between two variables. A perfect positive correlation between variables would be written +1.00; a perfect negative relationship, −1.00; and a complete lack of association, .00. Perfect positive or negative correlations are, of course, rare.

Correlation coefficients do not provide us with any information about which variable *causes* the other. If we find a +.60 correlation between student ratings of physical attractiveness of college men and frequency of dating, we could not conclude that the large number of dates they had was a result of physical attractiveness. Physical attractiveness may also be positively correlated with intellectual ability, "ego strength," or general self-confidence and dominance, so that any one or a combination of these variables may have produced the high dating frequency. One of the primary advantages of employing the experimental rather than the correlational method is that is allows us to make causal inferences about variables with a higher degree of confidence.

Singer has provided us with a good example of correlational research in personality in a study designed to determine whether or not there was a relationship between the use of manipulative strategies by students and their academic grades (Singer, 1964, pp. 128–150). His study was based upon the undergraduate myth that some students get high grades by manipulating their professors. Singer asked large numbers of students to fill out a paper-and-pencil test called the Machiavellianism Scale in order to measure individual differences in the use of manipulative strategies in a wide variety of situations. This scale was based primarily on information adapted from Machiavelli's *The Prince*, in which a sixteenth-century statesman offered advice to monarchs on the proper ways to rule. Items used in the scale included the following: (1) it is wise to flatter important people; (2) never tell anyone the real reason you did something unless it is useful to do so; and (3) the best way to handle people is to tell them what they want to hear (Christie and Geis, 1970).

After obtaining the test scores, Singer proceeded to correlate them with grade-point averages. He found a correlation of +.39 for the men in his sample but not for women, which suggests that men who use manipulative strategies to attain their goals have higher grade point averages. The kinds of strategies they used were left unspecified. There are also a number of other possible explanations for the positive correlation. One is that bright people might tend to be manipulative so that brightness, in terms of academic ability, contributed to their higher averages. This alternative was ruled out by using a partial correlation technique that allowed the investigator to hold ability test scores constant. The initial correlational relationship was still obtained.

But even though there was a positive association between Machiavellian skills and high grade averages for men, what about the lack of such a relationship for women? Does this mean that women do not use manipulative strategies to attain their goals? Singer argued that women also probably manipulate, but they use strategies revolving around physical attractiveness and appearance rather than verbal deceit. Perhaps the more physically attractive the woman, the more likely her success in college. Singer tested his idea by using faculty ratings of physical attractiveness of the women in his study and then correlating these ratings with grade-point averages, with academic ability held constant. The results showed a significant correlation of $+.37$ for first-born women, but a nonsignificant correlation of $-.04$ for later-borns. But why did he find the relationship for first-borns and not later-borns? That question could not be answered precisely and directly, but further study did show that first-born women tended to sit in front of the class, to see the instructor after class, and to visit the instructor in his office more frequently than did later-borns. The general conclusion, then, was that college men and women probably do use manipulative strategies to secure their goals, but that the *kinds* of strategies used differ by sex.

These results also imply that the professor is a "poor soul" at the mercy of students as he or she tries to fulfill academic responsibilities. As Singer notes: "He is seemingly caught in a maelstrom of student intrigue and machination. The picture is bleak." In the professor's defense, it should be noted that when faculty members were administered the Machiavellian Scale, their scores were higher than those of the students, indicating that the faculty is even more manipulative than the students. Perhaps, as Singer points out, the "battle" is not at all that one-sided.

Finally, we should note that psychologists use many other correlational techniques in their research, some of them considerably more sophisticated than the Pearson product-moment coefficient. Examples include *partial* and *multiple correlation* techniques, as well as a variety of factor-analytic methods (see Chapter 7 for the rudiments of the factor-analytic procedure).

Case Study Method

Intensive study of an individual's behavior over a period of time and in various situations is called a case history or *case study*. Such studies are frequently used in clinical and medical research to provide descriptions of a person's actions. One of the primary advantages of the technique is that it allows for a "rich" or complex and integrated treatment of the individual. Personality studies using the experimental method examine average or typical differences between individuals. The case method, then, provides a view of the uniqueness of the person, in the sense that it describes both the consistencies and inconsistencies of individual behavior and the ways in which characteristic experiences are organized. Since it focuses on the unique characteristics of the individual, the data it yields are difficult, if not impossible, to apply to people in general. The procedure also lacks the systematic control of variables inherent in laboratory experiments. Although this is a major source of weakness because it makes causal inferences impossible, it is also a source of strength because it may lead to serendipitous findings that, in turn, may lead to new testable hypotheses and further research.

A good example of the use of the case study method is Freud's analysis of Leonardo Da Vinci's personality, with special focus on his alleged homosexuality. The famous genius of the Renaissance had been accused and acquitted by authorities of forbidden sexual relations with other boys while he was an apprentice in the house of his master, Verrocchio. From this information and a few other biographical fragments, Freud brilliantly reconstructed much of Leonardo's unconscious life in an attempt to determine the truth or falsity of the accusation. Since Freud assumed that early childhood experiences were critical determinants of later personality development, he focused on Leonardo's only writing about his earlier life. As Leonardo described the flight of the vulture, he interrupted himself to discuss an early memory:

> It seems that it had been destined before that I should occupy myself so thoroughly with the vulture, for it comes to my mind as a very early memory, when I was still in the cradle, a vulture came down to me, opened my mouth with his tail and struck me many times with his tail against my lips.

To Freud, this infantile fantasy meant that the

> "tail," or "coda," is one of the most familiar symbols, as well as a substitutive designation of the male member, in Italian no less than in other languages. The situation contained in the fantasy, that a vulture opened the mouth of the child and forcefully belabored it with its tail, corresponds to the idea of *fellatio*, a sexual act in which the member is placed into the mouth of the other person. Strangely enough, this fantasy is altogether of a passive character; it resembles certain dreams and fantasies of women and of passive homosexuals (who play the feminine part in sexual relations) (Freud, 1947).

Freud then described this fantasy as an elaboration of another situation he assumed everyone has experienced; namely, the pleasurable sensations derived from sucking mother's nipples during infancy. Thus, Da Vinci's fantasy suggested to Freud that Leonardo may have been a passive homosexual whose sexual life had been inhibited by an extraordinarily close relationship with his mother, in the absence of his father. "Mother," according to Freud, was depicted in Egyptian hieroglyphics by the picture of a vulture, so that Leonardo's fantasy was a memory of a time when his own mother (the vulture) held him close and kissed him passionately on the lips many times. Since the erotic feelings of the young Leonardo for his mother could not continue to develop consciously, they were repressed by putting himself in her place and then mirroring her behavior in the selection of a sexual object. Furthermore, Leonardo sublimated much of his sexual feeling by taking into his employment as apprentices "pretty" boys. He selected strikingly handsome boys as apprentices and "nursed" them as his mother had protected and cared for him during his childhood.

Some people concluded Freud had proved scientifically that Leonardo Da Vinci was a homosexual. The conclusion is wrong. Freud has presented an interesting and ingenious, but *post hoc*, interpretation of the dynamics of Da Vinci's homosexuality. It is an interpretation tacked on to certain information about the master's life. A retrospective analysis does not prove anything scientifically, although we cannot help but admire Freud's intriguing formulations. A scientific analysis, on the other hand, would demand that *a priori* predictions about the relationship between early childhood experiences and events be made and then the relevant data collected. These points are important because they tell us that we should be cautious in accepting conclusions made by the post hoc method. While we may marvel at the creativity of some of these speculations and acknowledge that they can be used to generate testable hypotheses, we should not assume that they provide absolute proof for a theory, despite claims to the contrary.

CRITERIA FOR THE EVALUATION OF SCIENTIFIC THEORIES

Comprehensiveness. There seems to be general agreement among theoreticians that a "good" or formally adequate theory encompasses and accounts for a wide range and diversity of data—that is, it is *comprehensive*. Since no theory can cover all the *phenomena* related to human personality, decisions must be made concerning the importance of the events to be studied (Pervin, 1975, p.18). For example, is it more important that the theory adequately describe and explain eyelid conditioning or human aggression? The answer seems obvious—investigators should focus on the study of aggression because an understanding of aggressive acts would allow us to account for behaviors that have important implications for human welfare. If we gain knowledge about the parameters that control eyeblinking, what have we accomplished? The answer to that question for most people is "Not much." Yet we should exercise some caution in making this judgment until we hear the other side of the argument. Many scientists have argued that in science there is no unambiguous criterion which allows us safely to exclude phenomena from study on the basis of triviality. They argue that what may be a trivial undertaking for someone else may be an important re- search investigation for you, and vice versa. Furthermore, and more im- portant, no one knows for certain what will happen in the future. Work on a seemingly trivial problem may also bear fruit at some future point in time. In the eyeblink example, an understanding of the parameters or characteristics that control eyeblinking could give us information about the principles of classical conditioning, principles which can be used to explain the origins of many irrational fears and phobias.

As you can see, there is no clear-cut answer to this problem. One prominent personality theorist, Salvatore Maddi, has suggested that investigators can minimize the risk of triviality by relying on naturalistic observation. Such observation would include the gathering of informa- tion about human behavior by studying people in their daily surround- ings and, to a lesser extent, in therapeutic settings (Maddi, 1972, pp. 562–564). In this way, we can make tentative judgments about the worth of personality theories on the basis of comprehensiveness.

Precision and Testability. Besides being comprehensive, a good theory should contain concepts that are clearly and explicitly defined. It should also contain *relational statements* and *propositions* that are consistent and logically related to one another. It is generally recognized that in the early stages of theorizing, investigators may rely heavily on analogies and metaphors as an aid to thought, but in the final analysis they may only create inconsistencies and ambiguities which hamper understand- ing (Maddi, 1972, p. 569). Examples include Jung's *shadow*, which lurks around in the *darkness* of the collective unconscious, and Freud's treat- ment of the ego as a *battlefied* where mortal *combat* takes place between the *forces* of the id and superego.

Not only must the concepts in the theory be defined precisely, but the hypotheses containing them must be capable of being empirically studied—that is, they must be linked at some point with external reality (Hall and Lindzey, 1970, p. 12). The link between conceptualization and observation is accomplished through the use of *operational definitions*. In brief, a good theory contains hypotheses that are testable.

Simplicity. A good theory should be stated economically; that is, the theory should contain only those concepts and assumptions necessary for the explanation of the phenomena within its domain. The inclusion of unnecessary concepts or assumptions may lead an investigator to waste great amounts of effort studying meaningless relationships. At the very least, the data may be accounted for by existing concepts, so that the creation and use of new concepts may be unnecessary. A theory can also be considered inadequate in terms of economy or *parsimony* if it contains *fewer* concepts and assumptions than are necessary to account completely for the phenomena in its domain. Thus, the parsimony cri- terion is not met just because an investigator uses fewer concepts and assumptions in an absolute sense. He may have ignored the complexity of the data to be explained.

Empirical Validity. Good theory must be capable of generating predictions that have *empirical validity*. This is a key function of theory and involves the testing of *hypotheses* by making observations to determine if the investigator's conjectures are correct. Of course, the determination of validity is not always easy. First, research findings are always determined probabalistically. This means that we can place a certain amount of confidence in our findings, but we are never completely certain. If we confirm the hypothesis, it generally means that we have some confidence that the predicted relationship exists. Successful *replications* increase our confidence. On the other hand, failure to confirm may mean that we will not place much confidence in the relationship. Successive failures to replicate may mean that we will become even less certain that the relationship exists. At what point do we conclude that the theory has been disproved? To date, no absolute standard has been accepted by scientists.

Second, the determination of the validity of a theory is difficult because investigators can argue that the measures used to assess the concepts were unreliable and invalid. They may be measuring the concepts poorly or not at all. It should be noted that an investigator's claims involving poor measurement of concepts may be legitimate or illegitimate. In fact, the measurement procedures may be unreliable and error-ridden. On the other hand, a few theorists and their advocates have such strongly vested interests in their own formulations that they dismiss out of hand any evidence disproving those theories on the ground that the concepts tested were not adequately measured. Such self-serving statements run counter to the ideals of science and in the long run are overruled by the body of evidence accumulated by independent researchers.

Heuristic Value. A good theory is also stimulating and provocative. It may seem so blatantly inadequate that it stirs investigators into action to reveal its inadequacies. Alternatively, it may be the source of new ideas for some researchers and lead them into new paths that may prove enlightening and useful.

Applied Value. Finally, a good theory should be one that leads to new approaches to the solution of people's problems (Kelly, 1955, p. 24). This criterion is not universally endorsed by scientists, especially by those who work in the various areas of experimental psychology. Yet it seems particularly germane to the various theories in the area of personality. There can be little question that an adequate theory of personality will focus on abnormal as well as normal development and that an overriding concerns of virtually all personality psychologists will be helping people to overcome their problems.

At this juncture, equipped with information about the essential ingredients of the scientific process and the standards used to evaluate the worth of the various theories, we proceed to examine the major perspectives in personality.

DISCUSSION QUESTIONS

1. What are some of the results of investigators bringing their own particular perspectives to the study of personality?
2. Why is the definition of personality in terms of social attractiveness inadequate for use by psychologists?
3. What is science? In what ways does the scientific enterprise involve the use of theory and research?
4. Why do most psychologists use the scientific approach to study individual difference problems?
5. Discuss some of the inadequacies of the commonsense approach to the study of behavior.
6. Discuss the importance of operational definitions and replication in the study of personality.
7. What are the basic elements of the experimental method?
8. What is the correlational method, and when and how is it used in the investigation of scientific problems?
9. Explain the differences between the experimental and case study methods.
10. List and describe six criteria commonly used by investigators for the evaluation of scientific theories.

NOTES

E. Aronson and J. M. Carlsmith, "Performance Expectancy as a Determinant of Actual Performance," *Journal of Abnormal and Social Psychology*, 1962, **65,** 178–182.

R. Christie and F. L. Geis, *Studies in Machiavellianism* (New York: Academic Press, 1970).

J. M. Darley and B. Latané, "Bystander Intervention in Emergencies: Diffusion of Responsiblity," *Journal of Personality and Social Psychology*, 1968, **8,** 377–383.

L. Festinger, *A Theory of Cognition* (Evanston, Ill.: Row, Peterson, 1957).

S. Freud, *Leonardo Da Vinci: A Study in Psychosexuality,* trans. A. A. Brill (New York: Random House, 1947).

C. S. Hall and G. Lindzey, *Theories of Personality,* 2nd ed. (New York: Wiley, 1970).

G. A. Kelly, *The Psychology of Personal Constructs,* Vol. I (New York: Norton, 1955).

F. N. Kerlinger, *Foundations of Behavioral Research* (New York: Holt, Rinehart and Winston, 1967).

S. R. Maddi, *Personality Theories: A Comparative Analysis,* rev. ed. (Homewood, Ill.: Dorsey, 1972).

S. Milgram, "Behavioral Study of Obedience," *Journal of Abnormal and Social Psychology,* 1963, **67,** 371–378.

L. A. Pervin, *Personality: Theory, Assessment, and Research,* 2nd ed. (New York: Wiley, 1975).

J. E. Singer, "The Use of Manipulative Strategies: Machiavellianism and Attractiveness," *Sociometry,* 1964, **27,** 128–150.

R. B. Vacchiano, P. S. Strauss, and D. D. Schiffman, "Personality Correlates of Dogmatism," *Journal of Consulting and Clinical Psychology,* 1968, **32,** 83–85.

SUGGESTED READINGS

Carlsmith, J. M., Ellsworth, P. C., and Aronson, E. *Methods of Research in Social Psychology.* Reading, Mass.: Addison-Wesley, 1976.

Hendrick, C., and Jones, R. A. *The Nature of Theory and Research in Social Psychology.* New York: Academic Press, 1972.

Kerlinger, F. N. *Foundations of Behavioral Research.* New York: Holt, Rinehart and Winston, 1967.

Neale, J. M., and Liebert, R. M. *Science and Behavior: An Introduction to Methods of Research.* Englewood Cliffs, N. J.: Prentice-Hall, 1973.

GLOSSARY

Applied Value. Criterion or standard for judging the scientific worth of a theory. An adequate theory is capable of providing creative solutions that are of interest and concern to people.

A Priori Prediction. Hypothesis of the relationship between events that is made prior to the actual collection of data to test its validity.

Case Study. Research technique involving the intensive study of a single person in order to understand his or her unique behavior.

Cognitive Dissonance. Painful motivational state created within a person when two or more thoughts, attitudes, or behaviors are inconsistent with one another.

Comprehensiveness. Criterion or standard by which to judge the worth of a scientific theory. An adequate theory must encompass and account for a wide range and variety of phenomena.

Control Group. In an experiment, the group that does not receive the experimental treatment. A control group is designed to provide baseline data against which the effects of the experimental manipulation can be judged.

Correlation Coefficient. Statistic designed to measure the direction and degree of a relationship between variables.

Correlational Method. General procedure for establishing the noncausal nature of the association or relationship between events. Statistics involving correlations can vary in complexity from simple correlation coefficients to complicated factor-analytic techniques.

Dependent Variable. Change in behavior that occurs as a result of the manipulation of conditions by an experimenter.

The changes are dependent upon the manipulation of the independent variables by an experimenter.

Empirical Evidence. Observations of phenomena made by investigators.

Empirical Validity. Criterion used to judge the worth of a theory in which the various hypotheses are tested by experiments or observations to determine whether or not they are correct. Confirmation of the hypotheses lends support to the theory's validity.

Experimental Method. Scientific method for studying the nature of cause-and-effect relationships between and among variables. It involves the manipulation of independent variables and the observation of the effects on dependent variables.

Heuristic Value. Criterion or standard for judging the scientific worth of a theory. An adequate theory should stimulate new ideas and new research.

Hypothesis. Tentative theoretical statement about how events are related to one another. Hypotheses are often stated as predictions about how the operation of one set of events will affect the operation of others.

Hypothetical Construct. Term used to signify internal events, e.g., hunger or thirst, that are assumed to have a real basis in the physiology of the organism. They are events that exist and can be discovered.

Independent Variable. The variable actively manipulated by the experimenter so that its effects on individual behavior can be observed.

Mediating Event. Phenomenon presumed to occur between an external stimulus and an external response. A mediating event typically is conceptualized as signifying the unique learning history of the individual, which influences the ways in which he or she interprets external stimuli and responds.

Multiple Correlation. Statistical technique in which it is possible to determine the relationship between one variable and a combination of two or more other variables simultaneously.

Operational Definition. Procedures or operations used to define particular concepts. For example, a person's intelligence could be operationally defined in terms of his or her scores on a verbal reasoning test.

Parsimony. Criterion for judging the scientific worth of a theory. An adequate theory should be as parsimonious or economical as possible and still adequately account for the phenomena in its domain.

Partial Correlation. One of many correlational techniques designed to measure the nature of the association between events. The partial correlation technique allows the investigator to assess the nature of the relationship between two events by eliminating or "partialing out" the influence of a third variable.

Phenomenon. Observable fact or event capable of being studied scientifically.

Post Hoc Explanation. Explanation of a phenomenon given *after* its occurrence. The explanation presumes that certain factors caused the occurrence of the phenomenon, but there is no evidence that they actually did. The proof that the explanation has validity would await the outcomes of further experimental testing.

Precision. Criterion or standard for judging the scientific worth of a theory. An adequate theory should contain concepts and relational statements that are clearly and explicitly stated and measured.

Proposition. General theoretical statement about the relationship between events that may be true or false. Propositions or assumptions are the ground rules of the theory and, as such, are accepted as true.

Relational Statements. Theoretical proposition or hypothesis that links or relates concepts. For example, the concepts of frustration and aggression might be linked as follows: Increases in frustration lead to increases in aggressive behavior.

Replication. Duplication or repetition of an experiment to determine whether or not the original findings are reliable.

Self-Report. An individual's written or verbal description of his or her behavior.

Testability. Criterion or standard for judging the scientific worth of a theory. An adequate theory must contain hypotheses that can be defined, measured, and checked in terms of observable events.

Theory. A number of interrelated, conceptual statements that are created by investigators to account for a phenomenon or a set of phenomena.

2

PSYCHOANALYTIC AND NEO – ANALYTIC PERSPECTIVES

O nly a few people in the history of human endeavor have done work so creative and provocative that it shapes the course of human values and thought. Copernicus, the eminent sixteenth-century Polish astronomer, was such an individual because he discovered that the earth was not the center of the universe and forced us to reexamine our beliefs about our own omnipotence and omniscience. Darwin, the English naturalist of the nineteenth century, was another who forced us to realize that we too are part of the natural world and governed to some extent by our biology. Sigmund Freud belongs in this august company because he compelled us to acknowledge that we are often irrational and impulsive and characterized by conflicts of a sexual and aggressive nature. It was a shock to many scholars in the humanistic tradition of Western thought, which emphasized rationality and the virtues of ethical conduct, to learn that human beings are often irrational and that they continuously engage in internal struggles to keep their sexual and aggressive impulses in check. Freud bared the baseness of the human soul for everyone to see, and some people have never forgiven him his "treachery." He removed us from our pedestals and forced us to examine the dark and impulsive side of our natures. For his efforts, he was publicly reviled and scorned. Eventually, however, investigators in many disciplines began to explore the validity of his statements. Today, Freud's influence is worldwide. Scholars in literature are fond of using psychoanalytic concepts to explain the motives of their characters. Anthropologists focus on child-rearing practices in various cultures and use a Freudian model to understand adult personality. Philosophers and sociologists have used the Freudian concepts of repression and anxiety in their analyses of problems confronting modern society. Freudian concepts have also been adopted by ordinary people. We are all aware of the importance of "Freudian slips" and the ways in which the unconscious influences behavior. Sometimes we talk glibly—and incorrectly—

about ego trips, phallic symbols, penis envy, and Oedipal conflicts. The important point is that Freudian thinking has had a revolutionary impact on our lives and that Freud deserves his place in history, whether we ultimately accept or reject his view of human behavior and functioning.

In Chapter 2, we review the basic concepts of Freud's theory. We examine his attempts to construct a theory of personality based upon interpretations of self-reports by his patients. The chapter includes a description of the basic constructs (the id, ego, and superego) in his model and some of the important ways in which they interact to produce internal conflict. The use of various defense mechanisms to protect the ego and reduce the anxiety generated by the conflicts is also considered. Freud's theory of psychosexual development is reviewed, with special emphasis on the origins and nature of the various character disorders. These disorders are then distinguished from the neuroses, and a key example of Freud's treatment of an obsessive-compulsive presented. Finally, we consider the research evidence for the theory of psychosexual development.

Chapter 3 on Carl Jung examines the nature of the individual's psyche, all the interacting systems within human personality that are needed to account for the mental life and behavior of the person, and the life-process energy that motivates him or her to action. Although both Freud and Jung used the term *libido* to describe the energy that propels the person into action, Jung's conceptualization of it was much broader than Freud's. Jung thought of it not just in terms of sexual impulses that try to force their way into consciousness, but as forces generated by continuous conflicts within the psyche. Once created, this energy can move in a variety of directions. In short, Jung treated libido as a force that can split and move erratically through the psyche, as an unpredictable force. The result is that the person may at times exhibit bizarre and impulsive behavior. This conceptualization also adds a certain mystery to the person, since autonomous forces, often operating capriciously, do not allow outside observers to identify clearly the causes of his or her behavior.

In addition to the discussion of libido, the chapter examines the major structures of the psyche and describes the evolution of the self as the conflicts between the various oppositional forces are resolved via transcendence. Jung also believed that in the attempt to evolve toward selfhood, people adopted different orientations or attitudes toward life and utilized different psychological processes or functions to make sense out of their experiences. Eventually he combined the attitudes and functions in a theoretical scheme of psychological types and discussed the ways in which introverted and extraverted individuals try to deal with the world and their own conflicts. This theoretical scheme is examined in considerable detail in the chapter materials and includes a review of the major research evidence based upon it. Following this, the chapter delves into Jung's views on disordered behavior and therapy and closes with a consideration of the major strengths and weaknesses of his position.

In contrast to Freud and Jung, Alfred Adler, whose work is the subject of Chapter 4, presented a simplified scheme to account for the development of personality. He came to believe that all individuals felt inferior and strove to overcome these feelings and to become superior. Neurotic strivings were associated with attempts to achieve personal superiority at the expense of others, whereas healthy strivings included attempts to reach for perfection via efforts to improve the lot of others. Although Adler emphasized human rationality and consciousness in making decisions and discussed in detail the ways in which our goals inspire us to improve ourselves, we should not conclude that his position was totally optimistic in tone. Specifically, Adler was never able to break completely with his Freudian origins, and so he concluded that our life styles were set by the end of our fifth year. Such a stance has pessimistic overtones, since it implies that there is not much one can do to change oneself drastically after early childhood. Thus, a person with a destructive life style is essentially doomed to a life of misery and conflict. Therapy can be beneficial, but only to a certain extent. This point should be borne in mind when we consider the implications of Adler's position in relationship to the treatment of human suffering.

Despite his adherence to this aspect of Freudian theory, the general tone of Adler's writings is optimistic. Chapter 4 reveals his essential humanism and points out his socialist political orientation, as well as his constant attempts to help oppressed people. In particular, it focuses on his concept of social interest—that is, it focuses on his belief that we have an innate need to help others, and on his wish for an ideal society in which cooperation, harmony, and equality would be the rule.

The final chapter in this part, Chapter 5, contains a consideration of the basic concepts in Erich Fromm's position. Fromm was chosen in preference to other neo-Freudian theorists such as Horney, Sullivan, Murray, and Erikson because he focuses on the ways in which a society's political and economic structures influence development. Although in many respects he retains the Freudian focus on inner conflicts and attempts to cope with them, he attributes the origins of these conflicts not so much to underlying sexual and aggressive impulses as to the imposition of social and economic controls on the individual. The materials in this chapter also provide an opportunity for us to examine the unique ways in which Fromm combines elements of existentialism and psychoanalysis in his theory of personality development.

Sigmund Freud (The Bettmann Archive, Inc.)

CHAPTER 2

Freud's Psychoanalytic Theory

1939
18 56
—————
83

BIOGRAPHICAL SKETCH

Sigmund Freud was born in 1856 in the town of Freiburg, Moravia (now Czechoslovakia), of Jewish parents. His father was a wool merchant who married twice, and Sigmund was the oldest son of the second wife. The family consisted of five daughters and two other sons. He was a serious boy who excelled in his studies throughout his early schooling. Upon entering the University of Vienna, he reluctantly decided upon a medical career and was graduated in 1883. He maintained that he never felt comfortable playing the "doctor game," but he was impressed with the scientific attitude of people in the medical professon. Freud yearned to answer the great problems of the world and to learn all he could about human nature (Jones, 1963, p. 3–4, 22). From his perspective, science provided the means of securing such solutions.

During his medical school days, he came under the influence of the eminent physiologist Ernst Brücke, and worked as his assistant on neurological problems in lower animals. Although quite content in his work at Brücke's laboratory, Freud soon realized that his chances for advancement were poor and that the monetary rewards would always be minimal. Since he was seriously interested in a lovely young woman at the time and believed he should be earning enough money to support her before he committed himself to marriage, he was naturally quite distressed. After a series of attempts to secure money from his superiors failed, Freud, with Brücke's friendly encouragement, left the laboratory and entered private medical practice in the hope of raising his income. Shortly afterward, in 1885, he applied for a postgraduate traveling stipend to work with the renowned French neurologist Jean Charcot on the treatment of nervous disorders. The competition for the grant was fierce, despite the fact that it provided the winner with only $240 to cover traveling expenses from Vienna to Paris and all living expenses over a six-month period. Eventually, after much haggling and debate by

25

the committee authorized to make the decision, Freud was declared the winner. He was elated and wrote the following note to his fiancee, who lived in Hamburg:

> Oh, how wonderful it is going to be. I am coming with money and am staying a long while with you and am bringing something lovely for you and shall then go to Paris and become a great savant and return to Vienna with a great, great nimbus. Then we will marry soon and I will cure all the incurable nervous patients and you will keep me well and I will kiss you till you are merry and happy—and they lived happily ever after. (Jones, 1963, p. 50)

It should be mentioned at this point that Freud and Martha Bernays were married in 1886 and lived together happily for more than half a century.

In Paris, Freud observed Charcot's use of hypnosis to treat patients who had been classified as hysterics; that is, people who had bodily symptoms such as total or partial paralysis of the limbs and total or partial loss of sight or hearing. These symptoms were the behavioral signs of distress presumed to be caused by underlying motivational conflicts. Charcot could create or eliminate such symptoms through hypnotic suggestion. He at first thought they were caused by physical damage to parts of the nervous system, but intensive investigation revealed that this was not the case. He finally concluded that the symptoms were psychological, but it was left to Freud to spell out the dynamics of the problem. It was he who determined the complex, interrelated system of underlying motives that produced the symptoms.

Freud then tried hypnosis with his own patients at the suggestion of a mentor and physician named Breuer. Breuer had treated a young woman, Anna O., for a group of physical symptoms that had arisen in connection with the death of her father. The symptoms included paralysis of her limbs and disturbances of sight and speech. Breuer found, to his astonishment, that the woman's symptoms disappeared if she talked about them while in a hypnotic trance. In this state, she would relive the terrifying experiences that gave rise to her symptoms and express the accompanying emotions fully. This physical expression of emotion was labeled a catharsis. Eventually Freud and Breuer severed their relationship because of Freud's insistence that the basis of such disorders was sexual in nature (Jones, 1963. pp. 147, 165).

Between 1892 and 1895, the method of free association gradually evolved in Freud's thinking. He used the cathartic method in his treatment for several years, but he found there were many patients he could not hypnotize. As a consequence, he began to ask patients to concentrate on a particular symptom and to try to recall any early experiences that might explain its origins. Eventually he asked his patients to free associate, that is, to express every thought which occurred to them, no matter how irrelevant, unimportant, or unpleasant (Jones,

1963, pp. 157–158). Despite the fact that the patients' recollections seemed aimless and accidental, Freud felt intuitively that there must be some definite force controlling the thoughts. He had been thoroughly trained in medicine and neurology to accept the principles of *determinism* and causality, so that he could not now bring himself to believe that the thoughts of the patients were unrelated. In addition, Freud was impressed by the unwillingness of many patients to disclose memories that were painful to them. He labeled this opposition *resistance,* and came to believe that his patients were "repressing" certain important memories. His job, then, was to probe their unconscious and uncover the reasons for their active resistance.

In the course of his analyses, Freud also discovered that patients insisted upon tracing the origins of their traumatic experiences to early childhood. To his surprise, he found that many of these memories involved sexual experiences. Until this time, most people believed that childhood was a time of innocence, devoid of sexual urges. Freud disagreed strongly:

> We do wrong entirely to ignore the sexual life of children; in my experience children are capable of all the mental and many of the physical activities. Just as the whole sexual apparatus of man is not comprised in the external genital organs and the two reproductive glands, so his sexual life does not begin only with the onset of puberty, as to casual observation it may appear to do. (Jones, 1963, p. 172)

Freud at first believed that the early childhood seduction scenes described to him by his patients were literally true. Eventually, however, he began to have doubts. He found it difficult to believe, for example, that all his women patients' fathers were sexually perverse. He also found that literal acceptance of these accounts and subsequent suggestions to the patients of how they must deal with them did not always have therapeutic benefits. He noted in a letter to a friend that he had to renounce his explanations of hysteria and his hopes of becoming a famous physician. But he eventually faced up to the situation and revised his *libido theory.* The major revision was his acceptance of the fact that the descriptions were not literally true; they were instead fantasies which were nevertheless psychically real and valid in their own right (Jones, 1963, pp. 172–173).

In asking his patients to free associate, Freud also discovered that they often mentioned their dreams. He found that dreams provided the best means of unlocking the secrets of the *unconscious.* They yielded invaluable information about the nature of the person's conflicts and the mechanisms by which they were concealed from awareness (Jones, 1963, p. 129). In 1900, Freud published *The Interpretation of Dreams.* In it he noted that dreaming was neither an idle activity nor as chaotic as it seemed. Dreams serve as wish-fulfillment devices, and their latent content can be used to help a patient understand his or her problems.

In 1902, the Vienna Psycho-Analytical Society was formed. Initially, a small group of scholars from various disciplines met in Freud's office to discuss their work. When the membership grew, this practice was abandoned for meetings in larger, more formal settings. The period of 1905–1906 was a highly productive one for Freud; he published several books, including *Jokes and Their Connection with the Unconscious*, the well-known *The Psychopathology of Everyday Life*, and *Three Essays on the Theory of Sexuality*, as well as some articles. *Three Essays* in particular made Freud almost universally unpopular. The book was labeled "shockingly wicked," and Freud was branded as a man with an obscene and evil mind. The primary focus of the criticism was Freud's assertion that children are born with sexual urges and that the parents are selected as their first sexual objects. Freud believed, however, that he was right and that eventually his arguments would be accepted (Jones, 1963, pp. 240–243).

By 1910, Freud had gained an international reputation, but internal dissension among members of the Psycho-Analytical Society concerning his libido theory was beginning to occur. The defections began with Adler and Stekel, who were followed by Jung and others. Adler's defection was precipitated by his disagreement with Freud over the importance of the sexual factor in determining behavior. Adler minimized its importance and elevated the concept of a struggle for power in its place. He also deemphasized or discarded the concepts of repression, the unconscious, and infantile sexuality. Such major differences led inevitably to a separation between the two men. The split with Jung was much more distressing for Freud. He had been closer personally to Jung than to Adler and believed that Jung was superior in intellect and knowledge so he took the defection more seriously (Jones, 1963, pp. 313–314, 318).

Jung was disturbed by the uncompromising way Freud treated the question of sexuality in his public discussions of patients' neuroses. As Jung saw it:

> We should do well not to burst out with the theory of sexuality in the foreground. I have many thoughts about that, especially on the ethical aspects of the question. I believe that in publicly announcing certain things one would saw off the branch on which civilization rests; one undermines the impulse of sublimation . . . . Both with the students and with the patients, I get on further by not making the theme of sexuality prominent. (Jones, 1963, pp. 318–319)

Eventually, Jung deemphasized the sexual factor in the determination of neurosis. He considered libido or sexual energy as a designation of general tension and rejected Freud's belief that the Oedipal conflict involved incestuous yearnings on the part of the child. But despite the defections of some of his disciples whose positions came to be known as

an inclination to emphasize
adverse aspects, or to expect
the worst possible outcome

the *neo-analytic perspective,* Freud's fame continued to grow and the Psycho-Analytical Society flourished.

World War I had a profound impact on Freud's thinking and research. He was acutely distressed by the mass killing and suffering and eventually came to attribute these experiences to the operation of a universal death instinct on the part of human beings. Despite his pessimism about the future of humankind, Freud continued to elaborate his ideas in a long series of books. Among the more important ones, we find *Totem and Taboo* (1913), *Introductory Lectures on Psycho-Analysis* (1917), *Beyond the Pleasure Principle* (1920), *The Ego and the Id* (1923), *Future of an Illusion* (1927), *Civilization and Its Discontents* (1930), *New Introductory Lectures on Psychoanalysis* (1933), and *An Outline of Psycho-Analysis* published posthumously in 1940. In the late 1930's, encouraged by his supporters to flee the Nazis, he escaped to London. His remaining years were spent in considerable pain, as he suffered from cancer of the jaw and mouth. He persisted in his work, despite more than thirty operations, until the very end. He died in London on September 23, 1939.

PSYCHOANALYSIS AS A THERAPEUTIC TOOL

Psychoanalysis began as a method of therapy designed to help people experiencing problems in living and then evolved into a theory of personality. Most of the theory is based upon Freud's intensive examination of the lives and past experiences of a few neurotic upper-middle-class Viennese women, as well as on a detailed self-analysis. Via dream analysis, Freud discovered that the root of virtually all these neuroses was sexual conflict which originated because of traumatic (highly disturbing) experiences in early childhood. In the course of helping and advising his patients to confront and understand the nature of their conflicts, he also found that they began to see him as a reincarnation of important figures in their past. As a result, they began to transfer to him the kinds of feelings and behavior they had shown to these early authority figures. In Freud's view, this *transference* phenomenon could be of inestimable value in helping the therapist to cure patients. Yet it could also be a possible source of danger, if the patients decided to act out their hostile feelings toward the therapist.

In brief, the transference process was characterized by *ambivalence* on the part of the patients. Typically, they had attitudes of both affection and hostility toward their parents, and these shifting orientations were transferred to the analyst. The analyst's job was to promote positive transference and to use it to encourage patients to cope with their unpleasant experiences while actively discouraging them from dwelling on their negative attitudes. If the therapist was successful, the result was increased self-understanding by the patients and a more accurate assessment of reality. The patients would also eventually be able to function more effectively in everyday life (Freud, 1969, pp. 31–35).

BASIC CONCEPTS AND PRINCIPLES

In order to understand the dynamics of a person's conflicts, it was necessary for Freud to postulate constructs that allowed him to describe the ways in which these conflicts originated and affected behavior. Although Freud intended to use these constructs as explanatory devices, in reality they were post hoc interpretations superimposed on experiences related to him by his patients. In addition, there was a tendency to reify the constructs and to discuss them as though they were real entities that operated and determined the person's behavior.

Id

Id - biological instinct of personality
a) Eros - various sexual instincts
b) Thanatos / death instinct - aggressive impulse
usually, a & b may operate jointly
Id - seeks expression in reality continuously
- amoral
- operates according to pleasure principle

For Freud, the *id* was conceptualized as the original aspect of personality and was considered to be rooted in the biology (Jones, 1963, p. 2). It was thought to consist primarily of unconscious sexual and aggressive instincts. The various sexual instincts were further classified by him under the heading of Eros, while the aggressive impulses were classified under the heading of Thanatos or death instinct, although the latter term was suggested by Freud's followers and not by Freud himself. For any of us, Eros and Thanatos might operate jointly in different situations to affect our behavior. For example, we might find ourselves hating and acting aggressively toward parents whom we dearly love, or we might feel sexually attracted to an *proud* arrogant and obnoxious male with whom we are continually arguing.

Freud likened the id to a "seething cauldron" which contained ever-bubbling primitive urges and desires. He believed that these urges insistently and indiscriminately sought expression in external reality. The id was thus conceived of as amoral, since it was unconcerned with the niceties and conventions of society. It operated according to the pleasure principle: the aim of these impulses was always immediate and complete satisfaction. The pleasure principle appeared to be an outgrowth of the concept of philosophical hedonism, a doctrine which states that people always strive to maximize pleasure and minimize pain.

Ego

battlefield - 1. id & superego

It is clear that we do not live in a social vacuum and cannot simply do whatever we wish whenever we want something. Adults who act impulsively are called immature or childish. Mature conduct, on the other hand, appears to demand that we control our impulses in a wide variety of situations. For Freud, this control became possible when the *ego* was differentiated from the id. The ego comes into existence because the needs of the person require an appropriate transaction with the environment if they are to be satisfied. The ego therefore develops in order to carry out the aims of the id. It also keeps the impulses of the id in check until a suitable object is found. The conscious ego is characterized by realistic thinking; and it copes not only with the id impulses, but with the demands of the superego as well. As Freud saw it, the ego was similar to a battlefield where the armies of the id and the superego continually clashed. While much of the ego operates in consciousness, some of its processes are unconscious and serve a protective and anxiety-reducing function for the ego (Freud, 1960, p. 7).

Superego

The *superego* is the construct Freud used to describe the learning of moral values. These values are instilled in the person primarily by his parents. He learns which behaviors are appropriate or inappropriate in given situations. The superego represents learned ideals and was eventually conceptualized by Freud as having two primary components, *conscience* and the *ego-ideal*. Conscience is acquired through the use of punishment by the parents; the ego-ideal is learned through the use of rewards. When the person does something wrong, his conscience makes him feel guilty, but when he obeys his parents and seeks to win their approval by performing in socially accepted ways, he feels proud. The main functions of the sugerego are to inhibit the urges of the id, to persuade the ego to substitute moralistic goals for realistic ones, and to strive for perfection. The superego is considered to have both conscious and unconscious aspects.

Ego Defense Processes

One of Freud's key contributions to psychology involved his treatment of the many ways in which the individual uses protective maneuvers to reduce anxiety-arousing threats to the ego. We turn now to a discussion of the basic ego defenses he postulated.

Repression. *Repression* is an attempt by the ego to keep undesirable id impulses from reaching consciousness. In the course of analyzing dreams, Freud discovered that certain thoughts were blocked from consciousness—that is, repressed—because they were too painful to acknowledge and that attempts by him to make patients aware of these experiences met with "resistances." In Freudian terms, the battle for supremacy between the ego and the id involved an opposition between energy forces. The driving forces were called *cathexes*; the restraining forces were labeled *anticathexes*. In other words, certain unconscious wishes or ideas were energized and drove for expression in consciousness, but were met by other ideas energized by restraining forces seated in the ego. If the ego forces dominated, the wishes would be repressed; that is, forced back into the unconscious. If the id forces dominated, the person would "act out" his or her socially unacceptable impulses. For example, a person who hated her father might repress her hostility and anger, and thus be totally unaware of her actual feelings. If these feelings broke through to the surface, the individual might physically attack her father. The battle would be centered on her attempts to express her feelings and the ego's attempts to repress them because their expression could lead to serious problems. The ego would attempt to protect the individual by forcing her to repress her unpleasant thoughts. Freud considered repression the most fundamental of all defense mechanisms. As he put it, "the theory of repression is the pillar upon which the edifice of psycho-analysis rests" (Freud, 1938a, p. 939).

Freud also distinguished between repression and suppression. *Suppression* is the conscious blocking of unpleasant matters from awareness. The individual has some control over his behavior and actively seeks to avoid thinking about unpleasant matters. Repression, in contrast, occurs entirely on an unconscious level and involves unpleasant experiences that are repulsive to the ego. Memories which have been suppressed can be brought quite readily into awareness by cues from the environment, whereas repressed memories cannot be triggered into awareness in the same way.

Denial. Denial is the person's refusal to perceive an unpleasant event in external reality. It is a primitive defense. For example, a loved one dies and the grieved partner may refuse to accept it. Or a child is told by his parents to leave the playground and go home, and he conveniently ignores their instructions.

Often parents unwittingly teach children to use such a defense. They inform their little son that he is a "big boy" and that he is "just as strong as father." They also reassure him after he is hurt that he is really "all right" or that some food he despises is "really very good." As a result, the child learns to apply such thinking to painful experiences (A. Freud, 1946, pp. 90–91). Although the occasional use of such a mechanism to protect the ego is healthy, it becomes unhealthy if it is used continually and indiscriminately.

Displacement. Freud discussed the concept of displacement in the context of dream analysis (Freud, 1938b, pp. 336–339). It is the substitution of acceptable ideas for unacceptable ones. For example, a patient who hated her mother, whose first name was Rose, and unconsciously wanted to kill her, might dream about the plucking of roses from her garden and the cutting of their long stems before setting them into a vase for display. On another level, displacement would involve the use of a convenient and alternate outlet for one's energies and tensions when the direct path to a target is blocked. For example, a woman who feels hostile toward her husband but who cannot express her feelings openly to him may become irritable with the children as a result.

(A) *Sublimation.* Sublimation is a form of displacement in which an unacceptable impulse is transformed into one that is creative and socially acceptable (A. Freud, 1946, p. 56). A man with a strong need for aggression may channel his energies into activities that are socially acceptable. He may become, for example, an outstanding scientist or a first-rate novelist. By so doing, he may be able to dominate and control the behavior of others and to satisfy his need for aggression.

(B) *Projection.* When a person protects his ego by attributing his own undesirable characteristics to others, we might infer that projection has taken place (Freud, 1938c, p. 625). For example, a student who is very stingy might claim that it is other people who are really stingy. A girl who hates her mother may be convinced that it is her mother who hates her. A student who cheats on examinations may continually assert that other students received high grades because they cheated.

(6) *Reaction-Formation.* Reaction-formation involves the conversion of an undesirable impulse into its opposite. Freud considered it a lower form of sublimation (Freud, 1938d, p. 625). The man who hates his wife and yet is exceedingly kind to her would be a pertinent example. He could be said to be "killing her with kindness." Another example might be the parent who knows that his son hates violence of any kind and gives him a "gift" of karate lessons at the local YMCA for his birthday.

(7) *Rationalization.* Rationalization is the justification of behavior through the use of plausible, but inaccurate, excuses. A young athlete fails to stay on the football team because of a lack of ability and comes to the conclusion that he did not really want to stay on the team because it is going to lose many games. Or a young fellow flunks out of college and then claims that self-made men with practical experiences are superior to college graduates with little "real-life" experience. Finally, a person who loses a tennis match and blames it on the inferior quality of the ball or racquet would be rationalizing if, in fact, the ball and racquet were superior in quality. All these examples illustrate the "sour grapes" form of rationalization. The other form has been called the "sweet lemon" rationalization. In this kind of defensive maneuver, the person protects himself against feelings of inadequacy by claiming that an unpleasant experience is exactly what he or she wanted. A man who wins a llama on a television program and proclaims that it is the answer to his dreams might be using the "sweet lemon" type of rationalization.

(8) *Intellectualization.* Intellectualization is a process that allows individuals to protect themselves against unbearable pain. It involves a dissociation between one's thoughts and feelings. For example, a man may conjure up an elaborate rationale to "explain" the death of his young wife. By citing reasons and focusing on the logic of his argument, he may avoid, for a while at least, the tremendous pain associated with such a traumatic experience.

(9) *Undoing.* Undoing is a defense mechanism in which a person who thinks or acts upon an undesirable impulse makes amends by performing some action that nullifies the undesirable one. Such actions are typically irrational and can be seen in various superstitious rituals and in some religious ceremonies. By performing the undoing act, the person is convinced that the wrong he or she committed has been rectified. For example, a person who has continual thoughts about masturbation and believes that they are evil may wash his hands frequently as a means of "cleansing" himself.

(10) *Compromise Formation.* This defense involves the use of contradictory behaviors to gain some satisfaction for an undesirable impulse. The barbed compliment would be an example. Betty, who really hates Jane, comments: "My, what a pretty dress. How did *you* ever manage to select it?" Or a male student says to his professor, "That was an excellent test. How did *you* ever manage to construct it?" To apply the *coup de grace*, the student may add a few moments later, "Good lecture; I never expected it from you."

Freud postulated other defense mechanisms, such as identification, regression, and fixation. These defenses will be reviewed in the section on psychosexual development.

THE PROCESS OF PERSONALITY DEVELOPMENT

The Theory of Psychosexual Development

With this preliminary and rather sketchy review of the major structural components of personality completed, we turn to an examination of Freud's usage of these constructs in his scheme of *psychosexual development.* Before discussing the theory, however, we should note that it is biological in nature and based upon the inevitable unfolding of different stages at which particular behaviors occur. Normal development involves the coursing of libidinal or "sexual" energy through to a final stage called, aptly enough, genital. Between the phallic and genital stages lies the latency stage, in which sexual energy was considered to lie dormant. Abnormal development, on the other hand, occurs if the person undergoes traumatic experiences in early childhood, almost inevitably sexual in nature, which prevent the flow of significant amounts of libidinal energy through the various stages. The person's development is then said to be *fixated* at a particular stage, so that he or she is more vulnerable to crisis later in life. When subjected to stress, for example, he or she might regress by showing infantile kinds of behavior. For each stage in which conflict occurs, Freud postulated a corresponding adult character pattern.

Oral stage. The infant is practically all id, according to Freud, and cannot initially distinguish between himself and the environment. He is controlled by biological impulses and is basically selfish. The focus of pleasurable sensations or "sexual" impulses during the first, pregenital stage is the mouth, (Freud, 1969, p. 10). Of course, the mouth is also the source for food and water intake and thus is critical for survival, but this fact is not emphasized by Freud. Obviously, the parents are typically the primary sources of gratification for the infant, and their behavior is critical in determining whether or not the infant will experience personal difficulties in later life. These difficulties may occur as a result of parental overindulgence or underindulgence of the infant's needs during the first year or so. For example, conflict could be generated if the mother resents nursing the baby and proceeds to wean it abruptly. In such an instance, portions of the libidinal energy available to the individual become fixated around this conflict, while the remaining energy flows through to the next stage.

Anal Stage. During the second and third years, pleasurable sensations are focused on the anal cavity. The chief pleasures for the child involve retention or expulsion of feces (Freud, 1957, p. 324). It is during this stage that ego processes are being differentiated from the id and the child begins to assert his independence. This independence does not, however, involve rational decision-making in which the child weighs the conflicting evidence and comes to reasonable conclusions. Rather, it is a negativistic independence in which the child rejects out-of-hand whatever is being offered by the parents. If the child is asked, "Will you please tie your shoelaces?" the answer is an immediate "No." If the child is then asked "Do you want a candy bar?" the answer, once again, is a resounding "No," even though he or she may be hungry and had been seen by the mother foraging in the kitchen for candy only moments earlier. It is a period, in short, for a contest of wills and the assertion of ego control.

According to Freud, the primary contest revolves around toilet training. In this culture and others, cleanliness is a virtue and parents typically place heavy stress on regulating defecation and urination. The child can resist these demands by retaining the waste matter or by expelling it inappropriately; for example, by wetting or soiling his pants. Conflicts during this stage precipitate the occurrence of particular kinds of behavioral difficulties in adolescence and adulthood, as we shall soon learn.

Phallic Stage. During the fourth and fifth years, sexual tension is focused on the genital area. Both boys and girls are considered to derive pleasure from self-manipulation (Freud, 1957, p. 327). For boys, there is a developing longing for sexual contact with the mother. In the broadest sense, this longing involves a seeking of affection and love from the mother. At the same time, there is an increasing awareness on the part of the child that there is a sexual relationship between his parents and that father is his rival. But the father is bigger and stronger physically, *sexual intercourse / persons so closely / related that / to many they're forbidden by law*

and the child is fearful that he will be punished for his desires and that his penis will be cut off. The child can alleviate his castration anxiety by *identifying* with his father. His sexual desire is thus shunted into more socially acceptable channels. These strong, conflicting feelings and the process by which they are more or less adequately resolved Freud termed the *Oedipal complex,* a term borrowed from Sophocles' tragedy, *Oedipus Rex,* in which the Greek king and hero, Oedipus, unwittingly kills his father and commits incest with his mother. The development of the superego is an outgrowth of the resolution of this complex, in which the child takes on the values of his parents and their attitudes toward society.

Freud saw support for the Oedipal conflict in the kinship ties and practices within clans in various primitive societies (Freud, 1950, pp. 144–145). Using anthropological and historical evidence as a guide, he speculated that the brothers of a clan in a primal horde banded together in order to kill their father, their chief rival for the affection of the women. After committing the deed, they realized that a new social organization was necessary if they were ever going to live in harmony and avoid mutual destruction in a frantic effort to possess the women. As a consequence, a law against incest was implemented. Freud theorized that all cultures had instituted two taboos; namely, a law against incest, and a law protecting the totem animal. The totem animal was seen by Freud as a symbol of the father and worship of it allowed tribal members to allay their sense of guilt for their deed. In Freud's view, worship of the totem animal also symbolized a covenant between tribal members and their father. On the one hand, the father promised them protection and care; on the other hand, the members promised to respect the father's life. That is, they promised not to repeat the deed which had destroyed their real father. The covenant between tribal members and their fathers bears some resemblance to the male child's eventual identification with his father as a means of resolving his own basic conflict over the mother.

The process for girls is very different, according to Freud. It is the lack of a penis which is the source of their problems. Girls are considered to envy boys their possession of a penis and to seek its attainment. At first they try to compensate for their "deficiency" by emulating boys and also by masturbation of what Freud calls their "stunted penis," their clitoris. While mother is their first love object, they come to resent her, in Freud's opinion, for bringing them into the world without a penis. They then begin to love their father, since he has the desired object. They then identify with their mothers as a means of vicariously obtaining the desired object (Freud, 1969, pp. 44–51). Although initially they seek his penis, Freud argues that this desire is transformed into another fantasy—the wish to have a baby by him as a gift. Finally, the girl wishes to have a male baby since he would bring the longed-for penis with him. Since these desires can never be fulfilled, all girls were considered by

Freud to have relatively inadequate superegos. These "mutilated little creatures," as he called them, had little sense of objectivity and justice. This special conflict process in girls was called the Electra complex by some of Freud's supporters. In Greek mythology, Electra induced her brother to murder their hated mother. Perhaps one reason Freud was reluctant to apply the term Electra complex to the conflict process in girls is that the analogy seems weak and at variance with his own description of the process.

In any event, for many people, the Freudian proposal concerning the mechanisms and outcomes of the Oedipus complex, especially for girls, is absolutely absurd. Freud has been severely criticized for maintaining that the Oedipal conflict is biologically based and occurs universally in all human beings. There is, for example, some cross-cultural evidence that the Oedipus complex is not universal in the species and that, in some cultures at least, the resentment of the boy toward his father is based upon his powerful position in the family and not upon sexual jealousy.

Next, advocates of the women's movement in this country have correctly pointed to Freud's chauvinistic outlook toward women and the fact that such an attitude was not unexpected since he lived in a strongly patriarchal society. Women in Vienna in Freud's time were second-class citizens and subject to all the degrading treatment that accrues to members of minority groups. His concept of "penis envy" is particularly galling to women because it implies that anatomy is destiny and that constructive personal growth is virtually impossible. If you are inherently inferior, it makes little sense to expend great amounts of effort to try and improve yourself.

Karen Horney, a prominent neo-analyst, took particular issue with Freud over this matter many years ago. Her arguments are, in general, echoed by leading feminists today. Horney maintained that the Freudian position is bogged down in faulty biology. She asks why a biologically healthy female would show such psychological qualities. Further, she maintains that the Freudian interpretation does not allow for the social and cultural factors that affect the psychology of women. Penis envy is presumed to manifest itself in the behavior of the "castrating female" by tendencies to dominate and humiliate men and to be ambitious and competitive. In the course of her observations, Horney noted that tendencies toward dictatorial power and egocentric ambition are characteristic of neurotic *men* as well as of neurotic women (Horney, 1937, p. 204). These problems stem, in her opinion, from an excessively competitive society in which status is conferred upon those who are achievement-oriented, dominant, and ambitious. What normal women actually envy is the status of men and the psychological and physical rewards associated with the positive aspects of its attainment. This argument was also advocated by Alfred Adler in some of his later writings.

Finally, some recent research questions the validity of Freud's contention that women of all cultures desire a male child. Psychotherapist Max Hammer asked married and single college students and married non-college adults the question: "If you knew for sure that you could have only one child, would you prefer that child to be a male or a female?" and recorded their answers (Hammer, 1970, pp. 54–56). Table 2.1 presents the results in detail. In general, Hammer found that the results for the noncollege adults disconfirmed the Freudian hypothesis, since 70 percent of these women said they would prefer a girl. Of course, a Freudian would probably disagree with this conclusion, since it is based upon individual self-reports. He would argue that the women who said they preferred a girl were actually repressing their true desires. Even if one replicated this finding many times with large numbers of women, the Freudian might still maintain that the women participating in these studies were repressing their "true" desires. Although there is no way actively and directly to disprove the Freudian contention, it does not seem reasonable to expect that *every* woman in the world has such desires, given the incredibly complex and varied motivational life of human beings.

Latency Stage. This stage ranges from the sixth year to puberty and is a period in which the sexual instincts were assumed by Freud to be dormant (Freud, 1969, p. 10). He believed that the person's characteristic ways of behaving are established during the first five years of life and that radical personality change was extremely difficult, if not impossible, thereafter. Sexual energy is not lessened, but is sublimated or channeled into other pursuits, including the learning of various skills from school experiences.

Genital Stage. With the advent of puberty, sexual tension increases dramatically. The reproductive organs have matured and both sexes are

TABLE 2.1 Preference for Sex of Child, by Social Factors and Sex of Adult Respondents

Preference	Unmarried College Students		Married College Students		Married Non-college Adults	
	Men	Women	Men	Women	Men	Women
Boy	156 (90%)	184 (78%)	24 (83%)	15 (73%)	16 (90%)	8 (30%)
Girl	18 (10%)	52 (22%)	5 (17%)	6 (27%)	2 (10%)	18 (70%)
Number	174	236	29	21	18	26

Adapted from Hammer, 1970, p. 55.

now capable of procreation. The aims of the sexual instincts have been predominately autoerotic, but now the goal is mating with an appropriate sex object. At this point, an adequate heterosexual adjustment depends upon the amount of libidinal energy available to the person. If there have been no severe traumatic experiences in early childhood, with corresponding libido fixations, an adequate adjustment is possible. Upon adulthood, the person typically marries and settles into family life. For Freud, the normal person is one who makes satisfactory adjustments in two major areas, love and work. As mentioned earlier, an inadequate adjustment, on the other hand, involves libidinal fixations and the development of particular character disorders (Freud, 1969, pp. 12–13). We turn now to a discussion of these character types.

Character Types

The Oral Character. Persons who are fixated at the oral stage have problems in later life related primarily to receiving or taking of things from the external world. Concretely, individuals who have had their needs overindulged become habituated to receiving support and encouragement from other people. They are people who have been overindulged and thus are excessively dependent upon others for gratification (Blum, 1953, p. 160). They tend to be trusting, accepting, and gullible. People with such characteristics tend to admire strength and leadership in other people, but they make little attempt to fend for themselves. One could also conjecture that they tend to be rather incompetent, since most of their gratification is derived from what others do for them and not from what they themselves accomplish. There is a tendency on the part of such people to be overly optimistic, with the corresponding feeling that "Bad things can't happen to me." Obviously, a person with such a Pollyanna outlook will experience inevitable conflicts with others, since not everyone is nurturant and supportive like mother. How long could you expect others to remain your friends if you kept demanding all of their time, effort, and affection, without reciprocating in approximate measure?

Fixations may also occur because parents underindulge or severely frustrate the needs of their infants. In such instances, a person learns to exploit others. As neo-analyst Fenichel reports, people with such an orientation tend to have sadistic attitudes (Fenichel, 1945, p. 489). They tend to envy others their success and to try, through the use of manipulative strategies, to dominate them. Furthermore, such people tend to be stingy. They want "something for nothing." It is difficult to imagine liking and supporting a person who is continually manipulative and exploitative in interpersonal relations.

The Anal Character. Anal eroticism stems from difficulties during toilet training, as mentioned earlier. According to Freud, anal characters have three primary characteristics. They are exceptionally stingy, orderly, and obstinate (Blum, 1953, p. 161). Furthermore, each of these primary characteristics has a number of other traits associated with it. Their sense of orderliness is associated with both bodily cleanliness and conscientiousness in the performance of the most trivial duties. The tendencies toward parsimony may be associated, in extreme cases, with avarice, and obstinacy may give rise to active defiance of others. All these characteristics may be an outgrowth of reaction-formation defenses in which these persons may be unconsciously renouncing socially unacceptable impulses such as messiness, dirtiness, and stinginess. These impulses, in turn, are considered to be based upon the pleasurable sensations that accompanied early toilet training, in which the children kept their "prized possessions" from the parents and took delight in playing with their feces.

The Phallic Character. The difficulties experienced by phallic characters stem from inadequate resolution of the Oedipus complex. Phallic characters react to severe castration anxiety by behaving in a reckless, resolute, and self-assured manner (Blum, 1953, pp. 163–164). The penis is overvalued and this fact is reflected in excessive vanity and exhibitionism. Such males have to prove they are "real men." One way of proving it is by continuous conquests of women. The Don Juan type of male fits this description. For women, the primary motive is penis envy. Consequently, they are continuously striving for superiority over men. Such women are considered to be "castrating females."

The Genital Character. Genital characters are people who have made the necessary sexual adjustments. There is no damming-up of libidinal energies, since such people have located appropriate love objects (Blum, 1953, p. 164). They are also capable of modifying socially unacceptable impulses into acceptable ones. They have found satisfying careers and are performing creatively.

The Neurotic Person

People with the character types just described are not, technically speaking, neurotics. They are, instead, people who have learned habitual and immature ways of behaving as a means of coping. Continued severe stress, however, could result in the development of *neurosis* and eventually *psychosis*. For example, breakdown of the oral character might result in schizophrenia. Additional and severe stress might result in hysteria for the phallic character and *obsessive-compulsive* neurosis for the anal character. Thus, the origins of neurosis, as well as for the character types, are early-childhood conflicts during psychosexual development. These conflicts are inevitably sexual in nature, although a wish for death in the form of aggression toward others may also play a part.

The seeds for neurosis are sown by conflict between the id and ego and, to some extent, by the superego. This conflict involves an initial rejection by ego of inappropriate and powerful instinctual impulses. The ego then defends itself by the mechanism of repression. Working in tandem with the superego, it forces the unacceptable impulses out of awareness. The id impulses continue to struggle for expression and eventually the ego is forced to compromise by allowing them to be gratified in substitute ways through symptom formation. If this compromise is not forthcoming, the person will experience overwhelming *anxiety*. Thus, the mechanisms of compromise utilized by the ego result in a lessening of anxiety. Unfortunately, the use of defense mechanisms prevents people from learning the sources of their problems and ways of correcting them. Through analysis, however, what is unconscious and painful is made conscious. With strengthened egos, people are better able to deal with future problems and to function more adequately as members of society. At this point a review of a case of obsessive-compulsive neurosis will be presented as a means of providing you with a clearer picture of the workings of the Freudian model.

Obsessive-Compulsive Neurosis in the Rat-Man

Freud reported a case in which a young man with university education entered therapy because he suffered from various obsessions and compulsions (Freud, 1963, pp. 19–105). His primary fears were that his father might die and that a woman whom he loved would be hurt or killed. In addition, he had compulsions to cut his own throat with a razor and an impulse to kill an old woman. His attempts to cope with these problems caused him to expend considerable energy, and it was not surprising that his sexual life was less than adequate. He reported performing coitus irregularly and masturbating only rarely.

Freud secured a promise from the man to report everything that occurred to him, even if it was unpleasant, or seemed senseless or irrelevant. According to Freud, the man was unfamiliar with the analytic emphasis on sexual matters but began a discussion of his problems by recalling sexual experiences in his childhood. These episodes involved his fondling the genitals of a willing young family governess and watching another family governess undress as she prepared for her bath. He reported further that he enjoyed these experiences immensely, especially the ones which involved looking at the nude woman. At the same time, however, he had an uncanny feeling that his parents knew his thoughts and that he would be punished by his father for them. In general terms, then, we have a case in which strong instinctual impulses are experienced, but are warded off because the person anticipates superego-generated guilt feelings. In addition, Freud mentioned that the patient used other ego-defense mechanisms to protect himself.

In the course of the therapy, the patient also mentioned a current experience he had with a military officer during training maneuvers. He reported that he disliked and dreaded this man because the officer was obviously fond of cruelty. Furthermore, the patient told Freud that the officer advocated corporal punishment. During a conversation, the officer had told the patient of a horrible method of torture used by the military in other countries. The patient resisted telling Freud about it, but eventually relented and said that it involved putting a number of ravenous rats into a pot which had been turned upside down and attached to the person's buttocks. The rats then bored their way into his anus. Despite his reluctance to repeat the story, Freud noticed that the young man showed horrified pleasure as he told it. Furthermore, the patient mentioned that, as he related the captain's story to Freud, he had the idea that the punishment was happening to the woman he loved. Subsequently, the patient was forced to admit that the idea occurred to him that the punishment was being applied to his father as well. Why did the patient have these cruel and hostile feelings toward two people he loved?

Further probing by Freud eventually revealed the source of the patient's wish that the rat punishment happen to his father and loved one. First, the patient's father had been a noncommissioned officer who had been extremely cruel and violent at times. Freud suggested that the captain who first related the rat punishment story was disliked because he resembled the patient's father. At base, then, the patient hated his father. Freud then turned to the unraveling of these feelings. He believed that the problem lay in the sphere of sexuality and that some traumatic experience was responsible for the patient's feelings toward his father.

An examination of the onanistic or masturbatory history of the patient provided Freud with an important clue concerning the nature of the patient's conflicts with his father. The patient did not masturbate to any great extent during puberty, but a compulsion to practice it started when he was twenty-one, shortly *after* his father's death. In addition, the patient had fantasies that his father was alive and would reappear at any moment. Between twelve and one o'clock in the morning the patient would interrupt his work and take out his penis and look at it in the mirror. Freud conjectured that it was during this time period that the patient expected his father's ghost to appear. Since the father would then witness his son's exposure and would disapprove of it, Freud inferred that the patient's actions were defiant ones. Further probing revealed that the patient had been caught by his father in a sexual act connected with masturbation during his early childhood and that the father had beaten him severely for it. The patient had then repressed all memories of the event. Thus, the father had been perceived by the patient as trying to interfere with his sexual satisfaction, and so the son wished secretly for his death.

Freud found that rats had many meanings for the patient, but three were especially important. The patient recalled that, once when he visited his father's grave, he saw a rat gliding along over the grave. He assumed that the rat had been inside his father's grave and had just finished eating part of the corpse. The rat was a dirty and greedy animal, one that was mercilessly and cruelly persecuted by people. He felt that he was much like the rat, since when he was a child he had bitten people when he was in a rage, perhaps a rage similar to those generated by his father's physical beatings. In addition, rats were like children in his earliest recollections of them, and he was very fond of children. Unfortunately, though, his loved one could not have any children and this fact may have been the primary reason for his ambivalent feelings toward her. Finally, Freud conjectured that the rat could be considered a symbol of the male sex organ. This organ could further be symbolized as a worm, since as a child the patient had had an illness in which large roundworms had burrowed in his anus. Freud came to the conclusion that the rat obsession was also related to anal eroticism. Thus, Freud eventually revealed to the patient the multiple sources of his anal conflicts and, with the patient's consent, concluded that he was cured.

Research Evidence for the Theory of Psychosexual Development

We may agree that Freud created an interesting and provocative theory of human development, but the question of its empirical validity remains open and subject to examination. Even though the theory is relatively vaguely stated, it is still possible to derive hypotheses from it for scientific testing. First, the theory suggests that certain clusters of personality traits exist in mature adults (Kline, 1972, p. 7). For example, hypothesized traits in the oral receptive character include optimism, dependency, impatience, talkativeness, love of soft foods, and an intense curiosity. For the anal character, key characteristics include opposition to the influence from others, a drive to clean things, minute attention to detail, and a love of self-control. For the phallic character, typical traits include recklessness, pride, vanity, self-assurance, and courage. Can we identify people who have any one set of these traits and not the others? After surveying a great deal of research on the subject, Kline concludes: "There is good evidence for the anal character . . . some evidence for the oral character . . . and almost no support for the other psychosexual syndromes (e.g., the phallic character)" (Kline, 1972, p. 44).

Close examination of the data and findings in these studies, however, may lead us to a different conclusion in regard to the anal character. For example, in one of the most comprehensive studies on the anal character, the investigator found little relationship between parsimony and cleanliness and the general factor labeled anal character, although parsimony was considered by Freud to be one of the key elements of this character. In addition, most of the studies conducted on the anal character used only paper-and-pencil measures to assess the traits presumed to be an integral part of this character type. Although people may report that they have certain traits, we would have more confidence in the anal character construct if it could be shown that such character types actually behaved in a way suggested by their own traits. Does a person who reports that he is orderly and parsimonious actually show behavior that is considered by others to be orderly and parsimonious? Does he keep his room and office neat and clean? Does he wash regularly and appear neatly dressed? There is very little evidence to support the existence of such a relationship. Thus, it would appear that the evidence in support of the anal character is not as strong as Kline suggests. The general conclusion to be reached concerning the existence of the various character types is that, thus far, there is little support for this basic aspect of Freud's theory.

The second hypothesis seeks an answer to the question, "If these character types exist, can they be related to various child-rearing practices, as Freud surmised?" (Kline, 1953, p. 8). The results of a great many investigations show little or no support for Freud's speculations about the childhood etiology of the various character types. In fairness, however, we could maintain that the lack of support stems more from methodological inadequacies—for example, the use of unreliable and invalid measures—than from inadequacies of the theory (Kline, 1953, p. 94). In short, we could argue that the theory has never been put to a fair test. Another person could counterargue that many aspects of the theory itself are so vague that satisfactory measures of its constructs cannot be devised. Accordingly, it might be best to abandon the effort to test it. In any event, the evidence in support of this part of the theory is somewhat weak and unconvincing.

At this point let us turn to a discussion of some of the techniques Freud used to assess personality.

TECHNIQUES OF ASSESSMENT

Freud relied primarily on the case study method to understand the personalities of his patients. As mentioned earlier, this technique involved detailed and exhaustive examination and analysis of the lives and past experiences of his patients and the subsequent utilization of this information to help them overcome their problems.

Free association and *dream analysis* were the two major aspects of the case study procedure Freud employed. These techniques emerged only after considerable experimentation with lines of inquiry that focused on the physiological determinants of behavior and on hypnotic phenomena.

The free association technique involved self-reports by the patients of whatever thoughts and memories occurred to them, without any kind of self-censorship. The patients were told to report *all* thoughts, however trivial, unimportant, mortifying, and illogical they seemed to be. The emphasis was on honest reporting. During these sessions, Freud sat behind the patient, out of sight but in a position to watch facial expressions and gestures. This technique was used primarily because Freud wanted to be certain that he did not elicit particular forms of behavior through the use of gestures and facial expressions. He wanted the patients' responses to be spontaneous and not to be controlled by him (Ford and Urban, 1963, p. 168). Freud then interpreted the patients' remarks and provided them with an explanation of their behavior in an attempt to help them find solutions to their problems.

Freud's discovery that his patients often mentioned dreams has been described earlier. His task, as he saw it, was to analyze the symbols present in the manifest content of the dreams in an attempt to uncover their latent or hidden meanings. As a result of his extensive experiences, Freud believed that he had discovered dream symbols with universal, underlying meanings. Sticks, tree trunks, umbrellas, and snakes, for example, were thought to symbolize the penis; boxes, doors, and furniture chests represented the vagina. Symbols depicting decapitation were indicative of castration. Despite their universal nature, Freud thought that all symbols had to be judged and interpreted in terms of the unique conflicts of the individual. Dreams not only had latent meanings; they also consisted of events presented in condensed and dramatic forms, events that had multiple meanings. Freud saw his task as the discovery of these hidden meanings and the interpretation of them to his patients.

APPLICATION OF THE THEORY TO THE TREATMENT OF PSYCHOPATHOLOGY

Neurotics and psychotics are individuals who have responded to anxiety created by the stifling of their instinctual impulses with various defense mechanisms. As a result, normal growth has been arrested and their functioning is ineffective and stereotypic. To cure such individuals, it is necessary to reduce their conflicts and defenses by relieving their anxieties. Under such conditions, their energies are directed away from the maintenance of defenses and made available for constructive growth. These conditions are made possible by therapists who help these individuals understand the sources of their conflicts and the fact that these internal struggles have weakened the ego and prevented them from coping effectively with the demands of external reality. They are helped to see that they are repeating old behaviors and using ineffective strategies in current situations.

To reinitiate movement toward normal growth, therapists help reexpose the patients to emotional situations they could not handle in the past. Patients relive their conflicts and interactions, although in less intense form, through their relationships with their therapists. There is the development of a transference neurosis on the part of the patients involving the emergence of attitudes toward the analyst that have their basis in patient attitudes toward their parents. By reliving their conflicts, patients begin to gain insight into the sources of their problems. Yet the transference relationship results in more than intellectual insight; it involves an emotional awakening. Patients actively "work through" their problems and then experience changes. The results, if the transference has been successful, make conflicts that were unconscious conscious, and place id impulses firmly under the control of the ego. In brief, the ego is strengthened and is now prepared to mediate maximal instinctual gratification by helping such individuals function within the limits set by society.

CRITICAL COMMENTS

Freud's position can be evaluated in terms of how well it meets the six criteria outlined in Chapter 1 for judging the worth of scientific theories.

Comprehensiveness. Freud was an astute and original thinker who created a highly comprehensive theory. The range and diversity of behavior and experience described and interpreted is remarkable. Freud sought to understand not only various kinds of emotional and behavioral disorders, but other phenomena such as humor, marriage, war, death, friendship, myths and fairy tales, incest, societal mores, dreams, slips of the tongue, "bungled actions," suicide, bed-wetting, creativity, competition, and absent-mindedness. In short, Freud developed a system that explicitly sought to explain virtually all human behavior.

Although there is no question of the comprehensiveness of the theory in terms of the number of subject areas to which it has been and could be applied, there is a serious question concerning the adequacy of its explanatory power. It is a theory that does not allow for different and more parsimonious explanations of behavior. It is a "nothing-but" theory. The nothing-but refers to the fact that sex and aggressive tendencies are the sole determinants of behavior. Thus the motivational base of the theory is limited. It ignores the fact that people can be motivated by many different kinds of reinforcers. Despite these facts, Freud's theory remains one of the most comprehensive conceptual systems ever created by a personality investigator.

Precision and Testability. Part of the major problem with Freudian theory centers upon the relative vagueness of its concepts, the imprecision and ambiguities of its relational statements, and the difficulties it presents in allowing for the clear derivation and testing of hypotheses. Also, when results based upon such loose theorizing are secured, it is impossible to know whether they are supportive of the theory. When the results are contrary to the theorizing, however, it is always possible for advocates to claim that such outcomes are meaningless, since the hypotheses were not validly derived from the major theoretical propositions.

A related criticism is that much of the theory is presented in metaphors or in terms which do not lend themselves to scientific testing; for example, the love and death instincts. Frequently, "explanations" for observations are offered after the fact. The theory postdicts well, but has real difficulty in predicting in advance how people will behave. Much of the evidence for it is post hoc and secured through uncontrolled case study methods. In addition, Freud did not record the patient's observations as he recited them, thereby opening the door to the criticism that his memory of the events was distorted and drawn on the basis of observations of a few individuals. Finally, the universal conclusions that Freud drew about human behavior on the basis of extensive observations of a few patients seem incredible and naive. They can, however, be better understood if we realize the implications of a theory that is strongly rooted in biology. It is clear, then, that Freud's theory has some difficulty in meeting the precision and testability criterion.

Simplicity. Freud's theory fails somewhat to meet the parsimony criterion. Although it utilizes a number of assumptions and concepts to account for the phenomena in its domain, its proposed explanatory scheme is highly restricted in nature. In addition, the structure of human personality is divided into only three components and the interactions between and among these three facets are presumed to account for the nature of the underlying conflicts that hinder personality functioning.

Freud presented a generally pessimistic and one-sided stance concerning human nature. People were seen as essentially irrational and controlled by amoral forces. Although he recognized fully that human beings can be rational in their behavior, he chose to focus almost entirely on the irrational side of human nature in his work.

Empirical Validity. There have been literally thousands of investigations of various aspects of Freud's theory. Although the evidence in support of his theorizing on psychosexual development is weak, more convincing evidence shows that the less adequate an individual's defenses against sexual and aggressive impulses, the greater the likelihood of the appearance of psychopathology (Silverman, 1976, pp. 621–637). In addition, there is also evidence that sexual conflicts are present in some neurotics and that some of these disturbances arise from experiences during the early childhood period. All in all, the research evidence in support of the various aspects of Freud's theory is greater than many of his critics would be willing to admit.

Heuristic Value. Freud's theory has had tremendous heuristic value. He has served as an inspiration to many scholars by showing them the kinds of contributions that can be made to our knowledge of behavior through painstaking and courageous investigation. His theory has proved fascinating and stimulating to many people in many different disciplines. Scholars in literature, sociology, history, anthropology, religion, and political science have all made use of Freudian concepts.

Much of this fascination lies in the complicated picture of human beings that Freud has painted. Men and women are not simply rational animals, but curious mixtures of the irrational and rational. They often feel threatened by society and are continually searching for acceptable ways to express their innermost feelings. In an attempt to deal with their conflicts, they use various defense mechanisms which, while temporarily protective, prove damaging in the long run. Through painful confrontation with reality in a therapeutic setting, the limitations of their personalities are revealed and heroic attempts to overcome them are made with the help of the therapist. It seems clear that such drama was destined to excite and interest observers of human behavior and experience. This is a major part of Freud's legacy.

Applied Value. In addition to his seminal contributions to therapy and the treatment of emotional disorders, Freud's insights have been applied by anthropologists to cross-cultural phenomena. For example, Freudian concepts have been used to explain the effects of different weaning and toilet-training schedules on later personality development, as well as incestuous behavior. They have also been employed by sociologists and social psychologists to help them understand the dynamics of family life and the functioning of small groups. Freudian concepts have also been used fruitfully by historians, theologians, novelists, and economists. Thus, the psychoanalytic position has had considerable applied value.

DISCUSSION QUESTIONS

1. In what ways do the interactions between and among the id, ego, and superego create difficulties for the individual?
2. What are the primary defense mechanisms, as they were envisioned by Freud? Give possible examples of the operation of such mechanisms from your own experiences.
3. Cite some examples of the ways in which defense mechanisms can be used to help the person adjust to his or her environment.
4. What do you think might happen to a society in which id impulses were left unchecked by the superego?
5. How would you explain the behavior of a person who overeats continually in terms of the Freudian model of psychosexual development?
6. Do you agree that cleanliness is a virtue in contemporary society? If so, what are the possible reasons that people value it? If not, cite your reasons.
7. Do you think that Freud's concept of penis envy has any merit?

8.   What are the implications of the Freudian position for the ways in which society should treat homosexuals? Do you agree with Freud's position?

9.   Do you agree with Freud that the normal individual is one who is satisfactorily adjusted in two major areas—namely, love and work?

10.   Do you agree with Freud that the two major human motives are sex and aggression? State your reasons.

NOTES

G. S. Blum, *Psychoanalytic Theories of Personality* (New York: McGraw-Hill, 1953).

O. Fenichel, *The Psychoanalytic Theory of Neurosis* (New York: Norton, 1945)

D. H. Ford and H. B. Urban, *Systems of Psychotherapy: A Comparative Study* (New York: Wiley, 1963).

A. Freud, *The Ego and the Mechanisms of Defense,* trans. Cecil Baines (New York: International Universities Press, 1946).

S. Freud, "The History of the Psychoanalytic Movement." in A. A. Brill, ed., *The Basic Writings of Sigmund Freud* (New York: Random House, 1938a).

S. Freud, "The Interpretation of Dreams," in A. A. Brill, ed., *The Basic Writings of Sigmund Freud* (New York: Random House, 1938b).

S. Freud, "Totem and Taboo," in A. A. Brill, ed., *The Basic Writings of Sigmund Freud* (New York: Random House, 1938c).

S. Freud, "Totem and Taboo," trans. J. Strachey (New York: Norton, 1950).

S. Freud, "Three Contributions to the Theory of Sex," in A. A. Brill, *The Basic Writings of Sigmund Freud* (New York: Random House, 1938d).

S. Freud, *A General Introduction to Psychoanalysis,* trans. J. Riviere (New York: Permabooks, 1957).

S. Freud, *The Ego and the Id,* trans. J. Riviere and rev. and ed. J. Strachey (New York: Norton, 1960).

S. Freud, "Three Case Histories," in P. Rieff, ed., *The Collected Papers of Sigmund Freud* (New York: Collier Books, 1963).

S. Freud, *An Outline of Psychoanalysis,* trans. and ed. J. Strachey (New York: Norton, 1969).

M. Hammer, "Preference for a Male Child: Cultural Factors," *Journal of Individual Psychology,* 1970, **26,** 54–56.

K. Horney, *The Neurotic Personality of Our Time* (New York: Norton, 1937).

E. Jones, *The Life and Work of Sigmund Freud,* ed. and abridged L. Trilling and S. Marcus (Garden City, N.Y.: Anchor Books, 1963).

P. Kline, *Fact and Fantasy in Freudian Theory* (London: Methuen, 1972).

L. H. Silverman, "Psychoanalytic Theory: The Reports of My Death Are Greatly Exaggerated," *American Psychologist,* 1976, **31,** 621–637.

SUGGESTED READINGS

Fenichel, O. *The Psychoanalytic Theory of Neurosis.* New York: Norton, 1945.

Freud, S. *A General Introduction to Psychoanalysis* (English translation of the revised edition by J. Riviere). New York: Permabooks, 1957.

Freud, S. *The Standard Edition of the Complete Psychological Works*, J. Strachey (ed.). London: Hogarth, 1953.

Kline, P. *Fact and Fantasy in Freudian Theory*. London: Methuen, 1972.

Silverman, L. H. "Psychoanalytic Theory: The Reports of My Death Are Greatly Exaggerated," *American Psychologist*, 1976, **31**, 621–637.

GLOSSARY

Ambivalence. The mixed feelings of one person toward another that are characterized by alternation between love and hate.

Anal Eroticism. Feelings of sexual pleasure that have their source in the person's control over expulsion and retention of feces.

Anal Stage. Second pregenital stage of psychosexual development in which primary gratifications center around the anal orifice and the retention or expulsion of feces.

Anticathexis. Restraining force within the personality designed to keep unwanted impulses from reaching consciousness or awareness.

Anxiety. Painful feelings experienced by the person when the ego is threatened by unknown forces.

Cathexis. Driving energy force that attaches itself to an idea or behavior.

Compromise Formation. Defense mechanism which involves the use of contradictory behavior to attain some satisfaction for an unacceptable impulse.

Conscience. Punitive aspect of the superego, according to Freud.

Denial. Primitive defense mechanism in which the person protects him or herself against threats from the environment by blocking out their existence.

Determinism. Philosophical doctrine that all behavior is caused by the operation of other events and does not occur freely.

Displacement. Defense mechanism in which the person seeks gratification of impulses that are thwarted by shifting from the desired object to a substitute object.

Dream Analysis. Psychoanalytic technique used to probe the unconscious of the patient through the interpretation of his or her dreams.

Ego. Agency postulated by Freud to help the individual satisfy his or her basic urges in ways deemed appropriate by the members of society.

Ego-Ideal. Positive aspect of the superego involving the standards of perfection taught to the child by the parents.

Fixation. Defensive attachment to an earlier stage of psychosexual development that prevents the learning of new behaviors and the acquisition of new interpersonal relationships.

Free Association. Therapeutic technique pioneered by Freud in which the therapist encourages the patient to report without restriction any thoughts that occur to him or her.

Genital Stage. Final stage of psychosexual development in which an attempt is made to develop a mature love relationship with a member of the opposite sex.

Id. Reservoir of unconscious forces or urges that blindly seek gratification.

Identification. In Freudian theory, the defensive process whereby an individual takes on the characteristics of another in order to relieve his anxieties and reduce internal conflicts.

Intellectualization. Defense mechanism in which persons protect themselves against pain by isolating their thoughts about painful events from their feelings about them.

Latency Stage. Psychosexual period during which libidinal energy lies dormant and the primary focus is on the development of interests and skills through contact with childhood peers.

Libido. In Freudian theory, the basic energy source contained in the id that propels behavior. It was considered to consist of sexual impulses. For Jung, libido was conceptualized as a more general life-energy process consisting of sexual and self-preservative instincts.

Libido Theory. The view that the child has unconscious sexual urges that seek expression through intimacy with the parent of the opposite sex.

Neo-Analytic Perspective. Theoretical positions that have their origins in Freudian psychoanalytic theory, but that have evolved new concepts and ways of examining and understanding human personality which are significant departures from Freud's original theory.

Neurosis. Behavioral disorder characterized by underlying conflicts and anxieties that prevent the individual from coping effectively with his or her everyday problems.

Obsessive-Compulsive. A kind of neurotic who experiences repetitive thoughts and actions he or she cannot control.

Oedipal Complex. The process during the phallic stage in which the male child desires sexual contact with the mother, feels threatened by the father, and eventually resolves the conflict by identifying with the father.

Oral Stage. First pregenital stage of psychosexual development in which primary gratifications center around the mouth.

Phallic Stage. Third pregenital stage of psychosexual development in which primary gratifications are derived from manipulation of the genitals.

Projection. Defense mechanism in which a person attributes his or her undesirable characteristics to others.

Psychoanalysis. Theory of personality development, functioning, and change created by Freud. It places heavy emphasis on the roles of biological and un-conscious factors in the determination of behavior.

Psychopathology. Disordered behaviors, e.g., neuroses or psychoses.

Psychosexual Development. Theory devised by Freud to account for psychological and personality development in terms of changes in the biological functioning of the individual.

Psychosis. Severe kind of behavior disorder characterized by an inability to relate effectively to other people.

Rationalization. Defense mechanism in which the individual provides plausible, but inaccurate justifications for his or her behavior.

Reaction-formation. Defense mechanism in which an impulse or behavior is converted into its opposite.

Repression. Basic defense mechanism that keeps unpleasant experiences from entering consciousness.

Sublimation. Form of displacement in which a socially acceptable goal is substituted for one that is unacceptable.

Superego. Agency postulated by Freud to represent the incorporation by the individual of the moral standards of society and the ways in which the internalized standards control his or her behavior via reward and punishment.

Suppression. Defense mechanism involving the conscious removal of unpleasant thoughts from awareness.

Transference. Phenomenon postulated by Freud to account for the development of positive and negative feelings toward the therapist by the patient during the course of treatment, feelings originally presumed to be directed toward another person (usually one of the parents).

Unconscious. In Freudian theory, the depository of hidden wishes and impulses that govern the behavior of the individual.

Undoing. Defense mechanism in which a person makes amends for a socially unacceptable act by performing a related socially acceptable act that nullifies the misdeed.

Carl Gustav Jung (The Bettmann Archive, Inc.)

CHAPTER 3

Jung's Analytical Psychology

BIOGRAPHICAL SKETCH

Carl Jung was born in Kessewil, Switzerland, in 1875. His father, a pastor in the Swiss Reformed Church, was characterized by Jung as a weakling who was dominated by his wife. Jung described his mother as an insecure woman who frequently contradicted herself and treated members of the family inconsistently—that is, she alternated between being loving and kind and being harsh and aloof. When Jung was three years old, his mother entered a hospital for several months with an illness Jung attributed to the difficulty in her marriage (Storr, 1973, pp. 1-2). He also reported in his autobiography that the separation from his mother had a profound impact on him. He developed an ambivalent attitude of love and hate toward her, and reflections of his conflict are found in the image of women in his later works. In these works, women are frequently portrayed as destroyers and dominators as well as protectors; they are also depicted as unreliable and mistrustful:

> I was deeply troubled by my mothers being away. From then on, I always felt mistrustful when the word "love" was spoken. The feeling I associated with "woman" was for a long time that of innate unreliability. "Father," on the other hand, meant reliability and—powerlessness. That is the handicap I started off with. Later, these early impressions were [not] revised: I have trusted men friends and been disappointed by them, and I have mistrusted women and was not disappointed. (Jung, 1963, p. 8)

During his early school days, Jung lacked companionship, probably because he was far more advanced intellectually than any of the other children. He reported that he was not athletically inclined and did not engage in typical rough-and-tumble play with his peers. Instead, he spent much of his time in solitary pursuits, in long walks in which he gloried in the mysteries of nature. More important, Jung reports that he became fully aware of his own existence on one of his walks to school. He reveled in the experience that he was an autonomous being who controlled his own life, instead of being continually controlled by others:

53

> I was taking the long road to school . . . when suddenly for a single mo-
> ment I had the overwhelming impression of having just emerged from a
> dense cloud. I knew all at once: now I am *myself!* . . . Previously I had
> existed, too, but everything had merely happened to me. Now I happened
> to myself. Now I knew, I am myself now, now I exist. Previously I had been
> willed to do this and that: now I willed. This experience seemed to me
> tremendously important and new: there was "authority" in me. (Jung,
> 1963, pp. 32–33)

At this point, we can begin to see the beginnings of Jung's later focus
on the importance of "inner experience." Another incident during his
early school days made a marked impression on Jung and may explain
his later reliance on the concept of the unconscious. Jung was assigned a
composition topic in an English class. It interested him very much, so
that he spent a great deal of time and effort on it. He even hoped it
would receive one of the highest marks in the class. Instead, his teacher
accused him, in front of his classmates, of having copied it. Jung clung
to his innocence, but the teacher persisted in his accusations and
threatened to have Jung dismissed from school. For days afterward,
Jung thought about the incident and tried to muster proof of his innocence. But there was not a single way to prove he had written the
composition himself. At this point, his grief and rage threatened to get
out of control. Suddenly, he reported he experienced an "inner silence"
and something deep down inside him (his unconscious) began to speak.
It said:

> What is really going on here? All right, you are excited. Of course the
> teacher is an idiot who doesn't understand your nature—that is, doesn't
> understand it any more than you do. Therefore he is as mistrustful as you
> are. You distrust yourself and others, and that is why you side with those
> who are naive, simple, and easily seen through. One gets excited when one
> doesn't understand things. (Jung, 1963, pp. 65–66)

The picture that emerges of Jung as a boy is one of a person who was
sensitive and intelligent, but who neither understood nor was understood by his parents, teachers, and peers. As a result, he withdrew as
much as he could from the world of people and began to rely on his own
inner experiences to help him understand the world.

During his teens, Jung decided to become an archeologist, but his
family was too poor to send him to a university that included this
specialty in its curriculum. As a result, he entered the nearby University
of Basel and majored in medicine instead. He decided to specialize in
psychiatry because it seemed to provide an opportunity to reconcile two
important opposing tendencies within himself, an interest in natural
science and a preoccupation with religious and philosophical values.
This concern with conflict between opposites became a dominant theme
in his later theorizing (Storr, 1973, p. 5). In 1900, having obtained his
medical degree, Jung took a position as an assistant in a Zurich mental
hospital. There he became interested in the etiology of schizophrenia.

An extensive study of such patients led him to postulate the existence of a "collective unconscious" in people. He found the fantasies and delusions of the patients were in many respects similar to the myths and fantasies that guided people in contemporary and ancient cultures. Jung believed that the materials his patients revealed to him went beyond the recollection of their personal childhood and adult experiences (Storr, 1973, pp. 8–9).

In 1906, he published *The Psychology of Dementia Praecox,* a psychoanalytic treatment of schizophrenia. He also sent a copy of the book to Freud. A year later, Jung went to Vienna to meet Freud. The visit marked the beginning of a collaboration that lasted until 1913. The many reasons for the final split, catalogued in Jung's *Psychology of the Unconscious,* include his basic disagreement with Freud over the importance of the sex instinct in people. Jung could not accept Freud's belief that such an urge was virtually the only determinant of behavior. He also grew tired of Freud's concern with the pathological side of human nature. Jung wanted to develop a psychology that dealt with human aspirations and spiritual needs. In this respect he was an important forerunner of the humanist movement. He also argued that the way to self-realization was through the rediscovery of the spiritual self.(Storr, 1973, pp. 12–13). Between 1913 and 1917, Jung went through a mental crisis in his own life that culminated in his resigning from a lectureship at the University of Zurich. The crisis was precipitated by the break with Freud. Jung felt he could no longer rely on Freud's approach to therapy, that he needed to develop a new attitude or orientation toward treatment. He decided to let his patients tell him everything about their fantasies and dreams, and tried not to interpret their self-reports in Freudian terms. Then Jung himself began to have dreams of a frightening nature. For example, he dreamed of corpses placed in crematory ovens, who were then discovered to be alive. He also dreamed of monstrous catastrophes befalling Europe and felt vindicated when World War I broke out (Jung, 1963, pp. 170–176).

This flight into grotesque fantasies and dreams soon caused Jung to resign his lectureship. He did so consciously and deliberately because he " . . . felt that something great was happening to me." In short, Jung began an attempt to probe the secrets of his unconscious and to unlock the mystery of his own personality. He was obsessed with understanding both sides of his personality—that is, the inner world of subjective experience and the unconscious and the outer world of contact with other people and material objects. Since he was already successful in his academic and writing career (in his outer world), an exploration of his unconscious and inner world beckoned. In other words, Jung felt that his development was too one-sided; he was overdeveloped in terms of the outer world, but underdeveloped in terms of his knowledge of the inner world. He began a quest for "wholeness" or an integrated personality in which both sides of his nature would be brought into harmony or balance with each other. Part of this journey of self-exploration also involved an acceptance of the inevitability of death and of the fact that its occurrence was beyond the control of his ego. As a result, Jung eventually adopted a "religious" attitude toward life in the sense that he had a greater appreciation of it and its mysteries. This inward turning and self-analysis at the middle stage of life is clearly reflected in his description of the *individuation* process.

It was only toward the end of World War I that Jung emerged from his inward journey. In his opinion, the principal factor in the resolution of his crisis was his beginning to understand his mandala drawings, which symbolized the self. The rest of his life was relatively uneventful, except for one period during the World War II in which some critics accused him of being a Nazi sympathizer. Jung vigorously denied the charges and was eventually exonerated. He spent much of his time traveling and lecturing throughout the world and died in 1961 at the age of eighty-five. (Fordham, 1960, p. 145).

THE COMPLEXITY OF JUNG'S POSITION

In contrast to Alfred Adler's relatively simple and easy to understand position (see Chapter 4), Jung's theory is complex, esoteric, and obscure in many respects. It may be the most unusual viewpoint in the entire body of work on personality. Part of the problem stems from the fact that Jung read widely in a number of different disciplines. As a result, he drew upon materials from literature, physics, chemistry, biology, archeology, philosophy, theology, mythology, history, anthropology, alchemy, and astrology in his attempts to understand human functioning. Since few investigators or readers have the background necessary to evaluate the materials he utilized, it has been easier for many people to ignore or dismiss his theorizing than to grapple with the incredible array of complex ideas that are an integral part of it. Still another difficulty lies in Jung's own failure to write clearly. He often used conventional terms in idiosyncratic ways without fully explaining the arbitrary shifts he had made in their meanings. At this point, and with these difficulties clearly in mind, we present a review of the basic ideas of the theory.

BASIC CONCEPTS AND PRINCIPLES

The Psyche and Life-Process Energy

For Jung, the total personality is called the *psyche.* In his conceptualization, it is a nonphysical space that has its own special reality. Through the psyche, energy flows continuously in various directions from consciousness to unconsciousness and back and from inner to outer reality and back. This psychic energy was also thought by Jung to be real. He considered the terms *psychic energy* and *libido* to be interchangeable. Unlike Freud, however, who maintained that libido was equivalent to instinctual energy that was basically sexual in nature, Jung considered it to signify a more general *life-process energy* of which sexual urges are only one aspect. (Jung, 1969, p. 17). Psychic energy, like physical energy, is an abstraction representing something real that cannot be touched or felt, but that we know exists through its effects. Just as physical energy manifests itself in the heating and lighting of the rooms in our homes, so psychic energy manifests itself in our various feelings, thoughts, and behaviors.

Most important, psychic energy is considered an outcome of the conflict between forces within the personality. Without conflict, there is no energy and no life. Love and hatred of a person can exist within a psyche, creating tension and new energy that seeks expression in behavior. Other values may also conflict, such as a desire to have premarital intercourse when one knows that significant others may strongly disapprove. The number of potential conflicts is virtually unlimited. Jung also maintained that the various structures of the psyche are continually opposed to one another. For example, consciousness and unconsciousness are interdependent. Further, the *shadow*, that is, the unconscious and often evil side of our nature, may conflict with the ego, while ego processes may operate to keep unpleasant memories from awareness. The psyche is therefore conceived of as a general entity that operates according to the *principle of opposites*.

Once energy is created, it moves in a variety of directions (Progoff, 1953, p. 63). It can be dissipated in outward behavior or it can continue to move within the psyche, first in one direction, then in another. It may split and move unsystematically through the psyche; go into the unconscious; attach itself to other energy sources which could then manifest themselves in bizarre psychological forms—for example, in hallucinations and delusions or "unaccountable" moods. The point is that some of the libidinal energy that courses through the psyche operates autonomously, and hence unpredictably, with various results.

Libido also operates according to the *principles of equivalence and entropy*. These psychological formulations are based upon the first and second laws of thermodynamics in physics. The principle of equivalence states that "for a given quantity of energy expended or consumed in bringing about a certain condition, an equal quantity of the same or another form of energy will appear elsewhere" (Jung, 1969, p. 18). In short, an increase or decrease in some aspect of psychic functioning is met by a compensatory increase or decrease in another part of the psyche. An increase in hatred for one person would involve an equal loss of love for him or her. It could also involve a loss of love for someone else. An increase in concern with achievement of occupational success might mean an equivalent loss in concern with one's spiritual life, and vice versa. In the area of sexuality, an erotic feeling for one person that cannot be freely expressed would be repressed, but would *sublimation*

e.g. in dream

continue to be active at an unconscious level. In another person, the expression of the same feeling might be sublimated or transformed into creative work. Jung's position is similar in this respect to Freud's notion of displacement.

The principle of entropy refers to the process within the psyche by which elements of unequal strength seek psychological equilibrium. If energy, for example, is concentrated in the ego, tension will be generated in the psyche to move the energy from the conscious to the unconscious in order to create a balance. The critical point is that any one-sided development of the personality creates conflict, tension, and strain. An even distribution, on the other hand, produces harmony and contentment. The aim of individual development is self-realization, which involves the integration of all aspects of the psyche. In such a harmonious state, the person would presumably be maximally happy and productive. This balanced state would also involve the evolution of a new center, the self, to replace the old one (the ego). The ego should not be considered useless or obsolete in the final system; it would exist, but in harmony with the other aspects of the psyche.

At this point, a review of the major structural components of the theory and their functions is in order.

Ego

Jung believed that the ego is a "complex of representations which constitutes the centrum of (the) field of consciousness and appears to possess a very high degree of continuity and identity"(Jung, 1923, p. 540). The term *complex* refers to a collection of thoughts that are united, often by a common feeling. Ego is a complex that is not synonymous with the psyche, but is only an aspect of it (Jung, 1969, p. 324). Nor is it identical with consciousness. Instead, the ego is a unifying force in the psyche which is at the center of consciousness. It is responsible for our feelings of identity and continuity as human beings. Thus, the ego contains the conscious thoughts of our own behavior and feelings, as well as memories of our experiences.

The Personal Unconscious

The personal unconscious is the region next to the ego (see Figure 3–1). It consists of all the forgotten experiences that have lost their intensity for some reason, possibly because of their unpleasantness. It also includes sense impressions that are too weak to be perceived consciously (Jung, 1969, p. 376). These unconscious materials are accessible to the person's consciousness under certain circumstances. For example, they could be elicited by a skillful therapist with the help of the patient.

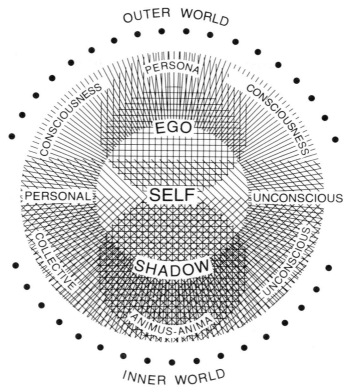

Figure 3.1.
Structural components of the psyche. Adapted from J. Jacobi, *The Psychology of C. G. Jung* (New Haven: Yale University Press, 1962), p. 126, Diagram 6.

The Collective Unconscious

Still deeper within the psyche lies the *collective unconscious*. It was characterized by Jung as "a deposit of world-processes embedded in the structure of the brain and the sympathetic nervous system . . .[which] constitutes in its totality a sort of timeless and eternal world-image which counterbalances our conscious momentary picture of the world" (Jung, 1969, p. 370). In other words, it is the storehouse of latent memories of our human and prehuman ancestry. It consists of instincts and archetypes that we inherit as possibilities and that often affect our behavior. The archetypes are themes which have existed in all cultures throughout history. According to Jung, such collective memories are universal in nature because of our common evolution and brain structure.

This concept has often been misunderstood. Writers usually refer to it as one of Jung's original contributions to psychology, although Freud had already utilized a similar concept, which he called the racial unconscious. Second and more important, Jung did not accept the idea of the French naturalist Lamarck that a person's characteristics were inherited, as some investigators have indicated. Instead, he argued that we inherit pathways that carry with them a tendency or predisposition to respond to certain experiences in specific ways (Progoff, 1953, p. 70). These tendencies come forth, sometimes spontaneously and sometimes when the person is under stress, in the form of archetypal motifs or themes. For example, Jung states that men and women in every culture have inherited the tendency to respond in ambiguous and threatening situations with some form of an all-powerful being that we call God. In Jung's words:

> God is an absolute necessary function of an irrational nature, which has nothing whatever to do with the question of God's existence. The human intellect can never answer this question, still less give any proof of God. Moreover, such proof is superfluous, for the idea of an all-powerful divine Being is present everywhere, unconsciously if not consciously because it is an archetype. (Jung, 1964, p. 81)

Jung then proceeds to argue that a person who renounces the idea of God will experience personal difficulties. Human beings must come to grips with such an idea if they are ever to achieve inner harmony. Thus, Jung would probably characterize atheists as people who have developed in a one-sided fashion and who are bound to experience difficulties eventually because they have failed to acknowledge this nonrational aspect of their nature. Searching for a rational answer in an irrational realm is a doomed quest. Jung seems to suggest that we accept the idea of an all-powerful being on faith; yet he also seems to contradict himself by suggesting that, since the idea of God has a reality within the psyche as an archetype, it is potentially knowable. This difficulty disappears if we keep the distinction between internal and external reality clearly in view. Jung maintained that we can never offer objective proof of God's existence; that is, tangible, material proof shared by others in the external world. But the idea of God has validity in a subjective or inner reality sense because it has its roots in human experience on a universal basis.

The idea of God is not like the idea of a chair with clearly discernible properties, however. God is a universal symbol, and such symbols, while real, can never be understood completely (Jung, 1958c, p. 118). We may gain valuable information about their reality through persistent self-analysis, but we will never know them completely. They are really processes that take different forms. They have a kind of shadowy existence, a mysterious quality about them, that perhaps we must at some point come to accept. In brief, their reality is so complex and bewildering that rational inquiry is helpful only to a point. Beyond that, only faith and acceptance of their unknown and unknowable aspects is demanded, if movement toward a balanced psyche is to be achieved.

The Archetype

Although we have discussed this concept earlier, more elaboration is needed because of its central position in Jung's theory. As we now know, *archetypes* are universal themes that affect our behavior. At various points in his writings, Jung referred to such themes as "imagoes" (images), "primordial images," "root-images," "dominants," and "behavior patterns." Archetypes are essentially thought forms or ideas that give rise to visions projected onto current experiences. For example, one of the primary archetypes is the mother-child relationship, which is characterized by the mother's protection of the child. Dissolution of this bond must ultimately occur if the person is to attain adulthood. Jung maintains that the bond is broken in many primitive cultures when young men undergo rituals of rebirth and visits to men's houses (Jung, 1964, p. 208). In our culture we do not have comparable rituals. As a result, many men have never dissolved their basic dependency on their mothers. In married life, they may project the mother image onto their wives by acting in childish, dependent, and submissive ways. Or they may react in an opposite manner by acting in hypermasculine ways by rejecting any offers of help from their spouse.

Other major archetypes in the Jungian system include the persona, shadow, the anima and animus, the self, and the major attitudes of introversion and extraversion. While introversion and extraversion are considered by many theorists not to be archetypes, Jung believed that they were. They were innate dispositions, but ones often molded by experience (Jung, 1923, p. 286).

The Persona. For Jung, the *persona* is "a compromise . . . between the demands of the environment and the necessities of the individual's inner constitution" (Jacobi, 1962, p. 19). It is the mask we wear in order to function adequately in our relationships with other people. This mask may take as many forms as the roles we play in our daily routines. It also aids in controlling evil forces in the collective unconscious. The persona is an archetype presumably because it is a universal manifestation of our attempt to deal appropriately with other people.

But the persona also has negative features. We can, for instance, learn to hide our real selves behind these masks. Our personas can become split off from potentially enlightening forces in the personal and collective unconscious. From another perspective, we may become so committed to a particular role that we lose sight of our individuality. Jacobi provides an example of the stultifying aspects of such automatic and rigid role-playing:

> We all know the professor . . . whose individuality is exhausted in playing the professor's role; behind this mask one finds nothing but a bundle of peevishness and infantilism. (Jacobi, 1962, pp. 19–20)

In the Jungian view, so inflexible a person would have to become more accepting of his own and other people's feelings. He would further have to recognize and accept the limits of his rationality and intellect. He would also have to become more receptive to archetypes like the wise old man, who might teach him something about human fallibility, since this archetype is the embodiment of wisdom and understanding. Of course, the professor might argue that such a view is sheer nonsense and that he is feeling fine and functioning well. Jungians would probably retort that the professor is simply rationalizing. In any event, the general point is that, in Jung's system, excessive identification with the persona may have harmful effects on personal development.

The Shadow. Introduction to students of this term usually meets with chuckles and amused expressions, but for Jung, the concept had important and serious meanings. The term was chosen by him to indicate the dark, sinister, Mr. Hyde side of our natures. In contrast to the persona's affiliation with the ego and consciousness and its role in personal adaptation to the external world, the *shadow* represents the evil, unadapted, unconscious, and inferior part of our psyches. It has two primary aspects, one associated with the personal unconscious, and the other with the collective unconscious (Dry, 1961, p. 95). In terms of the personal unconscious, the shadow consists of all those experiences that the person rejects on moral and/or aesthetic grounds. For example, our egos may reject our sadistic impulses or we may repress socially unacceptable sexual or aggressive impulses. Jung believed, incidentally, that the shadow incorporated both Freud's sexual instinct and Adler's will to power.

In terms of the collective unconscious, the shadow consists of universal personifications of evil within our psyches. The Devil, in its various forms, would be a prime example. Jung maintained that we may never understand this unadapted side of our personality because we can never bring ourselves to confront absolute evil. Nevertheless, the shadow exists in all of us, and it manifests itself in a variety of ways— unaccountable moods, pains of unexplained origin, feelings of self-destruction, and desires to harm others. It should be clearly understood that we do not, at base, have control over these impulses. Jung believed that these repressed feelings operate independently in the unconscious, where they join forces with other impulses. The result may be a complex with sufficient force to erupt into consciousness and momentarily to subdue the ego. For example, a dignified and sophisticated executive may suddenly become highly abusive toward his colleagues during an important meeting. His arguments may become totally irrational, irresponsible, and not at all related to the issues under consideration.

Finally, as with all of Jung's concepts, there are positive features to the shadow as well as the negative ones we have discussed. The murderer who decides impulsively to spare his victim because she reminds him of a loved one would be an example of the positive aspects of the shadow, as would the selfish man who spends virtually all his time making money and who then generously decides to donate a large percentage of his earnings to a local charity, even though he does not realize a tax break from his action. The "sinner" who suddenly becomes "good" and is concerned with helping others would be still another example. More generally, the positive side of the shadow is sometimes evident when a person feels unaccountably vital, spontaneous, and creative. All these instances show that the shadow can operate as a positive force as well.

The Anima and Animus. Like Freud, Jung believed that all men and women have elements of the opposite sex within them. Each man has a feminine side, while each woman has unconscious masculine qualities. This concept was based, at least partially, upon the fact that both men and women have varying amounts of male and female hormones in their bodies. The feminine archetype in man Jung called the *anima;* the masculine archetype in woman he labeled the *animus.* Like all archetypes, the anima and animus can function in either constructive or destructive ways. The anima operates positively in man when she serves as "his inspiration . . . [when] her intuitive capacity, often superior to man's, can give him timely warning [presumably about harmful events], and her feelings, always directed towards the personal, can show him ways which his own less personally accepted feeling would never have discovered" (Jung, 1964, p. 199). The negative aspects of the anima concept is seen when men act in moody, "bitchy," and "catty" ways. The animus in women has positive manifestations when it produces arguments based on reason and logic. The negative side of the animus can be seen in these behaviors:

> In intellectual women . . . [when it] . . . encourages a critical disputatiousness and would-be high-browism, which . . . consists essentially in harping on some irrelevant weak point and nonsensically making it the main point. Or a perfectly lucid discussion gets tangled up in the most maddening way through the introduction of a quite different and if possible perverse point of view. Without knowing it, such women are solely intent upon exasperating the man and are, in consequence . . . completely at the mercy of the animus. (Jung, 1964, p. 220)

Despite Jung's claims that the anima and animus are universal phenomena, the descriptions sound suspiciously like our cultural stereotypes of the sexes. The masculine archetype includes those characteristics we associate traditionally with the role of man; namely, reason, logic, forceful argument, and social insensitivity, among others. The feminine archetype and traditional feminine behavior are closely associated in terms of attributes such as emotionality, social sensitivity, intuition, vanity, moodiness, and irrationality. Although Jung does catalogue the presumed negative characteristics of the animus, his major detailed arguments about the "weaknesses" of the anima suggest a pa-triarchal bias that we have already seen in the writings of Freud.

These a priori images may operate in dreams and fantasies, according to Jung, but often they are projected onto real-life objects. For example, the animus in a woman could be projected onto her lover, producing a discrepancy between them that could be harmful to both parties. Perhaps she sees her lover as the universal hero, a compassionate and sensitive being who will always protect her and look out for her interests. In actuality, however, her lover may be an insensitive boor who is concerned only with exploiting her sexually. From another perspective, the animus may take the form of the evil conqueror who, when projected on a kindly and sensitive suitor, will inevitably produce conflict and problems. The ability to differentiate these universal images from their real-life counterparts is an extremely difficult task, but one that is important if each of us is to progress toward selfhood.

The Self. The *self* is an archetypal potentiality in all of us. It is concep-tualized as an innate blueprint that, theoretically at least, is capable of being realized. This "destiny within us" involves a process that Jung calls the "way of individuation" (Jacobi, 1962, p. 100). Individuation is a "process by which a [person] . . . becomes the definite, unique being that he in fact is. In doing so he does not become "selfish" in the or-dinary sense of the word, but is merely fulfilling the peculiarity of his nature, and this . . . is vastly different from egotism or individualism" (Jung, 1964, p. 183).

Thus, the self is the final goal of our striving and, in this sense at least, is similar to the goal of perfection in Adler's system, as we shall soon learn. The movement toward *self-realization* is a difficult process, one Jung believed could not be attained by young people. It takes time and considerable effort to resolve the many conflicts between opposites within the psyche, so that the few people who come closest to the attain-ment of selfhood would be middle-aged at a minimum. With the attain-ment of harmony, a new center or midpoint evolves within the per-sonality; namely, the self, which replaces the old one, the ego. The ego now becomes a satellite of the self, much like the earth in rotation around the sun. Consciousness does not replace unconsciousness within the psyche. Instead, the principle of opposites remains viable, with consciousness and unconsciousness balancing each other.

In such a state, the self is conceptualized as the unifying force which has a *transcendent function* that provides stability and balance to the various systems of the personality. In other words, as the individual ex-plores the unconscious aspects of her psyche, she learns more about it and its functions. She thus begins to feel more comfortable with this side of her nature; for example, she begins to understand how her shadow operates to make her moody or impulsive or how her animus forces her to express herself forcefully and logically in arguments with men. This understanding involves a resolution, not a solution, of her conflicts. Through her new understanding, she transcends these conflicts and begins to live more harmoniously within herself and with others.

Much of Jung's interest in *symbols* like the shadow and the animus stems from his attempt to find the ways in which the self has been described and expressed in various religious and occult systems, psychologies, arts, and philosophies throughout history (Progoff, 1953, p. 153). The most important representations of the self are the *mandalas* or magic circles, symbols found in the writings and art of all cultures (see figure 3.2 for an example). These mandalas represent a synthesis or union between opposites within the psyche when individuals attain self-realization. According to Jung, the oldest mandala is a paleolithic sun wheel drawing, based on the principle of four (Jung, 1958a, p. 326). Mandalas are also found in Buddhism and Taoism, and in other reli-

Figure 3.2.
Mandala of awakening consciousness. Adapted from J. Jacobi, *The Psychology of C. G. Jung* (New Haven: Yale University Press, 1962), p. 114, Plate 14.

gions of the Orient. In these religions, the golden flower is often placed in the center of the mandala, signifying the "heavenly mansion, the realm of the highest bliss, the boundless land, and the altar on which consciousness and life are brought forth." In the Middle Ages, mandalas often included Christ, with four evangelists around him.(Jacobi, 1962, pp. 131, 128).

Medieval alchemy was also involved in Jung's search for unique expressions of the self. He saw the alchemists' transmutation of base metals into gold, for example, as similar to the " . . . transformation of personality through the blending and fusion of the noble with the base components, of the differentiated with the inferior functions of the conscious with the unconscious" (Jung, 1964, p. 232). Finally, Jung stated that many of his patients spontaneously reported mandalas in their dreams and also painted them during therapy sessions. Thus, by drawing upon materials from an incredible variety of sources, Jung believed he had discovered a universal synthesizing phenomenon that transcended personal experience.

In an attempt to evolve toward selfhood, Jung believed that people adopted different ways of relating to experience; that is, they adopted different attitudes toward life and utilized different psychological processes or functions to make sense out of their experiences. Jung spelled out the details of the basic attitudes and functions used by people in his theory of psychological types, a topic to be considered next.

THE THEORY OF PSYCHOLOGICAL TYPES

Basic Attitudes

The two fundamental attitudes in Jung's typology are extraversion and introversion. *Extraversion* refers to "an outgoing, candid, and accommodating nature that adapts easily to a given situation, quickly forms attachments, and, setting aside any possible misgivings, will often venture forth with careless confidence into an unknown situation." Introversion, in contrast, signifies "a hesistant, reflective, retiring nature that keeps itself to itself, shrinks from objects, is always slightly on the defensive and prefers to hide behind mistrustful scrutiny" (Jung, 1964, p. 52). Jung points out that people are not purely introverted or extraverted. Instead, each person has both introverted and extraverted aspects to his or her nature, and both factors involve complex variations. One set of characteristics, however, is dominant (that is, conscious), while the other set is inferior or unadapted (that is, unconscious). The dominant side is compensated for by the inferior side, and vice versa. If too much libido is invested in the dominant side, for example, energy forces are set up and activated in the unconscious, typically with harmful results for the individual.

Jung's typology is based upon his conceptualization of the flow of libido within the psyche. One way energy can flow is outward toward life; another is inward toward subjective experience. For Jung, however, extraversion and introversion are not to be equated with outward libidinal flow or progression and inward flow or regression, respectively. Instead

> . . . movement can occur in two different forms: either extraverted, when the progression is predominately influenced by objects and environmental conditions, or introverted, when it has to adapt itself to the conditions of the ego (or, more accurately, of the "subjective factor"). Similarly, regression can proceed along two lines, either as a retreat from the outside world (introversion), or as a flight into extravagant experience of the outside world (extraversion). (Jung, 1969, pp. 40–41)

Thus, extraversion and introversion have their own "special dynamics," and both attitudes have progressive and regressive properties. What precisely is Jung talking about here? He is arguing that introversion and extraversion can have both "good" or healthy and "bad" or unhealthy consequences for our development. Like all Jung's concepts, this one has positive and negative features. Perhaps a concrete example will illuminate the arguments. Introversion may have progressive effects when a person creates a unique and useful product, like a first-rate novel. Introversion may have regressive effects when it leads to excessive brooding and indecisiveness in an individual who needs to make a firm judgment. Witness the student who is doing poorly in a course and hesitates to ask a more competent classmate or the instructor for help. Failure in the course may well be the outcome. Extraversion may have progressive effects when it leads us to make decisions like asking for assistance. Extraversion may have regressive effects when it leads to injudicious actions, like accepting virtually every pronouncement of authority in order to secure approval. Such people are so committed to the "object," namely, the authority figure, that they accept his comments uncritically. An example would be the student who changes her or his career on the advice of neurotic relatives.

The Four Functions

In addition to his ideas about introversion and extraversion, Jung postulated the existence of four functions or ways in which people may make sense of their experiences. As modes of relating to the world, they include thinking, feeling, sensing, and intuiting. Sensation is our initial experiencing of phenomena, without evaluation. Thinking proceeds from this point and is the interpretation of events through the use of reason and logic. Such interpretations also involve evaluation along an affective or feeling dimension. Finally, in the mode of intuition we relate to the world directly, with a minimum of interpretation and reasoning (Progoff, 1953, p. 100).

Jung called thinking and feeling the *rational functions,* since they involve a process of making judgments about experiences. Sensation and intuition are the *irrational functions,* because they involve passive recording, but not evaluating or interpreting experience. Although many of us tend stereotypically to associate thinking with rationality and feeling with irrationality, Jung makes the point that both thinking and feeling involve the assessment of the worth of any experience. Thinking is primarily concerned with the truth or falsity of our experience; feeling implies the degree to which we like or dislike something. There is a further semantic difficulty in that Jung does not want the term "irrational" to convey the idea of excessive or "mindless" emotionality. Instead, he uses the term to mean modes of relating to experience that are unrelated to reason. Perhaps "nonrational" would have been a more suitable designation for Jung to have used.

These functions are articulated or differentiated to varying degrees within the psyche. As Jung envisioned it, one function of the rational or irrational pair is *dominant* or superior, with its counterpart being inferior. The members of the remaining pair exist on an intermediate or auxiliary level. The dominant function is the primary mode of adjustment for the individual and exists in consciousness; the inferior function is unconscious or beyond the person's ability to make conscious. The members of the remaining pair exist in a kind of twilight zone, partly conscious and partly unconscious. The superior function is the most highly differentiated, followed by the auxiliary pair, with the inferior function being least differentiated. It should be noted that any one of the functions can be dominant; that is, there are thinking, feeling, sensing, and intuiting kinds of individuals. Of course, each of these types lacks full development. The "whole" or integrated person would be one capable of utilizing all the functions in dealing with his or her experiences.

Typology Derived from the Basic Attitudes and Functions

Out of the two major attitudes and four functions, Jung fashioned an eightfold classification scheme. In reality, there are sixteen possible personality types, if we take into account the fact that either member of the auxiliary pair can exist in a somewhat differentiated and conscious form. In his classic work on the subject, however, Jung focused his attention on eight of the possibilities—namely, the introverted and extraverted thinking, feeling, sensing, and intuitive types.

The Extraverted Thinking Type. The extraverted thinking type is characterized by a need

> . . . to make all his life-activities dependent on intellectual conclusions, which in the last resort are always oriented by objective data. . . . This kind of man . . .[lives by an] . . . intellectual formula. By this formula are good and evil measured and beauty and ugliness determined. . . . If the

formula is wide enough, this type may play a very useful role in social life, either as a reformer or a ventilator of public wrongs . . . or as the propagator of important innovations. But the more rigid the formula, the more does he develop into a grumbler, a crafty reasoner, and a self-righteous critic. (Jung, 1923, pp. 346–347)

Such a person also has repressed his feelings in his or her pursuit of ideas and ideals and tends to deny "aesthetic activities, taste, artistic sense, cultivation of friends, etc." (Jung, 1923, p. 348). Jung argues further that a person who is developing in such a negative fashion may appear concerned about the welfare of other people, but in reality is concerned only with the attainment of his or her goals. The self-serving activist who exploits the friendship of other people to further his or her aims would be an example.

The Introverted Thinking Type. According to Jung, the introverted thinker,

> like his extraverted counterpart, is strongly influenced by ideas, though his ideas have their origin not in objective data but in his subjective foundation. He will follow his ideas like the extravert, but in the reverse direction: inwards and not outwards. (Jung, 1923, p. 383)

The subjective foundation of the introverted thinker is the collective unconscious. Creative ideas spring from this source and not from outside sources like traditional moral authority. As a result of this concern with internal forces, the introverted thinker appears cold, aloof, and inconsiderate of others. In addition, he tends to be socially inept and inarticulate in his attempts to communicate his ideas.

The Extraverted Feeling Type. Jung believed that women were the best examples of this type. They live according to "objective situations and general values" (Jung, 1923, p. 356). In other words, their feelings and behavior are controlled by social norms—that is, by the expectations of others. As a consequence, their feelings change from situation to situation and from person to person. A prime example would be the college woman who breaks her engagement because her parents object to the man. Her feelings toward the young man are based upon her parents' judgments. If they like him, fine; if they do not, she feels compelled to reject him. In such people, thinking is largely repressed. If our woman thought about her action toward the man, it would be most upsetting.

On the plus side of the ledger, Jung maintains that extraverted feeling types can make adequate marriages. "These women are good companions and excellent mothers, so long as [their] husbands and children are blessed with the conventional psychic constitution" (Jung, 1923, p. 357). By "conventional psychic constitution," Jung seems to mean husbands and children who follow the rules and regulations society prescribes for the "well-adjusted" family.

The Introverted Feeling Type. Jung also gives the honor to women for being the prime examples of this type:

> They are mostly silent, inaccessible, and hard to understand: often they hide behind a childish or banal mask, and their temperament is inclined to melancholy. They neither shine nor reveal themselves. (Jung, 1923, p. 389)

Although they may appear unsympathetic to others, in reality they are capable of intense feeling, but their feelings have their origins in the collective unconscious. They have the depth of feeling that could erupt in religious or poetic form.

The Extraverted Sensing Type. Jung visualized men as the prime examples of this type. They are primarily reality-oriented and typically shun thinking and contemplation. Experiencing sensations becomes almost an end in itself. Each experience serves as a guide to new experience. Such people are usually outgoing and jolly and have a considerable capacity for enjoyment, some of which revolves about good food. In addition, they are often refined esthetes, concerned with matters of good taste in painting, sculpture, and literature, as well as with food and physical appearance. When they become overenamored with the object—for example, in the area of food or physical appearance—they develop into ". . . crude pleasure-seeker[s] or . . . unscrupulous, effete aesthete[s]" (Jung, 1923, p. 365). The novelist Rabelais' young fictional character, Gargantua, presents a perfect example of the negative aspects of extraverted sensing types:

> He spent his time like other small children: namely, in drinking, eating and sleeping; in eating, sleeping and drinking; in sleeping, drinking and eating.
> He was forever wallowing in dirt, covering his nose with filth and begriming his face. . . . He used to piddle on his shoes, brown up his shirt-tails, wipe his nose on his sleeve and clear his nostrils into his soup. . . . Often he coughed up, figuratively and literally. Fat? Another ounce of wind and he would have exploded. Appreciative? He would piss, full-bladdered, at the sun. Cautious? He used to hide under water for fear of the rain. (Rabelais, 1936)

The Introverted Sensing Type. In Jung's view, introverted sensing people are irrational types guided by the "intensity of the subjective sensation-excited by the objective stimulus" (Jung, 1923, p. 395). These appear to be people who overreact to outside stimuli. They may take innocuous comments from others and interpret them in imaginative or bizarre ways. They may also appear rational and in complete control of their actions because of their unrelatedness to objects—for example, people in the environment. Such people may also treat the objective world (external reality) as mere appearance and even as a joke. Libido from primordial images affects their perception of events. Positive manifestations of libido are found in creative persons, whereas negative manifestations are seen in psychotics.

The Extraverted Intuitive Type. These people are most concerned with exploiting external opportunities. In Jung's words, they have "keen nose[s] for anything new and in the making" (Jung, 1923, p. 368). Politicians, merchants, contractors, and speculators are examples of this type. Women are also more likely than men to have such orientations. According to Jung, such women "understand the art of exploiting every social occasion; they make the right social connections, they seek out men with prospects only to abandon everything again for the sake of a new possibility" (Jung, 1923, p. 369).

Positive features of these types include the fact that they are the initiaters and promoters of promising enterprises. They often inspire others to great accomplishments. They also champion the causes of minority group members because they sense the immense potential for personal growth in them. But there are also serious dangers for people with this orientation. Although they may enliven and encourage others, they do little for themselves. In addition, they are impatient and always seek new possibilities. Consequently, they often do not see their actions through to completion.

The Introverted Intuitive Type. In this type of person, there is an intensification of intuition that often results in estrangement from external reality. Such people may be considered enigmatic even by close friends. On a positive level, they may become great visionaries and mystics; on a negative level, they may develop into artistic cranks who espouse their own idiosyncratic language and visions. Such people cannot be understood by others, and since their judgment functions (their thinking and feelings) are relatively repressed, they are incapable of communicating effectively with others.

Research Evidence for the Theory of Psychological Types

In order to assess the validity of Jung's proposed typology, it was necessary for investigators to construct a scale that measured the various concepts. A personality inventory called the Gray-Wheelwright was developed first by Jungian analysts, but it has been largely replaced by the more popular Myers-Briggs Type Indicator (MBTI). Considerable work has been done with the MBTI to establish its reliability and validity. It is an inventory that consists of 166 items with a forced-choice format. Sample items for use in identifying introverts and extraverts and the sensing, thinking, feeling, and intuitive types are presented in Table 3.1.

Research has shown that occupational interests among college students are related in many instances to the Jungian typology. For example, one study showed that introverts had strong interests in mathematics and technical-scientific occupations, whereas extraverts gravitated toward sales and public relations jobs. Students who were intuitive preferred jobs as musicians and psychologists, whereas feeling, thinking, and sensing types leaned toward the occupations of minister, certified public accountant, and banker, respectively (Strickler and Ross, 1962).

TABLE 3.1   Sample Items from the Myers-Briggs Type Indicator (MBTI)

Introversion (I)-Extraversion (E) Items

1. When you have to meet strangers, do you find it
   a. pleasant, or at least easy (E) or
   b. something that takes a good deal of effort ? (I)
2. Are you naturally
   a. a "good mixer" (E) or
   b. rather quiet and reserved in company? (I)
3. In a large group, do you more often
   a. introduce others (E) or
   b. get introduced? (I)

Sensing (S)–Intuition (N) Items

1. Do you usually get along better with
   a. imaginative people (N) or
   b. realistic people? (S)
2. Do you get more annoyed at
   a. fancy theories (S) or
   b. people who don't like theories? (N)
3. Would you rather be considered
   a. a practical person (S) or
   b. an ingenious person? (N)

Thinking (T)–Feeling (F) Items

1. Which of these two is the higher compliment
   a. he is a person of real feeling (F) or
   b. he is consistently reasonable? (T)
2. Do you think it is a worse fault
   a. to show too much warmth (T) or
   b. not to have enough warmth? (F)
3. Do you more often let
   a. your heart rule your head (F) or
   b. your head rule your heart? (T)

Other recent research has provided additional evidence in support of Jung's typology. Two psychologists found introverted thinkers more effective in memorizing emotionally neutral stimulus material—that is, in memorizing a number of series of digits—than introverted and extraverted feeling types and extraverted thinkers. Extraverted feeling types were more accurate than the others in remembering new, emotionally toned material—that is, in memorizing a series of pictures of a female model portraying different emotions. A number of other predictions derived from Jung's theory were also confirmed, including one which showed that extraverted intuitive types were overrepresented among social service volunteers as compared with a matched sample of nonvolunteers (Carlson and Levy, 1973, 41, pp. 559–576). Thus, there is some support for the Jungian scheme, but much more research needs to be done in order to assess its validity properly.

THE PROCESS OF PERSONALITY DEVELOPMENT

We have already discussed in a rather sporadic fashion in earlier sections of the chapter some of Jung's thinking about the process of personality development. Here we will try to present a more coherent and focused summary of his views.

First, Jung conceived of personal development as a dynamic and evolving process that occurs throughout the life of the individual. The person is continually developing and learning new skills, and moving toward self-realization. Although Jung had little to say about the developmental process in childhood, it is clear he did not accept Freud's view that the individual's personality was relatively fixed by the end of the early childhood period. Neither did he accept Freud's view that only past events determine the person's behavior. For Jung, the individual's behavior was determined not only by past experiences, but also by future goals. The person was seen as one who continually planned for the future. But although the person can progress toward selfhood by developing differentiated psychological functions, he or she can also move backward as well. Such backward movement need not, however, necessarily have detrimental effects on the individual. As we have learned, some retreats into the psyche can provide the impetus for creative growth.

The movement toward actualization is often a difficult and painful process. It involves continual attempts by the individual to understand his or her experiences and to develop healthy attitudes. The person is often beset by crises, and Jung believed that many individuals experienced their most severe crises during the middle years. Adequate resolution of these crises helps move the person toward an accurate perception and full understanding of himself or herself. Under these conditions, the person becomes *individuated*, that is, all he or she is capable of becoming as a human being. The person is then able to reconcile the op-positing forces within the psyche through transcendence.

Progress toward self-actualization is not automatic. If the person grows up in an unhealthy and threatening environment, where the parents use harsh and unreasonable punishment, growth will likely be stifled. It is also possible that repressed evil forces within the psyche can erupt without warning to produce personality dysfunction. Under these conditions, the outcomes may be neurosis or psychosis. We turn now to a discussion of these disorders.

Neurosis and Psychosis

Jung considered neurosis and psychosis disorders that differ primarily in the severity of their consequences for people. Both result from one-sided development in which repressed forces create problems in func-tioning. In all of the eight types discussed earlier, for example, intense repression of one of the four functions would probably result in a form of neurosis. More specifically, when thinking is repressed in the in-troverted feeling type, Jung argued that the thinking function may eventually project itself onto objects, thus creating problems for the person. Why? Because the thinking function is archaic and undif-ferentiated, so that the person's judgment about the object or objects is bound to be gross and inaccurate. Such a person is unable to reason ac-curately about the intentions of others. As a consequence,

> other people are [assumed to be] thinking all sorts of mean things, schem-ing evil, contriving plots, secret intrigues, etc. In order to forestall them, she herself is obliged to start counter-intrigues, to suspect others . . . and [to] weave counterplots. Beset by rumours, she must make frantic efforts to be top dog. Endless clandestine rivalries spring up, and in these embittered struggles she will shrink from no baseness or meaness, and will even prostitute her virtues in order to play the trump card. Such a state of affairs must end in exhaustion. (Jung, 1923, p. 391)

The resulting form of neurosis is neurasthenia, or a disorder characterized by listlessness and fatigue. Jung saw psychosis as an ex-tension of neurosis that occurs when repressed and unconscious forces overpower consciousness. In his view, consciousness is a secondary phenomenon derived from unconsciousness. Therefore, consciousness is a rather fragile entity that can be "swallowed up" by unleashed forces in the unconscious. In such instances, the person collapses and the ego loses control when attacked by elements of the collective unconscious. Jung provides an illustration of the onset of psychosis with the case of a quiet young man who imagined that a woman was in love with him. When he discovered his love was unrequited, he

> was so desperate that he went straight to the river to drown himself. It was late at night, and the stars gleamed up at him from the dark water. It

seemed to him that the stars were swimming two by two down the river, and a wonderful feeling came over him. He forgot his suicidal intentions and gazed fascinated at the strange, sweet drama, and gradually he became aware that every star was a face and that all these pairs were lovers, who were carried along locked in a dreaming embrace. An entirely new under- standing came to him: all had changed—his fate, his disappointment, even his love, receded and fell away. The memory of the girl grew distant, blurred; but, instead, he felt with complete certainty that untold riches were promised him. He knew that an immense treasure lay hidden for him in the neighboring observatory. The result was that he was arrested by the police at four o' clock in the morning, attempting to break into the observatory.

What had happened? His poor head had glimpsed a Dantesque picture, whose loveliness he could never have grasped had he read it in a poem. . . . For his poor turnip-head it was too much. He did not drown in the river, but in an eternal image, and its beauty perished with him. (Jung, 1959, p. 126)

This illustration also shows that in Jung's scheme the collective uncon- scious has its attractive elements and can sometimes lure a person into its essentially fathomless inner reality.

Before reviewing the ways in which Jung's theory is applied in the treatment of psychopathology, let us examine briefly some of the major procedures he used to assess personality.

TECHNIQUES OF ASSESSMENT

Like Freud, Jung relied primarily on the case study as a personality assessment procedure. He also showed his Freudian roots by utilizing dream analysis and a focus upon the patient's life history in his attempts to understand the mechanisms and content of the unconscious. Yet, in a number of important respects, he developed his own assessment procedures. For example, early in his career he employed a word association list to help uncover the patient's complexes. This procedure involved having the patient respond to stimulus words with whatever words occurred to him. Jung recorded the time that elapsed between the initial presentation of the stimulus and the eventual response and used the time latency as an indicator of possible areas of resistance and conflict within the person. The assumption was that the longer the time interval, the greater the likelihood that important complexes or areas of conflict within the psyche were being tapped. In addition, Jung required his patients to recall all their responses to the word stimuli following a rest interval. Failure to reproduce the words or distorted reproductions were also considered reflective of underlying conflict (Jacobi, 1962, p. 38).

Although his dream analysis technique had much in common with Freud's, there were a few interesting differences. Instead of using the free association method, Jung relied upon amplification. This too is an association process, but it differs from the free association technique in that it involves associations provided by the therapist as well as by the patient. The therapist enriches the understanding of the meanings of the dream by suggesting additional images that may clarify the primary theme of the dream. He may enrich the process by suggesting relationships between the central theme and related symbols, myths, and legends (Jacobi, 1962, pp. 82-84). He does not rely upon the reproduction of early personal experiences by the patient, but directs the patient to incorporate new symbols and meaning into his responses.

In addition to dream analysis, Jung relied heavily on painting by his patients as a means of further encouraging them to express their unconscious feelings or thoughts. He maintained that these paintings had little artistic merit and was careful to point out that fact to the patients. Since the paintings were artistically worthless, the patients made sense out of them by coming to the conclusion that they must be expressions of their innermost selves. The painting exercises were also seen as forcing patients to cope actively with their problems. In Jung's view painting had real therapeutic effects. It moved patients off dead center and started them on the road to self-realization.

APPLICATION OF THE THEORY TO THE TREATMENT OF PSYCHOPATHOLOGY

The first point to be made is that analytical psychology is really a "psychology of the afternoon"; that is, a psychology that focuses upon the problems of the middle-aged. Thus, the forms of neurosis in young and old people, in Jung's view, were different:

> . . . the life of a young person is characterized by a general expansion and striving towards concrete ends; and his neurosis seems mainly to rest on his hesitation or shrinking back from this necessity. But the life of an older person is characterized by a contraction of forces, by the affirmation of what has been achieved, and by the curtailment of further growth. His neurosis comes mainly from his clinging to a youthful attitude which is now out of season. Just as the young neurotic is afraid of life, so the older one shrinks back from death. (Jung, 1954, p. 39)

As a result, therapy has to be tailored to the age of the person.

In general terms, however, Jung viewed therapy as a process in which both therapist and patient gained insights into themselves. He argued that the participants were equals in the sense that both parties had many limitations and that both were struggling toward self-realization. Consequently, he maintained that the therapist must give up all claims to superior knowledge, as well as desires to influence the patient, if substantial progress toward the *Tao* or fulfillment and harmony are ever to be attained. Progress toward the Tao refers to a process described by Chinese philosophers whereby individual conflicts and anxieties are transcended so that the person can live in state of perfect harmony and bliss.

Jung seems to contradict himself slightly later when he speaks of the therapist as a guide for the patient. A guide is defined as a person who has some special skills and knowledge that someone else can utilize for personal benefit. A guide should also, of course, be thoroughly familiar with the task he or she is undertaking. Hunters do not, for example, hire a guide who is ignorant of the woods where they are camping. In the best sense, though, Jung seemed to adopt a genuine attitude of humility toward an arduous and uncertain journey, the outcome of which is essentially unknown to the participants.

In his view, the therapeutic process had four key stages: confession, elucidation, education, and transformation (Jung, 1954, p. 55). Confession is a necessary first step in the healing process because it forces the individual to acknowledge his or her limitations to another. The person also becomes aware of his or her universal ties to human-kind, in the sense that all men and women possess certain weaknesses. The cathartic process also leads to the patient's reliance on the therapist; that is, transference occurs. In the process of understanding the transference, the patient brings to the surface certain contents of the un-conscious that the therapist clarifies; this is elucidation. During this stage, the person learns the origins of his or her problems. In the third stage, education, the person incorporates the insights into his or her personality in order to adapt to the social environment. Transformation occurs when the therapist and the patient have been through the first three stages. At this point, the dynamic interplay between the two can lead to exciting changes that move beyond adaptation to the environ-ment and toward self-realization.

CRITICAL COMMENTS

At this point, let us utilize our six criteria to evaluate the scientific worth of Jung's theory.

Comprehensiveness. Jung's position comes close to matching the one created by Freud in terms of the sheer number and diversity of phenomena it examines. In many instances, however, it is not as detailed in its treatment of the phenomena in its domain as is Freud's. Despite this fact, Jung's theory is quite comprehensive in nature. At various points in his career, he addressed himself to such diverse phenomena as marriage, creativity, religion, education, and the occult.

Precision and Testability. Jung's theory fails to meet this criterion. Its relational statements are vague and riddled with inconsistencies. The concepts are also extremely ambiguous. For example, the archetypes are metaphysical concepts that have multiple meanings and few clear referents in external reality. As Jung himself puts it:

> They can only be roughly circumscribed at best. . . . Every attempt to
> focus them more sharply is immediately punished by the intangible core of
> meaning losing its luninosity. No archetype can be reduced to a simple for-
> mula. It is a vessel which we can never empty, and never fill. It has a
> potential existence only, and when it takes shape in matter it is no longer
> what it was. It persists throughout the ages and requires interpreting ever
> anew. The archetypes are the imperishable elements of the unconscious,
> but they change their shape continuously. (Jung, 1958b, p. 145)

In addition to this inherent vagueness, Jung argued that some of our behavior is controlled by "autonomous forces" in the collective unconscious, forces that operate unpredictably. For instance, a man and a
woman may be having an enjoyable discussion about the virtues of the
sexes when they suddenly find themselves embroiled in a bitter controversy about the inherent superiority of one sex over the other. Jung
might account for this unexpected shift in behavior by maintaining that
the negative aspects of the anima in the man and the animus in the
woman had projected themselves onto their behavior. The man might
begin to argue in a "womanish" way and become completely irrational
and emotional about the innate superiority of men, whereas the woman
might become "mannish" and begin to argue dogmatically and in a
domineering fashion about the natural superiority of women. The bitter
argument might continue unabated for an hour or so and then suddenly
subside. Jung would maintain that the man was anima-possessed and
the woman, animus-possessed. The point at which such "possessions"
occur is completely unpredictable.

To scientists, such an assumption is totally unacceptable, since it violates their belief that all behavior is caused by previous events. Although
Jung believed that determinism was a useful concept in the explanation
of behavior, he also maintained that it had its limitations. In his view,
people lived by aims as well as by causes. Furthermore, Jung maintained
that some behavior was produced according to the *principle of
synchronicity* or coincidence. That is, events occur together in time, but
one does not cause the other. For example, thinking of the death of a
loved one does not cause the news received shortly afterward that the
person has just died. Or if a college woman thinks about meeting a
handsome man, the fact that he appears does not mean her thoughts
caused it. Is it any wonder that Jung is popular with spiritualists, clair-
voyants, and telepathists, but not with scientists?

In light of this discussion, it should not be surprising that Jung's
theory is difficult to test and that social scientists have conducted relatively few studies based on it. Most of the work has been concerned with
the establishment of a reliable and valid measure of his postulated
psychological types. Although the measure has proved useful for research purposes, there is currently some debate over whether or not it
even taps most of the dimensions in Jung's conception of the various
personality types.

Simplicity. Jung's theory also fails to meet the parsimony criterion. There seem to be more concepts than are necessary to explain its phenomena. Given kinds of behavior are readily "explained" by invoking a variety of archetypes. If a person behaves aggressively, for example, it could be the result of the activation of his shadow, his animus or anima, a mother archetype, a father archetype, and so forth. The behavior could be the result of the operation of one of these archetypes, several of them, all of them, or none of them. It could be due simply to the operation of un-known and uncontrollable forces within the psyche. When it's caused by the operation of an archetype, there is no systematic explanation of why or how one takes precedence over another.

Empirical Validity. As mentioned in the discussion of the second cri-terion, there is currently some debate concerning whether or not re-search measures of Jung's concepts have any validity. Because of these doubts and because there have been relatively few tests of the theory, it is not surprising that empirical support is weak. Where the theory has been put to the test, its weakness is compounded by the fact that the evi-dence is sometimes not consistently supportive.

Heuristic Value. Jung's theory has had considerable heuristic value. Al-though it has not been accorded high status by scientists, it has been ac-cepted by professionals from a variety of disciplines, including history, literature, art, anthropology, religion, and certain segments of the clinical psychology community. The ties between his position and reli-gion have been especially close, since for Jung spiritual concerns were the highest human value. He felt that Western people were too overdeveloped in the rational realm and grossly underdeveloped in the spiritual arena. Accordingly, Jung believed that many of us needed to turn inward and to meditate in a search for the meaning of our existence. It is not too surprising, then, that Jung has enjoyed popular success among many idealistic, middle-class students surfeited with material possessions and shaken by the war in Vietnam and by Wa-tergate and the CIA and FBI scandals.

Applied Value. Although the theory has been used with some degree of benefit by members of different disciplines, it has not been applied to different problem areas; for example, leadership and group process, as has the Freudian position. At present, its applied value remains largely restricted to therapy.

DISCUSSION QUESTIONS

   1. What is the psyche? How does psychic energy originate and how does it affect the person's behavior?

2. In the chapter some examples were given to show how the principle of equivalence operates in the personality. Can you think of any additional examples?

3. Do you believe that the collective unconscious exists?

4. One example of an archetype is the mother-child relationship. Can you think of any other experiences that are universal in nature?

5. How would you define the shadow? Is it possible to measure it objectively?

6. What kinds of individuals believe in the existence of evil forces within the person that control his or her behavior?

7. What is the nature of the relationship between the anima and animus and our cultural sex-role stereotypes?

8. Have you ever had a transcendent experience that helped you resolve a personal problem? Describe it as best you can and tell how it helped you overcome the difficulty.

9. Can you think of other examples of mandalas that are part of our culture?

10. Are you primarily an introvert or an extravert? In what ways?

11. Cite examples that show the negative qualities of introversion and extraversion.

12. What are superior and inferior functions? What are some of the problems an individual could experience if his or her thinking function was undifferentiated?

13. List the characteristics of the eight different personality types postulated by Jung.

14. Do you agree with Jung that neurosis in young people is due to their avoidance of setting and trying to attain concrete goals?

15. In what ways is Jung's position compatible with contemporary religion? Would you agree that there is a need for spiritual awakening among young people and adults?

NOTES

R. Carlson and N. Levy, "Studies of Jungian Typology: 1. Memory, Social Perception, and Social Action," *Journal of Personality*, 1973, **41**, 559–576.

A. M. Dry, *The Psychology of Jung* (New York: Wiley, 1961).

M. Fordham, *An Introduction to Jung's Psychology*, 3rd ed. (Middlesex, England: Penquin Books, 1960).

J. Jacobi, *The Psychology of Jung* (New Haven: Yale University Press, 1962).

C. G. Jung, *Psychological Types* (New York: Harcourt, 1923).

C. G. Jung, "The Practice of Psychotherapy," in *The Collected Works of C. G. Jung*, Vol. 16 (London: Routledge and Kegan Paul, 1954).

C. G. Jung, "Commentary on the Secret of the Golden Flower," in V. S. de Laszlo, ed., *Psyche and Symbol* (Garden City, N.Y.: Doubleday Anchor, 1958a).

C. G. Jung, "The Special Phenomenology of the Child Archetype," in V. S. de Laszlo, ed., *Psyche and Symbol* (Garden City, N.Y.: Doubleday Anchor, 1958b).

C. G. Jung, "The Psychology of the Child Archetype," in V. S. de Laszlo, ed., *Psyche and Symbol* (Garden City, N.Y.: Doubleday Anchor, 1958c).

C. G. Jung, "The Relations between the Ego and the Unconscious," in V. S. de Laszlo, ed., *The Basic Writings of C. G. Jung* (New York: Modern Library, 1959).

C. G. Jung, *Memories, Dreams, Reflections* (New York: Pantheon, 1963).

C. G. Jung, *Two Essays on Analytical Psychology* (New York: Meridian, 1964).

C. G. Jung, *The Structure and Dynamics of the Psyche*, 2nd ed. (Princeton: Princeton University Press, 1969).

I. Progoff, *Jung's Psychology and Its Social Meaning* (London: Routledge and Kegan Paul, 1953).

F. Rabelais, "The Five Books of Gargantua and Pantagruel," in *The Complete Works of Rabelais*. trans. J. LeClerog (New York: Random House, 1936).

A. Storr, *C. G. Jung* (New York: Viking, 1973).

L. J. Strickler and J. Ross, "A Description and Evaluation of the Myers-Briggs Type Indicator," *Research Bulletin* (Princeton, N.J.: Educational Testing Service, 1962).

SUGGESTED READINGS

Dry, A. M. *The Psychology of Jung*. New York: Wiley, 1961.

Jacobi, J. *The Psychology of Jung*, New Haven: Yale University Press, 1962.

Jung, C. G. *Collected Works* (Ed. H. Read, M. Fordham, & G. Adler). Princeton: Princeton University Press, 1953.

Jung, C. G. *Memories, Dreams, Reflections*. New York: Pantheon, 1963.

Storr, A. *C. G. Jung*. New York: Viking, 1973.

GLOSSARY

Analytical Psychology. Jung's unique brand of psychology that emphasizes the complex interplay between oppositional forces within the psyche and the ways in which these internal conflicts affect personality development.

Anima. The feminine archetype in men. It includes both positive and negative characteristics of the transpersonal female. In a positive sense, the anima involves a sense of warmth and intuitive understanding. In a negative sense, it involves moodiness and irritability.

Animus. The masculine archetype in women. It includes both positive and negative characteristics of the transpersonal man. In a positive sense, the animus involves an ability to reason and use logic to solve problems. In a negative sense, it involves an uncritical and dogmatic adherence to certain ideas and an irrationality in solving problems.

Archetype. Universal theme or symbol that can be activated by forces operating in the psyche, thereby generating visions that are projected onto current experiences.

Collective Unconscious. The depository of instincts and archetypes that go beyond personal experience. These transpersonal experiences are the residue of human evolutionary development and can be activated under the proper conditions.

Complex. Collection of thoughts united by a common feeling.

Dominant Characteristic. In Jung's theory, a developed, differentiated, and conscious part of the psyche.

Extraversion. Basic attitude postulated by Jung to account for people's attempts to relate to the world. Extraversion implies an outgoing and relatively confident approach to life.

Extraverted Feeling Type. Individual characterized positively by an acceptance of the standards of society and negatively by a change in emotions from situation to situation, along with an indiscriminate yielding to the expectations of others.

Extraverted Intuitive Type. Individual characterized positively by a quick grasp of the creative possibilities in various ventures and negatively by impatience and flightiness.

Extraverted Sensing Type. Individual characterized positively by an appreciation for the arts and negatively by crude pleasure-seeking.

Extraverted Thinking Type. Individual characterized in a positive way by a concern for social reform and in a negative way by a selfish and exploitative attitude toward others.

Irrational Functions. Modes of apprehending the world without evaluating it. For Jung, sensation and intuition were the irrational (nonrational) functions.

Life-Process Energy. All of the urges that are derived from conflict between forces in the psyche.

Mandala. Symbolic representation of the self or of the world.

Myers-Briggs Type Indicator. Paper-and-pencil test designed to measure the various types of individuals postulated to exist by Jung in his theory of psychological types.

Persona. Archetype consisting of the role human beings play in order to meet the demands of others. The persona also allows them to express their innermost feelings in ways acceptable to other people.

Personal Unconscious. In Jung's theory, the region that contains all of the personal experiences that have been blocked from awareness.

Principle Of Entropy. In Jungian theory, the idea that energy is redistributed in the psyche in order to achieve equilibrium or balance.

Principle of Equivalence. The idea that energy expended in one part of the psyche will be compensated for by an equal amount of energy in the same or different form in another part of the psyche. Thus, energy is neither created nor lost, but simply shifted from one region of the psyche to another.

Principle of Opposites. The idea that the energy which propels personality and behavior is derived from the interplay between opposite forces within the psyche.

Principle of Synchronicity. Belief that behavior is not caused but can be understood in terms of the coincidental juxtaposition of events.

Psyche. For Jung, a construct that was postulated to represent all of the interacting systems within human personality that were needed to account for the mental life and behavior of the person.

Psychological Types. Theory proposed by Jung in which people could be classified in terms of eight types based upon a combination of attitudes and functions.

Rational Functions. Modes of making judgments or evaluations of events in the world. For Jung, thinking and feeling were rational functions.

Self. For Jung, an archetype that leads people to search for ways in which to maximize the development of their potential.

Self-Realization. Process which involves the healthy development of the capabilities of people so that they can fulfill their own unique natures.

Shadow. The inferior, evil, and repulsive side of human nature.

Symbol. In Jung's psychology, a representation of a psychic fact. Each symbol was thought to have multiple meanings and to be incapable of being understood completely.

Transcendent Function. The process by which a conflict is resolved by bringing opposing forces into harmony or balance with each other through understanding.

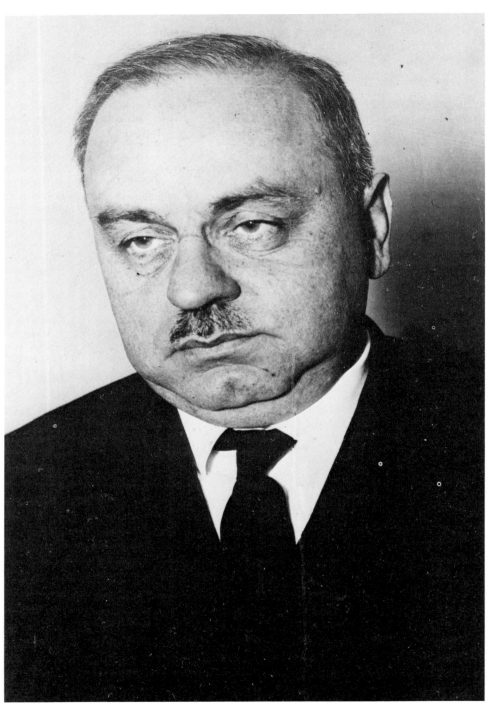

Alfred Adler (The Bettmann Archive, Inc.)

Adler's Individual Psychology

BIOGRAPHICAL SKETCH

Alfred Adler was born in Vienna in 1870, of Jewish parents. His father was a grain merchant whose work allowed the family to live an affluent, middle-class life. Alfred was the third of seven children, five boys and two girls, of whom the oldest was a boy and the second a girl. His early schooling proceeded without difficulty and without special academic distinction.

Later, at the Vienna Medical School, he came under the influence of a famous internist who stressed that the physician must always treat the patient as a whole, and not just the ailment. He was also fond of saying, "If you want to be a good doctor, you have to be a kind person." They were two lessons Adler never forgot. During his university days, he also acquired a socialist political orientation and endorsed much of Karl Marx's contentions about the nature of men and women, but not Marxist economic policies. Adler was attracted to the humanistic side of socialism, the side which stresses equality and cooperation between human beings and the maintenance of the democratic tradition in society. He became an unflagging champion of the common person and fought against oppression of the masses all through his life.

Once he had received his medical degree, Adler established a private practice in a lower-middle-class Vienna neighborhood near a famous amusement park. His patients included artists and acrobats from the park shows. Some of these extraordinary physical specimens told Adler that they had achieved their powers as a reaction to weakness and illness in childhood. It was these experiences which, at least partly, led Adler to focus on the concept of overcompensation in his theorizing. Adler's association with Freud apparently grew out of his defense of Freud's views on dreams, which had been attacked by critics in the local press. In 1902, he joined the small group of scholars who met in Freud's home. By 1910, he was elected the first president of the Vienna Psycho-

Analytic Society. Adler never established a warm personal relationship with Freud nor with most of the other members of the group. He was not a person to worship at the feet of the master, and his forthright questioning and criticism of some of Freud's concepts led to his resignation from the society in 1911.

Soon after, Adler formed a group called the Society for Free Psycho-Analytic Research, a title chosen to show his obvious displeasure with what he considered Freud's dictatorial ways. In 1913, Adler changed the name of the association to Individual Psychology to reflect his concern with understanding the whole personality, not just isolated aspects of behavior. One of the meanings of the word "individual" is total entity or indivisible entity, and it is this meaning which best reflects Adler's concern. Unfortunately, the term also suggests a study of the individual as contrasted with the study of group behavior. But Adler's theory is, in many respects, social-psychological in nature, so that for him, the individual can be understood only in terms of his or her participation with other members of society.

During World War I, Adler worked as an army doctor in a Vienna hospital. Largely as a result of these experiences, he discovered the importance of the concept of social interest. He saw the savage effects of the war on people, effects generated by lack of trust and cooperation. He returned to his writing and research activities with renewed purpose, and focused much of his energies on disseminating information to the "common man" about the need for cooperation, love, and respect between people. He was also instrumental in helping to establish some thirty child guidance clinics in the Vienna school system in which counseling with the entire family was conducted. By the early 1920s, Adler had gained international recognition and acceptance. He began to accept invitations to lecture in European cities and later discussed his views with audiences in the United States. He succumbed to a heart attack while on a European lecture tour in Aberdeen, Scotland, in May 1937 (Furtmuller, 1973, pp. 330–394).

BASIC CONCEPTS AND PRINCIPLES

The Aims of the Theory

According to Adler, *individual psychology* is a science that attempts to understand the experiences and behavior of each person as an organized entity. He believed further that all actions are guided by a person's fundamental attitudes toward life. True to his interest in improving the lot of humankind, he said that he also aimed at the correction of faulty or mistaken attitudes through use of the basic knowledge accumulated by tests of the theory. Thus, in addition to collecting basic information about human behavior, Adler was greatly interested in applying such knowledge in a practical way.

Basic Theoretical Scheme

Out of Adler's efforts to understand "that mysterious creative power of life—that power which expresses itself in the desire to develop, to strive and to achieve—and even to compensate for defeats in one direction by striving for success in another" came a simple, yet interesting, set of theoretical propositions. (Adler, 1969, p.1). These propositions emphasized that an understanding of human personality was possible only if we were aware of the individual's goals. In contrast to Freud, who was a strict determinist, Adler adopted the *teleological* position that it was the individual's goals which directed his current behavior. People have a purpose in life; namely, to attain perfection or completion. Furthermore, this movement toward perfection is generated by feelings of inferiority. We are continually struggling, according to Adler, from minus to plus. We are all engaged in the "great upward drive."

In his earliest writings, the final goal of our struggle was to be aggressive and all-powerful, to dominate others. Humans were seen as selfish and concerned with their own self-aggrandizement. Later, Adler revised his thinking and claimed that the final goal was to be superior. But the striving for *superiority*, in the best sense, did not involve personal domination of others; it was only the neurotic who strove for such a mistaken goal. The striving for superiority by the healthy person involved movement toward perfection in a way that contributed to the welfare of others. In such a motivational scheme, sexuality became a secondary phenomenon. The primary emphasis was on those constructive or destructive family experiences during the first five years of life which contributed to the individual's later development and movement toward or away from a final goal.

Feelings of Inferiority and the Striving for Superiority

While he was still involved in the practice of medicine, Adler noted that individuals with defective organs typically tried to compensate for their weaknesses by intensive training. A girl with a speech impediment might try to overcome her problem by intensive and persistent practice until, one day, she was able to excel, perhaps by becoming a national news broadcaster. Or a boy with puny legs might strive to become an outstanding distance runner. The qualifiers in these examples are necessary, since Adler firmly believed that it was not the defect itself which produced the striving, but the person's *attitude* toward it. The person was free to interpret the deficiency in many ways or even to ignore it. If he ignored it, then it would not result in overwhelming striving behavior.

Adler later expanded the concept of *organ inferiority* to include exaggerated strivings caused by feelings of unmanliness. *Masculine protest* was the term he used to describe these compensation behaviors. In Adler's thinking, superiority tended to be equated with masculinity and behaviors such as assertiveness, independence, and dominance, while inferiority and femininity tended to be equated. Feminine behavior included passivity, submissiveness, and dependence. His thinking was probably based upon the roles enacted by males and females in Viennese society at the time. Adler was not a male chauvinist. He used the concept of masculine protest to show that women were placed in an inferior position by society and that, as a consequence, they often tried to overcome feelings of inadequacy by aping masculine behavior. Examples include women who spout obscenities continuously and who often swagger and act tough. Lesbianism was considered an extreme manifestation of the masculine protest. On the other hand, similar compensatory behavior could be found in women who act in an exaggeratedly feminine manner. Thus "superfeminine" women may have adopted this life style as a means of luring and then dominating and humiliating men. Adler's concept described the behavior of men as well as of women. Men who felt insecure could also acquire exaggerated ways of behaving to prove that they were "real men." The Don Juan type would try to "prove" his manhood by countless seductions. For either sex, then, such manifestations were neurotic in character. In line with his equalitarian orientation, Adler abhorred the thought of treating anyone, male or female, as inferior, and argued vigorously that such bias had to be eliminated.

Eventually he broadened the concept of organ inferiority even more and argued that all of us experience feelings of psychological and social inferiority, beginning with our earliest participation in family life. Our parents and most others are not only bigger physically than we are, but more sophisticated and adept at solving problems. Out of these feelings of inferiority, whatever the basis, comes a striving for superiority. Feelings of inferiority can be largely constructive or largely destructive. Acknowledging the fact that we all feel inferior at some point in our lives could serve as a basis for mutual help and cooperation to overcome problems in living. But if we dwell excessively on our inferiorities, real or imagined, we are less likely to trust others or ourselves. As a consequence, we are likely to operate on the "useless side" of life; we are more likely to *overcompensate* for our deficiencies and to develop an exaggerated sense of superiority that others find loathsome.

Fictional Finalisms

Adler's *fictional finalism* concept is based upon the writings of the philosopher Hans Vaihinger. Vaihinger published a book entitled *The Philosophy of "As-If"*. In it, he argued that people create ideas which guide their behavior. Adler adopted this view and came to the conclusion that all people's various strivings could not occur without the perception of goals. Goals give direction to all our behavior and are necessary for individual advancement and development. These goals,

Piaget, Jean

BF 723 C5 P52813   The Child-d reality; problems of genetic psychology

BF 721 P5   The Child's conception of the world

LB 1117 P5 1965   The moral judgments of the child

BF 721 P462 1962a   Play, dreams and imitation in childhood

BF 721 P4813   The Psychology of the child

955695000
TITLE   WORLD BULK CARRIERS.
PLACE   OSLO, NORWAY.
HOLDINGS   1968-1971.
CALL NO.   HE 563 A3 T732
NOTES   SUPERSEDED BY WORLD BULK FLEET. WITH 1972.

955700000 V
TITLE   WORLD BULK FLEET.
PLACE   OSLO, NORWAY.
HOLDINGS   1972-1977.
CALL NO.   HE 563 A3 T7321
           /LATEST REF/.
NOTES   SUPERSEDES IN PART WORLD BULK CARRIERS WITH 1972.

955705000 V
TITLE   WORLD BULK TRADES.
PLACE   OSLO, NORWAY.
HOLDINGS   1972-
CALL NO.   HE 563 A3 W67.

955710000 A
TITLE   WORLD BUSINESS.
PLACE   NEW YORK.
HOLDINGS   1968-1970.
NOTES   CEASED PUBLICATION WITH 1970.

intellectual Cmn.
diff. field

CAROLINE LEUNG

GOT
I HAVE A BROKEN HEART
II
MY HEART IS BROKEN

Adler believed, are ideals and not something tangible. They can be healthy fictions or mistaken ones. For example, you could believe that your goal was to help people and to engage in activities that would prove beneficial to others. Or you could believe that you are Casanova and that your goal is to "prove" your superiority over women through an endless and indiscriminate procession of seductions.

Social Interest

Adler firmly believed that we are related to one another from the first day of life. We cannot escape the fact that everyone of us is, or has been at some time, dependent upon others for help. He claimed that our *social feeling* or *interest* is innate and that it can come to fruition only with the proper guidance and training. As he stated it: "[Social interest] means a striving for a form of community which must be thought of as everlasting, as it could be thought of if mankind had reached the goal of perfection" (Adler, 1973c, pp. 34–35). By striving for the completion of others, we help ourselves move toward the same goal. This striving would also imply that we have respect and consideration for all human beings. As Brennan maintains, "We remain open to the other and welcome him as a host would a guest, according to his own meaning, whose life is respected as equally valid as one's own" (Brennan, 1969, p. 10). It is this humanistic view which Adler strongly defended throughout his later writings, the implications of which we will discuss in greater detail in later sections of this chapter.

Style of Life and the Creative Self

These two concepts are closely interrelated in Adlerian theorizing. The *style of life*, originally called the "life plan" or "guiding image," refers to the unique ways in which people pursue their goals. An actress attempts to attain perfection through study and stage and film appearances. A scholar tries to become superior by intensive reading, studying, and thinking, and by the discussion of ideas with her colleagues. Our unique styles of life are formed during the first five years after birth. All our later experiences are then assimilated and interpreted in accordance with these established patterns of behaving. These styles emerge as reactions to our inferiorities, real or imagined. Once established, they are virtually impossible to modify.

The concept of the *creative self* appears to be an outgrowth of Adler's concern with the mechanistic nature of his style of life construct. This statement means that Adler was probably dissatisfied with a strict stimulus-response learning interpretation of the acquisition of the individual's unique behavior patterns, because it implied that the person was a passive recipient who did not interpret or act upon his experiences. The concept implies that each of us creates his or her own personality, that we actively construct it out of our experiences and heredities. People are, in the final analysis, responsible for their destinies. They are often quite aware of the alternatives available to them in solving problems and act in a rational and responsible manner. It is primarily the neurotic whose goals are unconscious and who is often unaware of the available alternatives in given situations.

THE PROCESS OF PERSONALITY DEVELOPMENT

The Importance of Early Childhood Experiences

Adler believed that both parents played crucial roles in discouraging or encouraging the development of the distinctive life styles of their children (Ansbacher and Ansbacher, 1956, pp. 372–381). The parents are charged with nourishing the child's increasing awareness with accurate conceptions of work, friendship, and love. In Adler's view, these are the three basic problems of life, and the healthy or courageous person is the one who confronts and attempts to cope with them.

The mother's role is particularly important since she is usually the first person to have extended, intimate contact with the child. She introduces the child to social life. If she loves the child, she is more likely to be interested in teaching the child the skills necessary to secure his or her welfare. If she is dissatisfied with her role, on the other hand, she may be preoccupied with trying to prove her own personal superiority. She may then try to prove to everyone that her child is more intelligent and handsome than all others and that he or she crawled, stood, and walked sooner than anyone else. Unfortunately, most children react adversely to such pressure, and the result is typically natural hostility and resentment.

For the father, the primary task is to prove that he is a worthwhile human being by contributing to the welfare of his wife, his children, and his society. Furthermore, he must treat his wife as an equal and cooperate with her in meeting the problems of life. Of course, she must also value him as an equal. If she is afraid of losing the affection of her children and forces him to be the sole administrator of punishment for their misdeeds, she is not fulfilling her obligations as a wife and mother and is acting, instead, on the "useless side" of life. She is guilty of pampering her children because of her own weaknesses and exploiting her husband. The same argument would apply to a husband who pampers his children.

Adler believed further that each child was treated uniquely by his parents, depending upon his order of birth within the family. The eldest child tends to be the center of attention in the family before the birth of other siblings. With their births, he or she is placed in the position of the "dethroned monarch" who has to share the affection and attention of the parents with others. As a consequence, the oldest child may feel resentment and hostility toward the younger ones. Such negative feelings are likely to occur if the parents have not properly prepared the child for the arrival of another or others. If they have adequately prepared him, the oldest child may adopt a protective and supportive attitude instead. He will often play the part of father or mother with the younger ones and feel responsible for their welfare.

According to Adler, the oldest child understands best the importance of power and authority, since he has to undergo their loss within the family. Consequently, the oldest child will be highly supportive of and dependent on authorities in later life and will be a person who tends to desire the maintenance of the status quo. Such a person is likely to be politically conservative. The second child is likely to view the oldest brother or sister as a competitor to be overcome. If the oldest child is protective and supportive of his younger sibling's attempts to excel, healthy development is more probable. If the eldest resents the second child and acts maliciously, movement toward neurosis for the younger one is more likely to occur. Adler also felt that the second child may set unrealistically high goals, thereby virtually ensuring ultimate failure.

The youngest child has many models and tends to develop a competitive orientation, according to Adler. He or she tends to commandeer most of the family's attention. Adler believed that parents tend to pamper and spoil the youngest members of their families. The result is a person who is excessively dependent on others for support and protection, yet who wants to excel in everything he or she does. Such a child tends to suffer from extreme feelings of inferiority, since others are bigger and more experienced. The only child has no models or rivals and is likely to be the center of attention in the family, assuming that his or her birth was a welcome event. If the child was unwanted, neglect or active rejection by the parents will probably occur. In most instances, however, the only child is likely to be pampered by the parents, especially the mother. Later, the child may experience considerable difficulty if he or she is not universally liked and admired.

Birth Order Research

It would be encouraging to report that tests of Addler's *birth order* thesis have yielded overwhelming support for his major arguments. This has not been the case, as a recent review of the research literature by Schooler has shown (Schooler, 1972, pp. 161–175). One general finding which has received considerable support, however, is that first-borns and only children tend to become more anxious than later-borns in threatening situations and, as a result, tend to affiliate more with others.

The earliest support for this hypothesis was found in an investigation by Schachter (Schachter, 1959). In his study, female subjects were introduced to a medical doctor who informed them that they were about to participate in an experiment concerned with the effects of electric shock on pulse rates and blood pressures. In one condition, the experimenter informed half the subjects that the shocks would be very painful; in the other, he told the remaining half that the shocks would be very mild and would only tickle. All subjects were then informed that they would have to wait ten minutes before the part of the experiment which involved shocking would begin and were given the option of waiting alone or together with other women. In addition, a third category on their checklist was available for those subjects who did not care whether they waited alone or together. (Incidentally, none of the subjects ever received any shock.) As expected, first-borns and only children not only reported being more anxious than later-borns, but a larger percentage of them chose to affiliate with other women. Figure 4.1 depicts the data in graphic form. Other research has also shown that first-borns perform less effectively under stress and that they are less likely than later-borns to participate in dangerous sports.

Although Adler was one of the first theoreticians to explore the possible effects of birth order on behavior, much of the research makes little or no mention of his seminal contribution; nor does it utilize his theorizing. Schachter, for example, based his hypotheses on the contention that parents tend to be uncertain and worried about the proper ways to treat their first-borns. They give them inordinate amounts of attention in order to reduce their own anxiety and the anxiety they have generated in the child. Presumably, then, first-born children learn to depend upon others as a means of reducing their own anxiety. Adler, on the other hand, argued that first-born children are often the center of attention and are made anxious not by inept parental handling, but by the loss of their central position to younger rivals. They begin to make attempts to regain their original status by performing in accordance with parental expectations. Thus, the theoretical basis for the hypothesis that first-borns will tend to affiliate more than later-borns under stress is different. The point is that Schachter's results are not to be interpreted in the strictest sense as supportive of Adler's theory. A related point is that it is all too easy to assume that because Adler was interested in birth order effects, any research outcomes in this area must be taken as evidence in support or nonsupport of his theory. The major asset of his theory may be its heuristic value—that is, its ability to stimulate further thinking and research—rather than the amount of scientific evidence which has been accumulated in its support.

Personality Development of the Neurotic

Out of this incredible welter of family experience and the person's interpretation of it emerges a guiding goal and a distinctive style of life

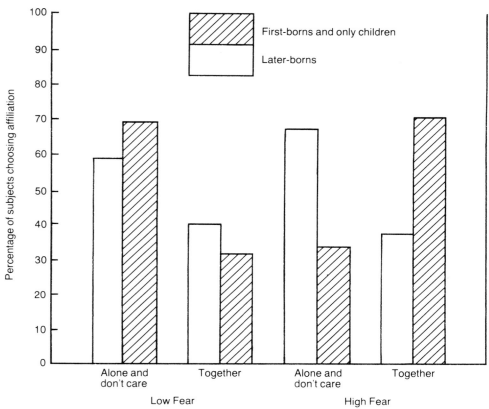

Figure 4.1.
Percentage of first-borns (including only children) and later-borns choosing to affiliate under nonstress and stress conditions. Adapted from Schachter, *The Psychology of Affiliation*, 1959, pp. 44, 45.

which can be changed only rarely. As hinted earlier, the three major sets of environmental factors that may give rise to severely mistaken or neurotic life goals are (1) organ inferiority; (2) neglect or rejection; and (3) pampering. Adler believed that pampering was especially damaging. In any event, the neurotic person is one who feels very acutely his own inferiority and who compensates for these feelings by establishing unrealistically high goals that he believes will enable him to demonstrate personal superiority over others. He is characterized further as an individual who is grossly inaccurate in his self-evaluations. He may continually either underestimate or overestimate his own worth. He is continually tense and fearful. He fears decisions, tests, and defeats. In the final analysis, he is terrified of being unmasked and recognized by others as inferior. Such a person does not act in accordance with social interest; he is not courageous. Instead, he continually adopts safeguarding or defensive strategies to protect himself.

In order to make his developmental process clear, let us briefly examine some of the experiences of a hypothetical male student. He is a first-born who received a great deal of attention from his parents, who always told him he was more intelligent than any of the other boys or girls his age, that he was superior to other children at solving problems, and that he was destined to become a great leader. They almost invariably praised him for his successes. Relatedly, they ignored, minimized, or distorted his failures by blaming someone or some aspect of the environment. If he struck out in a Little League baseball game, for instance, it was because the umpire made a poor call or because he neglected to use his favorite bat. If he did not receive the highest marks on his school tests, it was because the teacher was incompetent. Although he felt keenly inadequate and inferior at times in a variety of situations, he told himself that his parents were correct in their exaggerated appraisal of his skills. He did this as a means of safeguarding himself from the painful knowledge of his limitations. Beginning at an early age, then, his faulty style of life was set and he began to focus most of his energies on his goal to become a godlike person. His fictional goal would not permit him to admit mistakes. He came to believe that he was personally superior to others and to expect attainment of success in all his activities.

In college, he dated a few girls, invariably with poor results. He expected them to acknowledge his personal superiority, his vast knowledge of events, and to pay attention to his pronouncements. When they became resistive and resentful, he dismissed them as too simple-minded to understand the profundity of his thinking. Sex was considered a weapon one used to demonstrate complete superiority over women. Women were supposed to acknowledge his mastery of them, and he was surprised when they refused to comply with his demands. Eventually, he stopped dating altogether and concentrated instead on "proving" his superiority by excelling in his studies. He began to narrow his activities to those in which he was certain to excel. His competitiveness for grades was incredibly intense, and he continually downgraded his fellow students for their academic shortcomings. He began to turn his social activities with them into competitive battles. For example, he would turn a casual stroll to a morning class with a classmate into a competitive race in order to prove his superiority. He would not lend books to other students for fear they would attain higher grades. His professors were hardly worthy of him, and unless they praised his brilliance, he considered them incompetents who should be expelled from the university. Eventually, he was graduated and got a job as a journalist. Persistent conflicts with his boss and co-workers, however, finally led him to seek therapy. Examination of the origins of his faulty life style eventually produced a willingness to attempt to correct his mistakes. He came to understand the sources of some of his conflicts and to modify, to a certain extent, his life style.

Personal Development of a Constructive Life Style

The person who develops a healthy life style was seen by Adler as one who experienced a family life in which the parents treated him or her with respect and consideration. Under such conditions, Adler believed the person was likely to learn the importance of equality and cooperation between people. Such a person would therefore be likely to acquire a life style that had as its aim the attainment of goals in accordance with social interest. Adler often left the nature of these goals unspecified; they could vary from adoption of the principle that "honesty is the best policy" to movement toward specific occupational goals such as professor, doctor, silversmith, auto mechanic, used car salesperson, and television repairperson. Although recent research by the author and psychologist Martin Sherman has shown that members of the general public have little respect for the last three occupations (Ryckman and Sherman, 1974, pp. 351–364). Adler would argue that individuals could fill these roles in line with social interest—that is, by expending maximum effort and utilizing their abilities for the welfare of society.

Adler also maintained that the healthy person could change his or her fictional goals if circumstances demanded it. Would you act dishonestly and steal a loaf of bread to feed a starving child? Adler would probably answer "Yes," but only if you had exhausted every other avenue in trying to solve the problem. The healthy person is one who lives by principles, yet who is realistic enough to modify them under exceptional circumstances. We turn now to a discussion of the primary techniques used by Adler to assess personality.

TECHNIQUES OF ASSESSMENT

Like Freud, Adler sought to understand the individual's personality by focusing on an examination and analysis of early childhood experiences. He used three main techniques to gain access to these crucial experiences. One procedure involved asking the patient to recall his or her earliest experiences. Adler would then compare these recollections with facts the patient had already given him about his or her more recent life experiences to understand the common themes or goals that, often unconsciously, guided the person's behavior. Adler also utilized dream analysis as a major technique for understanding the patient's personality. Unlike Freud, however, he did not focus on sexual interpretations of manifest dream content. Instead, he thought that the person's dreams were determined by his or her goal of superiority. More specifically, dreams reflect the individual's unconscious attempts to achieve personal goals in accordance with his or her unique style of life. The goal may be constructive or destructive, of course. The student who is courageous and unafraid of examinations, for example, may have dreams involving the successful climbing of mountains and of enjoying the view from the top, whereas the student who is a quitter and who wants to postpone examinations may have dreams of falling off the mountain (Adler, 1969, p. 70). Each student's dreams are thus controlled by his unique style of life. Adler's third technique was birth order analysis as a means of understanding the personality. Information gained from the use of this procedure was subsequently employed to help individuals correct mistaken life styles.

APPLICATION OF THE THEORY TO THE TREATMENT OF PSYCHOPATHOLOGY

Neurotics and psychotics, according to Adler, are people who have faulty life styles, usually acquired via contact with parents who had either pampered, neglected, or rejected them during early childhood. In many instances, these parents showed erratic behavior, sometimes mixing pampering and rejection. As a consequence of this treatment, Adler believed that these children became highly anxious, felt insecure, and began to develop protective devices to cope with feelings of inferiority. Most often, they developed a striving for personal superiority to compensate for these feelings. Thus, the neurotic individual begins to believe in an arrogant way that he is actually superior to others and to act in ways consistent with his belief. For example, he may strive to be perfect and belittle others. He avoids failure and being wrong at all costs. Other people are thus perceived as competitors who must be defeated in order for the neurotic to be satisfied, no matter how short-lived the feeling. The psychotic too views others with suspicion, but does not validate his worth so much through comparison with others as through the use of private logic and reasoning and delusions of grandeur.

According to Adler, the goal of therapy is the reorganization of the individual's mistaken beliefs about himself and others, the elimination of faulty goals, and the implementation of new goals that will help him to realize his potential as a human being. To accomplish these objectives, Adler believed that "[t]he patient must be guided away from himself, toward productivity for others; he must be educated toward social interest; he must be led from his seclusion from the world, back to existence . . .; he must be brought to the only correct insight, that he is as important to the community as anyone else; he must get to feel at home on this earth" (Adler, 1973d, p. 200).

The therapist acts as the client's guide to facilitate movement toward these ends. First, they jointly learn to understand the childhood origins of the person's difficulties and the reasons for the development of a faulty life style. They begin to see why the patient feels he *must* be superior to others and that his orientation is destructive. Encouraged by the therapist, the patient moves away from competitive self-centeredness and comes to realize that psychological health is contingent upon the development of a cooperative attitude toward others and upon attempts to contribute to the welfare of society. He begins to see that he is worthwhile and a part of the community and that there is great joy in accepting responsibility for his own actions. Under these conditions, the person is no longer a "taker"; he is a "giver." Slowly, the patient moves toward reorganization of his perceptions and begins to behave differently toward others.

Implications of the Adlerian Position for Our Society

Much of Adler's theorizing has an authentic ring to it, especially when it is considered in the context of our highly competitive and power-oriented culture. Many of us can see ourselves and others engaged in a race to outdo each other and to secure more prestige and status than our neighbors. In the words of one prominent Adlerian named Dreikurs:

> Everyone tries to be more . . . to reach higher, and as a consequence, we are all neurotic, in a neurotic society which pays a premium to the over-ambitious search for prestige and striving for superiority. This search inspires a desire for self-elevation and personal glory, thereby restricting our ability for cooperation and our sense of human fellowship. Yet underneath we are all frightened people, not sure of ourselves. . . . It is this doubt of oneself, expressed in a feeling of inadequacy and inferiority, which restricts our Social Interest and which is at the root of all maladjustment and psychopathology. (Dreikurs, 1963)

From a very early age, children are taught the importance of winning and of avoiding failure. Comparisons between individuals are continuously made and, although warnings are sometimes given not to feel badly or think less of oneself after losing and not to downgrade a defeated opponent, such distinctions are tremendously difficult to maintain. As a consequence, many individuals who acquire notable skills tend to feel smug and personally superior to others, while the inept tend to feel unworthy and inadequate. Even the person with superior skills is not spared these feelings of inadequacy, however, for he has been taught by his parents and others never to be satisfied with his accomplishments.

The harmful effects of excessive competition are manifested in a variety of ways. Cheating and lying may become ways of ensuring the maintenance or the enhancement of personal success. In this regard, it is interesting to note that even one of our most hallowed traditions, the National Soapbox Derby, has fallen prey to the excessive demands for success. It was disclosed in the media recently that the winner of the race had an illegal electromagnetic device installed in his racer to increase his chances of winning. Is nothing sacred anymore? Countless examples could be added to support the general contention that the need for personal enhancement at the expense of others may give rise to unethical actions. For students it may be sufficient to mention the large numbers of their peers who routinely cheat on examinations to achieve higher grades and do not feel guilty about it, and the perhaps equally large number of academics who have lied and cheated in similar situations and who now pontificate about the deceptive practices of their students.

The overwhelming moral suggestion in most of Adler's writings and those of his followers is that cooperation is "good" and competition is "bad." It would be easy to conclude, as a consequence, that adequate social interest involves only cooperation and equality. But can cooperation have negative consequences for people and competition positive ones? Is competition in any form compatible with adequate social interest and cooperation incompatible with it? A closer look at Adler's definition of social interest indicates that the answers to these questions may be yes, for his definition of the term includes not only striving for personal superiority, but for superiority in the sense of realizing one's potential. In this latter sense of the term, an argument could be made that the healthy person acts in accordance with social interest to attain standards which move him toward completion. This private competition would involve setting new standards as old ones are mastered. Thus, a painter or a craftsworker could compete in this restricted sense of the term and have the products of his labor contribute to the welfare and happiness of others. These attempts would be in harmony with Adler's idea that the attainment of perfection involves the overcoming of resistances with which the environment confronts the organism (Adler, 1973c, p. 75).

But although such arguments may make some sense, they do not address the problem directly since most competitive events involve interpersonal comparisons and evaluations. But even here an argument can be made for the idea that competition may be compatible with social interest. Such an outcome could theoretically be obtained if a person competed *with* others rather than *against* them. Such competition would involve feelings of accomplishment or defeat, but without the accompanying feelings of personal superiority or inferiority in relationship to others. Perhaps such an outcome is possible where there is mutual respect and esteem between opponents *before* the onset of the competition. There would still be a winner and a loser, but neither party would feel any compulsion to gloat after winning or to feel inferior after losing. Instead, they might even rejoice in the other's success or be dejected when the other loses. Both parties would also benefit from the testing of their skills. The winner would be likely to improve himself as a result of the contest, while the "loser" would learn something from his failure that could be used to enhance his performance in the future.

In contrast, cooperation may be incompatible with social interest to the extent that it prevents personal movement toward perfection. When groups force individuals to sacrifice their opportunities to excel, such coercion would be seen as incongruent with social interest. The bright student who settles for "gentlemen Cs" because his friends would ridicule him if he obtained mostly A grades would be one such example. He may cooperate with them, but such activity is detrimental to his personal development. The "team player" in business organizations may also at times stifle her own creative urges in the interest of cooperation. In such instances, participants appear interchangeable, and equality between people becomes a synonym for sameness. Adler considered equality an essential quality of adequate social interest, but he did not equate it with sameness. He recognized individual differences in abilities and advocated equality in the sense of our recognizing the essential validity of everyone's existence and the fact that there should be equality of opportunity for every person. People should have full opportunity to realize their potential, an ideal that is also fundamental in our democratically oriented society.

CRITICAL COMMENTS

We turn now to an assessment of the scientific worth of Adler's theory in terms of our six criteria.

Comprehensiveness. Adler addressed himself to a wide range of phenomena involving disordered behavior, and in this respect, his position rivals Freud's. He discusses at length the etiology and cure of many different kinds of neurosis and psychosis. But Adler also applied his thinking to an understanding of the ways in which political, educational, and religious institutions affect personality development. In his discussions, he tried not only to assess the impact of the destructive elements of these institutions on the individual, but to outline the ways in which they could be restructured to promote psychological health and well-being. In general, then, Adler's theory is comprehensive in nature, although like Freud's theory, its motivational base is very limited.

Precision and Testability. The concepts in Adler's theory are generally global in nature and poorly defined. For example, some individuals are thought to have "proof complexes." A proof complex, according to Adler, is " . . . found in many people who want to prove that they also have a right to exist or that they have no faults" (Adler, 1973b, p. 75). How would you measure the proof complex in people? Even if you could develop an adequate measure, it is readily apparent that it would be an extremely difficult task. Then think of the difficulties in operationalizing Adlerian concepts like the redeemer complex, the exclusion complex, the predestination complex, creative power, and style of life, and you will have a good idea of the problems with making the theory testable.

The relational statements of the theory are also vaguely stated. Witness a hypothesis such as "The law of movement and its direction originate from the creative power of the individual, and use, in free choice, one's experiences of one's body and of external effects, within the limits of human capacity" (Adler, 1973a, p. 51). How much creative power is needed to effect the person's unique movements? How much movement occurs if the creative power of the person is utilized? It is interesting to note that Adler believed this hypothesis had already been empirically validated.

Simplicity. Adler made a diligent effort to construct a scientific theory understandable to the ordinary person. The result was a "common-sense" psychology that utilizes only a few constructs. But although parsimony of explanation is considered a virtue in scientific psychology, the set of constructs must be adequate to the task of accounting for human behavior in all its complexity. By postulating a master motive—that is, the striving for superiority—his position has a reductionist quality that fails to do justice to the great diversity of reinforcers which motivate us. Relatedly, the fact that there are only a few constructs in the theory means that they are going to be applied in highly general and imprecise ways. For example, we have already reviewed a number of problems with various constructs in the theory, including the fact that they are defined so loosely that it is often unclear what dimensions they encompass and how those which can be identified are related to everyday situations.

Empirical Validity. Still another criticism of the Adlerian position is that there has been little attempt to verify it empirically. Many of the articles in journals devoted to the continuation and expansion of his initial formulations (the *Journal of Individual Psychology*, the *Journal of Humanistic Psychology*) present applications of his ideas to current psychotherapeutic theory and practice. Some writers tend to present particular case studies and then to "demonstrate" how the use of Adler's ideas increases our understanding of the dynamics of the problems confronting the patients under consideration. In addition, Adlerian "explanations" are occasionally offered for the development of particular value systems by members of other cultures. Famous characters in literature are also subjected to such analyses. In general, however, direct tests of the theory are relatively few and are generally preliminary and exploratory in nature.

Heuristic Value. Perhaps the chief contribution of Adler's theory is the number of subsequent investigators of human personality who claim to have been influenced by it. For example, Adler is considered by some individuals to be one of the founding fathers of the existential-humanistic movement in psychology, with its heavy emphasis on the individual's freedom to make choices in given situations and to deal creatively with his experiences. Adler has influenced either directly or indirectly such prominent psychologists and psychiatrists as Carl Rogers, Abraham Maslow, Rollo May, and Victor Frankl. He has also had considerable impact on the experimental work of Julian Rotter, as will become evident in the discussion of Rotter's position in Chapter 10.

Applied Value. In addition to its considerable heuristic value, Adler's theory focuses upon phenomena that could reasonably be considered to be crucially involved in the development of people in a highly competitive and achievement-oriented society. In short, it is a theory which addresses itself to problems and issues that matter in a culture such as ours. Despite this fact, the theory has not had much practical impact outside of its contributions in the area of psychotherapy.

DISCUSSION QUESTIONS

1. Do you agree with Adler that all of us have an innate need for achievement? Does any cross-cultural evidence cast doubt upon Adler's contention?

2. Adler maintains that we all have had feelings of inferiority. Do you agree? If so, what were the primary sources of these feelings for yourself and your friends?

3. What is the relationship between a person's attitude and his or her behavior, as Adler sees it?

4. What is the masculine protest? Explain why the concept is relevant in explaining the behavior of both men and women.

5. Do you agree with Adler that our behavior is guided by our goals? What are some of the major goals of college-educated people in America today?

6. Adler's view of the healthy society is based upon his concept of social interest. What is social interest? Does the concept differ in any way from the concept of "enlightened self-interest"?

7. One of Adler's most interesting concepts is that of birth order. Do you agree with him that a person's order of birth can have a dramatic impact on personality development because parents tend to treat older and younger children differently? How many children are there in your family? Have your parents treated you and your brothers and sisters differently? If you are an only child, do you think that fact has made any difference in the way your parents reacted to you?

8. Do you think that we are all neurotic and that we strive too much for success?

9. Is competition necessarily destructive? How is social interest compatible with competition?

10. Is it possible for people to treat each other as equals in a capitalistic society such as ours?

NOTES

A. Adler, *The Science of Living* (Garden City, N.Y.: Doubleday Anchor, 1969).

A. Adler, "Advantages and Disadvantages of the Inferiority Feeling," in H. L. Ansbacher and R. R. Ansbacher, eds., *Superiority and Social Interest* (New York: Viking, 1973a).

A. Adler, "Complex Compulsion as Part of Personality and Neurosis," in H. L. Ansbacher and R. R. Ansbacher, eds., *Superiority and Social Interest* (New York: Viking, 1973b).

A. Adler, "On the Origins of the Striving for Superiority and of Social Interest," in H. L. Ansbacher and R. R. Ansbacher, eds., *Superiority and Social Interest* (New York: Viking, 1973c).

A. Adler, "Technique of Treatment," in H. L. Ansbacher and R. R. Ansbacher, eds., *Superiority and Social Interest* (New York: Viking, 1973d).

H. L. Ansbacher and R. R. Ansbacher, eds., *The Individual Psychology of Alfred Adler* (New York: Basic Books, 1956).

J. F. Brennan, "Autoeroticism or Social Feeling as Basis of Human Development," *Journal of Individual Psychology*, 1969, **25,** 10.

R. Dreikurs, "Individual Psychology: The Adlerian Point of View," in J. M. Wepman and R. W. Heine, eds., *Concepts of Personality* (Chicago: Aldine, 1963).

C. Furtmuller, "Alfred Adler: A Biographical Essay," in H. L. Ansbacher and R. R. Ansbacher, eds., *Superiority and Social Interest* (New York: Viking, 1973).

R. M. Ryckman and M. F. Sherman, "Locus of Control and Attitudes of Workers and College Students toward Members of Selected Occupations," *Journal of Applied Social Psychology*, 1974, **4,** 351–364.

S. Schachter, *The Psychology of Affiliation* (Stanford: Stanford University Press, 1959).

C. Schooler, "Birth Order Effects: Not Here, Not Now!" *Psychological Bulletin*, 1972, **78,** 161–175.

SUGGESTED READINGS

Adler, A. *The Practice and Theory of Individual Psychology*. New York: Harcourt, Brace & World, 1927.

Adler, A. *The Science of Living*. Garden City, N.Y.: Doubleday Anchor, 1969.

Ansbacher, H. L. and Ansbacher, R. R. (eds.). *The Individual Psychology of Alfred Adler*. New York: Basic Books, 1956.

Ansbacher, H. L. and Ansbacher, R. R. (eds.). *Superiority and Social Interest: A Collection of Later Writings*. New York: Viking, 1973.

GLOSSARY

Attitude. Learned tendency to respond to an object in a consistently favorable or unfavorable way.

Birth Order Effects. Adler's belief that each child was treated uniquely by the parents depending upon order of birth within the family. As a result, order of birth was considered to be an important personality determinant of behavior.

Creative Self. Term used by Adler to reflect his belief that people had the ability actively to create their own destinies and personalities.

Fictional Finalism. Imagined goal that guides the person's behavior.

Individual Psychology. The name for a psychology advocated by Adler that seeks to understand human behavior by recognizing its complexity and organization.

Masculine Protest. Attempt by an individual, male or female, to compensate for feelings of inferiority by acting superior.

Overcompensation. Exaggerated attempts by individuals to overcome their feelings of inferiority by acting as though they were superior to others.

Organ Inferiority. Biologically based defect of an organ in the body that gives rise to feelings of inadequacy on the part of the individual.

Social Interest. Innate tendency in human beings to help and cooperate with one another as a means of establishing a harmonious and productive society.

Style of Life. The distinctive personality pattern of the individual that is clearly established by the end of early childhood.

Superiority. The striving to attain perfection. For Adler, superiority is categorized into two types, personal superiority and superiority in a perfection sense. Personal superiority is considered harmful because it implies attempts to achieve satisfaction at the expense of others, whereas superiority strivings in the perfection sense are considered healthy because they imply the fulfillment of the individual's potential as a result of helping others.

Teleology. Belief that goals determine behavior. More generally, the doctrine that behavior is directed and shaped by a designing force.

Erich Fromm (Courtesy of Erich Fromm)

CHAPTER 5

Fromm's Humanistic Psychoanalysis

BIOGRAPHICAL SKETCH

Erich Fromm was born in Frankfurt, Germany, in 1900, the only child of Jewish parents. His father was an independent businessman; his mother, a homemaker. As a boy, Fromm was an ardent student of the Old Testament. He was aroused by the compassion and the possibility for human redemption in the stories of Abraham and Jonah, of Adam and Eve, and by the words of the prophets. In particular, he was impressed by the promise that one day nations "shall beat their swords into ploughshares and their spears into pruning hooks: nation shall not lift sword against nation, neither shall they learn war any more" (Hausdorff, 1972, p. 11). This prophecy had special meaning for Fromm because of the anti-Semitism and isolation he experienced. He sought consolation in the Old Testament and began to long for a universal peace and brotherhood he hoped would help him transcend the present. This longing can be seen clearly in his later writings about the nature of mature love and the establishment of a utopian social order.

Fromm's family life was not one of harmony. A strong concern with spiritual values was matched by an equally strong concern with the attainment of material success. He described his household as "tense," his father as "over-anxious and moody," and his mother as "depression-prone" (Hausdorff, 1972, p.12). Fromm believes retrospectively that this conflict between spiritual and secular values in his boyhood provided the impetus for his later search for a harmonious social order. His concern with understanding the fundamental questions of life and society was increased dramatically at age twelve when a friend of the family, a beautiful and talented woman, committed suicide. Her death seemed incredible and senseless to him (Hausdorff, 1972, p. 13).

At thirteen, Fromm began fourteen years of study of the Talmud under two humanistic and socialistic rabbis. He then left organized Judaism but retained a lifelong interest in religious writings (Hausdorff,

1972, p. 13). He entered the University of Heidelberg at a time when the social sciences were enlivened by a burst of new ideas. Karl Marx's theories on the ways in which the political and social order affected the individual's development were by now widely known, and it is clear that Fromm was influenced by them, as will become apparent later in the chapter. Darwin's theory of biological evolution was also sweeping the academic world, as was Freud's new and startling formulations of human personality (Hausdorff, 1972, pp. 14–15). Freud's ideas were particularly intriguing to Fromm since they seemed to offer insights into problems he could not resolve. For example, Freud's concepts helped Fromm understand the suicide of the family friend. As he put it, "When I became acquainted with Freud's theories, they seemed to be the answer to a puzzling and frightening experience" (Hausdorff, 1972, p. 16). While he then continued his studies in sociology and received his Ph.D. from Heidelberg in 1922, his interest in psychoanalysis soon became paramount. In 1925 Fromm went through instruction in psychoanalysis and later was analyzed by Hans Sachs. He never had any formal medical training, a fact which has led some of his critics to speculate that this "lack" in his education accounted for his "de-biologizing" the Freudian position (Hausdorff, 1972, p. 16). Fromm underwent still further psychoanalytic training in Berlin at the Psychoanalytic Institute in 1932. His teachers included some prominent Freudians—for example, Karl Abraham, Sandor Rado, Theodor Reik, and Franz Alexander—although he never met Freud himself (Hausdorff, 1972, pp. 20–21).

While increasing his knowledge of psychoanalysis, Fromm lectured at several institutes in Frankfurt and wrote papers utilizing both Marxist and Freudian ideas. It was at this point that he began to develop his theory of character formation. In 1931, Fromm wrote *The Development of the Dogma of Christ,* in which he adhered to the Freudian idea that religion was illusory, an infantile attempt to seek psychic gratification (Hausdorff, 1972, p. 22). He continued to publish papers compatible with orthodox psychoanalytic ideas throughout the 1930s.

In 1934, Fromm emigrated to the United States and became an American citizen. Over the years, he has held a variety of academic and clinical psychology positions. He has lectured at Columbia University, Bennington College, Yale, Michigan State, New York University, and at the National University of Mexico. He has also held positions at the International Institute of Social Research in New York City, the American Institute of Psychoanalysis, the William Alanson White Institute of Psychiatry, and the Mexican Institute of Psychoanalysis (Hausdorff, 1972, pp. 7–8). But he is today perhaps better-known as a theorist and writer than as a lecturer and therapist.

In 1941, he published the beginnings of his new theory in a popular book called *Escape from Freedom*. In it, Fromm discussed the ways in which modern society and ideologies mold the social character of the individual. In his view, men and women are primarily social beings who have been historically conditioned but who also have human needs that occur prior to the socialization process. We are born with certain potentialities whose development is fostered or hindered by the prevailing social order. Fromm believed Freud was correct in his contention that the family was the primary agent of society, but wrong in his assumption that instincts govern the behavior of the individual. Likewise, Fromm thought that Marx's emphasis on the power of ideas in bringing about social change was incorrect. For Fromm, ideas "are answers to specific human needs prominent in a given social character" (Hausdorff, 1972, p. 36). In general terms, Fromm's analysis is truly social-psychological in nature. It is an attempt to construct a theory in which the physiological and psychological needs of the individual and the needs and goals of society are mutually satisfied. His ideas about the development of social character are more precisely formulated in *Man for Himself* (1947). Most of the types he postulates bear a close resemblance to the Freudian character types, as we shall see. Numerous other books followed: *Psychoanalysis and Religion* (1950), *The Forgotten Language: An Introduction to the Understanding of Dreams, Fairy Tales, and Myths* (1951), *The Sane Society* (1955), *The Art of Loving* (1956), *The Heart of Man* (1964), *The Revolution of Hope* (1968), *The Anatomy of Human Destructiveness* (1973), and *To Have Or to Be?* (1976).

In *The Sane Society*, Fromm continued the analysis of society he had begun in *Escape from Freedom*. He pointed out that contemporary Western society is "sick" because its citizens are alienated from themselves and others. Using a historical analysis of capitalism, he stated that the emphasis on competitiveness and the accumulation of material wealth in the nineteenth century led to the exploitation of workers and to the establishment of an industrial and political order whose primary concern was economic advance at the expense of human relationships. This alienation process continues in the twentieth century, but its causes take a different form. In fully industrialized societies, big business and big government are the rule, and their existence and modes of operation often lead to special forms of estrangement and alienation. In Fromm's view, workers in these complex bureaucracies are faceless entities who have little input into their organizations. They are "managed" by bureaucrats as though they were objects or things, manipulated and treated as nonthinking automatons. The result is widespread apathy and destructiveness. Workers long to escape from their tedious jobs and to get involved in meaningful and creative activities. But, unfortunately, these desires are never realized. Even in their leisure time, they remain passive and alienated *consumers*. They consume football games, films, books, lectures, and social gatherings in an abstract and sterile way.

What can be done to overcome such malaise? How can we move

toward sanity? For Fromm, the answer lies in "humanistic communitarian socialism," a social, legal, political, economic, and moral system in which working people are active and responsible participants in the economic structure and in which the primary emphasis is on harmonious and cooperative relations between people. In such a society, people would be productive and capable of mature love. To reach this utopian state, Fromm calls for a humanization of technological society. This humanization process involves an altering of the administrative structure of big government so that grass-roots participation becomes possible and desirable. (We will discuss Fromm's views of the utopian society in more detail later in the chapter.) Currently, Fromm lives in Mexico, where he spends his professional time writing and lecturing at the National University.

BASIC CONCEPTS AND PRINCIPLES

Human Beings, "Freaks" of Nature

For Fromm, the most powerful motivating force for men's and women's behavior stems from their attempts to find a reason for their existence. In his view, we are all animals with certain biological needs that must be satisfied—and yet, we are more than animals. We can be aware of ourselves and we can also use reason to solve our problems. In addition, we have the capacity to imagine and to create new and useful products. These abilities, according to Fromm, are both a blessing and a curse. Although our self-awareness and reason can be used to solve our problems, they also make us conscious of our limitations, including the fact that we must inevitably die (Fromm, 1947, p. 49). Each of us must deal with this problem, and we all resolve it in relatively constructive or destructive ways. Our reason makes us aware of other problems, including the fact that we cannot possibly realize all our potentialities in the time available to us. It also informs us that we can no longer be unified with nature like the other animals. It impels us to deal with our frailties and to engage in a painful struggle with life.

In Fromm's view, these capacities provide us with a fundamental choice. We can choose to lead healthy and productive lives by developing our potentialities, or we can choose to escape from our freedom by submitting ourselves to others or by trying to destroy them. Using our freedom to develop into productive citizens can be painful, but it is also genuinely satisfying, whereas escaping from freedom by blind obedience to others, while it produces temporary security, is in the long run counterproductive and stifles our basic nature. We need to relate productively to one another if we are to maintain our sanity.

Human Needs

Because we are no longer one with nature, Fromm argues that we all feel isolated and alone at times (Fromm 1955, p. 35). We are aware of our ignorance, our limitations, and the role of chance in our births and deaths. To remain in such a state would lead to insanity; we must unite ourselves with others if we are to survive. Thus, the *need for relatedness* is a direct outgrowth of our existential condition. This relatedness can be relatively constructive or destructive in nature. We can achieve union by submission or by domination over others. In Fromm's view, both forms of relatedness are symbiotic and involve harmful dependencies. The passive form of symbiotic fusion is masochism (Fromm, 1956, p. 16). The person with masochistic tendencies feels alive only when he or she submits to the commands of others. It is almost as if the person says "You are everything: I am nothing." Perhaps you have known someone like this. Such a person tends to worship or adore others. The other is absolute perfection and can do no wrong. The masochistic individual feels alive primarily when he or she is being hurt by the other. Fromm also maintains that one can masochistically submit to fate, sickness, and to the orgiastic state produced by drugs. The active aspect of symbiotic relatedness is sadism. The sadistic person overcomes his aloneness, according to Fromm, by dominating and humiliating others. "I am everything and you are nothing" seems to be his battle cry (Fromm, 1956, p. 16).

Both these character types provide evidence of union without love. In contrast, Fromm believes that *mature love* is the embodiment of productive relatedness. He defines such love as "union under the condition of preserving one's integrity, one's individuality" (Fromm, 1956, p. 17). Its basic elements are "care, responsibility, respect and knowledge" (Fromm, 1956, p. 22). Mature love involves care and concern for the welfare of others. Although we often think of responsibility as a duty imposed by others, Fromm views it as the ability to respond voluntarily to the needs of others. Respect is also a term that sometimes has negative connotations, but Fromm uses it in the root sense of an ability to see others as they are and to be concerned with their growth and unfolding. Finally, Fromm maintains that we cannot respect and love a person if we do not know him (Fromm 1956, p. 24). Such a criterion means that mature love requires considerable time and effort, as well as a gradual, mutual self-disclosure.

In contrast, Fromm treats romantic love as pseudo-love because of its immediacy and the fact that it requires no effort. Such "love" is based primarily upon physical attractiveness and not upon intimate knowledge of the "loved" one. Althought there is intense commitment, that commitment is usually temporary. Fromm's definition of mature love suggests that we be leery of "instantaneous friendships" or situations in which we arrive at the simplistic conclusion that we truly love someone we have known for six months. Mature love should be treated as an ideal goal to be sought, instead of one presumptuously claimed. In a positive sense, Fromm's conception tells us that there is always something to be known about ourselves and the other person, and that we can delight in the exploration of the mysteries of another.

Another aspect of the human condition is the *need for transcendence*. For Fromm, we overcome our passive natures by acting creatively. To act creatively, however, we must love ourselves as well as others. The negative side of transcendence is destruction. Fromm maintains that the impotent person, that is, the one who feels powerless and incapable of creation, can transcend his environment only by destroying it. People have within them the potential for happiness and the capacity for self-destruction (Fromm, 1955, pp. 41–42).

The *need for rootedness* is also one of our basic needs. In discussing this aspect of our natures, Fromm builds on Freud's treatment of the potentially incestuous ties between mothers and their children and on historical evidence of the relationships between individuals in patriarchal and matriarchal societies. Fromm says our most fundamental relationship is with our mothers. As infants, we are physically helpless and completely dependent upon them for the gratification of our needs. As he put it: "Mother is food; she is love; she is warmth; she is earth. To be loved by her means to be alive, to be rooted, to be home" (Fromm, 1955, p. 43). It is therefore extremely difficult to separate ourselves from her so that, even as adults, we sometimes long for this former security. Fromm credits Freud with recognizing the importance of the relationship between mother and child in his formulation of the Oedipal conflict, but he says that Freud placed too much emphasis on its sexual roots and not enough on its irrational, affective origins. In brief, Fromm maintains that an intense and irrational dependency upon the mother, which may or may not have sexual overtones, is a universal problem for people (Fromm 1955, pp. 45–46).

He continues his discussion of rootedness by examining the positive and negative features of the individual's historical behavior in matriarchal and patriarchal cultures. In cultures ruled by women, Fromm claims there is a positive sense of equality and freedom. In his words, "the mother (in the generic sense) loves her children not because one is better than the other, not because one fulfills her expectations more than the other, but because they are her children, and in that quality they are all alike and have the same right to love and care" (Fromm, 1955, p. 48). In the negative sense, a matriarchal structure implies an answering loyalty to blood and soil (mother earth), so that creative development is stifled. In patriarchal cultures, people look upon male authority figures with fear and awe. Such relationships were and are negative because they encourage inequality and oppression. Positively, such cultures promote reason, individualism, and discipline. Fromm believes that loyalty to authority, when it places country above humanity, is destructive. In his judgment, a world of peace and understanding is possible only when we can experience rootedness in our brothers and sisters. In short, we must transcend boundaries that cripple us and keep us from experiencing solidarity with others (Fromm, 1955, pp. 60–61).

People also have a *need for identity*. They have to be able to say to others "I am I" and not "I am as you desire me." Each of us has a degree of self-awareness and a knowledge about our capabilities. Fromm would maintain that we should value our abilities and use them productively. We should also avoid, at all costs, basing our identities on what others expect of us. Such identities are shaky and create problems. In Fromm's view, identity based upon "herd conformity" is unfortunately widely present in our culture. We learn to accept uncritically the pronouncements of authority and to "buy" truth as others see it without engaging in our own thinking.

Finally, we all need a perspective on reality or, in Fromm's terms, a *frame of orientation and devotion*, if we are to live productively. Such orientations are necessary because we need to make sense out of our many experiences. The frame of orientation develops gradually in early childhood, to the point where we learn to use reason and imagination effectively in coping with our problems or to rely instead on rationalization to help us justify our behavior. Productive individuals utilize reason as well as feelings in their attempts at adaptation. In addition, Fromm maintains that we need an object for devotion and that the form and content of that object differ widely among peoples. Some use systems of animism and totemism; others worship monotheistically (Fromm, 1955, p. 66). Devotion to a humanistic ethic, an ethic in which "there is nothing higher and nothing more dignified than human existence" is apparent in Fromm's orientation (Fromm, 1955, p. 23). For him, God is seen not in traditional terms, but in the form of ideals such as love, truth, and justice that we all struggle to attain. Consequently, Fromm believes that "God is I, inasmuch as I am human" (Fromm, 1956, p. 59).

THE PROCESS OF PERSONALITY DEVELOPMENT

The Development of Character Orientations

In his formulations of the developmental process, Fromm discarded Freudian libido theory. Instead, he focused on the unique social and cultural conditions that affect the character development process and the satisfaction of our basic, existential needs. This process parallels Freud's position in some respects, as will become clear, but the etiological factors underlying it differ. It would be tempting to conclude that whereas Freud emphasized the biological determinants of personality, Fromm was concerned only with the cultural aspects. Such a conclusion would be incorrect for two reasons. First, Fromm does recognize individual differences in temperament; he argues that character, which is based on one's experiences, and temperament, which is constitutional, combine to affect behavior. Despite the lack of scientific evidence for the typology of temperaments developed in ancient Greece by Hippocrates, Fromm utilizes it in his theorizing. For example, the choleric individual who is capable of mature love would tend to react very strongly and quickly when he loves (Fromm, 1947, p. 60).

Second, and more important, Fromm argues that people have innate needs and potentialities which unfold in the course of development, provided social conditions are right. In particular, Fromm maintains that the norms of society are initially communicated to the child through the parents. The development of nonproductive orientations in children is the result of living with parents who are largely incapable of love. The acquisition of a productive orientation stems from experiences with loving parents. Although the following descriptions are presented as though they were ideal types, Fromm makes it clear that people are typically blends of these orientations, although one type tends to predominate (Fromm 1947, p. 69).

Nonproductive Orientations. In Fromm's view, the *receptive* orientation is found in people who believe that the source of all good or satisfying events lies outside of themselves. A similar formulation is seen in Freud's description of the behavior of infants during the oral-receptive stage of development. In his opinion, such people relate symbiotically to others and expect to be loved and appreciated without any effort on their part. They are continuously "falling in love" and being hurt in the process when the other person begins to resent the one-sided nature of the affair. Neo-Freudian Karen Horney also describes a type of individual who attempts to adjust to feelings of basic anxiety by indiscriminately "moving toward people."

The *exploitative* orientation is seen in people who believe that the source of all satisfactions lies beyond themselves, but do not wait passively to be gratified. Instead, they actively take whatever they want from others by force or cunning. A similar description is found in Freud's treatment of the oral-aggressive person. Fromm believes that such people relate to others symbiotically and that they cannot produce (Evans, 1966, p. 4). As a result, they tend to rob and exploit others in order to attain their ends. Examples include the man who "steals" the affections of another's wife and the person who plagiarizes the works of others. Once again, Horney describes a similar type, but she calls it the aggressive type. Such people, according to Horney, experience momentary satisfaction by "moving against people."

The *hoarding* orientation has its parallel in the Freudian anal character. Such people, in contrast to the previous types, do not have faith in the outside world. Instead, they "relate" to the world in a negative way by withdrawing from others. They are obsessively concerned with protecting themselves. In regard to love, Fromm maintains that they treat others as possessions. Like Freud's anal character, they are also excessively concerned with orderliness and cleanliness. Horney's description of the detached type who tries to adjust by "moving away from people" bears a close resemblance to Fromm's hoarding type.

Fromm's description of the *marketing* orientation represents a clean break with his Freudian roots. He states that this orientation has developed only recently in industrial societies. In such societies, people learn to treat themselves and others as commodities with a certain exchange value in a way that parallels the interchanges in the economic marketplace. In short, we all become buyers and sellers in an ever-fluctuating and uncertain "personality market." Appearance becomes the reality for us; substance becomes illusion. Commercials bombard us with messages about products which, if used, will make us more acceptable to others. Many of us go to considerable lengths to heed the current pronouncements. Films and popular magazines tell us how to dress and act if we are to be "successful." Business executives and other professionals have a definite image of how they should appear if they are to win promotions. Some students are not immune to such social pressures; they indiscriminately wear the "uniform of the day," usually worn blue jeans and workshirts. Such clothes seem to signal that they are properly anti-Establishment and properly on the side of the poor and oppressed. Fortunately, it's relatively easy to be a romantic when one is supported by affluent parents. Finally, people with marketing orientations have little genuine interest in the welfare of other people. Others are treated as "objects" to be used for their own selfish purposes. As a consequence, marketing relationships are typically characterized by indifference.

The Productive Orientation. In Fromm's opinion, a person who is generally productive has a fundamental attitude or mode of relatedness in all areas of human experience. Such an attitude encompasses his or her "mental, emotional, and sensory responses to another, to oneself and to things" (Fromm, 1947, p. 49). It involves the use of one's powers and the maximum realization of inherent potentialities. He states further that we can use our powers or capacities only if we are free and independent of control by others. Under these conditions, we are able to use our reason and imagination to penetrate to the essence of our experiences. We are also capable of mature love, of understanding another on an intellectual and emotional level.

Society and Human Productiveness

Although the character types postulated by Fromm are acquired initially through contact with parents, he also discusses the ways in which the nature and organization of society dramatically affect the development of individual potentialities. At the risk of oversimplification, Fromm argues that we live in a "sick" society in which indiscriminate competition and exploitation prevail and in which individuals feel powerless to correct the situation. In Fromm's view, a sick society tends to produce sick people, while a healthy one produces healthy people. Like Marx, he believes that work and mental health are intimately linked. In a sick or insane society such as ours, men and women tend to be alienated from their work. They are exploited by members of the ruling class; for example, entrepreneurs and powerful politicians, and treated like commodities. In his view, these "rulers" live by the sweat of the workers and treat them as inferiors. Such exploitation leads the workers to feel intense resentment and hostility toward their "oppressors," with revolution as the outcome. For Marx, the goal of the workers should be personal liberation from such tyranny through violent revolution. Fromm appears to be much more of a moderate in this regard, calling instead for reform via the humanization of the means of production. Such reform will not be easy, in Fromm's opinion, because people are generally unaware of the forces that determine their behavior. Yet the task must be undertaken if we are ever to live in harmony and understanding with one another.

In order to understand the process by which society hinders our self-development, Fromm conducts a historical and Marxist analysis of capitalism. He notes that nineteenth-century captialism was characterized by ruthless exploitation of the workers. It was considered virtuous to maximize profits at the workers' expense. The worker presumably had a choice, namely, to work or not to work. In reality, of course, he had to work in order to survive, and so he accepted the wages offered by the boss. Not only were wages low, but there was little correlation between personal effort and pay, so there was little incentive to improve oneself. Exploitation also took other forms, including the abuses of child labor and the callous unwillingness on the part of many owners to rectify unsafe working conditions. Capitalists then used their profits to seize new opportunities for expansion and to acquire property for production and consumption (Fromm, 1955, pp. 86–87).

The result of such social and economic tyranny was the formation of exploitative and hoarding types among the elite. The hoarding types are considered by Fromm to have been people who were "unimaginative, stingy, suspicious, pedantic, obsessional and possessive" (1955, p. 87).

The exploitative types were characterized by arrogance, conceit, exploitativeness, and egocentricity (Fromm, 1947, p. 120). Each type also had a positive side. For example, the positive aspects of the hoarding orientation included the need to be "practical, economical, careful, reserved, cautious, tenacious, imperturbable, orderly, methodical, and loyal" (Fromm, 1955, p. 87). The positive features of the exploitative character included the ability to take the initiative, pride, and self-confidence (Fromm, 1947, p. 120).

Vestiges of the hoarding and exploitative types are found today, according to Fromm, but they are not the primary types. Instead, the twentieth century is characterized by the emergence of the receptive and marketing orientations. In this century, Fromm maintains that capital and the means of production have come under the control of fewer and fewer companies. These companies have grown so large that management has been separated from ownership. We are also living in an era of big government. Bureaucracy reigns supreme under these conditions, and the result is increased *alienation* among the workers. The current emphasis, Fromm believes, is on efficiency and smooth operation. As a consequence, capitalism in our time seeks men and women with marketing orientations, people who mesh well with the organization. The bureaucratic mentality does not tolerate the risk-taker. Such people are perceived as troublemakers who need to be replaced by others who are more "adjusted." In brief, bureaucracy demands conformity from its personnel.

Fromm also thinks that the emphasis on bigness in institutions and in the media has led to a relative standardization of tastes and interests among the citizenry. We read the same papers, watch the same television programs and films, and listen to the same radio broadcasts. We are more concerned with consuming goods passively and with having entertainment spoon-fed to us than we are in actively participating in the process. More specifically, we rely in rather uncritical fashion upon instant analyses of political events by news commentators, instead of trying to do our own thinking about these issues. We also pay people large sums of money to entertain us so that we do not have to make the effort to create our own diversions. Many of us buy art for investment purposes and have not the slightest knowledge of aesthetics. In all these areas, and many more, the indiscriminate and passive incorporation of events has led to the acquisition of a receptive orientation. In the final analysis, then, these social conditions have produced people who are alienated from themselves and others. They are security conscious to the point of dullness. Most of all, they feel powerless.

Humanistic Communication Socialism as the Solution to Alienation

How then do we satisfy our psychic needs and learn to subsitute a productive orientation for a nonproductive one? According to Fromm, the answer lies in a drastic reordering of society and in an awakening on our part. It involves creating "an industrial organization in which *every working person would be an active and responsible participant, where work would be attractive and meaningful, where capital would not employ labor, but labor would employ capital*" (Fromm, 1955, p. 248). Under such conditions, men and women would be productively related to one another. In order to ensure relatedness, Fromm contends that workers should be organized into groups sufficiently small so that they can learn to know one another, even though there may be thousands of workers in the factory. In addition, the worker should be informed not only about the various aspects of his job, but about the various facets of the entire production process. He should know now his organization is related to the economic needs of the entire society. Most important, the worker must be given an active role in the decision-making process of the organization. Fromm points out that he is not advocating that workers own the means of production, but that they participate in the formulation and review of company policy. His solution involves a blend of centralization and decentralization in which all individuals participate actively in the process—a *humanistic communitarian socialism*. Finally, the primary purpose of any organization, according to Fromm is to "serve people and not to make a profit" (Fromm 1955, p. 35).

In addition to massive changes in the area of work, Fromm urges the transformation of the political system. He notes that the voter today is alienated from politics; the whole situation is beyond his comprehension. As Fromm puts it:

> . . . nothing makes real sense or carries real meaning [to the citizen]. He reads of billions of dollars being spent, of millions of people being killed; figures, abstractions, which are in no way in a concrete, meaningful picture of the world. (Fromm, 1955, p. 295)

To overcome this impersonal and unreal situation, we must recognize that the best decisions cannot be made via mass voting. Instead, we can make good decisions only in relatively small groups, much like the old town meeting (Fromm, 1955, p. 296). The voters must also have the necessary information to make meaningful decisions. Above all, their decisions must be capable of influencing our leaders.

Finally, Fromm states that society will also have to be changed on a cultural level. There must be an " . . . opportunity for people to sing together, walk together, dance together, [and to] admire together" (Fromm, 1955, p. 303). There must also be a spiritual renewal. This renewal would involve an increased commitment to the aims of Judaism and Christianity that includes " . . . the dignity of man as an aim and end in itself, of brotherly love, of reason and of the supremacy of spiritual over material values" (Fromm, 1955, p. 304). A commitment to these ideals, whether one believes in a monotheistic God or not, would eventually lead to a sane society in which all people would be productively related.

TECHNIQUES OF ASSESSMENT

In some respects, Fromm remains close to his Freudian roots in his attempts to assess personality functioning. Like Freud, he focuses on the ways in which traumatic experiences in early childhood hinder personality development. He also agrees with Freud that the unconscious conflicts responsible for the patient's problems must be made known if he or she is ever to recover and that free association and dream analysis are useful tools for achieving that objective.

Yet, Fromm goes well beyond Freud in his assessment attempts. In addition to his use of psychological methods of inquiry, he also employs a historical method that emphasizes the role political, religious, economic, sociological, and anthropological factors play in molding personality. It is this continued and systematic effort at utilizing a multilevel approach to the understanding of personality that makes Fromm and his *humanistic psychoanalysis* unique. The goal he seeks is a theoretical construction of human nature through the observation and interpretation of actual behavior in a cross-cultural and historic context (Fromm, 1947, p. 33). In more concrete terms, he hopes to infer our basic natures by watching our behaviors in a variety of contexts.

APPLICATION OF THE THEORY TO THE TREATMENT OF PSYCHOPATHOLOGY

According to Fromm, the causes of pathology are primarily sociocultural in nature. On a microscopic level, they involve symbiotic relationships between parents and children. On a macroscopic level, they involve those economic and political forces within society that stifle personal growth. These diverse forces, in Fromm's view, are largely responsible for the individual's inability to achieve a productive orientation. They create repressions of his or her needs for love and relatedness and generate instead brutal and exploitative strivings. The person comes to see others as threats to his own existence—that is, as obstacles to be overcome or removed. Under these conditions, the person is alienated from himself and from others. He does not understand the sources of his problems or that his behavior is at variance with his basic nature.

To achieve positive growth, the person must be made aware of the many family and societal conditions that have stifled his development. In addition to self-awareness, the person must actively change those life conditions reponsible for his illness. He must change his values and the norms and ideals that block his growth (Fromm, 1955, p. 240). Fromm believes further that the chances for positive growth depend not only on changes within the person and in his particular life circumstances, but on more general changes within society. As mentioned earlier, he thinks that a sane society produces sane people, and that a society based on humanistic ethics is desperately needed. In such a society, qualities like greed, narcissism, and exploitativeness would be nonexistent, and people would live in harmony and cooperation (Fromm, 1955, p. 242).

CRITICAL COMMENTS

We now evaluate Fromm's theory in terms of our six criteria.

Comprehensiveness. Fromm has created a comprehensive theory that attempts to show how biological and sociocultural forces mold our personalities. He focuses on the conditions responsible for positive mental health as well as those that produce pathology, and in the process discusses many different phenomena; for example, work performance, ethics, justice, cooperation and competition, self-love, power, and prestige.

Precision and Testability. Fromm's theory is dotted with imprecise terms—for example, "potentiality," "inner voice," and "love." Love is defined as "primarily giving, not receiving" (Fromm, 1956, p. 18). Fromm himself points out that this definition is ambiguous. He then proceeds to attempt to clarify the meaning of the term and ends his argument by declaring that "giving is more joyous than receiving, not because it is a deprivation but because in the act of giving lies the expression of my aliveness" (Fromm, 1956, p. 9). Even here the meaning is not very clear. Other definitions are equally confusing. Note, for example, his definition of conscience:

> Conscience is thus a reaction of ourselves to ourselves. It is the voice of our true selves which summons us back to ourselves, to live productively, to develop fully and harmoniously—that is, *to become what we potentially are.* (Fromm, 1947, p. 163)

Simplicity. Fromm's theory is not very parsimonious. It seems as though he has been reluctant to abandon concepts of dubious value in helping us to understand personality functioning. For example, he still utilizes the typology of temperament propsed by Hippocrates many centuries ago (see Chapter 15). In addition, he continues to employ Freudian concepts in his discussions of the causes of nonproductive orientations when it is clear that he favors the utilization of sociocultural explanations. Are both sets of concepts necessary for the adequate explanation of individual behavior? Even if they are, the criticism may still be valid, since Fromm also employs a set of existential concepts to explain the same behaviors.

Empirical Validity. There have been very few attempts to test Fromm's theory directly. One interdisciplinary field study conducted recently, however, did provide support for his theory of character development. But in general Fromm's strategy is to cite scientific evidence to support some of his speculations. As he notes, there are studies in the social psychological research literature which support the idea that workers are most satisfied with their work situations when they have actively and fully participated in decision-making related to their jobs. In addition, there is a considerable body of evidence which shows that self-alienation is associated with other socially undesirable personality characteristics; for example, low self-esteem and high anxiety are directly associated with poor performance in a variety of situations. Nevertheless, the citing of evidence is post hoc in nature and geared to fit preexisting theoretical formulations. Fromm has seldom utilized his theorizing to generate testable hypotheses that could lead to the general acceptance or rejection of his notions. He seems more clearly to be a social philosopher than a scientist.

Heuristic Value. The primary value of his theory, despite its weak empirical base, is its ability to stimulate the thinking of others. It is a complex set of formulations that rests firmly on moral issues which are important to each of us and which Fromm correctly concludes must be grasped and understood if we are to live in a more harmonious relationship with one another.

Applied Value. Fromm's writings have been read by countless academicians and their students and by millions of ordinary people as well. It is difficult to assess whether they have had a positive impact on the lives of those readers, but editorial comment in the media has been generally favorable and his readership has continued to increase. In personal terms, I and many of my students have found Fromm's writings provocative and interesting. They strike a responsive chord in us because they encourage us to aspire to the creation of a more humane society. Thus, Fromm's theorizing seems to have considerable applied value for many people.

DISCUSSION QUESTIONS

1. In what ways are human beings "freaks" of nature? What are our fundamental existential concerns?

2. Do you believe that most people have a need to relate to others? If so, why do they?

3. What is meant by the "need for transcendence"? In what ways have you acted creatively?

4. Do you agree with Fromm that we must place love of humanity before love of country if we are to behave productively?

5. Have you ever engaged in "herd conformity"? What were the determinants and consequences of your actions?
6. List the nonproductive character orientations, as envisioned by Fromm, and describe the ways in which they are similar to the Freudian character types.
7. Is the marketing personality type obsolete in contemporary society?
8. Would you agree that the owners of big business are oppressing poor people? Can you muster some arguments that show both the harmful and the beneficial results of the consolidation of power in the hands of a relatively few large corporations?
9. Do you feel that many people today can be characterized as receptive in their orientations? Do you and your friends take primarily an active or passive part in recreational activities?
10. Is Fromm's utopian dream of a humanistic communitarian socialist society possible or desirable?

NOTES

R. I. Evans, *Dialogue with Erich Fromm* (New York: Harper & Row, 1966).

E. Fromm, *Man for Himself* (New York: Holt, Rinehart and Winston, 1947).

E. Fromm, *The Art of Loving* (New York: Harper & Row, 1956).

E. Fromm, *The Sane Society* (New York: Holt, Rinehart and Winston, 1955).

D. Hausdorff, *Erich Fromm* (New York: Twayne Publishers, 1972).

SUGGESTED READINGS

Fromm, E. *Escape from Freedom.* New York: Rinehart, 1941.

Fromm, E. *Man for Himself.* New York: Holt, Rinehart and Winston, 1947.

Fromm, E. *The Art of Loving.* New York: Harper & Row, 1956.

Fromm, E. *The Revolution of Hope.* New York: Harper & Row, 1968.

Fromm, E. *The Sane Society.* New York: Holt, Rinehart and Winston, 1955.

GLOSSARY

Alienation. Feelings of powerlessness and aloneness experienced by individuals who have rejected the traditional values and are incapable of instituting a social and political system compatible with their own values and principles.

Frame of Orientation and Devotion. Development of a consistent and meaningful set of values and principles that help individuals to make sense out of their worlds.

Humanistic Communitarian Socialism. An ideal democratic society in which all individuals would have input into the decisions that affect their lives and in which they would also be able to develop their potential to the fullest, without fear of exploitation.

Humanistic Psychoanalysis. Theoretical position advocated by Fromm that draws upon Freudian principles to explain the conditions within early family life and within society that restrict or facilitate the healthy development of the individual.

Mature Love. For Fromm, an active concern for the well-being of the other and the ability to give generously of oneself for the benefit of the other without expectation of return. It also involves a knowledge of the other and an acceptance of the other's weaknesses as well as strengths.

Need for Identity. Need on the part of a person to become aware of his or her own characteristics and capabilities.

Need for Relatedness. In Fromm's theory, the basic human need to be in contact and share experiences with one another.

Need for Rootedness. In Fromm's theory, the basic human need to feel that we have a place within society.

Need for Transcendence. Need on the part of the person to resolve conflicts by acting in a creative or destructive manner.

3

TRAIT PERSPECTIVES

T he earliest attempts to explain human behavior probably involved
the use of typologies and traits. Typologies are the classification of
behavior into discrete or all-or-nothing categories—for example, Hippocrates' classic distinctions among choleric, melancholic, sanguine,
and phlegmatic types. Trait classifications involve the use of graduated
dimensions along which individual differences can be quantitatively arranged. These quantitative arrangements reflect the degree to which
people are assumed to possess a given amount of some particular
characteristic. For example, people may vary considerably in terms of
laziness, intelligence, and dominance. Some people are not very intelligent, others are moderately intelligent, and a few possess a great intellectual abilities.

The use of typologies and traits as an aid to understanding phenomena is in the best tradition of science, since virtually all the disciplines that use the scientific method began with classification schemes.
In zoology, for example, living things are classified into various phyla,
classes, orders, families, genera, and species. In terms of human personality, the efforts of Hippocrates, Gall, Kretschmer, Sheldon, and
many others can also be viewed as part of this tradition (see Chapter 15).

Classification schemes are important because they serve to identify or
accurately describe phenomena and because they help to organize
events in ways that make them more amenable to study. They are
considered a vital first step in the process of trying to understand relationships between events. Unfortunately, however, such schemes can
also be misused. Trait names, for instance, can be used as a means of
classifying certain behaviors. For purposes of description, such a procedure is perfectly valid. But when the trait names used to *describe* behavior are then employed as *explanations* for the same behavior, we have
a clear misuse of classification procedures. A concrete example might
make these points much clearer for you. Say that we observe a student
studying her course assignments for many hours on numerous
weekends. We might then describe her behavior as "hard-working." So

far, so good. The trait "hard-working" is used as an adjective to describe her behavior. Soon, however, many of us might be tempted to generalize beyond the behavior and to make inferences about her as a person. Many of us might conclude that she *is* hard-working. The final step in the process might be to invoke the trait "hard-working" as a *cause* of her behavior and conclude: "She behaves in a hard-working way because she has a hard-working disposition." Such a statement is circular and does not provide an adequate explanation for her behavior. Such "explanations" are often used by ordinary people as a means of making sense of their experiences, but scientific investigators who utilize the trait approach have sometimes been guilty of the same mistake.

The trait approach has three other major problems that should be considered here. First, traits have been treated as convenient constructs conjured up by investigators to increase the explanatory power of their theories about personality. In this view, traits are considered abstractions that account for relatively permanent consistencies and differences in behavior. They are not necessarily thought to have real existence in the person. Theorists like Allport and Cattell, however, believe that traits do have real existence inside the person and do act as causes of behavior. The constructs are the theorists' attempts to designate clusters of observable behaviors thought to be manifestations of underlying traits or dispositional attributes that really exist. If the traits do, in fact, exist, it should be possible through diligent study to identify them.

Investigators like Cattell have used sophisticated factor analytic techniques to analyze reams of data collected primarily through a variety of paper-and-pencil, self-report measures of behavior and have then claimed that the factors which emerged reflect real underlying personality traits. Such conclusions are clearly debatable. For one thing, the measures of behavior are based on self-report data that may or may not be valid. Furthermore, Cattell's results depend on the kinds of tests he chose to acquire the raw data for his statistical analyses and the kinds of subjects employed for the testing, as well as the kinds of statistical procedures he selected to generate these so-called real, underlying traits.

Second, and perhaps more important, trait theorists have tended to assume that their postulated global traits manifest themselves in a wide variety of situations. As a result, they have not paid much attention to the role that the environment plays in modifying behavior. They assume, for example, that a man who is aggressive will be aggressive in virtually all situations and that a child who is honest will be honest in all situations. Although research has shown that people will act consistently in a relatively narrow band of similar activities, much of our behavior is modified by changes in environmental conditions. Thus, a man may act aggressively in a variety of similar athletic activities, but be subdued in the presence of his parents, his wife, or his boss. A child may steal from his peers at school, but be scrupulously honest in his dealings with his relatives. In fact, his behavior may vary even more subtly. He may steal money from schoolmates he dislikes and be quite honest with those he likes. The point is that much of our behavior may be more situation-specific than we ordinarily think.

Despite these deficiencies, it would be incorrect to conclude that the study of traits is a worthless undertaking, as some psychologists have been prone to do. First, the traits postulated by certain theorists may reflect their own limited and inaccurate conceptions of dispositions residing within people, but it is equally clear that most people have had certain experiences and do show given behaviors that can be accurately summarized through the use of trait labels. A person may, for instance, have a history of experiences that predispose him to act in aggressive ways. He is more susceptible to provocation in certain situations than a person who has a reinforcement history that conditions him to avoid acting violently. The previous experiences of these two people in regard to the use of violence can be roughly ascertained through the use of self-report measures and then they can be classified as more or less aggressive than one another. In other words, we can measure the trait of aggressiveness in two men through the use of a test and then use this information to predict aggressive behavior in other situations. These predictions would tend to be low-level ones because we would simply be correlating self-reports of aggressive behavior in the past with aggressive behavior that ignores the influence of the current situation. For example, a person may report high incidences of aggressive behavior in the past and may or may not act aggressively in the present, depending upon current circumstances. We may not see aggressive behavior if we observe him in a church setting, but we may see violent actions if we observe him during a football game. The general point is that the most accurate predictions of behavior will be forthcoming when we account for both the personal dispositions or traits of individuals and the specific situational parameters they encounter.

Part III reviews and evaluates the positions of two of the most prominent trait theorists, Allport and Cattell. Like the Freudian and neo-Freudian theorists we considered in Part II, Allport and Cattell focus most of their attention and effort on internal, underlying personality states. Both psychodynamic and trait theorists assume that these underlying characteristics and motives exert generalized influences on behavior. In terms of the content of their positions, Allport and Cattell endorse some of the Freudian concepts. Both accept the notion that people sometimes act defensively and that some behavior is determined by unconscious motives. But Allport, more than Cattell, shows a clear and basic break with the Freudian model in regard to the extent to which he focuses on unconscious and defensive behavior. He believed Freud and others placed far too much emphasis on the irrational in personality functioning and not enough on the rational. For him, the Freudian model best described the behavior of people with behavioral disorders, but had little of substance to say about the behavior of healthy, mature individuals.

Allport set out to correct this imbalance by establishing the broad outlines of a humanistic psychology that focused on the uniqueness of the individual and the creative and rational aspirations of most people to realize their potentialities. In this regard, Allport must be seen as an important forerunner of the humanistic movement popular in psychology today. A discussion of his work could have been placed quite readily and appropriately in Part VI, where we will discuss the humanistic-existential positions. Since Allport believed that the trait concept was the most important in the construction of an adequate theory of personality, his position belongs within the trait perspective framework. Chapter 6 does, however, pay considerable attention to Allport's humanistic roots. It also details Allport's attempts to create an adequate definition of personality and outlines his theory of traits. The major gap in his theorizing about the developmental process of becoming and the role traits play in this emergent process is presented. The review of the process of development focuses on his conception of the mature personality. There is also coverage of the many techniques Allport used to assess personality. In this regard, differences between an idiographic and nomothetic approaches to data collection are reviewed. Finally, the application of Allport's theory to the treatment of people with behavioral disorders is presented.

In Chapter 7, the primary focus is on Cattell's belief that an adequate theory of personality must rest on solid measurement and statistical procedures. The chapter provides an introduction to the complex factor analytic methods he utilizes to "discover" the basic traits of personality. It also provides a discussion of each of his sixteen major traits or factors, as well as the results of some current studies obtained by utilizing a measure of these characteristics. There is an additional focus on the ways in which Cattell uses a specification equation as a means of combining traits and situations in an attempt to predict individual differences in behavior accurately. This multidimensional model includes a complex representation of the ways in which traits are dynamically interrelated within the person and how they operate across a variety of situations. Next, Cattell's emphasis on the role of heredity in personality development and functioning is outlined. There is a further presentation of the role of learning in personality development. In this regard, Cattell not only presents the usual ways in which classical and instrumental conditioning affect personality formation, but he stresses in original fashion the role of a complex form of learning called integration learning in changing personality. Finally, there is a discussion of the ways in which personality diagnosis through the use of precise measurement procedures can be used to identify disordered behavior so that the clinician would be in a better position to help clients. This discussion is followed by an assessment of the strengths and weaknesses of Cattell's position.

Gordon Allport (Courtesy of Harvard University)

Allport's Trait Theory

BIOGRAPHICAL SKETCH

Gordon Allport was born in 1897 in Montezuma, Indiana, the son of a country doctor. There were four boys in the Allport family, and Gordon was the youngest. He characterized his family life as marked by trust and affection, along with a strong emphasis on the virtue of hard work. Allport was scholarly from an early age; he was good with words, but poor at sports. He did not get along very well with his peers. In a show of utter contempt, one of his classmates even said of the young scholar, "Aw, that guy swallowed a dictionary" (Allport, 1968, p. 378).

Although he finished second highest academically in his high school class of one hundred students, Allport insisted that he was " . . . a good routine student, but definitely uninspired . . . about anything beyond the usual adolescent concerns" (Allport, 1968, p. 379). Following his older brother Floyd, who had graduated from Harvard, Allport squeezed through the entrance tests and matriculated there in 1915. The years at Harvard were stimulating and enlightening, according to Allport. He was overwhelmed by the intellectual atmosphere at the institution and its strict adherence to the highest academic standards. It was a real intellectual awakening for the small-town boy from the Midwest. Allport followed the example of his older brother and majored in psychology. Besides enrolling in courses taught by prominent psychology professors and being influenced by them, he also participated in a number of volunteer service projects (Allport, 1968, p. 381).

After receiving his baccalaureate in 1919, Allport took an opportunity to teach English and sociology at Robert College in Constantinople, Turkey. The following year he won a fellowship for graduate study at Harvard. Before returning to Cambridge, however, he decided to visit a brother who was working in Vienna at the time. He also decided to see if he could arrange a private meeting with Sigmund Freud. With the audacity of youth, he wrote a letter to Freud announcing that he was in

129

Vienna and implying that Freud would no doubt be glad to meet him. To his great surprise, Freud replied in his own handwriting and invited Allport to visit him at his office.

When Allport arrived, Freud ushered him into his famous inner office and sat staring at him expectantly. Not expecting the silence and not knowing what to say, Allport thought fast and told him of an episode on a streetcar on his way to the office. He reported that he had seen a four-year-old boy who displayed a conspicuous dirt phobia. The boy kept saying to his mother "I don't want to sit there . . . don't let that dirty man sit beside me" (Allport, 1968, p. 383). Since the mother was so clean and dominant looking, Allport assumed Freud would quickly see the point of the story—namely, that the boy's abhorence of dirt was a result of his mother's obsession with cleanliness. Instead, when he had finished the story, Freud hesitated and said kindly "And was that little boy you?" (Allport, 1968, p. 383). Allport, flabbergasted, realized that Freud was accustomed to thinking in terms of neurotic defenses, so that Allport's manifest motivation had completely escaped him. Allport reports that the experience taught him that depth psychology often plunged too deeply into the psyche and that psychologists might understand people better if they paid more attention to their manifest, conscious motives before probing into their unconscious natures.

Allport entered graduate school and finished the work for his doctorate in two years. He received his Ph.D. in 1922, at the age of twenty-four (Allport, 1968, p. 384). He was interested in developing a psychology of personality, but practically no one else in academic life had similar interests; he reports that his thesis was perhaps the first one devoted to an examination of the traits of personality. Immediately after receiving the degree, Allport had a shattering experience which he claims was a turning point in his life and career. He was invited to attend a meeting of a group of experimentalists at Clark University to discuss current problems and issues in sensory psychology. After two days of such discussions, the eminent psychologist Titchener allotted three minutes to each graduate student to describe his own investigations. Allport reported his work on traits of personality and was punished by total silence and stares. Titchener strongly disapproved of his presentation and demanded of Allport's major professor, "Why did you let him work on that problem?" Allport was embarrassed and mortified at these remarks, but later, when they had returned to Harvard, his professor consoled him by saying, "You don't care what Titchener thinks." And Allport found that in fact he did not (Allport, 1968, p. 385). The experience taught him another lesson—namely, not to be unnecessarily bothered by rebukes or professional slights and to pursue one's own interests. From that point on, Allport remained a maverick in psychology, a person who thought deeply and originally about issues and who stated his views candidly, no matter how controversial they were in the eyes of others.

Except for a brief stint at Dartmouth, most of Allport's professional life was spent at Harvard. During this period, from 1930 to his death in 1967, he wrote many scholarly theoretical and research articles on topics including prejudice, expressive movements, rumor, and attitudes and values. He also published a number of books, including *Personality: A Psychological Interpretation* (1937), *Becoming: Basic Considerations for a Psychology of Personality* (1955), *The Nature of Prejudice* (1958), and *Pattern and Growth in Personality* (1961). Fittingly, his work was recognized by his colleagues and he was awarded many honors. He was elected president of the American Psychological Association in 1939 and given the Distinguished Scientific Contribution Award in 1964. One honor he said he valued above all others. At the XVII International Congress of Psychology, which met in Washington, D.C., in 1963, fifty-five of his former Ph.D. students presented him with two handsomely bound volumes of their own writings with the dedicatory inscription: "From his students—in appreciation of his respect for their individuality" (Allport, 1968, p. 407).

BASIC CONCEPTS AND PRINCIPLES

Personality as Seen by a Humanist

Allport, like many investigators in the discipline, has commented on the virtual impossibility of defining the term personality precisely. After reviewing definitions offered by theologians, philosophers, lawyers, poets, sociologists, and psychologists, Allport proposed his own version in his first book. For him, personality was " . . . what a man really is." But this, too, was still too brief and vague. Accordingly, he presented a more precise definition: "Personality is the dynamic organization within the individual of those psychophysical systems that determine his unique adjustments to his environment" (Allport, 1937, p. 48). In a later book, he revised even this definition: "Personality is the dynamic organization within the individual of those psychophysical systems that determine his characteristic behavior and thought" (Allport, 1961, p. 28).

For Allport, the "dynamic organization" of personality refers to his belief that it was fruitless to consider personality as consisting of fragmented components independent of one another. Instead, personality is unified and constantly evolving and changing. Personality is also seen as an entity within the personality, a point which is obvious but which has interesting implications. Much of behavior was seen by Allport as caused by forces within the person. Although he did not deny that situational influences have an effect, he still felt it was the individual's own perception of these forces which determined his or her behavior. Furthermore, some behavior that seems to be controlled by external forces is really controlled by internal forces. An example might clarify this statement. Allport maintained that "if a child is a hellion at home, and an angel outside, he obviously has two contradictory tendencies in his nature, or perhaps a deeper genotype that would explain the opposing phenotypes" (Allport, 1968, p. 46). A situationist would simply predict that the child would behave differently depending upon which situation is salient. Allport argued that the differences in behavior may be caused by opposing tendencies or traits in the person's nature—for example, by his learned predispositions to act as a hellion or an angel in such situations.

Allport became more Freudian by suggesting that a unifying *genotype* may actually be responsible for the two *phenotypes* (behaving as a hellion at home or an angel outside). For example, the actual underlying tendency or genotype might be one of expedience, that is, the child may have the trait of expedience or the tendency to perform behaviors advantageous to him. Behaving like an angel at home might be pleasing to the child's parents; behaving like a hellion outside may win the approval of peers. As you can readily see, such trait "explanations" can be invoked easily on a post hoc basis and can be made to fit virtually any data under consideration. Another important point to remember in connection with this example is that although Allport recognized the role the situation plays in behavior, his primary allegiance remained with the ways in which the person's unique traits and other characteristics determined his behavior.

The reference to *psychophysical systems* in Allport's definition shows that he considered personality to consist exclusively of neither mental nor physical events, but of both "mind" and "body" elements, in an inextricable unity. These events are also organized into a complex he called a *system*.

Personality involves the characteristic or unique behavior or thought of the person. Allport argued that all the traits we apparently share with others are at base idiosyncratic and unique. He acknowledged that this aspect of the definition is very broad, but he wanted to take into account the fact that we not only adjust to our environment by behaving in certain ways, but we also reflect upon it. By so doing, we ensure not only survival, but growth.

Other Characteristics of Allport's Humanistic Psychology

Allport's emphasis on the uniqueness of the person is only one of the features of his position. In addition, there is a strong focus on the ways in which the internal cognitive and motivational processes of the person influence and cause behavior. These internal processes and structures include reflexes, drives, habits and skills, beliefs, intentions, attitudes, values, and traits. The person is conceived of as being active, creative, and characteristically rational. As the person matures, he becomes increasingly capable of making conscious and deliberate choices among the various alternatives for behavior. The person is seen as a self-reliant being who is relatively independent of the influence of others and who pursues goals in a thoughtful way. Allport chose this positive and opti-

mistic approach to the person in reaction to the more pessimistic con-
ceptualizations current when he was postulating his own position. He
believed these views of the person were too static, reductionistic, and
mechanistic, and placed too much emphasis on the unconscious and irrational side of human personality. Allport's theory was an attempt to
provide a much-needed corrective for this one-sided view.

The Theory of Traits

The major concepts in Allport's theory revolve around the different
kinds of traits possessed by each of us and the different properties of the
proprium or self. We consider first his theory of traits and follow it with
his treatment of the proprium and the developmental process, although
it should be noted that Allport never systematically related his trait concepts to his concepts of human development. Later we will try to make
some sense out of the irregularity in his theorizing, but first we should
consider the basic concepts in his *trait theory.*

What Precisely Is a Trait? For Allport, a trait is ". . . a generalized and
focalized neuropsychic system (peculiar to the individual), with the capacity to render many stimuli functionally equivalent, and to initiate and
guide consistent (equivalent) forms of adaptive and expressive behavior" (Allport, 1937, p. 295). Thus, a trait is something that actually
exists, but not something we see. It is located in certain parts of the
nervous system. Although we do not see it, we infer its existence by
watching the consistencies in a person's behavior. Dissimilar stimuli are
all capable of arousing a trait readiness within the person. The trait then
manifests itself through a variety of different responses. All these different responses are equivalent, however, in the sense that they serve
the same function—that is, expression of the trait (see Figure 6.1 for a
concrete example of the manner in which a trait generally operates). A
man's hatred of women is inferred from his bragging about male

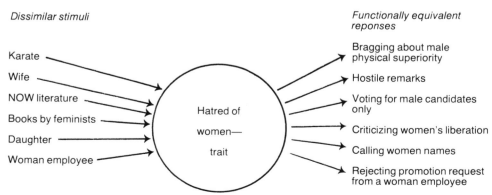

Dissimilar stimuli   *Functionally equivalent
                                                                reponses*

Karate   Bragging about male
                                                                physical superiority

Wife   Hostile remarks

NOW literature   Voting for male candidates
                                                                only
                              Hatred of
Books by feminists
                              women—   Criticizing women's liberation
Daughter
                              trait   Calling women names
Woman employee
                                                               Rejecting promotion request
                                                               from a woman employee

Figure 6.1.
The trait in action. Dissimilar stimuli arouse the trait. The trait then provides a variety of functionally equivalent responses.

physical prowess, by his voting for male candidates only, by his refusal to promote a woman employee, and by his name calling, criticism, and hostile remarks about women.

Cardinal, Central, and Secondary Traits. Allport also made a number of distinctions among various kinds of traits. Characteristics that are pervasive and dominant in a person's life he called *cardinal traits.* These are master motives, ruling passions, eminent traits (Allport, 1961, p. 365). For example, a person may have an overwhelming need to be powerful, and this need for power could be inferred from virtually all his behavior. Such a person would not only strive to attain a position of power within society, but would interact with his golf partner, his mail carrier, his children, and his marriage partner in a similar fashion. He would try to dominate his spouse and would even try desperately to win a game of ping-pong with his five-year-old daughter. A casual conversation with an acquaintance might lead to a bitter struggle on his part to win on some trivial issue.

Characteristics that control less of a person's behavior but are nevertheless important are called *central traits.* Such traits include possessiveness, ambitiousness, competitiveness, and kindness, among others. Although they do control the person's behavior in a variety of situations, they do not possess the generality of a central trait. Characteristics that are peripheral to the person are called *secondary traits.* Preferences, for example, are secondary traits. A person might "love" banana cream pie, so that this preference is aroused by a limited variety of situational stimuli around suppertime. He may prefer to vacation in Maine or Nova Scotia and therefore respond to advertising and conversation with friends about vacations in these areas with favorable comments.

Common Traits versus Personal Dispositions. Allport made yet another distinction among traits: He pointed out that they could be considered categories for classifying groups of people on a particular dimension (Allport, 1961, p. 349). We might say, for example, that some people are more dominant than others or that some people are more polite than others. Such comparative designations are really abstractions based on an identification of given dimensions. In short, they are *common traits* or traits we share with others. They are generalized dispositions and, in Allport's view, of limited usefulness in a science of personality.

Much more to his liking was the concept of the *personal disposition.* In contrast to the common or generalized trait, the personal disposition or individual trait concerned a unique characteristic of the person, a trait not shared with others (Allport, 1961, p. 358). Allport hoped that psychologists would stop paying so much attention to the role of common traits in a science of personality and would focus instead on those characteristics unique to the individual. Such a hope was based on his belief that common traits were categories into which the individual is forced, whereas personal dispositions more accurately reflect his own personality structure. As he stated it

> [B]y common trait methods, we find that Peter stands high in *esthetic interest* and *anxiety*, but low in *leadership* and *need-achievement*. The truth is that all these common traits have a special coloring in his life, and—still more important—they interact with one another. Thus it might be more accurate to say that his personal disposition is a kind of *artisitc and self-sufficient solitude*. His separate scores on common traits do not fully reflect this pattern. (Allport, 1961, p. 359)

For Allport, only by adopting an approach to the study of personality focused on the uniqueness of the person can we hope to make substantial advances in our understanding. By and large, though, investigators have argued that unique or individual constructs are impossible to imagine. If we used constructs that were unique to the individual, there would be no words in the language for them. We would have continually to invent new terms to describe each individual's motives and behavior—a hopeless undertaking. Of course, we can and do talk about the unique configurations or patterns of traits within an individual's personality, but even here critics have argued that a science focused on general differences between people can handle this problem; there is no need for Allport's highly personalized approach (Holt, 1962). Perhaps, though, these critics miss Allport's fundamental point about trying to focus more clearly on the uniqueness of the individual in their zeal to prove him wrong (further discussion of this issue is found later in the chapter in the section on Techniques of Assessment).

THE PROCESS OF PERSONALITY DEVELOPMENT

At this point, you know that there are a variety of ways of conceptualizing the development process. Freud, for example, focused on the development of strong sexual and aggressive needs as they related to various zones of the body—the oral, anal, phallic, and genital areas. Jung considered development in terms of the conflict between opposites within the individual that facilitated movement toward self-realization. For Allport, the discussion of the developmental process centers on the concept of the self. He acknowledged that the concept is a slippery one and that it has been used by different investigators in different ways. It has also encountered vigorous opposition from many psychologists. Wundt, the eminent nineteenth-century structuralist, thought the concept of self or ego or soul was hindering progress in psychology and declared that he favored a "psychology without a soul" (Allport, 1955, p. 36). Wundt's objection, and the objection of many behaviorists who came after him, was that there was a tendency on the part of some investigators to assign a primary role to the term in their theories and to discuss it as a mysterious central agency which unified our actions. In short, the term was reified by many investigators and treated as though it actually existed and could direct behavior. For example, a reified use of the term might be found in the following "explanation" of a person's behavior: "His strong sense of self caused him to give up smoking." In other words, he gave up smoking because of his strong ego.

Allport agreed that such reification is damaging to psychology, but he thought we could avoid this pitfall and still make good use of the term. In fact, he even maintained that we *must* use the term, for two reasons. First, the one certain criterion we have of our identity and existence is our sense of self. It is a fundamental experience; if we discard it, we discard the essence of personality. Second, contemporary theories of learning motivation and development need some form of the concept in order to account for differences in behavior produced by differences in individual experiences relevant or irrelevant to the self. Another way of stating this belief is that differences in learning and performance will occur as a function of the degree of "ego-involvement" on the part of the individual. If he is very ego-involved or if the task has greater self-relevance, he may learn to master it more quickly. Of course, theorists with a behavioral perspective would probably argue that Allport comes very close to reifying the concept of self in this kind of example.

A simpler and more precise way of discussing the differences in performance in this case might be to translate self-relevance into reinforcement terms and say that we might expect differences in performance if the person places different value or importance on the outcomes of the performance. He works quickly to master a task that yields valuable reinforcers, but does not learn as efficiently on a task in which the outcomes are relatively unimportant (see Rotter, Chapter 10, for a more detailed discussion of this point).

The Proprium or Self

Allport substituted the term *proprium* for self in his theorizing, and used it to mean a sense of what is "peculiarly ours." It includes "all aspects of personality that make for inward unity" (Allport, 1955, p. 40). The proprium or self is continuously developing from infancy to death and moves through the stages described below. (Note how the term has been endowed with magical powers in the previous sentences. It should be clear that we use it in this way because it is convenient to do so, and not because we believe an actual entity called the proprium guides our development.) At this point let us examine the various aspects of the proprium as Allport conceived them.

The Bodily Self. In infancy, the first aspect of selfhood, the bodily sense becomes salient, according to Allport. As infants, we are continually receiving sensory information from our internal organs, our muscles, joints, and tendons. These sensations become particularly acute when we are hungry, when we are frustrated, and when we bump into things.

In such situations, we learn the limits of our own bodies. As we mature, these recurrent bodily sensations provide information that confirms our own existence. In Allport's opinion, these sensations provide an "anchor" for our self-awareness. When we are healthy, we hardly notice the sensations; when we are ill, we are keenly aware of our bodies (Allport, 1961, p. 114). How intimate these sensations are is shown by Allport in an interesting example:

> Think first of swallowing the saliva in your mouth, or do so. Then imagine expectorating it into a tumbler and drinking it! What seemed natural and "mine" suddenly becomes disgusting and alien. Or picture yourself sucking blood from a prick in your finger; then imagine sucking blood from a bandage around your finger! What I perceive as belonging intimately to my body is warm and welcome; what I perceive as separate from my body becomes, in the twinkling of an eye, cold and foreign.(Allport, 1955, p. 43)

Later in the developmental process, we experience sensations from our bodily growth. In adolescence, when these changes are abrupt, some of us feel we are puny, ugly, and awkward; others feel they are strong, beautiful, and graceful. Girls may try to hide breasts they consider too large or accentuate ones they consider too small. Boys may test their prowess in physical games and exaggerate their sexual exploits. Allport believed strongly that this bodily sense forms the core of the self and is an important aspect of selfhood throughout life.

Self-Identity. The second aspect of the proprium also occurs during the first eighteen months of life and is called *self-identity.* Despite the vast changes that occur in our lives as we grow older, there is a certain continuity and sameness in the way we perceive ourselves. As Allport saw it: "Today I remember some of my thoughts of yesterday; and tomorrow I shall remember some of my thoughts of both yesterday and today; and I am certain that they are the thoughts of the same person—of myself" (Allport, 1961, p. 114). This information about self-identity seems obvious and even trite, but there have been useful discussions by the neo-analyst Erikson of the crises faced by people, especially adolescents, who doubt or are confused by their identities.

In Erik Erikson's view, adolescents are forced to overthrow the identifications of childhood and to develop new identities that prepare them for the obligations and privileges of adulthood. They exist in a suspended state in which society provides them with opportunities to establish commitments to life. The inability to settle on an occupational identity is the most disturbing, according to Erikson. For many young people, it is also a period of " . . . tortuous self-consciousness, characterized at one time by shame over what one is already sure one is, and at another time by doubt as to what one may become." Erikson argues that, in such an unsettled period, youth also try to establish their identities by over-identifying with an assortment of heroes. They also become defensive in their behavior in a variety of ways:

> To keep themselves together they temporarily overidentify . . . with the heroes of cliques and crowds. On the other hand, they become remarkably clannish, intolerant, and cruel in their exclusion of others who are "different," in skin color, cultural background . . . and often in entirely petty aspects of dress and gesture arbitrarily selected as *the* signs of an in-grouper or out-grouper. It is important to understand . . . such intolerance as the necessary *defense against a sense of identity diffusion*, which is unavoidable at a time of life when the body changes its proportions radically . . . and when life lies before one with a variety of conflicting possibilities and choices. Adolescents temporarily help one another through such discomfort by forming cliques and by stereotyping themselves, their ideals, and their enemies . . . .It is difficult to be tolerant if deep down you are not quite sure that you are a man (or a woman), that you will ever grow together again and be attractive, that you will be able to master your drives, that you really know you are, that you know what you want to be . . . and that you will know how to make the right decision without, once (and) for all, committing yourself to the wrong friend, sexual partner, leader, or career. (Erikson, 1968, p. 200)

In short, Erikson sees the typical adolescent as a person with identity problems. Although he paints a one-sided picture of the debilitating aspects of youth and neglects to point out the kind of joy in one's strength and vitality and the commitment to ideals that also characterize many young people, Erikson has picked out some of the important difficulties of this time in our lives.

Self-Esteem. The third aspect of the proprium to emerge from the second through the third year of life, according to Allport, is feelings of *self-esteem.* At this point, we have become more familiar with our environments; we experience pride when we master available tasks, and humiliation when we fail. Allport also thought that one symptom of our growing self-awareness is the outpouring of opposition to virtually any suggestion the parents may make. It is a time for testing the limits of our environment and for refusing to take orders from others. In Allport's view, we are typically very negativistic at this stage. Moreover, many of us do not outgrow our oppositional tendencies, and they reappear, usually in adolescence. Then our "enemies" typically are our parents and other members of the "establishment."

Self-Extension. From approximately four to six years of age, we enter a phase in which our primary concern is possessions. We are typically very egocentric. "I know the moon is following us, Daddy!" "No, I want *all* of the candy!" "He can't come into *my* house!" "Get out of *my* room, Billy!" These are just some of the manifestations of our unreasoning selfishness.

Later, we extend our loyalties to our families, our churches, our nation, and our career groups. We also become immersed in material possessions. It is not that unusual to see adolescents and adults kissing their cars, patting them, and encouraging them to perform in superior fashion. Imagine the symbolism a Freudian would see in such behavior! All these possessions become warm, acceptable parts of ourselves. Praise them, and you praise us; ridicule them and you ridicule us.

Self-Image. The next aspect of the proprium is the self-image. This part of ourselves evolves during the same period as our sense of self-extension. The self-image has two components, according to Allport; learned expectations of the roles we are required to enact and the kinds of aspirations for the future we seek to attain (Allport, 1955, p. 47). The self-image evolves slowly in conjunction with the development of conscience. We learn to do the things that others expect of us and to avoid behaviors that will bring disapproval. We begin to formulate plans for the future and to make tentative decisions about careers and the values we will embrace.

The Self as Rational Coper. During the period between six and twelve, we begin to engage in reflective thought. We devise strategies to cope with problems and we delight in testing our skills, particularly our intellectual ones. We are also capable of distortion and defense. Nevertheless, the thrust of Allport's argument is that we are, at this stage, beginning to sense our rational powers and to exercise them (Allport, 1955, p. 46).

Propriate Striving. Finally, Allport discusses the aspect of the self called *propriate striving*. This facet of the self occurs from twelve on and can be understood if we concentrate on Allport's treatment of human motivation. He distinguishes between propriate and peripheral motives. Peripheral motives are our impulses and drives and our striving toward the immediate gratification of our needs. They include our attempts at tension reduction. We are hungry and eat. We are thirsty and drink. We are cold and put on clothing. We are fatigued and fall asleep. These are simple and automatic acts aimed at reducing our tensions. Propriate motives, in contrast, consist of our "ego-involved" behavior. They include our attempts to increase or maintain rather than decrease tensions and our striving for important goals. We strive to attain a college degree, sometimes at tremendous personal cost. We may try to become the best athlete in a given sport. We may yearn to be a great artist or novelist. Propriate striving is characterized by the unification of personality as we pursue our major goals. In Allport's view, "The possession of long-range goals, regarded as central to one's personal existence, distinguishes the human being from the animal, the adult from the child, and in many cases the healthy personality from the sick" (Allport, 1955, p. 51).

The emergence of propriate striving is closely related to the development of conscience. In the child, the evolving conscience is a "must" conscience or what Fromm calls an "authoritarian conscience" (Fromm, 1947). It is also similar to Freud's conception. It is a conscience based upon fear of punishment. The child begins to incorporate or internalize the values and standards of his parents. He feels guilty if he violates their rules. As the person matures, however, there is a marked change in his perception of the world and other people. There is an emergence of the "ought" conscience, or what Fromm calls the "humanistic conscience." In this stage, obedience to the external standards of authority gives way to internal or self-generated rules. The person's conduct is guided by his own values and self-image.

The shift from a "must" to an "ought" conscience is not automatic. Many people who are adults in terms of age are still children in terms of conduct. They are still reacting in terms of parental prohibitions. They still suffer from unresolved guilt feelings and a rehashing of old conflicts with authority figures (Allport, 1955, p. 74). They have not learned to rely on their own judgment and to orient themselves toward the attainment of challenging goals.

Although the seven aspects of the proprium seem to emerge at different stages of life, Allport felt that they do not function separately. Several, even all of them, can operate simultaneously, as the following example shows.

> Suppose that you are facing a difficult and critical examination. No doubt you are aware of the butterflies in your stomach (bodily self); also of the significance of the exam in terms of your past and future (self-identity); of your prideful involvement (self-esteem); of what success or failure may mean to your family (self-extension); of your hopes and aspirations (self-image); of your role as the solver of problems on the examination (rational agent); and of the relevance of the whole situation to your long-range goals (propriate striving). In actual life, then, a fusion of propriate states is the rule. (Allport, 1961, p. 137)

The Development of the Mature Personality

Allport talked about the developmental process as one of *becoming*. The development of the mature personality takes time, according to him, so that only the adult is capable of coming close to self-realization. These shifts in development are not always smooth and even; they are, instead, often abrupt and discontinuous. The normal or mature person is qualitatively different from the abnormal or immature one.

Initially, the infant is an unsocialized being:

> Even at the age of two the child is, when measured by standards applied to adults, an unsocialized horror. Picture, if you can, an adult who is extremely destructive of property, insistent and demanding that every desire be instantly gratified, helpless and dependent on others, unable to

share his possessions, violent and uninhibited in the display of all his feelings. Such behavior, normal to a two-year-old, would be monstrous in a
man. Unless these qualities are markedly altered in the process of becoming
we have on our hands an infantile and potentially evil personality. (Allport,
1955, pp. 28–29)

During this early stage of development not only is the person dependent
on others, but most of his behavior is designed to aid his adjustment or,
in more understandable terms, to help him survive. He performs those
behaviors that will reduce hunger and thirst, for example. He also learns
what Allport called our "tribal conformities"—for example, the wearing
of clothes or brushing of teeth (Allport 1955, p. 63).

As his proprium develops, the person also learns to protect himself
against threats by the use of various defensive strategies. In this regard,
Allport accepted the validity of the Freudian ego-defense mechanisms,
but he felt that excessive and indiscriminate use of these strategies was
indicative of an abnormal or immature personality. The mature personality, in contrast, was characterized as being relatively free of these
debilitating tactics. Allport granted that sometimes adult behavior was
motivated by sexual and aggressive needs, but once again he felt that
such motivation played a relatively small part in the functioning of the
mature person. In his view, the mature individual's functioning was
directed more by events that affected him currently. Thus, if you want to
understand behavior, focus on current rather than past motives. For
example, a student may eat too little not because she is fixated at the oral
stage, but because she has a contract with the university or college to eat
in the dining halls and the food there is relatively unappetizing.

Functional Autonomy. The early development of the person, then, is
characterized by the presence of peripheral motives. Later, as the proprium develops, there is a shift from reliance on such learnings and motives to ones which are more central to ourselves. These propriate strivings include the use of our creative and spontaneous energies to move
us toward full maturity. The key question now becomes "How do we
free ourselves from these infantile motives so that we can function as
mature adults?" The answer, according to Allport, is found in his
general law of motivation called *functional autonomy.* As he put it, "Functional autonomy regards adult motives as varied, and as self-sustaining,
contemporary systems, growing out of antecedent systems, but functionally independent of them" (Allport, 1961, p. 227). Through the use
of this concept, Allport hoped to show that, as the person matures, her
bonds with the past are broken. The mature person no longer depends
on her parents. She has become functionally autonomous—that is, her
behavior is independent of her parents' wishes. She also no longer
needs to use defensive tactics to protect her self-esteem from attacks by
others. She is independent of them because she is now capable of judg-

ing her conduct by self-generated rules. A few examples may clarify the concept:

> An ex-sailor has a craving for the sea, a musician longs to return to his instrument after an enforced absence, a miser continues to build up his useless pile. Now the sailor may have first acquired his love for the sea as an incident in his struggle to earn a living. The sea was "secondary reinforcement" for his hunger drive. But now the ex-sailor is perhaps a wealthy banker; the original motive is destroyed and yet the hunger for the sea persists and even increases in intensity. The musician may first have been stung by a slur on his inferior performance into mastering his instrument; but now he is safely beyond these taunts, and finds that he loves his instrument more than anything else in the world. The miser perhaps learned his habit of thrift in dire necessity, but the miserliness persists and becomes stronger with the years even after the necessity has been relieved. (Allport, 1961, p. 227)

Thus, Allport's concept of functional autonomy serves as a bridge between the phase of development controlled by immature strivings and that characterized by mature motives. It should be noted that Allport's concept provides a description of shifts in the developmental process and not an explanation of why the shift occurs, as he contended. For Allport, it was because the miser's hoarding behavior has become functionally autonomous that he continues to save money. Obviously, functional autonomy may describe the miser's behavior, but behavior does not exist in a vacuum. Another event or other events control it. Perhaps the miser continues to save not for food to ease his hunger, but to buy other material objects. The important point is that the behavior may no longer be under the control of basic needs, but this does not mean that it occurs independently of other motives. For Allport, people who are able to free themselves from excessive reliance on these earlier motives show movement toward maturity. He developed six criteria for judging whether or not a person is mature (Allport, 1961, p. 283). A discussion of each follows.

Extension of the Sense of Self. The truly mature person, according to Allport, is able to participate in activities that go beyond himself. He is concerned not only about his own welfare, but the welfare of others. As Allport saw it:

> True participation gives direction to life. Maturity advances in proportion as lives are decentered from the clamorous immediacy of the body and of egocenteredness. Self-love is a prominent and inescapable factor in every life, but it need not dominate. Everyone has self-love, but only self-extension is the earmark of maturity. (Allport, 1961, p. 285)

Warm Relatedness to Others. The mature individual is also capable of relating warmly to others. Allport distinguished between two kinds of
warmth. The first is intimacy. The mature person is characterized by the
capacity for love, whether it be love of family or friends. The second
kind is compassion. Allport believed that the mature person has a
certain detachment in his dealings with others that allow him to be
respectful and appreciative of individual differences in behavior and
thought.

Both kinds of warmth suggest that the mature person would not be
possessive, gossipy, or intrusive on the privacy or rights of others. He or
she would avoid constant complaining, criticizing, and sarcasm. Putting
it another way, the mature person, according to Allport, would follow
the rule, "Do not poison the air that other people have to breathe." Such
respect for other people is in evidence because the mature person

> . . . comes to know that all mortals are in the same human situation: They
> did not ask to come into the world; they are saddled with an urge to survive
> and are buffeted by drives and passions; they encounter failure, suffer, but
> somehow carry on. No one knows for sure the meaning of life; everyone is
> growing older as he sails to an unknown destination. (Allport, 1961, p. 285)

Self-Acceptance. The mature person is also emotionally secure. He
avoids overreacting on matters that are beyond his control. He has a
high frustration tolerance level. The immature person, in contrast, tends
to act impulsively and to blame others for his own mistakes. Unlike the
mature person, he does not bide his time or make plans to circumvent
obstacles in his path. In brief, he lacks the kind of self-control that
characterizes the mature person.

Realistic Perception of Reality. The mature person is also accurate in his
perception of events. He does not continually distort reality. He has the
knowledge and skills that are necessary for effective performance and
living. Along with these skills, he also has the capacity to lose himself in
his work. In short, he is problem-centered, not ego-centered.

Self-Objectification. The mature person knows himself. He is blessed
with insight into his own abilities and limitations. Correlated with his
insight is a sense of humor. The mature individual has the ability to see
the absurdity in life and not be overwhelmed by it. He can be amused by
his own mistakes and not deceived by his own pretentiousness.

Unifying Philosophy of Life. The mature individual also has developed "a
clear comprehension of life's purpose in terms of an intelligible theory"
(Allport, 1961, p. 294). He noted that the sense of "directedness" was

present in mature people and that such a set of life goals are typically vaguely defined in adolescents. Young people do have ideals, but they are sometimes not clearly delineated. Moreover, once they seek to implement these ideals and fall short, they begin to experience disappointment. In their late twenties they begin to learn that they must compromise with reality. They find that their jobs are not as challenging or rewarding as they had hoped, that their marriages or living arrangements fall far short of their desires, and that they have not been able to overcome some of their personal limitations (Allport, 1961, p. 295). They find their goals and values changing and a revised and clearer set of principles beginning to emerge. The mature person has a fairly clear self-image and a set of standards that guide his conduct.

In regard to the relationship between traits and the proprium, we can only speculate. Since the beginning of the proprium occurs in infancy and most of our complex traits are learned later in the developmental cycle, it seems reasonable to assume that the proprium is the guiding force in our lives, whereas traits are more an outgrowth of its functioning. Since some of our traits are cardinal or central ones, it is also clear that some of our characteristics are bound in important ways to proprium functioning. In short, some traits are integral parts of ourselves. It is also clear that, although the proprium guides our conduct, new experiences can also have an impact. For example, a person may be guided by a self-image that requires him to be kind to others, but changes in both the self-image and his central trait of kindness may be modified by experiences with a series of individuals who exploit him.

TECHNIQUES OF ASSESSMENT

Because Allport considered personality to be a dynamic and interrelated entity, he thought it pointless to focus only on one or two of its facets. Since it was so complex, he believed that investigators must employ every "legitimate method" to study it (Allport, 1961, p. 395). Legitimate methods include reliable and valid assessment procedures based upon objective and systematic observations of given phenomena. Illegitimate methods, according to him, include ". . . gossip, prejudiced inference, the exaggerated single instance, unverified anecdote . . . [and] 'character reading' " (Allport, 1961, pp. 395–396).

Some of the legitimate methods are (a) constitutional and physiological diagnosis; (b) studies of sociocultural membership, status, and roles; (c) personal documents and case studies; (d) self-appraisal techniques such as self-ratings and Q-sorts (see Chapter 13); (e) conduct samplings such as behavior assessments in everyday situations; (f) observer ratings; (g) personality tests and scales; (h) projective tests; (i) depth analysis such as free association and dream analysis; (j) expressive behavior measures; and (k) synaptic procedures (Allport, 1961, p. 458). Synaptic procedures involve combining the outcomes of a variety of assessment techniques to produce a general picture or profile of the individual's personality (Allport, 1961, p. 445).

Although some of these techniques focus on the typical case or the average person, Allport's own orientation centered on the uniqueness of the individual. As he said, "Each person is an idiom unto himself, an apparent violation of the syntax of the species" (Allport, 1955, p. 19). As a result, he fought an uphill battle against the prevailing view in American psychology that a science of personality should seek to establish universal laws of human functioning. It should seek to understand the behavior and experience of people in general, to focus on the typical case or the average person. Such an approach Allport labeled *nomothetic*. He distinguished this approach from one in which the primary goal is to understand the functioning of a specific individual. Such a science he labeled *idiographic*.

The two views also generate different kinds of information about people. The nomothetic approach, for example, relies heavily on the use of statistics in the analysis of human behavior. It can tell us that, in comparison to Bill or Jane, John has a lower need for achievement since he scored only at the tenth percentile on a paper-and-pencil test designed to measure this characteristic, whereas the other two people scored well above the ninety-fifth percentile. Further testing could tell us that John is above average in intelligence, as compared to other adolescents of the same age. But Allport argued that although such testing may give us information about John that is useful, its usefulness is quite limited; it does not tell us anything about John's uniqueness. The information we obtained is abstracted from a unique personality. The idiographic approach, in contrast, would provide us with information about the ways in which these and many other characteristics interact within John's personality. It would give us a view of the dynamic and organized personality that is peculiar to John. Thus, Allport would seek to establish the lawfulness in John's behavior and experiences through the use of such techniques as personal records, pattern analysis of expressive movements, graphology, and case studies (Allport, 1937, pp. 369–399).

In Allport's view, we should develop methods compatible with the subject matter. The data collected by such methods could then by used to predict John's behavior in various situations. Of course, it would be invalid to try to draw any conclusions about the behavior of other individuals through the use of such methods, since the inferences are based upon the experiences of a single individual. A current review of clinical studies utilizing case history methods to predict the behavior of patients shows that, in general, they are not very successful or accurate in their prognostications (Mischel, 1968, pp. 103–148). Most of these studies, however, relied on psychodynamic inferences about states and traits, and not on direct self-reports. Allport was a staunch supporter of direct self-report measures in psychological research and would have expected psychodynamic procedures not to prove very useful. But he also acknowledged that the methods currently available to study personality idiographically are primitive. He would probably have argued that, despite the current limitations in idiographic study, it was still essential to study personality from this perspective and that improvements in methodology would come eventually.

APPLICATION OF THE THEORY TO THE TREATMENT OF PSYCHOPATHOLOGY

For Allport, the healthy or mature person is one who is continually in a state of becoming; the unhealthy or immature person is one whose growth has been stifled. He believed, like Freud, that the person's development could be arrested as a result of faulty relationships with his or her parents, and especially the mother, in early childhood. Allport believed that each of us needs to be secure and protected and that deprivations of love and affection can have a lasting and harmful impact on our growth:

> All in all a generous minimum of security seems required in early years for a start toward a productive life-style. Without it the individual develops a pathological craving for security, and is less able than others to tolerate setbacks in maturity. Through his insistent demanding, jealousy, depredations, and egoism he betrays the craving that still haunts him. By contrast, the child who receives adequate gratification of his infant needs is more likely to be prepared to give up his habits of demanding, and to learn tolerance for his later frustrations. Having completed successfully one stage of development he is free to abandon the habits appropriate to this stage and to enter the mature reaches of becoming. (Allport, 1955, p. 32)

To overcome these deprivations, Allport believed that the person must come to feel that he is ". . . accepted and wanted by therapist, family, and associates." The person must feel loved and must learn to love. As Allport put it, "Love received and love given comprise the best form of therapy" (Allport, 1955, p. 33).

But this is only one side of the picture. There are many people who have had secure and loving backgrounds who later become neurotic. Although their secure backgrounds make them free to grow, other problems crop up. Pressures are exerted on individuals to adjust to the norms of society, and often these adjustments preclude positive growth. Why? Because, according to Allport,

Society itself is sick. Why . . . make a patient content with its injustices, hypocrisies, and wars? And to what society shall we adjust the patient? To his social class, thus making him provincial and depriving him of aspiration? To his nation, thus giving him no vision of mankind as a whole? It is doubtful that we can accept society (any society) as a standard for a healthy personality. A head-hunter society demands well-adjusted head-hunters as citizens, but is the deviant in this group who questions the value of decapitation necessarily an immature human being? (Allport, 1961, p. 305)

Indiscriminate acceptance of these demands produces a person with restricted self-extension, a distorted self-image, a defensive self, and stunted propriate striving. That is, the person's loyalties become circumscribed, producing an intolerance of other people and groups outside the favored few. The person also sees himself and his goals in terms of the values established by others. For example, he sees himself as a lawyer and pursues that goal because his parents demand that he do so. In the process, important goals that he actually desires to pursue are shunted aside. The person experiences considerable conflict and uses defensive manuevers to alleviate the suffering. Movement toward self-realization is hindered. The task of the therapist, in Allport's view, is to help the person become aware of the sources of his distorted goals and to assist him in the attainment of maturity and well-being.

CRITICAL COMMENTS

We turn now to a consideration of the scientific worth of Allport's theory.

Comprehensiveness. Allport's theory is comprehensive in the sense that it is incredibly eclectic, borrowing and using concepts from learning theory, psychoanalysis, and existentialism, but technically speaking most of its focus is on healthy development. In addition, the various developmental stages of the proprium are described in general terms, and there is little attempt to specify precisely the variables that control the occurrence, maintenance, or modification of self phenomena. The theory is also restricted in the sense that it recognizes the influence of the environment in the development of personality, but does not specify the ways in which the environment operates to affect functioning.

Precision and Testability. Allport's theory is populated with vague and ill-defined concepts and relational statements. Terms like propriate striving and the self as rational coper do not lend themselves readily to operational definitions. We have already seen that Allport was not explicit in stating the ways in which his trait concepts were related to his formulations about the development of the proprium. Given these problems, it is apparent that it would be difficult to design adequate tests of his theory.

Simplicity. Allport's theory fails to meet the parsimony criterion not because it is surfeited with excess concepts, but because it has too few concepts to account for the phenomena within its domain. It is doubtful that the complexities of the developmental process can be described adequately in terms of the seven major concepts he utilized in portraying the properties of the self.

Empirical Validity. We have already learned that Allport's emphasis on traits led him to ignore the role of social and environmental factors in determining behavior. Such exclusive emphasis on internal factors does not facilitate the accurate prediction of behavior, as recent criticism has shown. In many instances, behavior can be modified quite readily by environmental manipulations, so that strict reliance on the use of traits to predict behavior is of limited usefulness. (Much more will be said about the problems of a trait approach to the study of personality in Chapter 16.) Not only is the trait, as conceptualized by Allport, of limited usefulness in the prediction of behavior, but there have been very few tests of his theory to date. Thus, the empirical support for his theory is weak.

Heuristic Value. Allport's theory, although interesting and informative in certain respects, has not been very heuristic. It is poorly organized, vaguely stated, and limited in terms of comprehensiveness. As a consequence, it has not been very exciting to most investigators.

Allport was interesting and challenging to psychologists, however, when he addressed himself to issues concerning the nature of psychology as a science. He was a powerful and articulate spokesman for the humanistic viewpoint, and he generated considerable controversy within the profession by detailing the limitations of the psychoanalytic and behavioristic positions. Perhaps most important, he championed the idiographic approach to the study of personality:

> Psychology is truly itself only when it can deal with individuality. It is vain to plead that other sciences do not do so, that they are allowed to brush off the bothersome issue of uniqueness. The truth is that psychology is *assigned* the task of being curious about human persons, and persons exist only in concrete and unique patterns. . . .
>
> We study the human person most fully when we take him as an individual. He is more than a bundle of habits, more than a point of intersection of abstract dimensions. He is more than a representative of his species, more than a citizen of the state, more than an incident in the movements of mankind. He transcends them all. The individual, striving ever for integrity and fulfillment, has existed under all forms of social life-forms as varied as the nomadic and feudal, capitalist and communist. No society holds together for long without the respect man shows to man. The individual to-

day struggles on even under oppression, always hoping and planning for a more perfect democracy where the dignity and growth of each personality will be prized above all else. (Allport, 1961. p. 573)

Many investigators were forced by Allport's clear voice to reconsider their acceptance of the tenets of a nomothetic science and to agree with him that any worthwhile theory of personality has to focus on the uniqueness of the individual.

Applied Value. Allport's theory is weak in the applied area. For the most part, it has been ignored by scholars both inside and outside the discipline.

DISCUSSION QUESTIONS

1. Compare and contrast the nomothetic and idiographic approaches to the study of personality. What are the advantages and disadvantages of each view?
2. In what ways is Allport an important forerunner of the humanistic movement in psychology?
3. Describe the various phases of the developmental process, as postulated by Allport. How much research support is there for his theory of development?
4. Do you agree with Erikson that adolescence is an unsettled and often stressful period?
5. List the inadequacies of utilizing the notion of "functional autonomy" as an explanatory concept of behavior.
6. Describe the criteria used by Allport to characterize the mature person. Can you think of any others?
7. What is a trait? What kinds of traits are there, according to Allport? Give concrete examples of the operation of each kind in people you know.
8. Is it truly possible to have traits that are unique to the individual?
9. Do you agree with Allport that young children are "unsocialized horrors?" What are the implications of Allport's belief for the disciplining of children?
10. What are some of the major problems in utilizing trait concepts to explain behavior?

NOTES

G. W. Allport, *Personality: A Psychological Interpretation* (New York: Holt, 1937).

G. W. Allport, *Becoming: Basic Considerations for a Psychology of Personality* (New Haven: Yale University Press, 1955).

G. W. Allport, *Pattern and Growth in Personality* (New York: Holt, Rinehart and Winston, 1961).

G. W. Allport, "An autobiography," in G. W. Allport, ed., *The Person in Psychology: Selected Essays* (Boston: Beacon Press, 1968).

E. H. Erikson, "Identity and Identity Diffusion," in C. Gordon and K. J. Gergen, eds., *The Self in Social Interaction* (New York: Wiley, 1968).

E. Fromm, *Man for Himself* (New York: Holt, Rinehart and Winston, 1947).

R. R. Holt, "Individuality and Generalization in the Psychology of Personality," *Journal of Personality*, 1962, **30,** 377–402.

W. Mischel, *Personality and Assessment* (New York: Wiley, 1968).

SUGGESTED READINGS

Allport G. W., *Personality: A Psychological Interpretation*. New York: Holt, 1937.

Allport G. W., *Becoming: Basic Considerations for a Psychology of Personality*. New Haven: Yale University Press, 1955.

Allport G. W., *Personality and Social Encounter*. Boston: Beacon Press, 1960.

Allport G. W., *Pattern and Growth in Personality*. New York: Holt, Rinehart and Winston, 1961.

Allport G. W., *The Person in Psychology: Selected Essays*. Boston: Beacon Press, 1968.

GLOSSARY

Becoming. Developmental process involving movement toward self-realization.

Bodily Self. Feelings that people have about themselves as a result of feedback from their physical senses.

Cardinal Trait. Characteristic of the individual that serves as the motivating force for virtually all of his or her behavior.

Central Trait. Important characteristic that controls the behavior of an individual in a variety of situations.

Common Trait. Disposition we share with others.

Functional Autonomy. Process whereby a behavior that was once controlled by a motive no longer is dependent on the operation of that motive for its occurrence. It is now said to function or operate independently of the motive.

Genotype. Inherited characteristic that may or may not be reflected in the phenotype or outward appearance of the individual.

Idiographic View. Approach to science that seeks to understand the uniqueness of a given individual's behavior through intensive investigation.

Nomothetic View. Scientific approach to the study of behavior that seeks to establish laws by specifying the general relationships between variables.

Personal Disposition. Trait unique to the individual.

Phenotype. Outward appearance of a particular characteristic that may or may not reflect the underlying inherited genotype.

Propriate Striving. Motive that propels the individual toward attainment of important, long-range goals. These drives involve an increase, rather than a decrease, in tension.

Proprium. Term used by Allport to signify all the various aspects of the person that make him or her unique. A synonym for the self.

Psychophysical System. Way of conceptualizing the organization of inner experience through the use of psychological concepts to represent actual underlying states in the nervous system.

Secondary Trait. Peripheral characteristic such as a preference.

Self-Acceptance. Term used to describe the person's tolerance and understanding of his limitations, as well as a recognition of his strengths.

Self as Rational Coper. Time during which individuals see themselves as capable of rationally formulating and utilizing strategies in order to attain personal goals.

Self-Esteem. Feelings a person has about his or her worth.

Self-Extension. Feelings people have about their possessions. They are seen as an important part of their selves.

Self-Identity. Feelings people have about themselves that they are established human beings who have a past that is unique and that guides their judgments.

Self-Image. Roles people play in order to win the approval of others and the formulation of plans and behavioral strategies for the future that help people attain their goals.

Self-Objectification. Ability of an individual to divorce himself or herself from emotional entanglements in problems and to see them realistically. It also involves a recognition of one's own abilities and limitations.

Trait Theory. Conception of personality that postulates the existence of underlying dispositions or characteristics that direct behavior. Traits are typically inferred from overt behavior.

Raymond Bernard Cattell (Courtesy of Raymond Cattell)

7

CATTELL'S FACTOR ANALYTIC THEORY

BIOGRAPHICAL SKETCH

Raymond Bernard Cattell was born in Staffordshire, England, in 1905. He received a bachelor of science degree in chemistry from the University of London when he was nineteen and his Ph.D. in psychology from the same institution in 1929. While at the university, he served as a research assistant to the famous psychologist-mathematician Charles Spearman, who was keenly interested in determining whether there was one general ability or intelligence, or whether people were made up of many different and specific abilities. To answer that question, he gave a large series of tests pertinent to the issue, intercorrelated the test scores, and came to the conclusion that there was, indeed, a single general intelligence factor. Today in psychology the tendency is to focus more on the specific abilities people possess and to utilize their scores for particular skill measures to predict performance, but the point is that, in attempting to answer the question of general versus specific abilities, Spearman devised the method of factor analysis. Cattell has relied heavily on this technique in developing his own theory of personality.

From Spearman and his intellectual predecessors, British scientist Sir Francis Galton and statistician Karl Pearson, Cattell was introduced to the statistical study of personality and ability functioning. Galton conducted pioneer work on the origins of genius and used statistical analyses on biological data to show associations between phenomena. Pearson later developed a formal, mathematical technique called the Pearson product-moment correlation coefficient to measure the size and direction of the association between two events. This correlation coefficient procedure was later used in the creation of the factor analytic method.

Following his graduation, Cattell served as director of a psychology clinic in England before becoming a research associate of the learning theorist E. L. Thorndike at Columbia University in New York. Following his brief stay at Columbia, he held positions at Clark University, Harvard, and Duke, before accepting a post at the University of Illinois in 1944. He has remained at Illinois until 1973 when he established the Institute for Research on Morality and Self-Realization in Boulder, Colorado.

Two other influences on Cattell's thinking should be mentioned. First, his clinical experience has led him to accept many of the psychoanalytic formulations, so that his theory is an interesting blend of rigorous experimental work and clinical observation. He makes, for example, repeated attempts to apply factor analytic methods to Freud's tripartite scheme of id, ego, and superego. Second, it is clear that Cattell has been greatly influenced by the British social psychologist William McDougall, who espoused an instinct doctrine of social behavior. McDougall made an attempt to "explain" social behavior by postulating seven basic instincts—repulsion, curiosity, flight, pugnacity, self-abasement, self-assertion, and parenting. Through factor analysis, Cattell has argued that there are at least seven ergs or innate drives that influence behavior, including sex, gregariousness, parental protectiveness, pugnacity, curiosity, escape or the need for security, self-assertion, and *narcissistic sex*. Note the similarities between the two positions. Cattell also relies heavily on McDougall's concept of sentiment in his theoretical formulations, as will become apparent.

Over a period of approximately fifty years, Cattell has published dozens of books and literally hundreds of research articles. He has also been the author or coauthor of numerous personality tests, including the Culture-Free Test of Intelligence, the Object-Analytic (O-A) Personality Test Battery, the Institute for Personality and Ability Testing (IPAT) Anxiety Scale Questionnaire, and the popular Sixteen Personality Factor Questionnaire (16 PF).

Among his more notable books, *Description and Measurement of Personality* (1946), is an early attempt to encourage good, solid, empirical research in the area of personality by presenting the basic concepts of his theory and attendant research findings. Published shortly afterward (in 1950), *Personality: A Systematic Theoretical and Factual Study* attempted to build the foundation laid in the earlier work and, in addition, to evaluate data and theories other than his own. These other positions included psychoanalysis, observations from cultural and physical anthropology, and formulations from sociology. Next, Cattell published a text entitled *Personality and Motivation Structure and Measurement* (1957), which presents the most comprehensive treatment of his position. In 1965, he published a popular version of his theory in a text entitled *The Scientific Analysis of Personality*. Some of his recent opinions on the usefulness of the multivariate approach to the study of personality are found in a text he edited called the *Handbook of Multivariate Experimental Psychology* (1966). Cattell continues to be active in research and is currently trying to integrate science with moral and religious issues (Cattell, 1965).

BASIC CONCEPTS AND PRINCIPLES

The Importance of Multivariate Experiments

In order to appreciate fully Cattell's perspective on personality, we must recognize his intense commitment to measurement and statistical analysis in the development of theory. For him, the methodological tail wags the theoretical dog. In other words, Cattell strongly believes that all scientific advances depend upon exact measurement (Cattell, 1950, p. 4). Thus he is disdainful of "armchair speculation" that has no ties to measurement. Measurement provides the foundation from which theories spring, and not the reverse. Before we try to determine *why* a person behaves as he or she does, we need to be able accurately to describe and measure the behavior itself (Cattell, 1950, p. 3).

In order to build a theory, then we start with empirical observation and description and then generate tentative hypotheses based upon this procedure. This in turn leads to certain deductions that we proceed to test empirically. Following our observations, the process begins again. Cattell calls the entire process the *inductive-hypothetico-deductive spiral* (see Figure 7.1). This theory-building technique is in contrast to the hypothetico-deductive model presented in Chapter 1, since it begins with a set of general propositions from which hypotheses are then deduced and tested. Although this model is the one generally employed in the social sciences, Cattell's point is that all too often such theories demand that the researcher have a fully developed hypothesis before starting the research. Such a requirement fails to teach the neophyte investigator about research as an exploratory process.

Second, it leads him to believe that confirmation of his hypothesis rests upon some single measurement difference. According to Cattell, this latter belief is particularly misleading because it encourages the researcher to think that the behavior under consideration was caused by a single event, when in fact it had multiple origins. Of course, Cattell may be knocking down a straw man, since few investigators in contemporary psychology are naive enough to believe that behavior is usually caused by a single event. Nevertheless, one of the important points Cattell raises is that excessive reliance on *bivariate experiments* to test hypotheses leads to oversimplified interpretations of the way events operate in reality. Cattell prefers instead that investigators utilize a multivariate approach to the study of behavior.

In making his case for the use of *multivariate experiments* in psychology, Cattell argues that the bivariate method—that is, the method that relies on the manipulation of an independent variable and the assessment of its impact on a dependent measure—artificially considers "bits" of human behavior and ignores studying the "total organism" (Cattell, 1965, p. 20). In contrast, the multivariate experimenter considers the "whole person" and the complexity of his or her behavior. He ". . . actually *measures* all the variables and . . . then

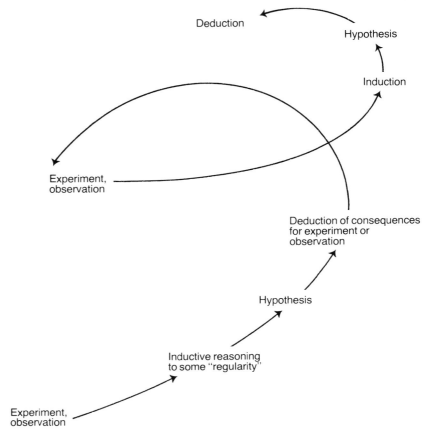

Figure 7.1.
The inductive-hypothetico-deductive spiral. Adapted from R. B. Cattell's
"Psychological Theory and Scientific Method," in R. B. Cattell, ed., *Handbook of Multivariate Experimental Psychology* (Chicago: Rand McNally, 1966), p. 16.

set(s) an electronic computer to abstract the regularities which exist"
(Cattell, 1965, p. 22). In the main, he uses various forms of *factor analysis*
to study multivariate problems.

What Is Factor Analysis?

In general, factor analysis is a statistical method in which many different
measurements are obtained from a single subject or a large group of subjects and then intercorrelated to determine the common or underlying
factors that determine the variation in the surface variables or the variables that appear to be related. In Table 7.1, for example, it is clear that
two clusters of variables appear to go together. Cluster 1 consists of tests
A, B, and C; cluster 2 consists of tests D, E, and F. Thus, the investigator

starts with a large number of surface variables and seeks to reduce them to a few common source factors that can be used to predict the variation in the original measures. Variables that are strongly intercorrelated are considered to be measuring, to a great extent, the same entity or factor. The problem facing the investigator is that he must then eventually label these underlying factors. Since his judgments are subjectively based interpretations that have important implications for future theorizing and research, considerable skill and care must be exercised in the labeling process. Inaccurate interpretations can be costly.

TABLE 7.1   Intercorrelations between Six Test Variables

Test	A	B	C	D	E	F
A Mistrust	—					
B Ego instability	.72	—				
C Guilt	.45	.49	—			
D Verbal comprehension	.02	.04	.07	—		
E Mathematical ability	.08	.18	.00	.58	—	
F Word fluency	.16	.04	.10	.62	.48	—

Once the intercorrelations have been determined, further factor analytic computations are employed to derive a factor matrix, such as the one shown in Table 7.2. The degree of association between each surface variable and the factors are called *factor loadings*. Loadings of .30 and above are usually considered substantial and significant. In Table 7.2 we can see that guilt, is associated with factor I, which we will tentatively label anxiety, at .66, while verbal comprehension is associated with factor II, which we will label intelligence, at .88. Once the factors have been tentatively identified, further research on other samples of subjects is usually conducted in an attempt to refine the factors even more. There will also be attempts to cross-validate the factors by using subjects of different ages, ethnic and cultural backgrounds, and so forth. In addition, other tests may be thrown in the factor analytic "basket" in an effort to discover new variables that load significantly on the factor. Interestingly, too, the primary factors themselves may be further analyzed to yield what Cattell calls *second-order factors*. These higher-order factors control even more of the variation in test score behavior than the *primary factors*. Anxiety and introversion-extraversion are two key examples of second-order factors. Primary factors such as ego weakness, guilt-proneness, innate tension, and suspiciousness all load on the general second-order anxiety factor, for example.

With this preliminary information about the mechanics of factor analysis in hand, let us examine Cattell's definition of personality and some of the other major concepts in his theory.

TABLE 7.2 Loading of Six Tests on Two Factors Labeled Anxiety and Intelligence

Test	Factor I	Factor II
A Mistrust	.52	.15
B Ego instability	.81	.08
C Guilt	.66	.04
D Verbal comprehension	.11	.88
E Mathematical ability	.03	.69
F Word Fluency	.19	.47

The Formula for Defining Personality

Personality is defined as "that which tells what a man will do when placed in a given situation" (Cattell, 1965, pp. 117–118). In line with his concern with the mathematical analysis of personality, Cattell then presents the definition in terms of a formula, as follows:

$$R = f(S.P)$$

The formula signifies that the behavioral response (R) of a person is a function (f) of the situation (S) that confronts him and the nature of his personality (P). Although Cattell fully recognizes the nature of the situation as a vital concept in the prediction of behavior, he deemphasizes it in developing his theory and focuses instead on personality factors such as innate drives, interests, abilities, and especially traits.

What Are Traits and How Do They Come into Being?

Traits are relatively permanent and broad reaction tendencies, according to Cattell, and serve as the building blocks of personality. They may be determined by biology (constitutional traits) and/or by environment (environmental-mold traits). They can be further subdivided into abilities, temperament traits, and dynamic traits. *Ability traits* refer to the person's skill in dealing with the complexity of a given situation. Intelligence would be a good example of an ability trait in Cattell's scheme. *Temperament traits* refer to the stylistic tendencies of the individual. For instance, people may be either chronically irritable, moody, easy-going, or bold. *Dynamic traits* refer to the motivation and interests of the person. A person may be characterized, for example, as ambitious, power-oriented, or interested in athletics. (Cattell, 1965, p. 28).

In addition to these distinctions, Cattell, like Allport, thinks that categorizing traits as either common or unique is useful. Common traits refer to characteristics shared by many people—for example, intelligence, confidence, powerlessness; unique traits are those specific to one person—for example, Bill is the only person with an interest in collecting 1898 census records for the cities of Baltimore and Los Angeles. Virtually all of Cattell's work focuses on common traits, but the incorporation of the unique trait concept into his theory provides a means for him to emphasize the fact that our personalities are unique. He also points out that the organization of common traits within our personalities is always unique.

Surface versus Source Traits. The distinction between *surface* and *source* traits is perhaps the most important one Cattell makes. In his view, a surface trait is ". . . simply a collection of trait elements, of greater or lesser width of representation which obviously 'go together' in many different individuals and circumstances" (Cattell, 1950, p. 21). These are variables which, when intercorrelated, cluster together. The source trait, in contrast, is the underlying factor that controls the variation in the surface cluster of traits. Surface and source traits are measured by the methods of factor analysis. Once we have accurately identified the major source traits controlling behavior, we should be in a better position to predict the person's behavior accurately, assuming, of course, that we have sufficient information about his ways of reacting in a given situation.

Major Source Traits

To reveal the underlying structure of personality, Cattell and his co-workers have spent approximately forty years measuring the behavior of individuals who differ in age, occupational status, cultural background, and so forth by means of the three data-collection techniques outlined in the Techniques of Assessment section. They have found approximately twenty basic traits (Cattell, 1965, p. 64). These source traits were initially labeled factors A, B, C, D, E, and so on, but later, as more and more evidence accumulated, the factors were identified and given labels. Sixteen of the most basic traits were then used in the construction of the Sixteen Personality Factor Test (16 PF test). The trait names of these factors are shown in Table 7.3. The traits are listed in terms of their importance in controlling variation in behavior, starting with factor A and ending with factor Q. Thus, the possession of information about a person's intelligence (factor B) would allow an investigator to predict his performance on given tasks more effectively than would knowledge about his dominance (factor E).

TABLE 7.3   Major Source Traits on the Sixteen Personality Factor Test*

Low Score Description	Factor		Factor	High Score Description
Reserved* (schizothymia)	A−	vs	A+	Outgoing (affectothymia)
Less Intelligent (low "8")	B−	vs	B+	More Intelligent (high "8")
Emotional (low ego strength)	C−	vs	C+	Stable (high ego strength)
Humble (submissiveness)	E−	vs	E+	Assertive (dominance)
Sober (desurgency)	F−	vs	F+	Happy-go-lucky (surgency)
Expedient (low superego)	G−	vs	G+	Conscientious (high superego)
Shy (threctia)	H−	vs	H+	Venturesome (parmia)
Toughminded (harria)	I−	vs	I+	Tender-minded (premsia)
Trusting (alaxia)	L−	vs	L+	Suspicious (protension)
Practical (praxernia)	M−	vs	M+	Imaginative (autia)
Forthright (artlessness)	N−	vs	N+	Shrewd (shrewdness)
Placid (assurance)	O−	vs	O+	Apprehensive (guilt-proneness)
Conservative (conservatism)	Q_1-	vs	Q_1+	Experimenting (radicalism)
Group-tied (group adherence)	Q_2-	vs	Q_2+	Self-Sufficiency (self-sufficiency)
Casual (low integration)	Q_3-	vs	Q_3+	Controlled (high self-concept)
Relaxed (low ergic tension)	Q_4-	vs	Q_4+	Tense (ergic tension)

*Popular terms are not enclosed in parentheses; technical terms are.

Adapted from R. B. Cattell, *The Scientific Analysis of Personality*, 1965, p. 365.

To measure the traits, study participants are given hundreds, even thousands, of items. Then their scores are factor analyzed. Some sample items for factor A are given in Table 7.4. Once the factors begin to emerge, other items are added and given to additional large groups of normal study participants in order to refine the factors. That is, the items that load most heavily on each factor are retained; the ones that do not are eliminated.

TABLE 7.4 Sample Items on the 16 PF for Factor A (Reserved vs. Outgoing)

1. I would rather work as:	
a. an engineer	b. *a social science teacher**
2. I could stand being a hermit.	
a. True	b. *False*
3. I am careful to turn up when someone expects me.	
a. *True*	b. False
4. I would prefer to marry someone who is:	
a. a thoughtful companion	b. *effective in a social group*
5. I would prefer to read a book on:	
a. *national social service*	b. new scientific weapons
6. I trust strangers.	
a. sometimes	b. *practically always*

*A person who answers the items by choosing the italized alternatives has an outgoing temperament.

Adapted from R. B. Cattell, *The Scientific Analysis of Personality*, 1965, p. 70.

Factor A. The largest factor, factor A, turned out to be a dimension long recognized by psychiatrists as important in the differentiation of individuals who had been committed to mental hospitals. As Cattell notes, the German psychiatrist Kraepelin first defined schizophrenia in terms of withdrawal, and later the Swiss psychiatrist Bleuler devised a classification scheme in which "insane" people were categorized as either cyclic or schizophrenic types. In the 1920s, Kretschmer, a German psychiatrist who did pioneering research on the relationship between physique and psychopathology, insisted that the types recognized by Bleuler were also found in less extreme form in normal individuals. Kretschmer showed that these types were associated with certain body builds; schizothymes (schizophrenics) tended to be tall and thin, while cyclothymes (manic-depressives) tended to be plump (Cattell, 1965, pp. 65–66). Thus, a long history of clinical observation and research findings supports the differentiation of individuals as either reserved or outgoing.

Factor C. Another main personality factor that emerged via statistical analysis was ego-strength (factor C). This source trait is very similar to the psychoanalytic concept of ego-strength. Research in many different laboratories in this country and in Great Britain shows that people who are neurotic or highly anxious also tend to have low ego-strength. Cattell points out that alcoholics, narcotics addicts, juvenile delinquents, and school dropouts are abnormally low in ego-strength. The essence of the factor involves an inability to control one's impulses and to deal realistically with problems (Cattell, 1965, pp. 73–74).

Factor E. People who have scores high on factor E, submissiveness-dominance, show these characteristics: Those who are dominant (E+) are self-assertive, boastful, conceited, aggressive, vigorous, forceful, willful, and egotistical; those who are submissive (E−) tend to be unsure, modest, retiring, meek, quiet, and obedient. Note that almost all source traits have good and bad aspects at either pole. This means that a person whose scores load on the E+ pole may have both positive and negative characteristics, as may a person whose scores load on E− (Cattell, 1965, pp. 90–91). For example, a person whose scores indicate dominance (E+) has the positive characteristics of vigor and forcefulness and the negative characteristics of conceit and egotism. Similarly, a submissive individual (E−) has the positive traits of modesty and quietness and the negative traits of uncertainty and excessive meekness.

Cattell mentions that men and boys score higher on dominance than women and girls. So do firefighters, Olympic champions, and pilots. Neurotics who are improving also show increases in dominance. But dominance is also prevalent in psychopaths—for example, in con artists and incorrigible criminals (Cattell, 1965, p. 92).

Factor F. Factor F, surgency-desurgency, is the largest single factor in children, according to Cattell, and is quite important in the personalities of adults. *Surgency* people are characterized as cheerful, joyous, sociable, responsive, energetic, witty, humorous, and talkative. Those high in *desurgency* are characterized as depressed, pessimistic, seclusive, retiring, subdued, introspective, and worrying. In connection with his discussion of the surgency factor, Cattell poses the rhetorical question of why psychology creates so many neologisms like surgency; his answer is that the popular counterparts of these terms are often misleading. Although "sociable" might seem adequate to describe surgency, for example, Cattell argues that surgency includes not only sociability, but other traits as well. In addition, the *quality* of the person's sociability will vary depending on whether we are talking about his test scores on factor A or factor F. The sociability incorporated in factor A refers to a warm, gentle "liking to be around people" orientation, whereas the sociability covered in factor F refers to a person who is slightly exhibitionistic, the "life of the party," with a practical joking side bordering on crudeness (Cattell, 1965, pp. 92–93). These are the reasons, then, for Cattell's frequent invention of terms.

Factors G and H. Factor G, superego strength, is similar in many respects to Freud's concept of the superego. People who are high in superego strength tend to be persistent in their pursuit of ideals and concerned with exercising self-control over their actions (Cattell, 1965, p. 94).

Factor H, *parmia* vs. *threctia*, refers to a source trait Cattell believes to have the highest degree of inheritance among all the personality factors. This contention is supported by physiological data that show a smaller and slower reaction in H+ (adventuresome) individuals (Cattell, 1965, p. 95). To say that the data supporting Cattell's argument are meager would be an understatement. In addition, it is unclear why the trait must be attributed primarily to constitutional sources. Is it not possible that the threctic individual (H−), a person highly susceptible to threats, could have learned to show prolonged reactions to stress? In any event, the label "parmia" is derived from the contention that ". . . the H+ person is one in whom the normal parasympathetic performance predominance is not easily shaken by sympathetic system (threat) or other interrupting responses" (Cattell, 1957, p. 130). The word "parmia" is based upon a shortening of the term "parasympathetic immunity," while "threctia" comes from the term "threat reactivity." The parmic individual is characterized as bold, adventurous, gregarious, genial, and responsive; the threctic person tends to be shy, timid, aloof, and self-contained (Cattell, 1965, p. 95).

Factor I. Source trait I is labeled *premsia* (tender-mindedness) versus *harria* (toughmindedness). Premsia is short for *pro*tected *emo*tional *sen*sitivity; harria comes from the term *hard rea*lism. According to Cattell, people learn to be either tenderminded or toughminded. Tendermindedness is associated with parental overprotection and indulgence, whereas toughmindedness is related to strict parental disciplining. I+ individuals are impatient, demanding, immature, gentle, sentimental, imaginative, and anxious. I− people are mature, independent-minded, realistic, and self-sufficient. Cattell has also found that I+ people are more creative and more neurotic. In addition, he notes that older cultures tend to be more premsic, whereas pioneer cultures such as those of the United States and Australia are more harric (Cattell, 1965, pp. 96–98).

Factors L and M. Factor L, is labeled alaxia vs. protension. The word "alaxia" is apparently a shortening of the term *relax*ation, while "protension" is derived from the words *pro*jection and *ten*sion. Protensives tend to be suspicious, jealous, and withdrawn; alaxics are trusting, understanding, and composed (Cattell, 1957, p. 143).

Factor M is labeled *praxernia* vs. *autia*. "Autia" (M+) is derived from the term *aut*istic and refers to people who are unconventional, fastidious, absorbed, highly imaginative, and intellectual. "Praxernia" is derived from the term *pra*ctical and conc*ern*ed and refers to individuals who are conventional, practical, conscientious, logical, and worrying. In the neurotic, the M+ person has a tendency to become completely absorbed in his own thoughts and to have a disregard for practical planning. In other words, he is a person who tends to be removed, at times, from the demands of external reality. The M− person, in contrast, is very much concerned with the demands of the environment and tends to pay excessive attention to detail. Cattell contends that M− may be the basis for obsessive-compulsiveness (Cattell, 1957, pp. 147–149).

Other Factors. The remaining factors account for a small proportion of the variation in behavior and have labels that are largely self-explanatory. One factor of considerable interest to the general public and scientific investigators alike, however, is radicalism-conservatism. Cattell found that radicals tend to believe in evolution rather than in judgments given by authority figures in the Old Testament. They also rely less upon conventional rules than conservatives—that is, they conform less to society's expectations of them. Cattell also reports that other research has shown that radicals like to engage in self-analysis, prefer dealing with complicated problems, and enjoy discussing the serious questions of life with friends more than do conservatives (Cattell, 1957, p. 209).

In a recent study, investigators first hypothesized that conservatives have a generalized fear of uncertainty and, as a consequence, would be more likely than liberals to express an aversion to complex and abstract art works. They had college students express their feelings toward twenty paintings judged by an art expert to differ in terms of uncertainty. The paintings were categorized as simple representational, simple abstract, complex representational, and complex abstract. As expected, conservatives preferred paintings that were simple and representational (literal) in nature and strongly disliked paintings that were complex and abstract. Liberals, in contrast, tended to prefer the more complex and abstract paintings (Wilson, Ausman, and Mathews, 1973).

Recent Research with the 16 PF

Once these major factors had been identified and utilized in the construction of a reliable measure of personality, attempts were made to use it in generating hypotheses about the behavior of people. In one study, for example, researchers were concerned with examining the relationship between the quality of the marriage relationship and the personality of husbands and wives. Marriages were first defined as stable or unstable and then the personality traits of husbands and wives in both groups were compared. Stability was operationally defined as "any known step being taken toward dissolution." It was found that stable marriages were characterized by similarities in the personality traits of the couples, whereas unstable marriages were composed of individuals with dissimilar characteristics.

A more recent study (Burton and Cattell, 1972) tried to refine the work of earlier researchers by looking at specific marital dimensions and personality traits instead of at the global concept of stability-instability. The marital dimensions included ratings by married couples of the degree of sexual gratification in the marriage, the amount of togetherness and role sharing, wife adequacy (measured by the degree of interest shown by the wife in keeping her home neat and clean and in doing most of the housework), the degree of participation in community affairs, the degree of social and intellectual equality between the spouses, the stability of the marriage, amount of social integration, work performance, social influence, masculine dominance, wife adequacy II, and division of influence. Amount of social integration referred to the number of activities that all family members, including the children, could do together. Work performance was measured by items that revealed whether or not each member of the family had his or her own set of jobs to do. Social influence referred to the party who had most influence over the other in social matters. Wife adequacy II referred to the degree of participation by the wife in decision-making, and division of influence assessed which spouse was the main source of influence in such matters as sex, child rearing, spending, and so forth. Married students filled out the Marriage Role Questionnaire (MRQ), which contained these dimensions and the 16 PF. The data were then analyzed to determine how the personality traits were related to the specific marital dimensions.

In general, the results were as follows: Spouses who were guilt-prone, highly anxious, and low in ego-strength were dissatisfied sexually, findings which are not too surprising. In regard to the "togetherness and role sharing" factor, couples who were highly anxious, guilt-ridden, and shy were more likely to have difficulty in agreeing with their mates on a variety of issures and in sharing problems. Couples who were high on exvia (extraversion) and low on anxiety reported high participation in community activities. Subjects who were highly anxious also reported that they had marriages in which job responsibilities were clearly established, but that they did not have much say in choice of friends and in other matters relating to the household. Spouses who controlled such matters (number of children planned, the way money should be spent) tended to be dominant, enthusiastic, and venturesome. Such subjects were also high on contertia—that is, they tended to use cognition rather than feelings in problem-solving. Not unexpectedly, their marriages were most unstable.

Finally, in regard to the "home devotion" factor, spouses high on superego strength (conscientious and responsible spouses) and on extraversion and compulsivity were the ones who scored high on home devotion. The authors speculated that perhaps an easy-going nature is important because such a trait could help the person combat the repetition and drugery involved in keeping a home neat and tidy (Burton and Cattell, 1972). Attention to detail would also be an asset, assuming that it did not permeate the person's life and keep her or him from functioning effectively in other areas.

It should be mentioned in connection with this study and in many others involving factor analytic techniques that it is impossible to establish causal directions in these relationships. For example, it is possible that the lack of sharing of problems between the partners caused them to be anxious and not that their anxiety caused them to disagree and to withdraw from one another. Of course, other extraneous variables could have produced the relationship between high anxiety and high disagreement. In addition, we have to exercise caution in accepting the labels the authors attach to their factors. This is largely an impressionistic undertaking and can be misleading to the reader. Is a wife's adequacy really measured by the degree of interest she shows in keeping her house neat and tidy and by her doing most of the work? Not only the women's liberationists would take strong issue with that assessment! Perhaps a more appropriate label for the factor would be "traditional homemaker's responsibilities." In any event, keep these criticisms in mind as we continue to explore Cattell's theory.

Specification Equation

Although Cattell has been able to isolate and measure reliably a number of key source traits in personality, he still recognizes that any viable theory of human functioning must be able to predict individual differences in behavior accurately. Accordingly, he has devised a mathematical formula that allows investigators to make such predictions. It is called a *specification equation* because it specifies the ways in which traits are to be combined to predict any performance. The equation Cattell proposes is as follows:

$$R = b_1 A_1 + b_2 B_2 + b_3 C_3 + \ldots + b_n K_n$$

In the formula, R is the performance or "response" of an individual in a given situation, and A, B, C, through K are source traits pertinent to the specific prediction of performance for the person. The small *b*s are weights or behavioral situation indices. These weights are unique to each factor or source trait and show the degree to which each is involved in the situation under consideration (Cattell, 1965, pp. 78–80).

These weights for specific situations are generated by experimentation in which the performances of large groups of individuals are assessed and the relative importance of certain source traits is determined by factor analysis. Then these weights are used in the general equation, along with the individual's own scores, as a means of predicting performance. Suppose, for example, we are interested in predicting Jim's golf performance. On the basis of testing large groups of young male adults, let us assume we know that intelligence (factor B) is the most important factor in golfing effectiveness (that is, that intelligence is very highly correlated with golfing success), followed by stability (factor C), surgency (factor F) and assertiveness (factor E). Assume also that the weights can vary from .00 to 1.00, with a weight of 1.00 signifying maximum loading or highest importance. We might then assign the weights as follows:

$$R = .8B + .6C + .3F + .2E$$

We would insert the individual's own scores on these factors and solve the equation. If trait scores could vary between zero and 100, with scores of 100 indicating maximum intelligence, stability, surgency, and assertiveness, and if Jim's scores were intelligence 40, stability 10, surgency 40, and assertiveness 20, his golfing performance would be predicted as follows:

$$R = .8(40) + .6(10) + .3(40) + .2(20)$$
$$R = 32 + 6 + 12 + 4$$
$$R = 54$$

Maximum golfing performance would be predicted by the following equation:

$$R = .8(100) + .6(100) + .3(100) + .2(100)$$
$$R = 80 + 60 + 30 + 20$$
$$R = 190$$

Since a maximum performance score is 190 and Jim's score was 54, we conclude that Jim will perform rather poorly.

The trait combination model just presented is linear and additive in nature. Cattell says we should use it if it helps us to predict behavior accurately and we should modify or even abandon it if it does not. At this point, however, Cattell thinks that a linear model and not a curvilinear one is adequate for the prediction of much of our behavior (Cattell, 1965, p. 252). We could use it to predict academic performance and job success, for example. It is a multidimensional model that includes a complex representation of the ways in which traits are dynamically interrelated in the person and how they operate in various situations.

Dynamic Traits and the Dynamic Lattice

Dynamic traits are traits that "power" or propel the person into action. They are dispositions that motivate the person to behave in certain ways. In Cattell's theory, they are further subdivided into attitudes, sentiments, and ergs. Attitudes are defined as specific interests in particular courses of action toward certain objects in a given situation (Cattell, 1965, p. 175). Cattell views them as hypothetical constructs that intervene between environmental stimuli and eventual external responses. The attitude of a woman student, for example, might be "I want very much to kiss this handsome guy the next time we go out together." The attitude shows an intense interest (I want very much) in a particular course of action (to kiss) toward a specific object (this handsome guy) in a given situation (the next time we go out together). Ergs and sentiments are inferred from the factor analytic study of attitudes. For example, a man may have a timid disposition that is based upon an underlying fear erg (Cattell, 1950, p. 84).

Sentiments are large and complex attitudes, according to Cattell. Sentiments incorporate a host of interests, opinions, and minor attitudes. For instance, a man's sentiment about his home may be seen in his attitudes about his wife, his children, and about marriage in general, as well as in his interests in home repairs and landscaping and so forth (Cattell, 1950, pp. 161–162). Such a sentiment would be learned over a long period of time. Sentiments are characterized by Cattell as *environmental-mold* traits—that is, as traits learned via experience with people.

An *erg*, according to Cattell, is ". . . an innate psycho-physical disposition which permits its possessor to acquire reactivity (attention, recognition) to certain classes of objects more readily than others, to experience a specific emotion in regard to them, and to start on a course of action which ceases more completely at a certain specific goal activity than at any other" (Cattell, 1950, p. 199). In short, ergs are innate drives triggered by stimuli in the environment that cease when the goal of the erg is reached. For example, the parental erg is released by cries of distress from children and satisfied when they are out of danger. (See the biographical sketch for a list of the other drives Cattell maintains are innate.)

Why does Cattell think these drives are innate? He bases his judgment on findings in both naturalistic and clinical observation studies. Naturalistic studies involve observation of behavior in lower mammals analogous to behavior in human beings and general observations of human behavior in a wide variety of situations and cultures. It is inconceivable to Cattell that human beings who are clearly related structurally and functionally to the mammals and primates, could lack the instinctual equipment they possess. It should also be clear, however, that human beings possess a more highly developed and sophisticated brain, along with skills to communicate through language, which make them much more flexible and adaptable than the lower mammals.

Another argument voiced by Cattell to show that certain drives are innate concerns the universality of the behavior. If a particular behavior pattern—for example, pugnacity or aggressiveness—is seen universally, despite cultural variations, then it is usually considered to be innate. Finally, drives are considered to be innate if the behavior pattern persists in spite of environmental training. In light of these criteria, it is difficult to understand why Cattell continues to believe that aggressiveness is innate. First, there is considerable evidence that aggressive behavior is not predominant in all cultures. In some cultures aggression is devalued and people are punished for hurting others. Even within cultures, there is considerable diversity in socialization practices and consequently in the amounts and kinds of aggressive behavior shown. As social learning theorist Bandura (see Chapter 11) points out, different socialization practices among American Indian groups produced marked differences in aggressiveness between them. For example, the Comanches and the Apaches trained their children to be warriors, whereas the Hopi and the Zuni encouraged theirs to be cooperative and peaceful. In addition, some religious sects emphasize pacifism as a way of life. Bandura also notes that there are clear differences in the amount of aggression shown by members of different social classes in our society (Bandura, 1973, p. 112). Parents in many working class homes, for example, actively encourage and model aggressive behavior for their children, while middle-class parents tend to encourage verbal discussion as a means of resolving conflicts.

A great deal of research dealing with the learning and modification of aggressive behavior is reviewed in Chapter 11, so we will not dwell any longer on the inadequacies of Cattell's arguments. In fairness, we must point out that most social scientists today agree that behavior is a function of the interaction between biological and social factors. Cattell has not ignored that fact, but he has tried to show how innate tendencies, as well as learning experiences, affect behavior. But the evidence he cites in support of the biological determinants of behavior is one-sided and in some respects obsolete. There is little mention, for example, of the tremendous research literature on the ways in which social learning experiences affect behavior. From a physiological perspective, too, there are scholarly reviews that seriously question the findings of ethologists like Lorenz, Hess, and Tinberger who make inferences about instincts in humans and the lower animals on the basis of naturalistic observation, reviews Cattell never mentions (Lehrman, 1953; Meyer, 1955; Fletcher, 1957; Montagu, 1968). The dynamic traits he uses in his personality theory are further postulated to be organized in complex ways within the cognitive and motivational structure of the organism. The traits are interrelated in a *dynamic lattice.* He also relies heavily on Murray's concept of *subsidiation* to explain how the traits are intertwined. Subsidiation refers to a process whereby certain traits control and lead to the occurrence of other traits. In order for a person to achieve the goal of becoming a great concert pianist, he must first learn to serve deferentially as an apprentice to a master pianist. We say that his deference to the master is subsidiated to his achievement drive. We are, in brief, describing a step sequence of traits in which the occurrence of a particular trait is necessary before another trait can occur. Thus, Cattell believes that we must not only be able to describe and measure the various kinds of traits possessed by the person, but also be able to show how they are interconnected (Cattell, 1950, p. 156). To accomplish this latter goal, he thinks we must ask the person why a particular habit or trait is being shown. He also thinks that, although people may not know the answer to the question or may even distort their answers in order to protect themselves, often they will be able accurately to describe the process by which their traits are linked.

When they have described the process, we are left with a complicated and often bewildering intertwining of interests, attitudes, sentiments, goals, and drives. Figure 7.2 presents only a fragment of a dynamic lattice for a hypothetical person involving attitude subsidiation, sentiment structure, and innate goals. At the right of the diagram, we see the ergs; in the middle are the various sentiments; and at the left are a variety of attitudes. We can also note that numerous ergs give expression to various sentiments, that the sentiments are related to one another, that several attitudes converge on the same sentiment, and that a few attitudes are common to different sentiments. For the hypothetical person under consideration, we might speculate that love of his wife is based upon the fact that she satisfies his needs for sex, protection, and companionship. In addition, he knows that he must maintain a healthy bank account to ensure his security and to secure the material goods his wife needs to be happy. Perhaps, then, he will discontinue his frequent recreational trips to New York City for fear it will deplete his account

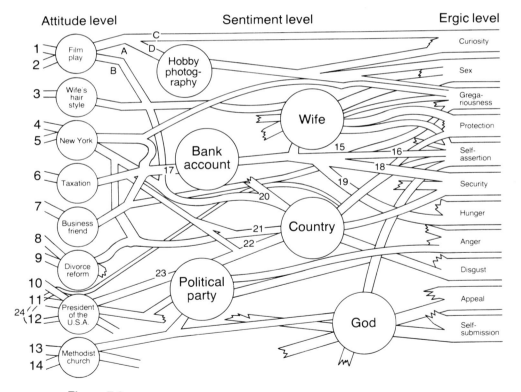

Figure 7.2.
Fragment of a dynamic lattice, showing attitude subsidiation, sentiment, structure, and ergic goal. Adapted from R. B. Cattell, *Personality: A systematic Theoretical and Factual Study* (New York: McGraw-Hill 1950), p. 158.

and create unhappiness for him. Alternatively, he may wish to talk to his business friend about the possibility of reinvesting the money in his account as a means of securing a higher rate of monetary return. Such a tactic, if possible, would ensure maximum satisfaction for both his wife and himself.

Finally, changes in the dynamic lattice can be brought about by changes in the person's environment. However, the attitudes of the person are more susceptible to change than the sentiments, according to Cattell, since sentiments are the deeper, underlying structures in personality. Occasionally, though, real changes in personality can occur. A person may lose his family in a catastrophe, for instance, and this traumatic event will trigger major changes in his functioning (Cattell, 1950, p. 160).

Before turning to a discussion of Cattell's views on personality development, it should be mentioned that the integration of all the attitudes, interests, drives, and sentiments continually at interplay within personality is handled by Cattell's postulation of a master motive called the *self-sentiment*. The self-sentiment interrelates the various attitudes, sentiments, and interests of the person and also regulates the expression of the ergs.

THE PROCESS OF PERSONALITY DEVELOPMENT

The Role of Heredity and the Environment

Unlike any of the other theorists reviewed in this text, Cattell discusses in some detail the physiological influences of the mother on the behavior of the embryo. He believes that such influences can have a tremendous effect on personality. For example, although the specific causes that produce mongolism in children are unknown, there is no doubt that failures in embryonic development are responsible for producing mongoloid human beings who have limited intelligence and personalities with severely restricted behavioral patterns. In addition, abnormalities in the person's metabolism can lead to mental retardation. Cattell also notes that the birth process can have a definite effect on personality. Injuries to the head at birth may produce deficiencies in intelligence and motor coordination, or even paralysis, for example. In regard to temperament, Cattell believes that it is related to the endocrine condition of the mother during the gestation period, although he is not sure about the nature of the relationship. Thus, personality seems to be shaped by the operation of the physiological condition of the mother upon the normal nervous system maturation of the individual *in utero* (Cattell, 1950, pp. 557–559).

In addition to biological influences on personality, Cattell discusses the tremendous impact of the environment. The impact of the environment, however, is not as great during the first year of life as it is later in the developmental process. At first, biological and maturational influences are paramount. Cattell points out research which shows that both in motor and verbal learning untaught twins quickly achieve the same levels of performance as those who have been thoroughly trained (Cattell, 1950, p. 561). His point is that the untrained child may learn particular skills very rapidly once he is mature enough to do so and that he can quickly achieve levels of proficiency which equal those of his well-trained counterpart. As the person grows older, however, the environment does have an increasing impact on the formation of personality.

Role of Learning

Cattell distinguishes between three kinds of learning that are involved in personality formation. They are *classical conditioning, instrumental conditioning* (reward learning), and *integration learning*. As many of you probably know from your introductory psychology course, classical conditioning involves pairing a neutral stimulus with a stimulus that provokes a particular response until the presentation of the neutral stimulus itself is capable of evoking the response. A classical conditioning interpretation has been used to account for the acquisition of many fears and phobias. Cattell believes that classical conditioning can account for some of our individual learning, but not for most of it. He thinks it plays a role in unconscious learning, in the formation of phobias, and in the acquisition of deep and powerful emotional attachments (Cattell, 1965, p. 268).

Much more of our personality learning, according to Cattell, occurs via reward learning. We perform a certain action in order to reach a goal. The rat in the Skinner box presses a bar and receives food pellets. It quickly learns to press the bar. Bar-pressing is instrumental to the attainment of the goal. Under other conditions, the animal presses the bar and is shocked. It quickly learns to avoid pressing the bar. Similarly, a person learns to diet because the weight loss will bring approval from his friends and from his doctor. Or a child takes a cookie without his parents' permission and is spanked. He rapidly learns not to take cookies from the cookie jar, at least not when his parents are in the vicinity.

Cattell argues that reward learning is paramount in the formation of dynamic lattices (Cattell, 1965, p. 269). A student may have a sentiment about his athletic prowess, for instance, and train hard and long. Such training may prove highly rewarding if he subsequently performs at a track meet and wins a race. As a consequence, his sentiment toward athletic prowess is satisfied and so is his erg for self-assertion—that is, his innate need to feel proud. The formation and maintenance of the dynamic lattice will depend upon *confluence learning*—that is, the acquisition of behaviors and attitudes which simultaneously contribute to the satisfaction of two or more different goals (Cattell, 1965, p. 270). For example, the student athlete may develop a positive attitude toward dieting and physical exercise because they satisfy his need for pride (self-assertion erg) and his need to do something different (curiosity erg). Thus, learning may involve the satisfaction of a number of goals within the person's dynamic lattice. The sentiments themselves are learned via reward learning. For example, the student's interest in proving his athletic prowess is perhaps acquired through successful performance.

Finally, Cattell postulates a complex form of learning called integration learning. It appears to be a form of cognitive and instrumental learning in which the developing person uses ego and superego processes to maximize long-term satisfactions. The person learns to seek realistic, alternative solutions to innate drives or ergs as a means of maximizing satisfactions (Cattell, 1965, p. 276). The similarity to Freud's position should be readily apparent. The development of the ego and superego also occurs during the second through the fifth years of life, according to Cattell. Cattell accepts as well Freud's observations that this period is marked by conflicts and is critical in the development of personality (Cattell, 1950, pp. 573–575).

With the shift in loyalty from parents to peers, Cattell sees the period of six through thirteen as a carefree one in which the child continues to strengthen his ego and extend his love beyond his parents and himself to others. It is a period of consolidation. During adolescence, there are rapid physical changes in boys and girls and increases in emotional instability, social awkwardness, and sex interests, along with augmented concerns about being altruistic and contributing to society. The primary sources of conflict during this period are "(a) the task of gaining independence from the parents; (b) the task of gaining status in an occupation, preparing for that occupation, and achieving economic self-support; (c) achieving satisfactory sex expression by winning a mate; and (d) achieving a stable, integrated personality and a satisfactory self-concept" (Cattell, 1950, p. 594). These conflicts are due, in Cattell's opinion, to both biological and environmental influences.

Maturity is the period from twenty-five to fifty-five and is a time of little basic personality change. Although there is a slight decline in biological efficiency (for example, increased problems with hearing and vision and a slowing of metabolic rate), Cattell believes that, due to learning and experience, increases in creativity are possible. There is an increase in emotional stability for both sexes (Cattell, 1950, pp. 610, 611, 613). Maturity also is a period in which adjustments need to be made. There is the discovery that adolescent dreams and aspirations are, in many respects, unrealistic. Near the end of maturity, when there is increased leisure time, there is a tendency to revive romantic interests.

Cattell cites the Kinsey Report as showing that men tend to have a revived interest in extramarital affairs. In women, with the approach of the menopause, there is a wistful longing for romance (Cattell, 1950, p. 616).

In old age, there is a more rapid decline in physical powers. Performance on tasks demanding ingenuity suffers, whereas performance on tasks requiring experience remains steady. Cattell supports the views of some modern psychiatrists who argue that the following characteristics are typical of people in old age:

Worry over finances

Worry over health

Feeling unwanted, isolated, lonely

Feeling suspicious

Narrowing of interest

Loss of memory

Mental rigidity

Overtalkativeness, especially of the past

Hoarding, often of trivial things

Feeling(s) of inadequacy, leading to feelings of insecurity and anxiety

Feeling(s) of guilt, irritability

Reduction of sexual activity but increased sexual interest, especially in the male

Untidiness, uncleanliness

Conservatism

Inability to adjust to changed conditions

Decreased social contacts and participation (Cattell, 1950, pp. 618–619)

While it is impossible to deny that there is physical deterioration in old age and that this deterioration may manifest itself in lessened performance in various situations, it is not at all clear that the negative characteristics frequently attributed to the elderly are accurate. Old people do not necessarily lack confidence or feel powerless, and they are not necessarily wracked by guilt and anxiety. Indeed, there are many old people who are competent, satisfied with their situations, and actively engaged in meaningful activities. In the final analysis, a more realistic appraisal of both the strengths and deficiencies associated with old age is needed. We need to move away from the concept of the elderly as "doddering old codgers" who cannot tie their shoelaces and also from the glorification of the period as the "golden years" when "senior citizens" flower and prosper without a care in the world.

The Theory of Abnormal Development

Cattell accepts the clinical notion that neurosis and psychosis are based on unresolved conflicts within the person, and seeks to develop quantitative techniques to aid the therapist in diagnosis and treatment. He envisions the conflicts of the person in Freudian terms—as involving struggles between the id, ego, and superego—and calls for the development of a "quantitative psychoanalysis" (Cattell, 1965, p. 230). For example, a man's interest in marrying one of two women is based on the operation of a number of ergs and other personality factors. Cattell gives a simplified version of the formula that could be utilized by a clinician to predict the way in which the man would resolve his conflict. The formulas, with slight modifications, are as follows:

$$I_{Jane} = 0.6E_{sex} + 0.5E_{Greg} + 0.3M_{superego}$$
$$I_{Sally} = 0.6E_{sex} + 0.3E_{Greg} + 0.3M_{superego}$$

In this example, the man is in real conflict because the various ergs and the superego sentiment are approximately equal in strength. Yet, since the gregariousness erg is slightly stronger for Jane, the decision would be in her favor. In ordinary language, both women satisfy the man's needs for sex equally and are respectable in the eyes of others, but Jane is a more pleasing companion socially than Sally, so he decides to marry Jane (Cattell, 1965, p. 232).

The situation that faces the clinician is much more complicated than this example would suggest, of course; it is provided only for illustrative purposes. Cattell also proposes that the clinician rely on diagnostic tools which have been empirically validated in trying to understand the clients' conflicts. These tools—for example, the 16 PF—provide a means of assessing the major factors in personality that includes not only the Freudian structures of id, ego, and superego, but also the various attitudes, interests, and sentiments of the client (Cattell, 1961, chap. 14).

Definition of Neurosis. For Cattell, a neurosis is the "pattern of behavior shown by those individuals who come to a clinic for aid because they feel themselves to be in emotional difficulties (and who do not have that kind of disorder which a psychiatrist recognizes as psychosis)" (Cattell, 1965, p. 209). He uses such an operational definition because he is convinced that our understanding of neurosis must begin by identifying those measurements which differentiate this group from normal members of the general population. Using this initial criterion, both he and Eysenck, another prominent factor analytic theorist, have found that neurotics do indeed differ from both psychotics and normals on a number of personality dimensions. Thus, neuroticism and psychoticism are not just illnesses that differ in degree. They are different kinds of illness (Cattell, 1965, p. 210). Let us consider the primary factors that have been identified as contributing to neurosis before considering the factors involved in psychosis.

Factors Contribuiting to Neurosis. In terms of family background, Cattell presents evidence that neurotics grow up in families characterized by conflict, inconsistent discipline, and insufficient affection. They are also subjected to parental demands to adhere to excessively high moral standards. This fact, coupled with their genetically based lower than average emotional stability, leads eventually to neurosis (Cattell, 1950, p. 497).

On the basis of countless factor analytic studies by Cattell and scores of other investigators, the following factors have been tentatively identified as contributing to neurosis: Neurotics have been found to be low in ego-strength or emotional stability, high on autia and premsia, and low on surgency and dominance (Cattell, 1965, p. 211). In regard to autia, Cattell has found that neurotics tend to disregard externals and social necessities and to refuse to change their ideas to bring them into line with acknowledged facts. They are also high in premsia on the I factor, showing extreme and indiscriminate emotional sensitivity to others and a considerable amount of capricious behavior. Furthermore, Cattell claims that neurotics are shy and inhibited generally. He also points out that their low ego-strength means that they are easily overcome by their emotions, are subject to moods, and cannot adjust their behavior to the realities of given situations (Cattell, 1965, p. 212).

Above all, neurotics tend to be highly anxious. Cattell traces their anxiety to various sources. It may arise because the ergic tension of the person is unsatisfied. Cattell is true to his Freudian roots when he notes that ergic drives for sex and pugnacity (aggression) are more frequently punished in our society and, as a consequence, can give rise to high levels of anxiety. Consistent also with the orthodox Freudian position, Cattell maintains that anxiety can arise as a result of low ego-strength and a highly punitive superego. In very original fashion, Cattell also makes the major point that the high levels of anxiety most neurotics show may be partially a result of a constitutional proneness to threat reactivity. In other words, neurotics may be more biologically sensitive to threats than normals. Furthermore, Cattell argues that these high levels of anxiety may be partially caused by a self-sentiment with breadth. In short, a person who is committed to a great variety of activities is more vulnerable to threats than one who does not have such a broad range of pursuits. Finally, high levels of anxiety can arise if the individual is forced to deal with many trivial details in his life in order to achieve ergic and self-sentiment satisfactions (Cattell, 1961, pp. 18–22).

While generally in agreement with Cattell on the kinds of variables that contribute to neuroticism, Eysenck maintains Cattell has exaggerated the number of factors needed to account for neurosis. He claims that there are fewer factors and that Cattell found more because he failed to use a factor analytic method to extract second-order factors (Eysenck, 1953, p. 66). The important point, however, is that two major theorists, working independently, are in substantial agreement about the kinds of traits that characterize the neurotic.

Definition of Psychosis. According to Cattell, psychosis is ". . . a form of mental disorder different from neurosis, in which the individual loses contact with reality and needs hospitalization for his own protection and that of others" (Cattell, 1965, p. 373). In comparison to the neurotic, the psychotic lacks insight into his problems, is unable to take care of himself, and may be a threat to others.

Factors Contributing to Psychosis. Cattell points out that, since there are several distinct types of psychosis, we should not expect to find any single personality dimension that will distinguish the psychotic from the neurotic or the normal (Cattell, 1965, p. 223). It should also be clear that the various types of psychosis will have different etiologies—that is, the causes of the disturbance will be different for each type. Cattell presents evidence which shows, for example, that manic-depressive psychosis is highly inheritable, whereas there is a lesser association between heredity and schizophrenia. By implication, then, the emergence of schizophrenia will depend heavily on the operation of certain environmental factors. One study of thirty families with either schizophrenic or manic-depressive parents showed, for instance, that approximately 8 percent of the children with schizophrenic parents were schizophrenic, whereas 19 percent of the children of manic-depressive parents were manic-depressive (Cattell, 1950, pp. 128–129). We know, of course, that this study and many others like it are marred by serious methodological flaws. We might simply ask the question, "Was it possible for the investigator to control for differences in the family environments of these children, differences that may have conceivably produced the dissimilar disorders?" The answer would have to be "No," thus calling the genetic interpretation into question.

Cattell also points out that differences in family environments contribute to the onset of the two types of psychosis. He reviews evidence which shows that the parents of manic-depressives are warmer and much more overprotective of their children than are the parents of schizophrenics. In contrast, the parents of schizophrenics have been found to be much more ambivalent in their attitudes toward their children (Cattell, 1950, p. 542). In terms of scores on the 16 PF, Cattell reports on the findings of other investigators which show that schizophrenics are low in ego-strength, low in drive tension, and highly introverted and conceited. Manic-depressives, in contrast, are low in intelligence, conservative in temperament, and high on superego (Cattell, 1965, p. 225).

Finally, a factor labeled, appropriately enough, psychoticism has been found by Eysenck to distinguish powerfully between psychotics and normals. In terms of personality traits, Eysenck found that, in comparison to normals, psychotics were less articulate, poorer at solving mathematical problems, slower in tracing lines with a stylus, had poorer memories, and a greater inability to concentrate on the task at hand. They also read more slowly, tended to overestimate distances and test scores, and showed unrealistic levels of aspiration (Eysenck, 1952, p. 217). Cattell is in substantial agreement with Eysenck on these points.

TECHNIQUES OF ASSESSMENT

Cattell can rightfully be called a "psychometrist of personality," since he places such heavy emphasis on the use of various testing and statistical techniques. We have already seen how he uses factor analysis to derive the major traits of personality, for example. In order to apply the factor analytic procedures, however, masses of data must first be collected from large numbers of people. Cattell relies on three major procedures to obtain such data. He calls them the *L-data*, *Q-data*, and *T-data* methods. L-data or "life-record" data refers to the measurement of behavior in actual, everyday situations. Ideally such data would be collected without using rater judgments. Instead, the investigator would collect unobtrusive data, such as the number of automobile accidents the person had over the past twenty years, her marks in school, the number of civic organizations of which she is or has been a member, and so forth. However, Cattell believes such data would be difficult to obtain, so the investigator is forced to take secondhand data; that is, data in the form of a rating by someone who knows the person well. Different aspects of the person's behavior, such as her dependability on the job and her friendliness, would be obtained via trait ratings from coworkers and friends on, for example, ten-point, Likert-type scales.

The second source of information is called Q-data or questionnaire data. Such information is often gathered in an interview situation in which respondents fill out paper-and-pencil tests from which trait scores can be derived. The 16 PF is an excellent example of Q-data.

The third type of data is based upon objective tests and is called T-data. T-data is information gathered by an observer in a standard test situation from a subject who performs without being aware of the dimensions on which he is being scored. Whereas Q-data refers to information that is potentially "fakeable" by subjects, T-data refers to information that is essentially "unfakeable." For example, if a person is asked on a questionnaire whether or not he ever cheats on examinations and he is either too frightened or embarrassed to admit to such behavior, he may fake his answer and report that he never does so, even though he may on rare occasions. In regard to T-data, however, a person may be asked to respond to a Rorschach test in which the inkblots do not provide the subject with unambiguous information he can fake. That is, he does not know the dimensions on which he will eventually be scored by clinical psychologists (Cattell, 1965, pp. 60–62).

Data collected via these methods can then be integrated and utilized in the assessment of the major personality traits. The use of data from various sources makes it more likely that the complex interweavings of the various aspects of personality can be understood more fully.

APPLICATION OF THE THEORY TO THE TREATMENT OF PSYCHOPATHOLOGY

Cattell insists that skillful treatment of mental disorders relies on personality factor assessments which will not only provide a profile for diagnosis, but also a statement about the kinds of constitutional factors that influence behavior (Cattell, 1965, p. 228). In addition, it should not surprise you to learn that he believes the availability of reliable and valid measuring instruments can help the clinician make better judgments about the efficacy of treatment procedures. These judgments can be made by assessing the client's personality before and after therapeutic intervention and noting the amount of change in behavior (Cattell, 1961, p. 413). The P-technique is further suggested as the procedure best able to provide an accurate assessment of the complex changes occurring in the client as he or she moves through therapy. This technique involves testing the person repeatedly on a large number of personality dimensions on a number of different occasions. It provides a means of discovering the unique trait structure of the person (Cattell, 1965, p. 372; 1961, p. 415).

Although all therapy should rest on precise measurement, Cattell believes that astute clinical observation has merit and should be used, but always in conjunction with testing procedures. In this regard and in other respects, he is an eclectic. He appreciates and accepts many of Freud's clinical insights, but he maintains that a therapy built on pronouncements and not on measurement can, in the long run, do serious harm to society. In general, he is contemptuous of the ". . . fanciful and presumptuous theorizing of pre-metric, pre-experimental [theorists]" (Cattell, 1965, p. 333).

He thinks further that a search by the therapist for the causes of a disorder in early traumatic experiences, à la Freud, may be beneficial to the client. By reliving the experiences, the client is in a better position to reevaluate his own emotional reactions and eventually to change his destructive behavior. Some of these changes can be effected, in Cattell's view, via behavior therapy, in which the person is taught new responses to threatening stimuli. Thus, to a limited degree he accepts as valid therapeutic approaches that utilize historical analysis (for example, psychoanalysis) or a direct reconditioning approach (for example, behavior therapy).

Yet in the final analysis, Cattell opts for a view of therapy which recognizes that people with severe disorders are defective throughout their whole personality functioning (Cattell, 1965, p. 335). Measurement procedures must focus on the entirety of the person's trait structure; we cannot simply focus on traumatic experiences involving sex and aggression, nor can we focus only on certain limited and specific areas of behavior change. We must address ourselves to the full range of constitutional personality factors that set limits on the person's performance and to the complex interweaving of traits and sentiments that influence behavior patterns. Obviously, then, we need complex measurement procedures to assess complex underlying structures. Accordingly, some kinds of therapy will prove more effective than others, depending upon the kinds of factors that are causing the specific types of neuroses and psychoses. For example, in psychoses based largely on the operation of constitutional factors, therapy might involve the use of drugs, electric shock, and lobotomy (Cattell, 1950, p. 543). In certain neuroses, on the other hand, therapy might start with analyses of dreams and the reliving of traumatic experiences (Cattell, 1961, p. 415). Where the problem is of a minor and relatively restricted nature, in the sense that it does not involve deep-rooted trauma, behavior therapy might be effective. Thus, Cattell is clearly eclectic in his attitude toward the kinds of treatment to be used in therapy. But he is single-minded in his determination that all therapy should be based on solid measurement procedures.

CRITICAL COMMENTS

We turn now to an examination of the scientific worth of Cattell's theory.

Comprehensiveness. There is little doubt that Cattell has devised a comprehensive theory of personality. His theory addresses itself to a wide range of diverse phenomena, both normal and abnormal. Beyond that, it attempts to account for both the biological and sociocultural factors which jointly influence behavior. We cannot help but be impressed by the range of his interests and efforts in pursuing this formidable task. Although we can question the validity of some of the procedures used to assess these constitutional factors and the amount and quality of the evidence available to support his assertions, it is evident that Cattell has a deeper appreciation and understanding of the role biology plays in determining behavior than most of the other theorists in this book, with the possible exceptions of Sheldon and Freud.

Cattell fully recognizes the complexity of the motives that determine behavior and the fact that an adequate science of psychology must utilize measurement procedures which are equal to the task. As he notes, we can no longer afford to rely so heavily on the bivariate experiment in our research efforts. Its primary shortcomings include the fact that it sometimes precludes the study of vital human matters. Try to imagine doing controlled experiments on bereavement, for example. Next, many important psychological concepts, such as love, justice, or neurosis, cannot be adequately measured operationally by single variables. Third, investigators are occasionally presumptuous in assuming that controlled experiments can lead to results in which the causal connection between events can be determined absolutely. This, of course, is extremely unlikely; in reality, investigators never know whether this kind of control has been achieved (Cattell, 1957, p. 25).

Fortunately, Cattell has not taken an "either-or" position on the merits of the multivariate approach and the deficiencies of the controlled experiment. He does not suggest that investigators abandon the bivariate approach. Instead, he recognizes that both approaches have unique assets. The bivariate approach does allow investigators to make cause-and-effect inferences with greater certainty than do other approaches, for example.

It is thus reasonable to conclude that Cattell recognizes the complexity of personality, has developed a theory that seeks to approximate that reality, and attempts to utilize measurement procedures commensurate with the task.

Precision and Testability. Of all the theorists in this text, Cattell has demonstrated the most concern with the construction of a theory based upon precise measurement. He has steadfastly and painstakingly worked to define and refine his concepts through the use of sophisticated and elaborate factor analytic procedures. Despite this fact, critics have argued that his data are fraught with ambiguities and subjectivity. First, they question his claim that he empirically discovered the underlying traits in personality through the use of factor analytic methods. After all, he is the one who made the decision to include only certain traits in his analyses. This was a subjective and largely arbitrary decision on his part. Given his Freudian background, is it really surprising that he includes psychoanalytic items in his analyses and then labels the resulting factors ego-strength and superego strength? Even if other investigators, working independently, arrive at the same factors, can we really conclude that such factors exist? Maybe they were all profoundly influenced by Freud, a not unlikely possibility in light of his tremendous and revolutionary impact on personality psychology.

We must remember that we are dealing with constructs created by theorists to help them account for phenomena that exist in reality. The constructs are not identical with reality; they are representations of it. Accordingly, some constructs make for a better fit with reality than others. Cattell relies on one set of constructs in trying to understand personality; other investigators may use others. Eventually, we choose between construct systems on the basis of their ability to help us explain phenomena. Factor analyses of constructs, such as traits and sentiments, allow us to discover an underlying structure in a given body of data, but they do not allow us to conclude that the resulting factors give us the real underlying structures of personality. After all, if different researchers start with different assumptions and constructs, the observed factors will differ markedly.

Another related criticism of the factor analytic approach concerns the subjectivity involved in labeling factors. Despite all the concern with objectivity in his measurement procedures, Cattell must still, in the final analysis, use subjective judgment in interpreting the meaning of the factors by labeling them. Cattell recognizes this and advocates caution in applying labels until many different analyses are completed, but the labeling process is still interpretive and rests upon the wisdom of the researcher. As you undoubtedly know by now, some researchers are wiser than others, so that the amount of error in the labeling process will vary considerably. And despite Cattell's concern with accuracy of interpretation, our impression is that he has not paid as much attention to this aspect of his research as he has to the computational part.

These are some, but by no means all, of the criticisms that one can level at Cattell's use of factor analytic techniques. Looking beyond methodology, however, we can see other weaknesses in Cattell's position. With all his emphasis on the identification and measurement of the primary dimensions in personality, Cattell has not had enough time to pursue the creation and testing of hypotheses based on theorizing. The theorizing is in a relatively primitive state and there has been little attempt to generate explicit and systematic sets of propositions that would guide research efforts.

It seems ironic that an investigator who has spent a lifetime in the creation of a precise and explicit theory of personality can be so strongly and legitimately criticized on the precision and testability criterion. In fairness, it should be noted that his position, though flawed on this account, appears a model of elegance and precision when compared to the various psychodynamic and humanistic-existential theories.

Simplicity. Cattell has attempted to construct a theory that is parsimonious by using factor analytic procedures to "uncover" the major trait determinants of behavior, but it is doubtful that sixteen traits are adequate to the task. Thus, it seems that the theory suffers not because it has too many concepts, but because it has too few.

Empirical Validity. Cattell has spent most of his research career establishing the reliability and validity of the trait concepts to be utilized in the construction of an adequate theory of personality. Thus, there is considerable empirical support for these basic concepts. Yet, Cattell has not gone beyond this level and tried to generate systematic sets of theoretical propositions and hypotheses that could be tested, so that it is premature to discuss the empirical support for this aspect of his theory.

Heuristic Value. Many psychologists agree that there is a great deal to admire about Cattell and his efforts as a scientific investigator. He is seen as a first-rate scholar with wide-ranging interests and expertise in a variety of areas. There is little question that he has been incredibly productive as a researcher and prolific as a writer. He is perceived as a person with the kind of curiosity, intelligence, and boldness necessary in the pioneering investigator. Despite these beliefs, Cattell's theory has not had much impact on the thinking and work of investigators within psychology. There are several possible reasons for this situation. First, like Jung, Cattell's work is difficult to understand. The language of the theory is often technical and forbidding, and Cattell's penchant for using neologisms is not designed to endear him to readers. Second, although factor analysis is a relatively objective and precise statistical technique, the investigator's own biases and assumptions can influence the outcomes. Third, Cattell's measures are designed to tap personality traits assumed to operate across a variety of situations. This is strange, considering his explicit statements concerning the importance of situational parameters in determining behavior. The major point is that Cattell's focus is limited. According to critics, his concentration on transsituational traits in his research efforts can lead only to rather low levels of accuracy in the prediction of behavior, a point we will explore more thoroughly in Chapter 16.

Applied Value. Cattell's work has had some practical impact in the area of the clinical diagnosis of psychopathology; it has had even greater impact in providing management supervisors with diagnostic personality testing procedures that can be used to make decisions about the placement of workers in jobs suited to their talents and personalities.

DISCUSSION QUESTIONS

1. What is the inductive-hypothetico-deductive spiral? How does this approach to the construction of personality theory differ from the hypothetico-deductive model used by most investigators?
2. What is factor analysis? What are some of its strengths and weaknesses as a personality assessment procedure?
3. What is a trait? What are the primary sources of traits in personality?
4. How do source traits differ from surface traits? What are the major source traits?
5. Why does Cattell think it is necessary to invent new terms like parmia and threctia to describe personal dispositions?
6. What is Cattell's specification equation? Describe its use in the prediction of behavior.
7. What are the major aspects of the dynamic lattice?
8. List the three kinds of learning involved in the formation of personality. Give examples of each type.
9. Is there necessarily a decrease in physical and mental powers with the onset of old age? Do the elderly always feel powerless?

10. What kinds of family backgrounds are likely to give rise to neuroticism?

11. How do neurotics differ from psychotics? What are the major factors contributing to psychoticism, as espoused by Cattell?

12. What is the P-technique? How is it utilized in the treatment of people with behavioral disorders?

13. What are some of the advantages of using multivariate rather than bivariate experimental techniques to study human behavior?

14. What primary source traits would you attribute to the partners in stable and successful marriages? What primary source traits characterize people you like or dislike?

15. How does Cattell define personality? What are some of the limitations of his definition?

NOTES

A. Bandura, *Aggression: A Social Learning Analysis* (Englewood Cliffs, N.J.: Prentice-Hall, 1973).

K. Burton and R. B. Cattell, "Marriage Dimensions and Personality," *Journal of Personality and Social Psychology*, 1972, **21,** 369–375.

R. B. Cattell, *Personality: A Systematic Theoretical and Factual Study* (New York: McGraw-Hill, 1950).

R. B. Cattell, *Personality and Motivation Structure and Measurement* (New York: Harcourt, Brace, and World, 1957).

R. B. Cattell, *The Meaning and Measurement of Neuroticism and Anxiety* (New York: Ronald, 1961).

R. B. Cattell, *The Scientific Analysis of Personality* (Baltimore: Penguin, 1965).

H. J. Eysenck, *The Scientific Study of Personality* (London: Routledge and Kegan Paul, 1952).

H. J. Eysenck, *The Structure of Human Personality* (London: Methuen, 1953).

R. Fletcher, *Instinct in Man: In the Light of Recent Work in Comparative Psychology* (New York: International Universities Press, 1957).

D. S. Lehrman, "A Critique of Konrad Lorenz's Theory of Instinctive Behavior," *Quarterly Review of Biology*, 1953, **28,** 337–363.

D. R. Meyer, "Comparative Psychology," *Annual Review of Psychology*, 1955, **6,** 251–266.

M. F. A. Montagu, *Man and Aggression* (New York: Oxford University Press, 1968).

G. D. Wilson, J. Ausman, and T. R. Mathews, "Conservatism and Art Preferences," *Journal of Personality and Social Psychology*, 1973, **25,** 286–288.

SUGGESTED READINGS

Cattell, R. B. *Personality: A Systematic Theoretical and Factual Study.* New York: McGraw Hill, 1950.

Cattell, R. B. *Personality and Motivation Structure and Measurement.* New York: Harcourt, Brace, and World, 1957.

Cattell, R. B. *The Scientific Analysis of Personality*. Baltimore: Penguin, 1965.

Cattell, R. B. *Handbook of Multivariate Experimental Psychology*. Chicago: Rand McNally, 1966.

Cattell, R. B., and Dreger, R. M. (eds.). *Handbook of Modern Personality Theory*. Washington, D. C.: Hemisphere Publishing, 1977.

GLOSSARY

Ability Trait. Skill possessed by individuals that enables them to cope effectively with problems posed by the environment.

Alaxia. Source trait that predisposes a person to be trusting, relaxed, and understanding.

Autia. Source trait that predisposes a person to be imaginative and self-absorbed.

Bivariate Experiment. Investigation in which the experimenter tries to assess the impact of one variable on another.

Casual. Source trait possessed by some individuals that forces them to ignore protocol and to follow their own impulses.

Classical Conditioning. Type of learning pioneered by Pavlov in which an initially neutral stimulus becomes capable of evoking a response after continued pairing with a stimulus that naturally produces the response. This type of learning is also called respondent conditioning.

Confluence Learning. Acquisition of attitudes and behaviors that simultaneously contribute to the satisfaction of two or more goals.

Controlled (Source) Trait. Source trait possessed by certain individuals that enables them to act in socially precise and disciplined ways.

Desurgency. Source trait involving depression, pessimism, introspection, and worrying.

Dynamic Lattice. Complicated and organized system of traits that exist within human personality.

Dynamic Trait. Characteristic that embraces the motives and interests of people.

Environmental-Mold Trait. Characteristic learned through experiences with the environment.

Erg. Innate drive that controls behavior.

Factor Analysis. Statistical techniques designed to yield the intercorrelations between a number of variables. Factor analysis attempts to account for these intercorrelations in terms of underlying factors, usually fewer in number than the original number of variables.

Factor Loading. Term used in factor analysis to indicate the degree of association between a specific variable and a general factor.

Group Adherence. Source trait possessed by some individuals that compels them to seek answers to their problems by joining and participating in groups.

Harria. Source trait possessed by certain individuals that forces them to behave in a toughminded, direct, and forceful way.

Inductive-Hypothetico-Deductive Spiral. Approach to theory construction and validation in which facts are collected first and then generalized into hypotheses that can lead to deductions which can be tested empirically.

Integration Learning. Form of learning proposed by Cattell in which the person utilizes his or her reasoning abilities and value system in making judgments as a means of maximizing the attainment of long-range goals.

Instrumental Conditioning. Type of learning in which the presentation of a reinforcing stimulus is made contingent upon the occurrence of a response (operant conditioning, reward learning). Responses are strengthened or weakened by the application of various kinds of reinforcers.

L-Data. Life-record information obtained through observation of behavior in everyday situations.

Multivariate Experiment. Investigation in which the experimenter tries to assess the impact of a variety of variables on a given behavior.

Narcissistic Sex. Sex that is selfishly motivated, where the primary quest is for personal gratification and not for the gratification of the needs of the other.

Parmia. Source trait possessed by certain individuals that forces them to act in ways that can be characterized as adventurous and bold.

Praxernia. Source trait that predisposes a person to be practical, conscientious, and concerned.

Premsia. Source trait possessed by certain individuals that forces them to be impatient, impulsive, sentimental, and anxious.

Primary Factor. General factor that emerges following an analysis of the correlations between a number of surface variables.

Protension. Source trait that predisposes a person to be suspicious, jealous, and withdrawn.

Q-Data. Questionnaire information obtained through a subject's self-reports of behavior.

Second-Order Factor. Higher-order factor that emerges following an analysis of the associations between a number of primary factors.

Self-Sentiment. Concept used by Cattell to account for the organization of the various attitudes, sentiments, and motives of the person.

Sixteen Personality Factor Questionnaire. Factor analytically derived questionnaire created by Cattell to measure basic underlying traits of personality.

Source Trait. An underlying characteristic found as a result of conducting a factor analysis on a number of variables and finding that they are all interrelated. The commonality or unity among the variables is then interpreted as indicating the existence of a source trait.

Specification Equation. Formula that specifies the ways in which traits are weighted in relation to given situations and then combined to predict behavior.

Subsidiation. Process involving the interrelatedness of traits whereby the gratification of one motive is necessary before a related motive can be satisfied.

Surgency. Source trait encompassing cheerful, sociable, and energetic behavior.

T-Data. Objective test information based upon an observer's judgments of an individual's behavior.

Temperament Trait. Innate tendency on the part of individuals to react to the environment in a particular way.

Threctia. Source trait possessed by certain individuals that forces them to act in ways that can be characterized as shy, timid, and restrained.

Trait. Relatively permanent and broad reaction tendency that serves as a building block of personality.

PART 4

COGNITIVE PERSPECTIVES

I n order to understand the role of cognition in current theories of personality, it is first necessary to examine the meaning of the term. In ordinary language, cognition refers to the thoughts or ideas we have about the world around us. Thus, in the broadest sense, we are talking about events that occur inside us which help us make sense of the world. Technically, theories of cognition are concerned with the problem of how we gain information about events and how we act upon our environments on the basis of our processing of this information.

Since cognition involves internal events, it could be argued that the various psychodynamic and trait theories we have considered thus far in the text should be studied here. After all, Freud's concept of the ego deals in large measure with our attempts to understand external reality and to perform those behaviors which will result in maximum pleasure for us. The conflicts between the id and superego also involve the use of internalized rules to restrict the expression of inappropriate id impulses. These rules are frequently utilized in our decision-making and can be construed as cognitive in nature.

The concept of trait employed by Allport and Cattell to account for personality functioning is also a cognitive construct. Traits are motives assumed to guide behaviors and influence judgments about the environment. Allport goes beyond Cattell in postulating a developmental process of "becoming" that is largely cognitive. As we know, for him the mature person is one who is capable of making use of information in a rational way. The self-actualization theories created by Maslow and Rogers can also be construed as cognitive, as we shall see later in the text. So can the work of some of the social learning theorists reviewed in Part 5. These positions incorporate cognitive constructs like expectancy, imitation, verbal and pictorial imagery, memory, and so forth.

Why, then, not include these theorists and their positions in this section of the text? Why do we include only Kelly's theory? The answer is that, although many of these theories have elements of cognition, Kelly stands alone as the creator of a comprehensive and "pure" cognitive

187

theory of personality. His attention is focused solely on the ways in which we process information as a means of increasing our understanding of the world. His is an intellectualized view of personality which sees all of us acting as scientists in order to predict and control events. In Kelly's view, we are all continually trying to make sense out of our worlds by forming hypotheses about how they work, by testing them in the real world, and then revising them if they do not fit or work. Our aim, according to him, is to maximize our predictive accuracy about the ways in which the world operates.

To present this view, he built a theory with a brand new terminology and did away with many traditional concepts in psychology. For example, Kelly does not talk about learning, ego, motivation, reinforcement, drive, the unconscious, or need. Yet if one looks closely at his position, concepts like motivation, reinforcement, and drive are subtly present, but not emphasized or discussed in a traditional way. For example, although Kelly does not focus on a drive reduction concept of human thirst and hunger motivation, as do some of the traditional learning theorists, he does maintain that we seek to improve our constructs by increasing the number of concepts in our cognitive systems and by altering concepts at variance with our experiences. We have, in brief, a *need* to know, a *desire* to make accurate predictions about phenomena. These aims show clearly that Kelly believed human beings were motivated, but the focus is on cognitive motivation and not on biological drives.

Kelly also rejects the empirical Law of Effect, which states that behavior is more likely to occur if it has been followed by the application of a positive reinforcer and less likely to occur if it has been followed by a punishing stimulus. He rejected this view of reinforcement because it suggests that our behavior is under the control of external reinforcers, whereas he believes our actions are controlled by cognitive processes. Yet, Kelly does talk about reinforcement, but he discusses it indirectly in terms of the accuracy of the match between our conceptualization of the world and its actual state. In other words, it is positively reinforcing when we predict events accurately and punishing when we do not. For example, we will tend to feel satisfied if we can predict accurately that someone we dislike will behave dispicably either toward us or others, whereas we will be unhappy if our enemy behaves kindly and generously toward us or others because we do not expect such behavior. But this concept of reinforcement seems to have its limitations. Would we continue to be unhappy if our enemy presented us with a check for a million dollars or if he saved our lives during a catastrophe? Also, recent studies in social psychology have suggested that some people enjoy inconsistency and abhor consistency. Too much predictability would probably be boring.

Chapter 8 provides a close look at Kelly's unique and clearly stated theory. It begins by examining the fundamental assumption underlying

the theory, namely, the philosophical stance called constructive alternativism. The basic terms of the theory are outlined, followed by the
presentation of the fundamental postulate and the many corollaries of
his personal construct position. Next, there is a detailed examination of
Kelly's Role Construct Repertory Test (RCRT), a test designed to
measure individuals' personal construct systems. This section of the
chapter then leads to a discussion of Kelly's view of psychotherapy and
the role of therapist and client. We conclude with critical comments
about the strengths and weaknesses of his theory.

George Alexander Kelly (Courtesy of Brandeis University)

Kelly's Theory of Personal Constructs

BIOGRAPHICAL SKETCH

George Alexander Kelly was born in a small town in Kansas in 1905, the only child of a Presbyterian minister and his wife. He attended high school in Wichita, Kansas, and then Friends University, where he enrolled in courses on music and public debating. He was graduated from Parks College in 1926 with a degree in mathematics and physics. He flirted with the idea of becoming an aeronautical engineer, but eventually committed himself to education. He then held a variety of jobs, including teaching speechmaking to students in a labor college and teaching Americanization to a class of recent immigrants.

In 1929, he was awarded an exchange scholarship and spent a year at the University of Edinburgh. He earned a bachelor's degree in education and returned to the United States with a developing interest in psychology. As a consequence, he entered the graduate program in that field at the University of Iowa. In 1931, he was awarded his Ph.D. for a dissertation in the area of speech and reading disabilities.

His professional career in psychology began with his acceptance of a position at Fort Hays State College in Kansas. Soon afterward, he began an attempt to develop psychological services for the State of Kansas by establishing a network of traveling clinics throughout the state. It was during this period that Kelly largely abandoned the psychoanalytic approach to the understanding of human personality. He reported that his clinical experiences had taught him that people in the Midwest were paralyzed by prolonged drought, dust storms, and economic considerations, not by overflowing libidinal forces. He began to develop his theory, based in part on observation of a friend who took a part in a dramatic production in college, "lived it" for the two or three weeks the play was in rehearsal, and was profoundly influenced by it. Kelly noted that whereas many people would dismiss his friend's efforts as "sheer affectation," the fact of the matter was that the person's behavior was not false or without substance. It eventually expressed his "real self." This experience led Kelly to formulate a *fixed-role therapy* technique designed to help the person overcome his or her own limitations.

The crux of his theory of personal *constructs* was created when he observed that "people tended to have the symptoms they had read about or had seen in other people." When the terms or constructs of "inferiority complex" or "anxiety" were popular in the twenties and thirties, people began to describe themselves as having inferiority complexes or anxieties. These self-descriptions were subsequently used in their interpretations of reality. Kelly's preoccupation with the structure of language and the impact of language and roles on behavior led him to read the works of the eminent linguist Korzybski, and those of the role-playing theorist Moreno, and resulted in the refinement of his theory (Kelly, 1955, Vol. 1, pp. 360–366).

After a stint in the Navy as an aviation psychologist during World War II, Kelly was appointed associate professor at the University of Maryland. He left Maryland in 1946 to become professor of psychology and director of clinical psychology at Ohio State University. During the following two decades, he completed his major theoretical work, *The Psychology of Personal Constructs* (1959). He also traveled widely and lectured at many universities throughout the world. In 1965, he accepted the Riklis chair of Behavioral Science at Brandeis University. He died one year later.

BASIC CONCEPTS AND PRINCIPLES

Constructive Alternativism

The concept of *constructive alternativism* underlies Kelly's theory of cognition. Although it is an imposing term, the concept is really not too difficult to understand. It refers to the assumption that all of us are capable of changing or replacing our present interpretation of events (Kelly, 1955, Vol. 1, p. 15). In colloquial terms, we can always change our minds. But the assumption also implies that our behavior is never completely determined. We are always free to some extent to reinterpret our experiences. Thus, it is clear that Kelly believed in the primacy of the individual. Yet Kelly also believed that some of our thoughts and behavior were determined by other phenomena. In other words, his theory is constructed on a joint freedom-determinism base. As he put it, "Determinism and freedom are inseparable, for that which determines another is, by the same token, free of the other" (Kelly, 1955, Vol. 1, p. 21). A concrete example might make his point clearer. A student decides that the attainment of a college degree summa cum laude is important to her.

As a result, this subjective fact will determine certain other behaviors; for example, she will curtail her social activities and spend many hours in the library or her dormitory room studying. In brief, she was free to choose her goal, but once chosen, the goal determines certain related behaviors.

To put this example in terms of the terminology used by Kelly, we can say that the *superordinate construct,* namely, the attainment of the college degree, was freely chosen and then acted to subordinate or control certain other constructs, namely, the number of social activities and the number of hours spent studying. Since this is such an important point because it sets the stage for the description of his personal construct theory, we quote Kelly to make certain it is fully understood:

> The relation established by a construct or a construction system over its subordinate elements is deterministic. In this sense the tendency to subordinate constitutes determinism. The natural events themselves do not subordinate our constructions of them, we can look at them in any way we like. . . . The structure we erect is what rules us. (Kelly, 1955, Vol. 1, p. 20).

Theorists who adopt a behavioral stance argue that Kelly's argument is inadequate. They maintain instead that all behavior is determined and would ask Kelly simply, "How did the young woman come to 'choose' her goal of graduating with highest honors?" They would then proceed to suggest that this goal too was determined by certain experiences she had had or was currently undergoing.

Every Person as "Scientist"

Kelly believed that each of us, like the scientist, attempts to predict and control events. We are continually in the process of evaluating and reevaluating our experiences and trying to use our interpretations to understand and control the world about us. We have our own "theories" about human behavior. We "test" hypotheses based upon the theories, and we subsequently weigh the experimental evidence (Kelly, 1955, Vol. 1, p. 5). On the basis of this evidence, the world becomes more predictable or it becomes clear that we must change our concepts or constructs about it if we are to function effectively.

Of course, Kelly considered us scientists in a very special and limited way. As individuals and "scientists," we use our own highly personalized view of reality in making our judgments. These judgments and their revisions are rarely open to the scrutiny of others. Our constructs are also not as objectively defined as those used by research scientists. Our "theories," too, rarely meet the criteria set by conventional science. In short, we have rather commonsense views of ourselves and reality, and the possibilities for distortion and error are great (see

Chapter 1 for a review of some of these points). Nevertheless, Kelly maintained that there are certain similarities between ourselves and scientists, so that an understanding of these commonalities may help us to appreciate his system better. We should be cautious in accepting the scientist analogy because, as you undoubtedly know, every analogy has its own limitations.

In Kelly's view, then, we operate *like* scientists as we make efforts to understand the world. He also noted that many of us continually shift our view of reality to fit the "data." No matter how distorted our views of reality are, they are still real to us and we operate in terms of them. As he put it

> A person may misrepresent a real phenomenon, such as his income or his ills, and yet his misrepresentation will itself be entirely real. This applies even to the badly deluded patient: what he perceives may not exist, but his perception does. (Kelly, 1955, Vol. 1, p. 8)

Thus, Kelly embraced the phenomenologist position which characterizes the works of the humanist theorists reviewed in Part 6. Like the humanists, Kelly believed we are not passive organisms, but instead that we actively relate to the environment, often in a creative way.

The Nature of Constructs and Construing

In building our systems of personal constructs, we place interpretations on events. Through an abstraction process, we construct the meaning of events for ourselves (Kelly, 1955, Vol. 1, p. 50). We then utilize our constructions for dealing with new information from the environment. These interpretations are reality for us and we act in terms of them. They are also highly personalized; we often interpret the same experiences differently from others.

The constructs we form to make sense out of our experiences and use in order to deal with new experiences are based upon our previous experiences. For Kelly, constructs are ways in which we organize experiences in terms of similarities and contrasts. He noted that "in its minimum context a construct is a way in which at least two elements are similar and contrast with a third" (Kelly, 1955, Vol. 1, p. 61). In addition, he argued that constructs must contain at least three elements and may contain many more. Constructs are also bipolar, which means that they are construed in terms of contrasts as well as in terms of similarities. To say that an object is a chair implies, of necessity, that it is not also a table. To say that bearded men tend to be virile is to imply that clean-shaven men are impotent. To say that Beth and Marie are intelligent is to imply that someone else, perhaps Jane, is stupid.

Since constructs are primarily personal, people may apply different labels to the same experiences. For example, events certain people call "dependent" others may label "pleasant." Such an individual may believe that he or she is being pleasant in interpersonal relationships, when in fact his or her willingness to yield indiscriminately to the wishes of others in order to avoid their anger would be labeled "excessive dependence" by others. Kelly argued that there is also the possibility that, although two people may label an experience similarly, the contrast end of the dimension may differ. For example Bill and Jim may label certain of their behaviors and the behavior of others as "sincere," but Bill may see behavior on the opposite end of the spectrum as "insincere," whereas Jim may label it "morally degenerate." Thus, Bill might react to certain contrast behaviors of his construct with mild disapproval, whereas Jim would probably become angry and upset under the same circumstances. Their subsequent behavior toward the person exhibiting the contrast behavior may also vary. Bill might try to reason with the "insincere" person; Jim might attack or avoid the "moral degenerate."

Kelly believed that sometimes people formulate constructs before they can verbalize them. This is particularly true of children. For example, some children are capable of showing affection toward loved ones, but incapable of verbalizing their feelings. Kelly also maintained that people who are disturbed often "repress" or distort certain experiences and are unable or unwilling to deal with them on a verbal level. As a consequence, they undergo therapy with an expert who may be able to help them deal with the limitations inherent in their construct systems. A detailed example of how Kelly applied his theory of personal constructs in a therapeutic setting will appear later in the chapter. At this point, let us examine some of the other characteristics of constructs, as Kelly formulated them.

Additional Characteristics of Constructs

Constructs are arranged in a hierarchical manner within a particular person's cognitive world. There are ordinal relationships between them; that is, one construct may subsume another or other constructs (Kelly, 1955, Vol. 1, p. 57). For example, a person seen by others as a "moralizer" may actually use a superordinate construct of "good vs. bad" to control his other concepts. For him, a "good" person might be one who is intelligent, cooperative, kind, ambitious, sincere, and so forth; a "bad" person might be one who is characterized as stupid, competitive, cruel, unambitious, and insincere.

Constructs many also vary in terms of their range of convenience. By *range of convenience*, Kelly meant that a particular construct might be related to some constructs, but not to others; that is, a given construct has relevance for some constructs, but not for others (Kelly, 1955, Vol. 1, p. 68). A person might use the good-bad dichotomy to control many of his constructs but probably would not apply it to every construct. The good-bad dichotomy probably has a wide range of convenience for many people, but other constructs are much more limited. The construct of fat-thin might be a pertinent example here. We might think of fat people versus thin people or fat lions versus thin lions. But we do not ordinarily think of fat light versus thin light, fat weather versus thin weather, or fat crying versus thin crying.

Related to the notion of range of convenience is Kelly's idea about the *permeability* of constructs. A construct is considered permeable if it will allow additional new elements—that is, constructs currently excluded from its range of convenience—to be construed within that framework (Kelly, 1955, Vol. 1, p. 79). For example, a person's construct of right versus wrong may allow him to include new ideas and behavior by other people as right or wrong. He may be prepared to make a judgment concerning the moral validity of euthanasia, for example, a topic about which he had previously been ignorant. On the other hand, if the construct were impermeable, he would be incapable of making such a moral evaluation. Of course, it is rare that a construct is completely impermeable; usually, there are various degrees of permeability. By introducing the notion of permeability, Kelly made allowances for change in the system. Other ways of talking about change would include making allowance for "growth," "personal development," and "the realization of the self."

In short, Kelly has posited a complicated, hierarchical system of cognition populated by personal constructs derived from experience that now control or determine the ways in which the person will react to incoming stimuli or information. Although much of his behavior is determined by such constructs, there is also room within his system for change, since the superordinate concepts are free and often permeable. Change in these permeable constructs would then produce changes in the superordinate construct system.

In addition to the permeability-impermeability construct, Kelly proposed that constructs could be characterized as *preemptive, constellatory,* and *propositional.* A concept that includes only its own elements and maintains that these elements cannot be part of other constructs is called a preemptive construct. For instance, Kelly noted that a person may argue "Anything which is a ball can be nothing but a ball." Thus, balls cannot be "pellets", "spheres," or "shots" (Kelly, 1955, Vol. 1, p. 153). Unfortunately, such black-or-white thinking sometimes characterizes our interpersonal relationships as well. Occasionally, we hear people arguing that "Capitalism is nothing but exploitation of the masses by big business," or that "the Women's Lib movement is nothing but an attempt by a few frustrated and ugly hags to castrate men."

Kelly also proposed that a construct which ". . . permits its elements to belong to other realms concurrently, but fixes their realm memberships," be called a constellatory construct (Kelly, 1955, Vol. 1, p. 155). Stereotypes belong to this category. The point is that, once we identify a person or object as a member of a given category, we then attribute a cluster or constellation of other characteristics to him. Although we are fully aware of the fact that we tend to stereotype people in terms of ethnic and cultural backgrounds, do we also have reliable stereotypes of people on the basis of other characteristics, like hair color? A recent study has shown that indeed many of us do (Lawson, 1971). In this study, the investigator asked college men and women to rate fictitious people with different hair colors on a variety of personality characteristics. He found that men tended to see blondes as more beautiful, delicate, and feminine than either brunettes or redheads. Both men and women also rated brunettes most favorably and artificial or "bleached" blondes most unfavorably. For example, brunettes were seen almost in Girl Scout terms—that is, they were seen as intelligent, ambitious, sincere, strong, "safe," valuable, and effective. In terms of attributing personality characteristics to men, both men and women also rated dark-haired men most favorably. They saw them as more handsome, intelligent, ambitious, sincere, strong, rugged, valuable, effective, and masculine, in comparison to men with blonde or red hair. Men with blonde hair were generally rated more favorably than redheads. Thus, it seems clear that many of us tend to have constellatory constructs or stereotypes, even about hair color. The tragic implication is that such personal constructs may, under certain circumstances, produce unnecessary pain for the possessor of such a genetically endowed trait when he or she comes into contact with someone who possesses the stereotype.

Finally, Kelly stated that a construct which left its elements open to construction in every respect be called a propositional construct. "Any round object can be considered, among other things, to be a ball." But a ball can, for such a person, also be elliptical, worn, or small. Propositional thinking is flexible thinking. The person is continuously open to new experience and is capable of modifying existing constructs. For Kelly, the person best equipped to deal with his environment is the one who knows the circumstances under which propositional or preemptive thinking is appropriate. He pointed out that if a person relied exclusively on propositional thinking, he would be immobilized. He would continually be reevaluating and reconstruing his experiences and, as a result, would be indicisive. If he were a star receiver on a professional football team, for instance, it might be best if he were to consider the object being hurled at him as a football and nothing else. In such a case, preemptive thinking would be a necessity. On the other hand, sole reliance on preemptive thinking would lead a person to make dogmatic and unyielding judgments. Such a way of thinking would be fraught with danger for the person: Imagine what would happen to the low-ability student who maintained that he was brilliant and never needed to study for examinations in his courses.

Now that we have examined some of the fundamental characteristics of constructs, let us begin our review of the basic theory.

The Fundamental Postulate of the Theory

The basic assumption underlying Kelly's theory is that ". . . a person's processes are psychologically channelized by the ways in which he anticipates events" (Kelly, 1955, Vol. 1, p. 46). This statement suggests that Kelly believed we are behaving, changing organisms who operate in terms of our expectations about events. In short, our expectations channel or direct our actions. They provide the motivation for our behavior. In terms of Kelly's man-as-scientist analogy, we seek prediction and verification for our views of events. We generate a construct system by construing events and then we act in terms of that framework.

The following corollaries or propositions were then derived, in part, from the fundamental postulate as a means of elaborating the system.

Individuality Corollary. We not only anticipate events, but we may differ from one another in our anticipations. This proposition, according to Kelly, lays the groundwork for the study of individual differences. People differ from each other because they have had different experiences, and also because there are different approaches to the anticipation of the same event (Kelly, 1955, Vol. 1, p. 55). The construct systems people generate are idiosyncratic in many respects, but there are also commonalities between people in the way they construe events. People can and do share experiences.

Organization Corollary. Next, Kelly proposed that ". . . each person characteristically evolves, for his convenience in anticipating events, a construction system embracing ordinal relationships between constructs" (Kelly, 1955, Vol. 1, p. 56). People differ not only in their constructs, but in the way in which they organize them. Organization of constructs also serves to reduce conflict for the person. If a married man knows that his wife and family come first, even before his mother, then potential conflicts can be minimized. Doubt as to which construct is superordinate can be painful, as many husbands have learned.

Choice Corollary. Kelly assumed that all of us were continually making choices between the poles of our constructs. He assumed further that we tended to make a choice in terms of those alternatives which would allow us to deal most effectively with ensuing events. Should we be cautious or risk-taking in given situations? Should we marry or not marry? Should we pursue a college degree or drop out? Kelly maintained that people tended, in general, to make choices that would define and "elaborate" the system. In short, given an option, we choose alternatives designed to increase our confidence in our interpretations of the world, alternatives that also increase our understanding of it through "personal growth."

Fragmentation Corollary. According to Kelly, our construct systems are in a continual state of flux. Yet within these systems, we may successively use a variety of subsystems that are inferentially incompatible with one another (Kelly, 1955, Vol. 1, p. 104). What precisely is Kelly talking about here? He is saying, in effect, that our construct systems are not always completely consistent with one another, and that we may sometimes show behaviors that are inconsistent with our most recent experiences. For example, a young woman may decide that she loves a man and declare to friends that she has agreed to marry him. The following day, although we might expect her to show affection toward him, she might begin to revile him in front of friends, pointing out his limitations and declaring that the marriage is off. Here we have construct subsystems that are incompatible. Kelly might explain the inconsistency in her behavior by pointing out that, although she loves him, she also knows that he is selfish and inconsiderate and that he will eventually hurt her badly. Thinking about these limitations forced her to terminate the marriage plans. In brief, the construct "fiancé" subsumed the construct of "love" and also the construct of "despising his personal characteristics." Such fragmented and inconsistent construct systems can exist side by side within a person's cognitive world and show up in successive behaviors because other constructs in the larger system trigger them. In this case, the incompatible systems may have been triggered by the superordinate construct "mother," who brought the man's failings to her attention.

The important point to note here is that, in trying to predict behavior, we have to discover such ruling constructs as "mother" and show how, in the final analysis, they control the person's behavior. Kelly is taking issue here with some of the traditional learning views of the determinants of behavior. For some of the early learning theorists, behavior was determined by its immediate antecedents. What Kelly is saying is that the prediction of behavior is much more complicated and involves as assessment of the meanderings of the individual's "cognitive world" and that this world is not always composed of logical and consistent subsystems.

Commonality Corollary. Kelly also maintained that ". . . to the extent that one person employs a construction of experience which is similar to that employed by another, his psychological processes are similar to those of the other person" (Kelly, 1955, Vol. 1, p. 90). This corollary was proposed by Kelly to show that not only would people who differ in their construction of events behave differently (see individuality corollary), but they would behave in the same way if they interpreted events similarly. Thus, it is possible for people to act alike even if they have been exposed to different stimuli, if their constructs are similar.

Sociality Corollary.   Finally, Kelly maintained that ". . . to the extent that one person construes the construction processes of another, he may play a role in a social process involving the other person (Kelly, 1955, Vol. 1, p. 95). In other words, a person would be able to predict accurately what another would do and to adjust his own behavior accordingly to the extent that he understands the construct system of the other. Much of our behavior, Kelly maintained, consists of such mutual adjustment. These mutual understandings allow us to function effectively in society. Imagine what would happen if we disagreed about the meaning of traffic signals, for example. If the construct "red" implied "go" for some people, while the construct "green" implied "go" for others, we would soon learn the consequences of our lack of mutual understanding and adjustment.

These are some of the major ingredients in Kelly's theory. At this point, we turn to a discussion of the ways in which these propositions can be utilized to understand his views on human development.

THE PROCESS OF PERSONALITY DEVELOPMENT

Kelly assumed that the development of each person revolved around attempts to maximize his understanding of the world through the continuing definition and elaboration of his construct system. The rationale upon which this assumption is based is unclear. It may be that Kelly, like other major humanistic psychologists, simply assumed that this tendency was innate. Certainly he did not assume that it was learned, although the person's interaction with the environment was assumed to play the major role in helping to move the individual toward personal growth. Yet this point must be clarified if we are truly to understand Kelly's views on the relationship between the environment and personal development. He rejected outright the mechanistic learning view that behavior was determined solely by the operation of environmental events. The person does not simply react to the environment. Instead, he or she actively, uniquely, and systematically construes it and then utilizes these constructions to anticipate events. The individual uses previous experiences to create hypotheses about the possible occurrences of new outcomes. In Kelly's opinion, he or she does not respond to the environment in order to maximize pleasure and avoid pain, as reinforcement theorists assume. Instead, he or she actively seeks to maximize the accuracy of his or her views.

He developed several models to illustrate the ways in which the individual utilizes information from the environment in deciding upon a course of action. One of the more important ones he termed the circumspection-preemption-control (C-P-C) cycle. The cycle begins, according to Kelly, when the person considers all the possible ways to construe a given situation. That is, she considers a series of propositional constructs that might help her in dealing with the situation at hand. The preemption phase comes into play next when she reduces the number of constructs available to her and considers seriously only those that will help her solve the problem. Finally, she decides on a course of action by making a choice of that alternative in a single construct she believes will lead to action that will solve the problem (Kelly, 1955, Vol. 1, pp. 516–517). As an illustration, consider the case of a young woman who wants to become a world-renowned violinist. There are a variety of ways she could construe herself in the situation. She could see herself as a "future tennis great," a "lazy person," or a "popular local actress." Until she rejects these self-constructs and settles on one that paints her as a "dedicated student of music," she is unlikely ever to become successful and to realize her ambition. By making that choice, she exercises control over her behavior and anticipates the extension of her construct system.

In Kelly's view, people are continually acting in this way. That is, they are continually considering the alternatives in given situations, reducing the possibilities to those that will work, and acting in terms of their choices. The developmental process, then, is seen by him as a creative and dynamic interchange between individual and environment. It involves constructions and reconstructions in the light of new experiences. Its aim is to maximize the person's understanding and therefore his control over his environment. The healthy person is thus one who has an accurate and valid construct system and a flexible view of the world. More will be said about Kelly's beliefs about the unhealthy individual in a later section. Now, we turn to a consideration of his attempts to assess personality.

TECHNIQUES OF ASSESSMENT

Kelly used many different techniques to assess personality. Some of these procedures were devised by him; others were borrowed and adapted from the works of other major personality theorists.

The primary method used by Kelly in the assessment of personality in a therapeutic setting was the *interview*. Within that framework, the initial step is transitive diagnosis. That is, the therapist attempts not only to assess the realities of the client's life, but also to point out the directions in which he can proceed toward the solution of his problems (Kelly, 1955, Vol. 2, pp. 774–775). In using this procedure, Kelly makes clear that he is not simply interested in traditional diagnosis, in which therapists pigeonhole their clients by using a classification scheme. More specifically, he is not interested solely in having clients take various personality tests and then classifying them as manic-depressives, obsessive-compulsives, or hysterics. He maintains that such an approach is static and focuses on what the client has been in the past and what he is currently. It ignores the fact, in Kelly's judgment, that the person is forever changing, that he is in transition, and that the therapist must not only document the reality of the client's situation, but most also point out possible goals for him to attain.

The RCRT

This discussion should not lead you to the conclusion that Kelly ignored personality testing in his initial diagnosis. On the contrary, Kelly thought that such testing could be utilized with advantage, along with direct questioning, to increase his understanding of the person. In accordance with his belief, he made use of the Rorschach and the Thematic Apperception Test, as well as other more original techniques, to diagnose the client's problems accurately. One major diagnostic tool created by Kelly to assess the personal construct systems of people in clinical settings was the Role Construct Repertory Test (RCRT). A matrix or grid is created in which clients first list the names of the important people in their social environments. They are then asked to sort these people by successively considering three of them at a time, to make circles under their names, and to mark down in a space to the right of each row in the grid the way in which two of them are alike and yet different from the third. When they have decided on the two people and the important way in which they are alike, they are asked to put an X in the two circles corresponding to the ones who are alike. This identifies the "similarity" part of the construct. Next they are asked to write in a space to the right the way in which the third person is different from the other two. This is the "contrast" part of the construct.

Following this procedure, clients are asked to consider the other prominent persons in their environments and to place a checkmark ($\sqrt{}$), *not* an X, under the name of each person who has this important characteristic. If they do not place a checkmark next to some of these important people, it means that the contrast part of the construct applies to these people. Clients then proceed to sort all these people again on new dimensions. The number of constructs to be utilized depends upon the subjects. Some subjects will be able to sort important people in terms of a few dimensions or constructs; others will sort them on many dimensions.

For an illustration of how this assessment procedure works, turn to Table 8.1. This table represents the cognitive matrix of one of Kelly's clients. The columns list the important individuals in this person's life. The rows represent the constructs used by the client to construe them. Construct 2 can be termed an "education" construct. The client sees both a teacher he accepts ($\otimes$), and one he rejects ($\otimes$) as similar in terms of educational level. He sees his boss, in contrast, as having a different educational background (o). His brother ($\sqrt{}$), sister ($\sqrt{}$), friend ($\sqrt{}$), and a successful person ($\sqrt{}$) he knows are all similar to his teachers in educational background. The remaining figures (voids), including himself, mother, father, spouse, ex-girlfriend, ex-friend, a rejecting person, a pitied person, a threatening person, an attractive person, a happy person, and an ethical person, all have an educational background that is different from his teacher's.

Once the task has been completed by a subject, it is possible to devise a score in a variety of ways. One simple way used by psychologist James Bieri was to examine the check patterns across the various rows and to assume that similar patterns signified a lack of differentiation in his perception of others (cognitive simplicity). On the other hand, if the patterns were highly dissimilar, it was assumed that the person had a highly differentiated view of others (cognitive complexity) (Bieri, 1955). In a clinical setting, the person's cognitive complexity score can be interpreted by the therapist, along with other testing information, to illuminate his problems. An example of an interpretation of a client's repertory protocol is presented in the next section of the chapter. At this point, however, let us examine a study by Bieri that makes use of the test in an experimental setting.

In his study, Bieri sought to test the validity of Kelly's RCRT by first classifying the college students who participated as either "cognitively complex" or "cognitively simple" on the basis of their scores on the RCRT. Using Kelly's assumptions that a basic characteristic of human beings is to move toward greater predictability of their environments and that each person has a set of constructs to use in making those predictions, Bieri argued that those who are cognitively complex would be better able to predict the behavior of others than those who are cognitively simple. This prediction was based upon reasoning which maintained that those who can differentiate among many different events in the environment would be more capable of making discerning and accurate judgments than those who see many events in their environments as similar and who apply the same labels to them.

To test this hypothesis, the investigator had cognitively complex and cognitively simple subjects respond to a questionnaire depicting twelve social situations in which four alternatives were given. A typical item follows:

> You are working intently to finish a paper in the library when two people sit down across from you and distract you with their continual loud talking. Would you most likely:
> a. Move to another seat.
> b. Let them know how you feel by your facial expression.
> c. Try to finish up in spite of their talking.
> d. Ask them to stop talking.

After the subjects completed the questionnaire in terms of how they would respond in these situations, they were asked to guess how two of their classmates would respond in the same situations. The subjects' predictive accuracy was assessed by noting the number of times their predictions matched the responses of their classmates. As expected, the cognitively complex students were much more accurate in their predictions than the cognitively simple ones. It was also found that the cognitively simple or undifferentiated subjects were more likely than the com-

Table 8.1 Client's Repertory Grid

IMPORTANT PEOPLE IN CLIENT'S LIFE

People (columns): Self, Mother, Father, Brother, Sister, Spouse, Ex-girlfriend, Friend, Ex-friend, Rejected person, Pitied person, Threatening person, Attractive person, Accepted teacher, Rejected teacher, Boss, Successful person, Happy person, Ethical person

Constructs

#	Similarity Pole	Contrast Pole
1	Don't believe in God	Very religious
2	Same sort of education	Completely different education
3	Not athletic	Athletic
4	Both girls	A boy
5	Parents	Ideas different
6	Understand me better	Don't understand me at all
7	Teach the right way	Teach the wrong way
8	Achieved a lot	Hasn't achieved a lot
9	Higher education	No education

No.	(Similarity pole)	(Contrast pole)
10	Don't like other people	Like other people
11	More religious	Not religious
12	Believe in higher education	Not believing in too much education
13	More sociable	Not sociable
14	Both girls	Not girls
15	More understanding	Less understanding
16	Both have high morals	Low morals
17	Think alike	Think differently
18	Same age	Different ages
19	Both friends	Not friends
20	Both appreciate music	Don't understand music

Note: Circles containing Xs and checkmarks—similarity; empty circles and blanks—contrast.

From G. A. Kelly, *The Psychology of Personal Constructs*, Vol. 1, 1955, p. 270.

plex subjects to perceive inaccurate similarities between themselves and others; that is, they tended to assume that the predictions they made for themselves would also apply to others, even though this was not the case. In brief, cognitively simple subjects tended to be quite egocentric. This is but one example of research based upon Kelly's theorizing. There have been many other studies, and the findings tend to lend support to Kelly's formulations (Bonarius, 1965).

In addition to the RCRT, Kelly used other techniques to assess personality. Two of the major ones, self-characterization sketches and fixed-role therapy, are explored in detail next.

APPLICATION OF THE THEORY TO THE TREATMENT OF PSYCHOPATHOLOGY

The Aim of Psychotherapy and the Roles of Therapist and Client

In Kelly's opinion, the sick person was best construed as one who continued to use constructs that were invalid. Thus, the basic aim of psychotherapy is to help the client form new constructs or revise old ones so that he may deal more effectively with his environment. The therapist is primarily concerned with opening up the possibility of continual change in the client's construct system so that he can regain his health. His job is to diagnose the illness and to throw light on the "paths" by which the client can become well (Kelly, 1955, Vol. 2, p. 582).

In order to achieve these objectives, Kelly believed the clinician should conceptualize his role quite broadly. The therapeutic process, in Kelly's view, begins as both parties try to define their roles. If the client begins to conceptualize therapy as involving minor adjustments on his part, it will be virtually impossible for the therapist to get him to see the need for drastic change. The therapist therefore must begin with the client's limited view of psychotherapy and try to show him the need for revising it. The therapist does this by listening closely to the client's complaints and by using a variety of techniques to produce change. Techniques that produce minor changes include (a) threat; (b) invalidation; and (c) exhortation (Kelly, 1955, Vol. 2, pp. 583–587). By threat, Kelly meant that the client became aware of the possiblity of imminent change in his construct structures. Under such conditions, Kelly thought the therapist could take advantage of the situation by pointing out new ways for the client to construe his experiences to facilitate constructive growth. Change could also be produced if the therapist invalidated the client's constructs,—that is, showed him why and how his constructs won't work. Last, the therapist could produce minor change by admonishing the client for his actions and telling him to behave effectively.

To produce major change, the therapist must show the client that he accepts him and that he is willing to help the client "work through" his problems. Kelly's view of acceptance differs from that of other nondirective therapists, however. In the traditional view, the therapist assumes that everyone has the right to choose to become anything that he desires. Kelly would like to accept this view in principle, but is uncertain where such a commitment on the part of the therapist would lead. In his view, acceptance involves not so much approval of the client's characteristics *en toto*, but a readiness to understand the person's construct system and to use it to help him get well. One of the implications of this stance is that the therapist must have a clear and firm understanding of his own construct system. Furthermore, he must empathize with the client, but he does not surrender his own viewpoint. The therapist should instead try to subsume much of the client's system into his own viewpoint (Kelly, 1955, Vol. 2, pp. 585–587).

Kelly believed that major change could be effected if the therapist was willing to help the client "work through" his problems. To do this, Kelly would ask the client to "think through" his problems and to see how they would turn out in the end. He called such a procedure *controlled elaboration*. Its aim was to make the client's construct system internally consistent and communicable so that it could eventually be validated or invalidated by new experiences.

During the "thinking through" process, the therapist is not simply passive and accepting. He actively tries to help the client revise or discard old constructs and formulate new ones. He does this by skillfully suggesting new elements be added to the old constructs (for example, "Your view of your brother should also include the fact that he is highly considerate of your friends") or by helping the person formulate new constructs (for example, "Your minister is a person who might help you to better understand why you doubt the existence of God."). He also tries to challenge the client's system without precipitating a catastrophe (Kelly, 1955, Vol. 2, pp. 589–590).

The role of the therapist also requires that the client use current constructs to deal with problems experienced in childhood. Kelly maintained that all too often therapists allowed their clients to dwell on the past and to recount their experiences in childish terms. He proposed that revision of these constructs could happen only if client and therapist were willing to use new, adult thinking about the old experiences. The therapist also helps the client to design new "experiments," to "test" hypotheses with courage, and to weigh the "evidence" critically. The role of the therapist, therefore, is like the role of the experienced scientific investigator who is helping to initiate a beginner into the realm of science. The therapist also acts as a validator of the evidence the client accumulates. As Kelly put it

> It is . . . important that the therapist play his role, not only with an acceptance and a generosity possibly rare in the client's interpersonal world, but always with a kind of naturalness and faithfulness to reality which will not mislead the client who uses him as a validator. In a sense, the therapist must play a part as a reasonably faithful example of natural human reac-

tions, rather than one which is superhuman or divested of all human spontaneity. In a sense, the therapist takes the best to be found in human nature and portrays it in such a way as to enable the client to validate his constructs against it. Having identified the therapist's generalization of the acceptable values in human nature, the client may seek them out among his companions (Kelly, 1955, Vol. 2, p. 593).

In conclusion, the therapist must have a clear idea of his own system and its constructs. He must also be alert and sensitive to a variety of cues emanating from the client. As a scientist, he must be characterized by propositional thinking and be willing to change his views on the basis of the evidence. He must, in brief, be flexible. He must also be courageous, according to Kelly, because psychotherapy is often a distressing experience for him as well as for the client. Finally, he must possess verbal skills and an ability to utilize them, and he must be creative and energetic in the pursuit of his hypothesis, if the client is ever to get well (Kelly, 1955, Vol. 2, pp. 595–605).

Use of the RCRT to Appraise Client Experience

Kelly noted that there were two general approaches to the appraisal of the client's experiences. One focused on the client's past; the other tended to deemphasize the past and to concentrate instead on the present. Kelly agreed that the therapist should not dwell exclusively on the past, but he did think the clinician should make some use of it via the case history method. As he saw it, the past was important because its

. . . events are the validational evidence against which [the client] won and lost his wagers, against which he tested his personal constructs. They are the checkpoints he had to use in charting the course of his life. To understand what they actually were is to get some notion of the ranges of convenience of the client's constructs, what the system was designed to deal with, one way or another. Moreover, many of these events will have to be given some stabilizing interpretation in the new construct system produced under therapeutic intervention (Kelly, 1955, Vol. 2, p. 688).

Also, for Kelly, this procedure would give the clinician evidence of how the person's culture affected his or her life. He believed that the culture provided the person with much evidence of what is "true" or "false" in life. To assess the effects of culture on the person, Kelly turned to the RCRT.

At this point, let us examine possible interpretations of the meaning of it, as they apply to the actual client's matrix shown in Table 8.1. If we proceed down column 1 ("Self") and simply note the incidents ($\checkmark$) and voids (blanks), we can get some idea of how this person sees himself. Remember also the incidents refer to the similarity poles and blanks to the contrast poles of the constructs. He describes himself as a male who is similar in a few respects to his parents who, like him, are very religious. Unfortunately, he claims that he doesn't understand nor do his parents nor his wife nor ex-girlfriend understand him. He is not friends with his parents or his sister. He sees his brother as one of the few people who understand him. Although his brother has accomplished a great deal in his lifetime, the client does not think that he himself has been very successful. Unfortunately, the client, although he seems to admire his brother very much, does not consider him a friend or, alternately, his brother does not see him as a friend. He sees his friend and his wife as friends (See construct 19), but he does not see the person he calls "friend" as a real friend.

We might want tentatively to interpret his construct system to mean that the client sees himself negatively and as alone and isolated, even among people who are supposed to be close to him. He believes that his brother and friend understand him, but he is convinced that his parents do not. Even though his brother and "friend" understand him, they are not really seen as friends. Part of his problem might also stem from the fact that the client describes himself as not sociable. We have, then, a clinical picture of a young man who is possibly either lonely because his family and friends have failed to communicate with him or a person with whom friends and family cannot communicate because he is unsociable and withdrawn. Of course, it is also possible that his feelings of isolation are being produced by still other factors. In any event, his responses on the RCRT provide the clinician with only a clue to his problems. Other diagnostic techniques such as the self-characterization, which will be discussed next, as well as detailed interviews, help the clinician make more definite judgments. It is also clear that you may be able to draw other meaningful inferences from this RCRT protocol. The interpretation here was simply designed to give you some idea of Kelly's approach.

Self-Characterization Sketches and Fixed-Role Therapy as Aids to Effect Change

Once Kelly had made his diagnosis of the client's difficulties, techniques had to be devised to bring about needed change. We have already reviewed briefly some of the procedures that could be used to produce both major and minor adjustment changes.

The therapist not only accepts what the client says, he asks him to elaborate on his constructs through the use of a *self-characterization sketch*. It is a simple approach based upon Kelly's belief that ". . . if you do not know what is wrong with a person, ask him; he may tell you" (Kelly, 1955, Vol. 1, pp. 322–323). Thus, the clinician directly asks the client to write a character sketch of another person, say John Bolling, as if he were the principal character in a play. The client is asked to write it as a friend who knew the character intimately and sympathetically. This third-person format is followed to make the task as nonthreatening as possible.

Following the writing of the sketch and the interpretation of it by the therapist, the therapist uses the interpretation to write a fixed-role sketch for the client, which he is asked to enact. The sketch is designed to produce major changes in the client by making it a script that contrasts sharply with the client's current perception of himself, as revealed in the self-characterization sketch (Kelly, 1955, Vol. 1, p. 370). To accomplish this goal, the therapist focuses on those constructs in the self-characterization sketch that imply immobility. The sketch is designed to protect the client by leading him to believe it is only a fictitious character he is enacting. Kelly found that, with this disclaimer, clients were willing to try out the new role, and that later they began to see its implication for themselves and to act in terms of it.

Kelly also provided a clear example of how the self-characterization and fixed-role therapy techniques worked in the case of an actual client he called Ronald Barrett. An analysis of the self-characterization sketch revealed that Ronald was a compulsive individual who believed dogmatically that there was a reason behind all existence and that the only way to understand the causes of one's existence was to rely on rational thought and logic. Thus, the only way for Ronald to solve problems was to maintain control over his feelings and to rely solely on reason. Despite his attempts at maintaining strict control, however, Ronald saw himself "ready to explode" on many occasions and was disturbed by his feelings, since they would bring disapproval from others. Although he had no warm and friendly relationships with people, he thought that he must have their approval. Such approval could be gained, he reasoned, only by keeping his emotions in check and appearing calm and restrained. His concern with restraining his feelings even extended to his relationships with girls. To quote directly from his self-characterization sketch:

> He [meaning Ronald] has some ideas concerning girls that seem odd or just plain crazy to most people. He completely refrains from calling a girl "beautiful." She may be cute, pretty, attractive, or some other adjective in his mind, but he uses the word "beautiful" only (to) describe material things that have no "feeling" as humans have. Although he listens attentively to stories or general discussions about sex, he rarely enters into the conversation. One may say that he puts too much meaning and thought into kissing a girl. If he has gone out with a girl a couple of times, or even once, and doesn't continue to go out with her or to call her, he is very hesitant about asking her for a date again, say two or three months later. He is usually lost for conversation when meeting someone new, or seeing a girl he knows, but if he once "breaks the ice," he can usually talk freely. However, when he calls a girl on the telephone, no matter how well he knows her, he hates to have anyone around him or even within hearing distance. Furthermore, he doesn't like to practice anything, such as a musical instrument, any place where he can be seen or heard. (Kelly, 1955, Vol. 1, p. 328)

Kelly noted that Ronald was himself disturbed by some of his ideas about girls. He also mentioned that Ronald did attribute "feeling" to girls, but not to beautiful ones. This suggested that he saw girls, and all feeling things, as imperfect. As a consequence, he continually was hesitant and awkward in his relationships with women. To help Ronald overcome his problems, Kelly wrote a fixed-role sketch for him to enact in his daily life. The sketch was about a man called Kenneth Norton. The sketch was as follows:

Kenneth Norton

Kenneth Norton is the kind of man who, after a few minutes of conversation, somehow makes you feel that he must have known you intimately for a long time. This comes about, not by any particular questions that he asks, but by the understanding way in which he listens. It is as if he had a knack of seeing the world through your eyes. The things which you have come to see as being important he, too, soon seems to sense as similarly important. Thus he catches not only your words but the punctuations of feeling with which they are formed and the little accents of meaning with which they are chosen. . . .

Girls he finds attractive for many reasons, not the least of which is the exciting opportunity they provide for his understanding the feminine point of view. Unlike some men, he does not "throw the ladies a line" but, so skillful a listener is he, soon has them throwing him one—and he is thoroughly enjoying it.

With his own parents and in his own home he is somewhat more expressive of his own ideas and feelings. Thus his parents are given an opportunity to share and supplement his new enthusiasms and accomplishments. (Kelly, 1955, Vol. 1, pp. 374–375)

According to Kelly, the sketch centered on a simple theme, namely, the seeking of answers in the feelings of other people rather than in argument with them (Kelly, 1955, Vol. 1, p. 375). He asked Ronald to become Kenneth Norton for two weeks. First however, Kelly let Ronald rehearse in his office a number of times until he was thoroughly familiar with the sketch (Kelly, 1955, Vol. 1, p. 387). Of course, Kelly insisted on addressing the client as Kenneth throughout the rehearsal and enactment period. Kelly also held therapy sessions during the enactment time period to assess Ronald's progress or lack of progress. Progress was uncertain at first, but by the twelfth interview, Ronald reported feeling much less insecure in social situations and more willing to express his feelings. Shortly afterward, the therapist "broke" the client's Kenneth Norton role and told him how Kenneth Norton was, in a sense, supposed to be Ronald Barrett. Ronald accepted this opinion after some discussion and then thanked the therapist for all his help. Ronald returned to his everyday situation with a changed set of constructs and a more realistic assessment of his own behavior and the behavior of others (Kelly, 1955, Vol. 1, pp. 394–395).

CRITICAL COMMENTS

We turn now to an examination of the scientific worth of Kelly's theory.

Comprehensiveness. Kelly's theory is not very comprehensive, al-though it has the potential to handle far more phenomena than it does currently. Its perspective is primarily cognitive in nature, and it tends to deemphasize the role the situation plays in determining behavior. It is, in short, a personalistic rather than a situationist or interactionist ap-proach to the study of behavior. The emphasis on rationality is one-sided. It tends to downplay the irrational thoughts and desires that sometimes control our behavior. It is an intellectualized way of concep-tualizing human functioning. People do not often act as scientists. They are not always objective; they do not always weigh evidence critically. Most important, even if they do weigh it, they sometimes remain unaf-fected by it.

It is important to note, however, that Kelly could not bring himself to dismiss out of hand some of the Freudian constructs which allow inves-tigators to account for irrational behavior. Instead, he tried to retranslate some of the Freudian terms into terms compatible with his psychology of personal constructs. The concept of the unconscious is discussed, in part, as "preverbal constructs," for instance. These are concepts the person cannot articulate because of their poor symbolization. Another way of talking about the unconscious is in terms of the concept of sub-mergence. Kelly assumed that some of our bipolar constructs have poles which are not readily available to us (Kelly, 1955, Vol. 1, pp. 466, 467). For example, a client may believe that "Everyone is kind." This implies that nobody is ever cruel to him, an unlikely possiblity. The therapist might argue that the contrast end of the construct (cruel people) is sub-merged and that his job is to make this aspect of the construct conscious before the client can begin to regain his health. Of course, although Kelly believed his concepts of preverbal constructs and submergence were more specific and clearly defined than Freud's concept of the un-conscious, it is not readily apparent that this is indeed the case. Much of Kelly's discussion of the ways in which the therapist comes to under-stand the mechanisms by which the client submerges his constructs in order to avoid dealing with them is just as muddied as the interpreta-tions offered by some psychoanalysts.

Precision and Testability. In comparison to most of the theories reviewed in the text, Kelly's position is unusually clear and testable. The theory is housed within an explicitly stated framework so that hypotheses can be derived and tested. In addition, the RCRT provides a precise and reli-able way of measuring many of the basic ideas in the theory.

Simplicity. Kelly's position seems quite parsimonious. If anything, it ap-pears to have too few concepts to account for personality functioning. There are relatively few concepts used to describe the developmental process, for example. Kelly says little of an explicit nature about the kinds of learning experiences that move the individual toward maximum understanding of his world. The author also remains unconvinced that the concepts of motivation and reinforcement are totally superfluous and do not help us to understand personality functioning.

Empirical Validity. The experimental evidence in support of certain aspects of Kelly's theory is strong. Most of this research has been concerned with establishing the reliability and validity of the RCRT and some of the basic propositions of the theory. Despite these facts, two points should be made. First, this evidence is largely correlational and paper-and-pencil in nature. Thus, there is a definite need for more sophisticated experimental work in which behavioral criterion measures are used and interaction effects between cognitive functionings of the individual in specific situations are assessed. Despite the provocative nature of Kelly's formulations, research efforts have remained at a fairly unsophisticated level. Perhaps investigators will remedy this problem in the near future so that the worth of Kelly's theory can be assessed more adequately. Second, it should be pointed out that the RCRT is primarily a descriptive device; that is, it describes the constructs the client claims to use in articulating and ordering experiences. Interpretations of the meanings of the constructs, however, rest upon the clinician's skills and sensitivity. Kelly claims that the measure can be used to help clients improve their behavior, but the "evidence" that he offers is traditional in nature—that is, it is based upon the therapist's subjective judgment that the client has improved. In this respect, Kelly's use of case history materials to "prove" the validity of his views on psychotherapy is limited.

Heuristic Value. Kelly's theory has not proved very interesting and challenging to many investigators in the personality area, although there are a few former students and associates and a number of British psychologists who have been active in testing various aspects of it. Part of the difficulty may lie in the fact that the theory is original and too abruptly different from other existing positions in the discipline. It is not clear to many psychologists that the elimination of traditional concepts like motivation and reinforcement is a move in the right direction. Some psychologists believe further that the theory is too cognitive and presents a view of personality that is too one-sided and simplistic. They are intrigued by Kelly's attempts to measure the person's cognitive system, but find that his view does not account adequately for the social learning variables responsible for individual development and functioning.

Applied Value. Kelly's theory has had little impact on disciplines outside psychology and has not contributed very much to the solution of social problems. The theory is currently in its initial stages of verification, so that it may have more impact in the future, especially in the clinical area.

DISCUSSION QUESTIONS

1. Why do many people want to believe their behavior is free and not determined?

2. In what ways do we act as scientists in the prediction of our behavior? Cite limitations in applying this analogy as an aid in understanding our behavior.

3. What is a personal construct? Why must constructs contain at least three elements? Can you think of constructs that contain only two elements?

4. How do propositional and constellatory constructs differ? Give examples of each type of construct.

5. Make up a repertory grid that describes your own constructs in relation to the important people in your life. Did the activity provide you with any insights about your personality?

6. What are some of the strengths and weaknesses of using Kelly's Role Construct Repertory Test (RCRT) to assess personality?

7. What are some of the potentially harmful consequences to other people of your utilization of stereotypes about hair color?

8. Are the traits associated with stereotypes always negative ones? Can you think of sex-role traits that are positive, for example? Why do people rely on stereotypes to guide their behavior?

9. What are some of your superordinate constructs? In your view, is your social success superordinate to academic success or vice versa? Why?

10. Do you agree with Kelly that people are generally rational in their behavior?

NOTES

J. Bieri, "Cognitive Complexity-Simplicity and Predictive Behavior," *Journal of Abnormal and Social Psychology*. 1955, **51**, 263–268.

J. Bonarius, "Research in the Personal Construct Theory of George A. Kelly: Role Construct Repertory Test and Basic Theory," in B. Maher, ed., *Progress in Experimental Personality Research* (New York: Academic Press, 1965), pp. 1–46.

G. A. Kelly, *The Psychology of Personal Constructs*, Vols. 1 and 2 (New York: Norton, 1955).

E. D. Lawson, "Hair Color, Personality and the Observer," *Psychological Reports*, 1971, **28**, 311–322.

SUGGESTED READINGS

Bannister, D., and Fransella, F. *Inquiring Man: The Theory of Personal Constructs*. Baltimore: Penguin, 1971.

Bonarius, J. "Research in the Personal Construct Theory of George A. Kelly: Role Construct Repertory Test and Basic Theory," in B. Maher (ed.), *Progress in Experimental Personality Research*. New York: Academic Press, 1965, pp. 1–46.

Kelly, G. A. *The Psychology of Personal Constructs*, Vol. 1, 2. New York: Norton, 1955.

Mancuso, J. C. (ed.) *Readings for a Cognitive Theory of Personality*. New York: Holt, Rinehart and Winston, 1970.

GLOSSARY

Choice Corollary. The proposition that people select between alternatives in making their judgments about the ways in which reality operates.

Commonality Construct. The proposition that similar construct systems between individuals may lead to similarities or commonalities in behavior.

Constellatory Construct. Type of construct that allows its elements to belong to other constructs concurrently, but once identified in a particular way, these elements are fixed.

Construct. Abstraction defined in terms of the similarity and contrast of its elements.

Constructive Alternativism. Fundamental assumption that human beings are capable of changing their interpretations of events.

Controlled Elaboration. Therapeutic techinque in which the client is encouraged to clarify and "work through" his problems in consultation with the therapist. One of the outcomes of this consultation is the revision or discarding of old construct elements and the formulation of new and more effective ones.

Fixed-Role Therapy. Therapeutic procedure used by Kelly to produce personality changes in clients by constructing roles for them which help them overcome their weaknesses. It helps the clients reconstrue themselves and their life situations.

Fragmentation Corollary. Proposition that the personal construct subsystems of individuals may be disjointed and incompatible with one another.

Individuality Corollary. Proposition that people differ in their constructions of reality.

Organization Corollary. Proposition that the individual's constructs are arranged in particular ways within his or her personal system.

Permeability. Dimension concerned with the issue of whether new elements will or will not be admitted within the boundaries of a construct. A permeable construct is one that can admit new elements; an impermeable one cannot.

Preemptive Construct. Type of construct which includes only its elements and maintains that these elements cannot apply to other constructs.

Propositional Construct. Type of construct that leaves its elements open to alternative constructions.

Range of Convenience. All the events encompassed by a given construct.

Role Construct Repertory Test (RCRT). Test devised by Kelly to assess the personal construct system of an individual.

Self-Characterization Sketch. Initial step in fixed-role therapy in which the client is asked to write a brief character outline of himself but to phrase it in the third person so as to minimize threat to the client.

Sociality Corollary. Proposition that constructive interpersonal relationships depend upon the mutual understanding of the other's construct system by the participants.

Superordinate Construct. Construct that generally controls or subordinates many different constructs.

5

SOCIAL – BEHAVIORISTIC PERSPECTIVES

H istorically, two major lines of thought and investigation have shaped the course of personality psychology. One grew out of clinical practice, beginning with the work of the French physicians Charcot and Janet, and culminated in the efforts of Freud and his disciples. These investigators were medical men primarily concerned with understanding the etiology of their patients' abnormal behavior in order to help them overcome their problems. Thus, they emphasized behavior change. They also focused on some of the most interesting, important, and complicated phenomena in human functioning: love, hate, death, sexual behavior, aggressiveness, and so forth.

In contrast to this medical orientation, the other major line of investigation had its roots in the experimental laboratory. Theorists in this tradition were primarily concerned with the scientific understanding of the learning process. They assumed that most of our behavior was acquired and that the task of the psychologist was to specify the environmental conditions responsible for producing behavior. They were proponents of a simple stimulus-response (S-R) psychology in which an attempt was made to understand how given stimuli became linked to given responses.

The most important proponent of the S-R model in psychology was John B. Watson. Watson had been trained at the University of Chicago as a functionalist. The functionalists explained behavior in terms of "mental functions." Borrowing from Darwin's evolutionary theory, they argued that human beings, like the lower animals, were engaged in a constant struggle to survive. To do this, they had to learn to "adjust" their behavior. Such adjustment was possible because human beings possessed "minds" that encompassed the "ability to reason" and that helped them solve problems presented by the environment.

To Watson, such a position did little to advance psychology as a science. He believed that terms like "mind," "spirit," "soul," and "consciousness" were useless because the private events to which they referred could not be measured objectively and reliably. Psychology would advance only if it got rid of such "mentalism" and focused on public events that could be objectively validated. As a result, Watson proclaimed that psychology was the study of observable behavior and that references to private events were unscientific and unworthy of scientific investigation.

Watson's pronouncements had a significant effect on psychology during his lifetime, and vestiges of his viewpoint can be seen in the work of the various contemporary social-behavioristic theorists discussed in this part of the text. This statement is especially true of Skinner's work (Chapter 9), but it also applies in certain respects to the positions taken by Rotter and Bandura (Chapters 10 and 11).

Like Watson, Skinner has a basic aversion to the study of private events, even though he has recently concluded that such phenomena are important and would have to be included in any comprehensive theory of behavior. He would prefer to focus on observable behavior that can be reliably recorded. Like Watson, he is primarily concerned with trying to understand how environmental stimuli influence behavior in the hope of generating fundamental laws. To accomplish this goal, Skinner believes that systematic observation and experimentation are necessary, and that the experimentation must occur under controlled conditions. Such control can best be exercised by studying the behavior of lower animals in the laboratory. Because the behaviors most amenable to control are simple ones, Skinner believes that the investigator should proceed from the simple to the complex.

Such a position means that his followers will concern themselves primarily with a restricted set of phenomena and will not be actively engaged in attempts to explain phenomena like love and hate. Skinner argues that his approach has paid off handsomely, as principles of behavior painstakingly discovered in laboratory work with lower animals have been successfully applied to people in therapeutic and educational settings. It is only in recent years that Skinner's operant analysis has been applied to human problems, but we can now say with some conviction that he is gradually moving from a simple behaviorism focused only on lower animals to a more complex social behaviorism that addresses itself to important human issues. In line with this new development, we even see the tough-minded Skinner beginning to recognize, however reluctantly, the role that cognitive variables play in behavior.

The materials in Chapter 9 review Skinner's arguments about the need for a scientific technology of behavior and the dangers of mentalism. He does not, however, equate mentalism with cognition. Mentalism has a pejorative meaning for Skinner, but cognition is a far less negative term for him. What Skinner objects to specifically are "mentalistic" explanations that seem to help us understand behavior but in fact impede our understanding. Statements like "He was kind to you because he has a *pure soul*," or "She scored an A on her chemistry exam because she has a good *mind"* would be two examples of mentalistic explanations that lack scientific explanatory power. They are invoked on a post hoc basis and are meaningless from a scientific standpoint, as we pointed out in Chapter 1. Cognition and mentalism are similar in that both terms refer to private events; but whereas mentalism describes events that cannot be studied scientifically, cognition refers to events that can be objectively and reliably recorded and communicated clearly among scientists. The primary method of studying cognitive events is verbal reports, and Skinner accepts their use, as do Rotter and Bandura.

Chapter 9 also focuses on the major terms and principles in Skinner's operant analysis of personality. Of particular importance is his treatment of the effects of various kinds of reinforcers and reinforcement schedules on the acquisition and modification of behavior. Skinner is frequently lambasted by critics as advocating the use of punishment to control behavior, but this accusation is simply not true. As we shall see, Skinner does not consider punishment an effective means of altering behavior. The chapter also includes a discussion of the development of normal and abnormal personalities within Skinner's unique framework. Additionally, there is an extensive discussion of the ways in which operant principles can be applied in therapeutic and educational settings, and a review of critical comments about the worth of his position.

The work of Rotter and Bandura also has a number of features in common with the psychology advocated by Watson. First, both Rotter and Bandura believe that most of our behavior is learned. They also believe that the advancement of psychology as a science will depend upon the establishment of precise measurement procedures and the systematic observation of behavior under controlled conditions. Yet the theories advocated by both men rely heavily on the use of cognitive constructs, a position clearly in opposition to Watson's dictum that the study of such events has no place in psychology. Thus, their positions go far beyond Watson's simple, mechanistic model of human functioning. Whereas Watson leaned heavily on Pavlov's classical conditioning paradigm to explain the acquisition of behavior, Rotter and Bandura expand this position by incorporating the role of organismic variables into their formulas. Their position is a neo-behavioristic one that includes such cognitive constructs as expectancy, imitation, covert rehearsal of events, values, memory, and habits. These stimulus-organism-response (S-O-R) models attempt to deal with more complex phenomena than the ones studied by Watson and, to a certain extent, by Skinner. At the same time, however, Rotter and Bandura insist upon accurate and objective measurement of these complex phenomena.

The positions of Rotter and Bandura are a more direct outgrowth of learning theories propounded after Watson. Rotter himself traces the origins of his position to the work of the learning theorists Thorndike, Tolman, and Hull. From Thorndike, Rotter adopted the view that behavior is subject to modification by its consequences. In other words, Rotter accepts the concept of instrumental or operant conditioning. (For a fuller review of Thorndike's position, see the biographical materials on Skinner in Chapter 9.) It should also be noted that operant learning is the cornerstone of Skinner's theory and is accepted by Bandura as well, although Bandura does not give it the same status in his system that Skinner does.

From Hull and Tolman, Rotter adopted the idea of trying to increase our understanding of behavior by utilizing the concepts of intervening variable and hypothetical construct. Intervening variables and hypothetical constructs are terms that allow an investigator to discuss the role of organismic variables—for example, hunger, motives, expectancies, habits, drives, intelligence, prior reinforcement history, and so forth—in guiding or directing behavior. They are ways of discussing the operation of internal or private events that *intervene* between external stimuli and eventual external responses. They are the O variables in the S-O-R framework. Hypothetical constructs were used by Hull to signify his belief that an internal event such as hunger or a drive has a real basis in the nervous system of the individual and that this basis would eventually be discovered. Intervening events were used by Tolman to refer to a mathematical relationship between events that could be measured. A concrete example might make the differences between the terms clearer for you. For Tolman, the concept of hunger might be defined in terms of the number of hours of food deprivation. Thus, he might make a differential prediction concerning the running performance of rats: He might predict that animals deprived of food for twenty-four hours would run faster to reach food pellets than animals deprived of food for one hour.

Hull would agree with Tolman's mathematical definition, but would argue that hunger also involves specific chemical changes in body tissues that would need to be accounted for in order to predict the running performance of these animals accurately. Thus, even though all the animals in the twenty-four-hour deprivation condition are assumed to be equally hungry in terms of Tolman's definition, Hull would argue that differences in running performance *within* this condition are due to differential chemical changes which are also part of the meaning of the term hunger. Thus, Tolman uses mathematical definitions of variables such as hunger to avoid "excess meaning" in his theoretical constructs, whereas Hull's treatment of these variables is more complicated and probably more accurate in its assessment of the reality of the situation.

Yet Hull's position also poses problems. There is the danger that using terms with "excess meanings" can lead to fuzzy thinking and post-hoc interpretations of research results. In the example just cited, Hull's concept of hunger might lead to a post-hoc "explanation" of results which showed that animals deprived of food for twenty-four hours ran *slower* than animals deprived of food for one hour in terms of the amount of sugar in the blood. It could be argued that the contradictory results were due to a low blood sugar level in the rats deprived of food for one hour, a condition unknown to the investigators at the time they conducted the experiment. Or the results could have been due to a lack of norepinephrine in the bodies of the animals deprived of food for twenty-four hours. The possibilities are endless. The point is that terms like hunger with multiple meanings must be carefully assessed at the outset of experimentation. Their referents must be pinpointed, for failure to do so may lead to endless speculation about the actual causes of the behavior in question. The distinction between the hypothetical construct and the intervening variable is, in fact, not obvious to most students—or to many psychologists, for that matter—and today the terms are used interchangeably. These differences are, however, important, and you should bear them in mind, particularly as we attempt to understand weaknesses in the cognitive aspects of the Rotter and Bandura theories.

From Tolman and Hull, Rotter also borrowed the notion that behavior is purposive, that is, that we are guided by our motives to attain certain goals. Rotter's thinking is particularly close to Hull's in this regard. For Hull, the formula to predict the probability of the occurrence of behavior was as follows:

$$E = H \times D$$

E refers to the "excitatory potential" of behavior (the probability of behavior), *H* refers to habit strength, and *D* refers to drive strength. Thus, for Hull, the probability of a given response or movement toward a goal was seen to be a function of the animal's drive state (motive) multiplied by its habit strength. In Rotter's scheme, excitatory potential becomes "behavior potential," habit strength is roughly translated as "expectancy of the occurrence of reinforcement," and drive strength is reinterpreted as the "value of the reinforcement." Thus, the probability that a given behavior will occur is a function of the expectancies or habits that a person acquires, primarily as a result of the number of experiences she undergoes in a given situation and the importance of the reinforcer, which will affect her drive level as she moves toward her goal.

Chapter 10 includes a review of these and other concepts in Rotter's theory. The chapter focuses on one construct of particular importance in Rotter's social learning position, internal-external control of reinforcement, and provides a sampling of research findings based on the measurement of individual differences in focus of control.

Bandura's work, like Rotter's, places heavy emphasis on the role of cognitive mediation. This does not mean, however, that Bandura rejects the concept of reinforcement; he simply does not give it primacy in his theoretical system. He focuses instead on the role that observational learning plays in the acquisition, maintenance, and modification of be-havior. As he rightly notes, the study of imitation learning has been relatively ignored by traditional learning theorists. Historically, the con-cept can be traced to the work of Morgan in 1896, Tarde in 1903, and MacDougall in 1908. All these theorists believed that imitation was an innate tendency in human beings. As the instinct doctrine fell into dis-repute because of the popularity of Watsonian behaviorism, however, a few learning theorists, such as Humphrey, Allport, and Holt, tried to ac-count for imitation in terms of Pavlovian conditioning. In terms of this learning paradigm, imitative responses were the simple result of a person matching his behavior to the behavior of another. In other terms, imitation involved contiguous association between social stimuli.

Soon, however, the behaviorist focus shifted from classical condition-ing to instrumental or operant learning. This new view was advocated primarily by Miller and Dollard in their classic text, *Social Learning and Imitation* (1941). In essence, their position was that imitation learning oc-curred when a motivated person was positively reinforced for matching the behavior of a model during a sequence of random trial and error responses.

Bandura's objection to the classical and instrumental conditioning explanations of imitation centers around the fact that both positions fail to account for the acquisition of new responses through observation. In regard to the operant position, for example, Bandura contends the assumption is that the person makes a long series of random responses which are eventually shaped through reinforcement until they match the behavior of the model. Bandura believes this process is too com-bersome to account for the many responses we learn in the course of our lives. He suggests instead that imitative learning can often occur in the absence of external reinforcement. We acquire behavior without performing it overtly and without being reinforced for it. We simply watch the behavior of others, represent it cognitively (that is, sym-bolically), and then perform it under the appropriate conditions.

Chapter 11 begins by elaborating upon these points in a discussion of the major assumptions underlying Bandura's social learning position. Then the basic concepts and principles of his theory are outlined. The focus is on the ways in which behavior is learned when the person is exposed to single and multiple models with varying personality charac-teristics. It is noted that the impact of multiple models on children's be-havior is often complicated and difficult to assess, since the models often show contradicting behaviors. There is also a detailed discussion of the role of self-control processes in the acquisition of behavior in the chapter. This is followed by an examination of some applications of modeling principles and research to two major social problems: violence in the media and problem behaviors, with a focus on phobias in children. Bandura's recommendations for bringing violence under control and the use of modeling as a therapeutic technique are reviewed. Following this presentation, Bandura's treatment of the developmental process is given. Concepts of imitation, successive approximation, and schedule of reinforcement are used by Bandura to help us understand this process. Assessment of the primary strengths and weaknesses of his position follow.

B. F. Skinner (Courtesy of Harvard University)

CHAPTER 9

Skinner's Operant Analysis

BIOGRAPHICAL SKETCH

Burrhus Frederick Skinner was born in Susquehanna, Pennsylvania, in 1904. In his autobiography, he reports that his home life was warm and stable. He was never physically punished by his lawyer father and only once by his mother, and that was when she washed his mouth with soap and water after he said a "bad" word. Skinner also mentions that he liked school and acquired a strong background in English and literature, mathematics, and the sciences from a few fine teachers. As a boy, he was always building and creating things. He built roller-skate scooters, wagons, sleds, seesaws, merry-go-rounds, slingshots, blow guns, kites, and model airplanes. This fascination with mechanical objects can be seen in his invention and use of various devices in his experimental work, including the Skinner box, an apparatus designed to help investigators study the effects of different reinforcement schedules on animal behavior; the cumulative recorder, a device to assess the rate of responding of organisms; and the teaching machine, an instrument designed to facilitate learning in students.

Because he had a thorough grounding in literature, Skinner decided to major in English when he enrolled at Hamilton College in New York State. He notes, however, that he never really adjusted to student life. He joined a fraternity, but knew little about fraternity life. He was also inept at sports. Like many students then and now, he complained bitterly about unnecessary curriculum requirements. By his senior year, he reports being in open revolt. He participated in a number of activities designed to humiliate some faculty members the students thought pompous and arrogant. One of these incidents is particularly noteworthy. In order to deflate a name-dropping English professor, Skinner and another student printed posters that read, in part: "Charles Chaplin, the famous cinema comedian, will deliver his lecture 'Moving Pictures as a Career' in the Hamilton College Chapel on Friday, October 9." The lecture was reported to be under the professor's auspices. They plastered posters all over town, and then returned to the campus and went to bed. The next morning, the other student called the local newspaper and told reporters that the college president wanted the lecture publicly announced. By noon, the situation was completely out of hand. Swarms of children were taken by their parents to the railway station to greet the famous actor. In spite of police roadblocks, approximately four hundred cars got through to the campus. There were other escapades, along with threats of expulsion by the college president, but he was finally permitted to graduate.

After college, Skinner pursued a career as a writer. As a senior, he had met the famous poet Robert Frost, who had requested that Skinner send him samples of his work. Skinner sent the poet three short stories, and received encouraging comments in reply. He then spent approximately two years living in Greenwich Village in New York City and in Europe. Eventually he realized he would not be successful as a writer, presumably because he had nothing important to say. His interest in human behavior led him to enter Harvard to study psychology.

Skinner found the intellectual atmosphere at Harvard stimulating and challenging, and reports that, in order to improve his skills in a new field, he set up a rigorous study schedule and adhered to it for almost two years. He read nothing but psychology and physiology. Some of his academic mentors included the historian E. G. Boring, the clinician Henry Murray, and the physiologist W. J. Crozier. The writings of J. B. Watson, Ivan Pavlov, and E. L. Thorndike also had a considerable impact on the young psychologist. For example, he was impressed by Watson's concern with devising a technology of behavior. In one fell swoop, the noted behaviorist had thrown out all "mentalistic" concepts, including mind, spirit, and consciousness, and proclaimed instead that psychology was the scientific study of observable behavior. Skinner too has maintained that psychologists should focus on behavior that is observable and verifiable but, unlike Watson, he believes that psychologists must also account for internal or private events, as long as such events can be measured objectively and reliably.

The work of the Russian physiologist Ivan Pavlov on the conditioned reflex was also important to Skinner. Pavlov was originally interested in the process of digestion in lower animals and the conditions under which digestive juices were secreted. In the course of his work he discovered that the animals salivated not only when food was actually in their mouths, but also when it was shown to them by the experimenter. He called this phenomenon a "psychic secretion." His next step was to control the conditions under which such secretions occurred. As virtually every psychology student knows, Pavlov designed a room that minimized the intrusion of extraneous stimuli and was eventually able to demonstrate, through a precise series of maneuvers, that salivation could be brought under the control of specific stimuli such as a light or a bell. Previously neutral stimuli acquired the power to evoke responses originally evoked by other stimuli. The animals were "classically conditioned." Besides the fact that such respondent conditioning can account for a variety of behaviors, Skinner was impressed by the procedure Pavlov used to bring the behavior under control. He reports accepting fully then and now Pavlov's dictum, "Control your conditions and you will see order."

Although some of our behavior is learned via classical conditioning, most of it is learned after we voluntarily behave and find that our actions are followed by positive and negative experiences. Skinner's interest in operant behavior—that is, behavior that operates on the environment—was piqued by animal experiments conducted by the learning theorist E. L. Thorndike. Typically, cats were deprived of food and then placed in problem boxes and left there until they accidentally moved a mechanism that opened a door and allowed them to escape. The animals usually made a variety of responses before making the correct one. Thorndike explained this "trial and error" learning by maintaining that an association was acquired between the responses of the animals and their reinforcing consequences. Responses that resulted in pleasurable sensations Thorndike considered to be "stamped-in," whereas he considered responses followed by an annoying state of affairs to be "stamped-out." Skinner has adopted a modification of this *Law of Effect* to explain the acquisition of behavior. A primary aspect of his modification is the focus on changes in the probability of responding produced by the application of reinforcers.

Following years of intensive study, Skinner received his Ph.D. from Harvard in 1931 and then spent five postdoctoral years working in Crozier's laboratory. In 1936, he accepted his first academic position at the University of Minnesota; two years later, he produced his first book, *The Behavior of Organisms*, a work which presents his initial formulations for an *operant analysis* of behavior. While at Minnesota, Skinner also found the time to begin a novel entitled *Walden Two*, a story about a miniature utopian society based on operant principles.

After a brief stint as chairman of the psychology department at Indiana University, he returned to Harvard in 1948 and has remained affiliated with that institution ever since. Besides being accorded many honors by his fellow psychologists, Skinner was also one of the few behavioral scientists to win the President's Medal of Science. He has also been a prolific writer: his books include *Science and Human Behavior* (1953), *Verbal Behavior* (1957), *Cumulative Record* (1961), *The Technology of Teaching* (1968), *Contingencies of Reinforcement* (1969), *Beyond Freedom and Dignity* (1971), *About Behaviorism* (1974), and *Particulars of My Life* (1976). He continues to write and to be actively interested in the promotion and advancement of psychology to benefit human beings (Skinner, 1970, pp. 1–21).

THE NEED FOR A SCIENTIFIC TECHNOLOGY OF BEHAVIOR

Like virtually all of us, Skinner believes we are faced today with problems that threaten our very existence. But although we often misuse the products of a scientific technology, he argues that we can in fact utilize the same technological prowess to solve our problems. We have even taken a few small steps in that direction: To contain the population explosion, we are turning to a variety of birth control methods. We are beginning to utilize pollution control devices to clean up the environment. We are attempting to lessen the threat of world famine by devising better methods of crop production. We are continuously attempting, and sometimes succeeding, in controlling various kinds of diseases (Skinner, 1971, p. 1). Yet, in each of these areas, we have only scratched the surface. Why is this so? In Skinner's opinion, it is because the solutions to these problems lie not in the application of our physical and biological knowledge, but in an understanding of human behavior. He points out, for example, that birth control devices are useless if people do not use them. Pollution control procedures are also not helpful if people continue to ignore or resist them. What we need are drastic changes in our behavior (Skinner, 1971, p. 4).

The Dangers of Mentalism

If we grant the legitimacy of Skinner's argument, why have we not made more progress in understanding human behavior and using this knowledge to alleviate suffering? The answer, Skinner believes, lies in our refusal to give up "mentalistic" explanations of behavior that give the *appearance* of helping us understand our actions, but in fact hinder us in our quest. In Skinner's words

> We are told that to control the number of people in the world we need to change *attitudes* toward children, overcome *pride* in size of family or in sexual potency, build some *sense of responsibility* toward offspring, and reduce the role played by a large family in allaying *concern* for old age. To work for peace we must deal with the *will to power* or the *paranoid delusions* of leaders; we must remember that wars begin in the *minds* of men, that there is something suicidal in man—a *death instinct* perhaps—which leads to war, and that man is aggressive by *nature*. To solve the problems of the poor we must inspire *self-respect*, encourage *initiative*, and reduce *frustration*. . . . This is staple fare. Almost no one questions it. Yet there is nothing like it in modern physics or most of biology, and that fact may well explain why a science and a technology of behavior have been so long delayed. (Skinner, 1971, pp. 9–10)

Such explanations are post hoc in nature, according to Skinner. They seem to provide answers to questions, but they do not. Further, such *mentalism* also brings curiosity to an end (Skinner, 1971, p. 12). The problem seems to be solved. For example, if someone asks us, "Why didn't you study last night?" and we reply, "Because I didn't feel like it," she is likely to take our reply as a satisfactory explanation of our behavior. In fact, however, it would be much more revealing to know what in our past might have made studying aversive for us. Perhaps we did not do well on previous exams in the course or perhaps the materials were too difficult or too easy. Or perhaps we were looking forward to a party in the dormitory and studying for the exam would have prevented us from enjoying this experience. The possibilities are virtually endless. But the person accepts our comment, "I didn't feel like it," and does not inquire further into the details of our behavior. Of course, in ordinary conversation we may not want more information. What we should realize, however, is that she could have learned much more about the causes of our behavior if she had asked additional questions. She may have been lulled into accepting minimal information as an adequate explanation. Skinner maintains that a scientific approach to the study of human behavior must reject such false security. We must give up the nebulous inner "explanation" and search instead for the precise antecedent events that, in reality, produce our behavior.

Skinner does not, as we have pointed out, categorically reject the study of all private events. In a recent work, *About Behaviorism*, he takes pains to point out that Watson, in his zeal to establish psychology as a science, made an exaggerated and incorrect commitment to the elimination of the study of introspective life (Skinner 1974, p. 5). Skinner believes, albeit half-heartedly, that psychologists must provide adequate explanations of private events, but the events studied must be capable of being reliably and objectively recorded. Thus, verbal reports might provide acceptable data for Skinner and his followers, if the scientific criteria are met (Skinner, 1974, p. 31). But since other people have difficulty teaching us the appropriate labels for our private experiences, we must be cautious in accepting such reports at face value. Thus, contrary to popular belief, Skinner does not just accept Watson's simplistic *stimulus-response* formulation. He maintains that such an approach is obsolete and that he has been unfairly attacked. His critics, he says, are ignorant of the major changes in psychology in the past sixty years and continue mistakenly to criticize him for treating human beings as robots. Skinner says he recognizes the complexity of behavior and suggests that people, especially those in the humanities, "stop beating a dead horse."

It seems clear, then, that Skinner does not reject or accept the study of inner events in an all or nothing fashion. An example may help clarify what he would find objectionable or acceptable. Imagine a person sitting down at a table in a restaurant and eating a meal consisting of Fettucini Alfredo, Beaujolais, coffee, and spumoni. For illustrative purposes, a basic question might be: Why did he eat? The typical answer is that he ate *because* he was hungry. Skinner would reject this interpretation as mentalistic if we considered this explanation adequate. He would say that the term hunger would have to be explained by linking it to antecedent events in the environment—for example, to the number of hours since the time of the previous meal. His hunger did *not* cause the person to eat; rather, food deprivation, along with a host of other environmental variables, (the decor of the restaurant, the price of the food, its attractiveness) contributed to the probability that he would eat that meal at that particular time.

A behavioristic analysis would force us to focus on those events in the environment that help produce the behavior. The events can be current ones or ones that have occurred in the past. This information, coupled with data about our genetic endowments, where it is pertinent to the explanation of a given behavior, helps us in prediction. For example, if the diner had been allergic to the starches in the fettucini, he might have decided not to eat at all or to eat different food. Thus, inner events—that is, our prior histories, which are based upon transactions with the environment, and our unique genetic heritages—contribute to the prediction of behavior. You should be aware that although Skinner recognizes the legitimacy of such inner events for a behavioral psychology, he nevertheless deemphasizes them in his own analysis. He accords the same legitimacy to physiological events, but again pays little actual attention to them in experimental analysis. Besides the difficulty of reliable measurement the scientist cannot systematically manipulate them and watch their effects on behavior. Skinner believes that major advances will occur only when psychologists focus on the ways in which behavior and external environmental variables are causally related. What is needed, in brief, is a *functional analysis* of behavior.

Free Will Versus Determinism

According to Skinner, this search for order among events is offensive to many people. It is offensive because, once these relationships are specified, scientists can begin to anticipate and determine our actions (Skinner, 1953, p. 6). They can start to exercise control over our behavior. Such an idea runs counter to the long tradition we have of viewing ourselves as free agents. We do not like to believe our actions are the product of specifiable antecedent conditions; we prefer to believe we are free and capable of spontaneous inner change (Skinner, 1953, p. 7). As members of a democratically oriented society, we also resist anyone who says he or she wants to control our behavior.

Skinner states that this belief in our own autonomy has a number of unfortunate implications. First, acceptance of the belief may mean that our behavior is uncaused by events in the environment. We alone are responsible for our own actions, and thus we should be rewarded for behaving well and punished when we behave badly. This view, however, often obscures our perception of the environmental variables that in fact control our behavior (Skinner, 1971, pp. 19–20). For example, some of us "know" that members of minority groups are responsible for their own situation. We say that they should show some initiative and work like we do. We sometimes hear people say of juvenile delinquents, "Well, they got themselves into it, let them get themselves out of it!" The part played by an oppressive environment is lost in such accounts. The focus on the inner man or woman prevents us from seeing clearly the possible contributing causes of their behaviors. It is interesting that although many of Skinner's critics consider him a fascist, a reactionary, a Machiavellian, and the like because of his stand on determinism, he emerges instead, at least in this instance, more like a super-liberal.

A science of behavior that questions our autonomy also threatens beliefs about personal worth and dignity. A scientific analysis shifts the credit as well as the blame for our actions to the environment (Skinner, 1971, p. 21). We may not object to an analysis that absolves us of blame, but we would probably object to one that deprives us of a chance to be admired and loved (Skinner, 1971, p. 75). In addition, Skinner points out that the amount of credit we give someone for a performance is typically inversely proportional to the conspicuousness of the causes of the behavior: "We stand in awe of the inexplicable, and it is therefore not surprising that we are likely to admire behavior more as we understand it less" (Skinner, 1971, p. 53). For example, we may be more impressed by the performance of a young figure skater if we do not know that she practiced six hours a day every day of the week for the past eleven years to attain her current status. We are probably much more impressed with the "bright" and "creative" novelist if we do not know that he began writing at age ten and had received twenty-eight rejection slips from publishers before they decided to publish one of his manuscripts.

The rejection of ourselves as autonomous beings may also be threatening because it implies that we come under the control of others. Why should we fear such a consequence? First, the loss of freedom means for many of us that we will not be able to do what we want (Carpenter, 1974, p. 87). Skinner maintains that such an argument is false because it implies that we have free will. In reality, our wants are conditioned by external events. A homemaker, for example, does not buy a dishwasher because she simply and freely wants one. Instead, she may buy one because her old one has broken down or because she learns of a new model through advertisements in the media. Perhaps her mother-in-law has been pressuring her to sell "the old eyesore." Whatever the reason or reasons, her behavior is determined by events in the past or current environment.

Second, many of us have been taught to believe that all control of behavior is bad (Carpenter, 1974, p. 89). Skinner maintains that such a belief is stereotypic. There are many instances in which control is exerted over our behavior and we do not complain or think it bad. Parents restrain small children from diving into the twelve-foot end of the pool. Society controls driving behavior with elaborate rules and regulations. State governments require auto safety inspections. Compulsory vaccinations protect us against disease. Doctors exercise control when they operate on people. The list is endless, but the point should be clear. Yet, Skinner's critics continue to insist that a particular form of control—coercion—is bad because it involves the exploitation of one party by another. Skinner agrees wholeheartedly with this statement. He too would oppose control of this sort. What, then, are the objections to his position? There seem to be two primary points. One, that Skinner wants to manipulate people without their being aware of it, and two, that Skinner wants to set himself up as the arbiter of good and evil (Carpenter, 1974, p. 90). Skinner answers by pointing out that all our behavior is determined, whether we are aware of it or not. Second, he says we already have a general consensus on what is good and bad. Virtually everyone is against disease, poverty, war, and indiscriminate destruction of the environment. Conversely, nearly all of us prefer politeness to rudeness, generosity to greed, love to selfishness, and so on. Why quarrel over the obvious?

Despite the cogency of Skinner's arguments for a thoroughgoing determinism, the fact remains that the deterministic viewpoint is an assumption on his part, even though there is considerable evidence to support it. Most of the evidence is based on studies with lower animals, in which it is possible to control conditions and observe systematic changes in behavior. For human beings, however, the problem is much more complicated: The scientist usually does not have control over our previous environments and thus cannot observe the same changes in behavior that might occur in lower animals as a function of the manipulation of events in the current environment. In short, there is too much "noise" in the human system for us to argue conclusively that determinism is scientifically proved. Nevertheless, it appears to be a reasonable working assumption in light of the fact that it continues to lead to the accumulation of data which advances our understanding.

Personality from the Perspective of a Radical Behaviorist

We have considered some of the major reasons why Skinner opts for a scientific approach to the study of behavior, along with some of the provocative philosophical implications of his position. But what about the study of personality? Is it lost in Skinner's strict emphasis on a "cause and effect" analysis of behavior? The answer to the latter question is "No," but Skinner considers the study of personality legitimate only if established scientific criteria are met. He will not, for example, accept the idea of a personality or self that guides or directs behavior. He considers such an approach a vestige of animism, a doctrine that presupposed the existence of something like spirits within the body which moved it (Skinner, 1974, p. 167). Nor would he be satisfied with dead-end "explanations" of behavior such as this one: "Why did the robbers kill those helpless people?" "Because they are crazy."

Skinner considers the study of personality to involve a systematic examination of the idiosyncratic learning history and unique genetic background of the individual:

> In a behavioral analysis, a person is an organism . . . which has acquired a repertoire of behavior. . . . [He] is not an originating agent; he is a locus, a point at which many genetic and environmental conditions come together in a joint effect. As such, he remains unquestionably unique. No one else (unless he has an identical twin) has his genetic endowment, and without exception no one else has his personal history. Hence no one else will behave in precisely the same way. (Skinner, 1974, pp. 167–168)

The study of personality, then, would involve the discovery of the unique set of relationships between the behavior of an organism and its reinforcing consequences. Of course, such an analysis would have to be consistent with the organism's genetic capacity to respond to events in the environment.

BASIC CONCEPTS AND PRINCIPLES

Operant Behavior and Conditioning

All our behavior takes place in a setting and produces outcomes. In terms of Skinner's system, we operate upon the environment to generate consequences (Skinner, 1953, p. 65). The occurrence of reinforcers is said to be contingent or dependent upon our behavior. Operant behavior includes talking to people, reading, walking, writing, eating, kissing, dressing, hitting a baseball, singing a song, and countless other activities. When we are deprived of water, we drink and our behavior is reinforced by the water. We kiss another person and are reinforced for our behavior. We write a check and are reinforced for our action. If the check is good, people stop trying to collect payment. If it is bad, they will probably try to make things difficult for us. Criticizing someone is also reinforcing for the criticizer. Turning the house thermostat from 55 to 70 degrees on a winter morning is also reinforcing. The establishment of the linkage or association between the behavior and its consequences is called *conditioning*. Through operant conditioning, the occurrence of behavior is made more or less probable.

Operant Reinforcement and the Probability of Response

Behavior is made more probable if it is followed by the presentation of *positive reinforcers*—for example, food, water, or affection. It is also strengthened by the removal of aversive stimuli from the situation—for example, electric shock, criticism, extremes in temperature. These latter stimuli are called *negative reinforcers*. Both positive and negative reinforcers strengthen behavior. Behavior is made less probable through the

application of punishing stimuli or through the removal of positive reinforcers (Skinner, 1953, p. 73). Spanking a child would be a good
example of the use of punishment; taking a toy away from a child would
be an example of the removal of a positive reinforcer.

The Effects of Punishment

Skinner says that *punishment* is the most common technique of control in
modern life. Its use is familiar to all of us:

> [I]f a man does not behave as you wish, knock him down; if a child mis-
> behaves, spank him; if the people of a country misbehave, bomb them.
> Legal and police systems are based upon such punishments as fines . . .
> incarceration, and hard labor. Religious control is exerted through pen-
> ances, threats of excommunication, and consignment to hell-fire. Education
> has not wholly abandoned the birch rod. In everyday personal contact we
> control through censure, snubbing, disapproval, or banishment. . . . All of
> this is done with the intention of reducing tendencies to behave in certain
> ways. (Skinner, 1953, p. 182)

But why is the use of punishment so pervasive? Probably because it is
easy to apply and because it has immediate, observable, and satisfying
effects for the punisher. In addition, the technique is easily learned,
whereas alternative positive measures are more difficult to acquire. The
need for punishment also has the ostensible support of history, according to Skinner (1971, p. 80). For all these reasons, many of us resort to it.

But does punishment work? Certainly in the short run, it seems to be
effective. It stops the undesired behavior. Skinner maintains that this effect may be misleading, since the reduction in the strength of the behavior may not be permanent (Skinner, 1953, p. 183). The evidence for
this last statement is a study he conducted in which he trained rats of the
same sex, age, and genetic strain to press a lever in a Skinner box as a
means of obtaining food pellets (Skinner, 1938, pp. 151–160). After establishing the bar-pressing response, Skinner withheld the reinforcers
from these animals in order to *extinguish* their behavior. In a control
group, Skinner let some of the animals continue to press the bar without
punishment until they stopped responding completely. In the experimental group, each time the animals pressed the lever, they were
punished by a "slap" on the paws administered mechanically. This
punishment continued for the first ten minutes of the extinction period
and then was terminated. Skinner found an initial decrease in the rate of
responding for the animals while they were being punished. When the
punishment was ended, however, the experimental group began to
respond again. Eventually, this group produced as many responses as
the controls. The general point of the study seems to be that punishment
temporarily "suppresses" behavior, but the behavior is likely to reappear when the punishing contingencies are withdrawn. In Freudian

terms, we might speak of suppressed wishes that eventually appear, perhaps in sublimated form.

Punishment also has two other undesirable effects, according to Skinner. First, it may give rise to emotional responses that are incompatible with appropriate behavior (Skinner, 1953, pp. 186–187). For example, a man who as an adolescent is punished severely for masturbating while looking at pictures of nude women may later experience strong feelings of guilt in a situation with a member of the opposite sex where sexual behavior is appropriate. Or a child who has been beaten by his parents for reading poorly may later experience considerable resentment toward teachers who are trying to help him improve his reading skills. The feelings of resentment may then be correlated with behavior such as refusing to read, which leads to a continuation of the reading difficulties.

Second, punishment may also create strong conflict in people (Skinner, 1953, p. 190). It should be clear that such conflict would not, in a Skinnerian analysis, involve an "inner struggle," but rather an incompatibility between responses, one of which is positively reinforcing and one of which is potentially punishing. The male student who has been rejected by a number of women students but who continues to seek a relationship with women on campus would be a pertinent example. Such a person might be labeled in traditional personality terms as awkward, indecisive, and timid.

For all these reasons, Skinner believes we should shun the use of punishment to control behavior. Instead, we should focus on the use of positive reinforcers. (A detailed examination of Skinner's position in regard to the use of positive reinforcers in education will appear later in the chapter.)

Operant Extinction

The failure to reinforce a response affects the probability of responding by making its occurrence less and less frequent. Under such extinction conditions, Skinner points out that

> [a] person is . . . said to suffer a loss of confidence, certainty, or sense of power. . . . [He] is said to be unable to go to work because he is discouraged or depressed, although his not going, together with what he feels, is due to a lack of reinforcement—either in his work or in some other part of his life. (Skinner, 1974, p. 58)

We control the behavior of others through the use of such a procedure. To eliminate behavior we consider undesirable, for example, we ignore it. If our roommate acts in obnoxious ways, we may simply not pay attention to him. If a child has a temper tantrum, the parents may ignore her by reading a newspaper or turning on the television set. Such a procedure seems to make sense, but unfortunately it is often unworkable in practice. The reason is simply that the undesirable behavior is often very strong, since it has been reinforced many times in the past. As a consequence, it is highly resistant to extinction. Thus, the mother who tries to eliminate temper tantrums by ignoring her child's behavior is likely to "give in" eventually by listening to her child, comforting him, and giving him what he wants. Such an action on her part is positively reinforcing to her as well as to the child. Her behavior eliminates aversive stimuli for her and hence is strengthened. Unfortunately, by positively reinforcing her son, she has also ensured that the behavior will continue. An alternate strategy in this situation might be to send the child to his room for a brief period of time, a procedure known technically as a "time out," until he stops whining and complaining and then to show him a more constructive way to solve his problem and reinforce him for using it.

Schedules of Reinforcement and the Acquisition of Unique Repertoires

All of us are exposed to different environments and to different schedules or arrangements of reinforcement in our daily lives. Some parents, for example, consistently reinforce their children's behavior; others supply only intermittent reinforcers. These schedules have a tremendous impact on our responding. Numerous studies with lower animals, for example, have shown that behavior learned on a *continuous reinforcement* schedule—that is, a schedule in which each performance is followed by a reinforcer—produces higher rates of responding than behavior reinforced only intermittently. Behavior learned on an *intermittent* or *partial reinforcement* schedule, however, is much more resistant to extinction than behavior acquired on a continuous schedule (Skinner, 1953, p. 99). Animals trained on a continuous reinforcement schedule also show greater signs of "emotional reaction" or "low frustration tolerance" when their behaviors are subjected to extinction than do animals trained on intermittent schedules.

The implications for human functioning are quite straightforward. Affluent parents who raise their children on continuous reinforcement schedules should not be surprised that their offspring do not show behaviors we can label persistent, hardworking, ambitious, and competitive. Instead, we may hear them called spoiled, soft, weak-willed, and lazy, among other things. Descriptions such as persistent, hardworking, ambitious, and competitive are more likely to be applicable to children who have been subjected to partial or intermittent schedules of reinforcement (Carpenter, 1974, pp. 27–28).

There are a variety of forms of intermittent reinforcement. Two of the major ones are the *fixed-ratio* and the *fixed-interval*. In a fixed-ratio schedule, an absolute number of behaviors is required before reinforcement is applied (Ferster and Perrott, 1968, p. 525). For example, a student may have to complete two class projects before receiving a grade in the course. Or a worker may be placed on a fixed-ratio schedule by an employer. Such a schedule is commonly known as piecework pay. Unfortunately, a high rate of responding may be required by the employer before she pays her employees. Such an unfavorable schedule may in some instances be detrimental to the health of the workers. In addition, we might find that morale and interest in the job is very low. In traditional personality terms, we might say that the workers are discouraged or apathetic.

In a fixed-interval schedule, the first performance that occurs after an absolute amount of time has elapsed is reinforced (Ferster and Perrott, 1968. p. 526). There are many examples of the operation of such schedules in our daily lives. We eat at certain times of the day, go to bed and get up at a regular time. Sometimes we get paid by the hour. One of the interesting features of behavior regulated on fixed-interval schedules is that the rate of responding tends to be low just after reinforcement, but increases rapidly as the time for reinforcement approaches. A person who is reinforced on such a schedule could be characterized as inconsistent, erratic, opportunistic, or even "moody."

Self-Control Processes

Skinner has been interested not only in the ways in which schedules of reinforcement determine behavior, but in the role of *self-control processes*. For him, self-control involves an analysis of " . . . how the individual acts to alter the variables of which other parts of his behavior are functions" (Skinner, 1953, p. 229). The individual is said to exercise self-control when he actively changes those variables or "things" that determine his behavior. For example, we may find that we cannot study when there is a stereo blaring music. We get up and shut it off. We have actively changed the nature of the variable (loud music) that affected our behavior. Another example might be the obese person who exercises control over his behavior by buying and eating only low-calorie foods. He can also politely refuse to eat high-calorie foods when they are offered to him by others.

Skinner has outlined a number of the techniques we use to control our behavior (Skinner, 1953, pp. 231–241), some of which have subsequently been studied by social learning theorists interested in modeling (see Chapter 11). First, Skinner states that we control our behavior through physical restraint. For example, some of us clap our hands over our mouths to avoid laughing at someone else's mistakes. Others put their hands in their pockets to keep from biting their fingernails. Sometimes we simply remove ourselves from aversive situations. We walk away from someone who has insulted us lest we lose control and physically attack him. Physical aids can also be used to control behavior. For example, tools or equipment can be used to facilitate certain behaviors. Sometimes we use drugs to control undesirable behaviors. The overweight person uses appetite-depressant pills; the depressed person uses a variety of stimulants.

Another technique we can use to control behavior is to change the stimuli responsible for it. Some alcoholics "avoid temptation" by giving their liquor supply away. Some athlete-students put their athletic equipment out of sight when they sit down to study. Other students in a similar situation may draw the curtains in their rooms in order to avoid being lured out of doors on a bright spring day. In technical language, these people are removing *discriminative stimuli* that induce unwanted behavior. We not only remove certain stimuli in given situations, we also present stimuli in order to make certain behaviors more probable. For example, we enter dates and times in an appointment book in order to remind ourselves of our responsibilities. We may also listen to tapes of our voices in an attempt to improve our diction.

Skinner maintains that we sometimes induce emotional changes in ourselves for purposes of control. We may work ourselves into a "good mood" before a stressful meeting in order to increase the probability of emitting the "right" behaviors. Athletes frequently use this method of control when they "psych themselves up" before an important game. We may also control our behavior by doing something else as a way of refraining from actions that bring in punishment. To keep from verbally or physically attacking people we dislike intensely, we may find ourselves thinking and performing actions unrelated to our opinions about them. Or we may avoid talking about taboo topics—for example, telling nuns about the right of women to have abortion on demand—by talking about a less threatening subject—how to play a good game of bridge.

Yet another technique is to control our behavior by self-reinforcement; we reward ourselves for actions we consider commendable and punish ourselves for behavior we consider undesirable. For example, we may reward ourselves for studying hard and doing well on an exam by going to see a film acclaimed by the critics. If we fail to do well, on the other hand, we may punish ourselves by giving our tickets away.

We have now reviewed some of the basic concepts and principles in Skinner's theory. Let us see how he utilizes them in his treatment of personality development.

THE PROCESS OF PERSONALITY DEVELOPMENT

A Schedule of Reinforcement Approach

It should be clear at this point that Skinner would prefer to discuss changes in the individual's personality over time as involving his or her exposure to unique environmental schedules of reinforcement and not to the emergence of maturational stages, à la Freud and Piaget. Although he thinks such theories have some predictive value, Skinner generally opposes them because they do not allow for the control or manipulation of events, a procedure he considers crucial for a science of behavior (Skinner, 1974, p. 12). Such theories tend to be descriptive, not explanatory, and as Skinner sees it, the primary goal of science is the prediction and control of events (Skinner, 1953, p. 6). An example at this point may clarify his position.

In Piaget's stage theory, children from birth to about three years of age are observed to play games without any attempt to adapt to social rules. In stage 2, children between the ages of three and five simply imitate the play of the rule-regulated behavior of adults and regard the rules as sacred and immutable. In stage 3, children who range in age from seven to adolescence play the game with a mutually agreed upon set of rules, but understand that the rules can always be changed with the approval of the other players (Flavell, 1963, pp. 291–292). Now, with these descriptions of behavior at the various age levels, we can predict the kind of behavior a child will exhibit if we know his age. But we do not have an adequate explanation for his behavior—that is, we do not know why he behaves as he does. We have descriptive information of limited usefulness, not causal information. To ascertain why the child behaves as he does, we must be able to control and manipulate events that have an effect on his game-playing behavior.

For these reasons, Skinner prefers to study personality in terms of the learning of a multitude of behaviors that allow the organism to survive and prosper in his or her transactions with the environment. In rough terms, the person is learning throughout life which contingencies provide satisfaction and which produce pain in given situations. He learns to discriminate between stimuli or situations which are the occasions for the reinforcement of specific behaviors and those which do not lead to reinforcement for the same behaviors. His learned behaviors are then said to be under *stimulus control*. A child, for example, may learn to cry in public and not at home, since crying in the former situation usually brings immediate attention and comfort from his mother, whereas crying at home is generally ignored. Or a student may quickly learn that studying in a library and not in a noisy dormitory leads to passing grades. Simple skills are learned at first; later on, more and more complex behaviors are acquired and utilized. But people are not seen as passive organisms who simply respond automatically to reinforcement cues. Instead, they exercise self-control over their environments by actively selecting and changing environmental variables in order to satisfy their own needs.

The "Development" of Normal and Abnormal Personalities

Some people have had an unique set of transactions with the environment that results in the acquisition of *repertoires* we might label "normal." Others have had a set of experiences that result in the acquisition of unique response patterns we might label "abnormal." In Skinner's view, there is no qualitative difference between so-called normal and abnormal individuals. We do not need to devise a different set of reinforcement principles to account for their behaviors. He maintains that the same set of principles can account for the behavior of all individuals, irrespective of the labels we might use in describing their actions. According to him, we should focus more on the environmental determinants of behavior than on the inner determinants. We need to eliminate references to a "mental apparatus," such as the one employed by Freud. Such theorizing is imprecise, ambiguous, and leads to pseudo-explanations of behavior.

Skinner believes, however, that Freud contributed much to our understanding of behavior and that many of his ideas can profitably be translated into terms amenable to scientific inquiry. For example, the various ego defense mechanisms Freud postulated can be examined in terms of the person's attempts to avoid or escape punishment. In Skinner's view, punishment makes the stimuli created by punished behavior aversive. As a consequence, any behavior which reduces or eliminates that stimulation is subsequently positively reinforcing. Thus, repression simply involves the fact that ". . . behavior which is punished becomes aversive, and by not engaging in it or by not 'seeing' it, a person avoids conditioned aversive stimulation" (Skinner, 1974, p. 155). There is no need to talk about an inner process in which id impulses incapable of fulfillment are kept lurking in the unconscious. Another example is sublimation. In Freudian terms, sublimation is the " . . . discharge of instinctual energy and especially that associated with pregenital impulses through socially approved activities" (Skinner, 1974, p. 156). In Skinnerian terms, sublimation is translated in the following way: If two forms of behavior are positively reinforcing, but one of them is punished, the other is more likely to occur. For Freud, conversion involves "[t]he transformation of an unconscious conflict into a symbolically equivalent somatic symptom" (Skinner, 1974, p. 156). Such mental events are presumed to have the power to produce physical illness. Inner-directed rage, for example, is said to produce ulcers. But Skinner maintains "the condition felt as rage is medically related to the ulcer, and that a complex social situation causes both" (Skinner, 1974, pp. 156–157). Of course, "complex social situation" would have to be precisely and adequately defined. It might hypothetically, however, include a punishing boss, a nagging wife or husband, whiny kids, loss of a loved one, and so on. Once again, the general point is that many of the traditional clinical concepts can be translated into terms which make them amenable to scientific investigation.

TECHNIQUES OF ASSESSMENT

Skinner is primarily interested in the experimental analysis of behavior. This means he is concerned with the identification of those environmental variables that control the emission of behavior. These variables include situational factors which signal the organism that the emission of particular behaviors will lead to the occurrence of reinforcers and the reinforcement schedules themselves. Since the analysis of behavior is a complicated matter that involves the interplay of a multitude of variables, Skinner proceeds by focusing on specific behaviors and those environmental events considered to be controlling influences. In short, Skinner attempts to discover the nature of the cause-and-effect relationships between events. To accomplish this goal, Skinner first focuses on simple, observable behaviors that can be readily and reliably quantified and on those environmental stimuli thought to control the emission of these behaviors. Other variables thought to be irrelevant are eliminated or held constant.

Skinner believes that his approach can be implemented best by focusing on the behavior of non-human species, since their environments are relatively easy to control and many of their behaviors are simple and can be quantified. The environment usually used for study purposes is the so-called Skinner box, and behavior is quantified through the use of a cumulative recorder. The Skinner box is a small, soundproofed chamber usually containing a lever or bar that an animal such as a rat can depress to obtain food reinforcers. For work with pigeons, translucent disks that can be lighted with different colors are mounted on the wall. When the pigeon pecks at the "right" disk, that is, a disk of a particular color chosen by the experimenter as correct, food is delivered via a feeding disk. The frequency and rate of responding is recorded precisely and automatically by the cumulative recorder wired to the apparatus. A stylus or pen moves along a paper attached to a revolving drum.

Skinner maintains that the use of lower animals like the pigeon and rat to establish the principles of behavior is a good strategy, since these principles are generalizable to the behavior of human beings. In his view, a single set of principles can account for much, but not all, of the behavior of both non-human and human organisms.

APPLICATION OF THE THEORY TO THE TREATMENT OF PSYCHOPATHOLOGY

Psychopathology and Behavior Modification

Behavior modification is an attempt to apply learning principles derived from laboratory experiments to changing undesirable behavior (Krasner, 1970, p. 89). These principles are based on research in classical conditioning and observational learning, as well as on operant conditioning. For our purposes, however, the focus will be on the use of operant techniques, which have been utilized successfully in a number of problem areas. For example, investigators have demonstrated that it is possible to increase the social skills of retardates, to lessen the amount of aggressive behavior shown by delinquents, to improve the study habits of students, to enable obese individuals to lose weight, to curtail smoking in adults, to reduce stuttering in children and adults, and to control the undesirable behavior of psychotics. To alter the behavior of psychotics, for instance, investigators have designed special environments within institutions in which patients can earn tokens for performing socially appropriate tasks and then exchange them for goods and activities that are positively reinforcing. Such incentive systems are commonly known as *token economies*.

The Token Economy. At this point, let us examine the classical attempt by Ayllon and Azrin to design such an environment as a means of strengthening key behaviors in psychotics in a mental hospital (Ayllon and Azrin, 1965, pp. 357–383). They pointed out that the most important limitation in trying to develop a technology of behavior is the lack of standardization, since untrained personnel are used to observe and record the behavior, as well as to administer reinforcers. For example, attendants may define "grooming behavior" in different ways. One attendant might define satisfactory grooming as combing hair, brushing teeth, and wearing clean clothes. Another may not check the patient's teeth or clothing and yet conclude that she has earned a number of tokens because she has combed her hair. As a consequence, both attendants may give the patient the same number of tokens for appropriate grooming. It would not be unreasonable to find the second attendant swamped with requests from patients to check their grooming.

In addition, it is difficult to record and reinforce desired activities on a ward of approximately forty-five patients when they are all engaging in a variety of activities at the same time. Research has shown that reinforcers have the greatest impact on behavior and are most effective if they are applied immediately following the desired response. If different attendants reinforced the patients at varying time intervals following responses, the impact on behavior would be lessened or even nonexistent. If the attendants do not know which behaviors to reinforce, how much to reinforce, or when to reinforce, it seems unlikely that there will be much improvement. Accordingly, the investigators spent eighteen months developing their program in order to eliminate these and other problems. The final program included a standard list of behaviors to be changed, as well as a list of the reinforcers. The behaviors to be strengthened differed among patients and included helping serve meals to the other patients, washing dishes, cleaning tables, typing letters, answering the telephone and calling hospital personnel to the phone, washing sheets, pillow cases, and towels in the laundry, and so on. A list of the reinforcers to be given in exchange for tokens is shown in Table 9.1.

The results of the program showed, in general, significant improvement in patient behaviors over a forty-two-day period. In another experiment within the same program, the investigators demonstrated that, once the tokens were withdrawn, the behavior of the patients deteriorated. When the system was reinstated, performance levels rose again. This shift in performance shows the powerful impact of the tokens in changing behavior.

TABLE 9.1   List of Reinforcers Available to Patients for Tokens

Reinforcer	Number of Tokens Daily
I. Privacy	
Selection of room 1	0
Selection of room 2	4
Selection of room 3	8
Selection of room 4	15
Selection of room 5	30
Personal chair	1
Screen (room divider)	1
Choice of bedspreads	1
Coat rack	1
II. Leave from the ward	
Twenty-minute walk on hospital grounds (with escort)	2
Thirty-minute grounds pass	10
Trip to town (with escort)	100
III. Social interaction with staff	
Private audience with ward psychologist	20
Private audience with social worker	100
IV. Devotional opportunities	
Extra religious services on ward	1
Extra religious services off ward	10
V. Recreational opportunities	
Movie on ward	1
Exclusive use of a radio	1
Television (choice of program)	3
VI. Commissary items	
Candy, milk, cigarettes, coffee, and sandwich	1–5
Toilet articles such as toothpaste, comb, lipstick, and talcum powder	1–10
Clothing such as gloves, scarf, and skirt	12–400
Reading and writing materials such as pen, greeting card, newspaper and magazine	2–5
Miscellaneous items such as ashtray, potted plant, picture holder, and stuffed animal	1–50

Adapted from Ayllon and Azrin, 1965, p. 360.

But this study and other experiments with token economies, although generally successful, have spawned a number of serious questions. First, the behaviors that were changed seem trivial and unrelated to the major problems confronting psychotics. What is so wonderful about getting a patient to comb her hair or wash some dishes? The answer is that although major problem behaviors remain untouched, the behaviors that were strengthened represent a significant shift in functioning for the patients. In the beginning of these experiments, some of the patients refused to wash or groom themselves. A few of them lay in their own excrement. Some refused to utter a word. The application of operant techniques changed this state of affairs and was the first step toward recovery. It also increased the freedom of the patients, in the sense of providing them with an opportunity to perform a variety of activities for positive payoffs rather than simply sitting all day doing nothing. The changes in appearance are also beneficial because the staff may begin to treat patients better. As psychologist Krasner puts it, ". . . if you can't tell the patient from the staff without a score card, you will most likely react to him (or her) as if he (or she) were normal just like you" (Krasner, 1970, p. 97). The effort to establish and implement a method of treatment is monumentally preferable to providing no treatment at all, as is all too often true of most mental institutions. Behavior modification is not the only therapeutic method that can be employed to overcome this impasse, but it is one and it does work. On the debit side of the ledger, there is the problem of changing patients' more serious behavioral problems and of teaching them behaviors that will allow them to function adequately in the larger society. Too little research has been addressed to these areas.

Aversive Techniques. Behavior modification confronts us with some serious ethical questions, one of which concerns the use of aversive techniques. Is it morally correct to use punishment, for example, to change behavior? This is a complicated question, but it does not seem to be enough to argue, as some authorities do, that it is ethically legitimate to do so because society itself tends to rely more heavily on aversive control than on the use of positive reinforcement procedures (Kazdin, 1975, p. 237). That would be like the student who argues that cheating on exams is all right because "everybody does it and thinks it's OK."

The second argument often used is that behavior modification ". . . *deemphasizes* the use of aversive techniques in applied settings" (Kazdin, 1975, p. 237). The reasons include the undesirable side effects of punishment and its interference with other socially appropriate behavior. But this argument sidesteps the issue of whether punishment can be effective in changing behavior. In fact, there is considerable research evidence that aversive techniques can be used effectively to change undesirable behavior (Kushner, 1970, pp. 26–51).

At this point, let us examine an actual case history in which aversive control techniques were used so that you can decide for yourself whether or not the use of punishment can be justified under certain circumstances. The case involved self-destructive behavior in a severely retarded seven-year-old boy who was nonverbal and who functioned like a two-year-old (Kushner, 1970, pp. 42–44). The self-destructive behavior consisted of hand-biting severe enough to cause bleeding and infection. Hospital personnel tried to prevent the behavior by placing boxing gloves on the boy's hands, but when they were removed, he simply went back to biting his hands. The child also tried to prevent the behavior by sitting on his hands or by holding onto his nurse's hand. This strategy only worked temporarily, and he continued to bite his hands when they were free. Observation by the investigator indicated that the nurses' reaction to his crying following the hand-biting was to become very solicitous, to pick him up, and to give him a great deal of attention and affection, very much in the tradition of the Rogerians giving of "unconditional positive regard" (see Chapter 13). Discussion with the nurses about the reinforcing properties of their behavior met with great resistance. Since it was obvious that the nurses could not be convinced of the necessity to ignore the behavior and since the extinction process would be so slow that much more damage would be inflicted, the investigator decided to use electric shock to prevent the behavior. Electrodes were placed on the child's thigh and shock administered following any hand-biting behavior. After the initial application of shock, the mother was brought into the room and was asked to use the word "no" at the same time that the shock was being administered. The decline in hand-biting was rapid and dramatic. Later the nurses were instructed to use the word "no" whenever the child moved his hand to his mouth and to call him a "good boy" when he moved his hand away. Other behavioral methods were then applied to maintain the low rate of hand-biting.

Would you condone the use of punishment in this case? This is a difficult judgment to make. Was there an alternative, positively reinforcing method that would have worked as well? If there was, then it should have been employed (Kazdin, 1975, p. 241). In this example, however, the nurses had tried a number of less punishing strategies, and none of them worked satisfactorily. Of course, this does not mean that they or the investigator exhausted all the possibilities before proceeding. If all possibilities were tried and found wanting, aversive control might be considered as a serious alternative. Even then, however, it would be unethical to use cruel and unusual punishment as a means of controlling the behavior. Thus, if aversive stimuli are used, they should obviously not be immobilizing or have serious and permanent side effects (Kazdin, 1975, p. 239). If all these conditions are met and the rights of the patients are protected, then perhaps the use of punishment can be justified in certain instances. Obviously, any investigator employing aversive control techniques must continually be aware of his ethical obligations and act accordingly. There are no easy answers in this situation, but progress in helping people is not made by denying the efficacy of punishment in producing behavioral change, no matter how noble or worthwhile it makes us feel.

There have been abuses of the rights of patients in the past in programs using behavior modification techniques. Occasionally, cruel and unusual punishment has been administered by investigators. In one study, for example, patients were shocked without their consent and deprived of meals for a number of days. Even in the Ayllon and Azrin study reviewed in this chapter, there is a question of the abuse of patient rights. A reexamination of Table 9.1, which shows the kinds of reinforcers that could be bought with earned tokens, indicates that attendance at "extra" religious services could, theoretically at least, be prohibited by the investigators if the patient had not earned any tokens. This kind of prohibition comes very close to an abridgment of the patient's constitutional rights concerning freedom of religion. We should not conclude simplistically from these examples, however, that denial of patient rights or the administration of cruel and unusual punishment is pervasive and that therefore behavior modification procedures should be abandoned. Abuses are relatively few and the benefits to thousands and thousands of people have been tremendous. Instead, investigators must work to eliminate abusive practices, and to uphold to the best of their abilities the ethical ideals of the profession.

At this point, let us examine the ways in which operant principles have been applied to the problems of the educational system.

Education and Behavioral Technology

For Skinner, the history of education in this country and in many others shows clearly that teachers and administrators have tended to rely on aversive practices to control the behavior of students. According to him, fifty years ago children learned the prescribed materials to escape the cane or birch rod. Today, the rod is seldom used, but Skinner (1959, p. 149) maintains that we have not actually shifted from aversive to positive control, but from one kind of aversive control to another. In the lower grades, for example, the child fills in a workbook to avoid the teacher's displeasure or criticism, as well as the ridicule of his classmates. Low marks not infrequently result in "staying after school," a trip to the principal's office, or admonishments or spankings by parents. Homework is imposed by the teacher and is sometimes used as punishment for troublemaking. Many of the same practices occur at the college and university level, but in place of the principal, students face the college dean. In addition, the competition for marks in higher education is especially keen, and high marks for one student often mean low marks for another, because many teachers continue to grade in terms of the traditional bell curve.

These and many other practices are painful for large numbers of students and generate many unwanted by-products (Skinner, 1968, p. 97). First, the student may try to escape from the punishing situation by being tardy. Or he may eventually drop out of school altogether. Students who commit suicide are often the ones who have experienced difficulties in school. Subtler forms of escape include chronic daydreaming and "restlessness." A student may not be able to sit still for a few minutes in class, but will spend hours playing in the neighborhood park or watching television. Another serious result of aversive control, in Skinner's view, is that students may attempt to attack their controllers. They may become defiant, rude, or impudent to their teachers. They may use obscene language. In the more serious cases, they may even physically attack their teachers. For Skinner, vandalism is another indirect manifestation of attempts by students to weaken the control of powerful others.

As a consequence of the detrimental nature of aversive practices, many well-intentioned and concerned teachers have sought alternatives. According to Skinner, one major alternative to punishment accepted by educators in practice, if not in theory, is permissiveness. He maintains that permissiveness has a number of seeming advantages, including the fact that it saves the practitioners the labor of supervision and the enforcement of standards. But he suggests that

> [p]ermissiveness is not . . . a policy; it is the abandonment of policy; and its apparent advantages are illusory. To refuse to control is to leave control not to the person himself, but to other parts of the social and nonsocial environments. (Skinner, 1968, p. 84)

Another major alternative, which is related in many respects to permissiveness, is guidance, and its effects on the educational process are usually described with a horticultural metaphor. A person is said "to grow" like a flower or tree if his experiences occur in the right "soil." Behavior can be "cultivated," but only under the right conditions. It is also "developed" until "maturity" (Skinner, 1968, p. 87). You might want to review the materials in Chapters 12 and 13 on Maslow and Rogers at this point for good examples of the guidance position. Skinner says that this position has some convenient advantages for its practitioners:

> One who merely guides a natural development cannot easily be accused of trying to control it. Growth remains an achievement of the individual, testifying to his freedom and worth, his "hidden propensities," and as the gardener is not responsible for the ultimate form of what he grows, so one who merely guides is exonerated when things go wrong. (Skinner, 1968, pp. 87–88)

In Skinner's view, the primary disadvantage of this position is that it obscures the reinforcements actually responsible for the changes in behavior by attributing them to ". . . the unfolding of some predetermined pattern" (Skinner, 1968, p. 88).

Skinner himself opts for a detailed examination of the environmental determinants of behavior. In his opinion, education involves ". . . the arrangement of [the] contingencies of reinforcement under which students learn" (Skinner, 1968, p. 64). These contingencies can be effectively arranged by the use of teaching machines and other programmed instruction techniques. Complex subject matter is presented to the student in a series of small, easy to learn steps. In one form of programmed learning, a question is presented and the student writes her answer in a space provided by the program. Then she lifts a lever that moves her answer under a transparent cover and simultaneously exposes the correct answer. If the two answers match, the student punches a hole in the paper near her response to indicate that she has answered correctly. This procedure instructs the machine to allow the next question to appear. The student proceeds to answer all the questions following the same procedure. She then starts the series again and attempts to answer correctly those questions she answered incorrectly at first. The process is repeated until she has mastered the program materials (Skinner, 1959, p. 162).

Skinner maintains that such a format has many advantages over the traditional system. First, it is more efficient than the traditional instructional procedures. It is a labor-saving device because it can bring many students into contact with one programmer (Skinner, 1968, p. 37). Although programming may suggest mass production to some people, in reality it acts almost like a private tutor for the student. Unlike lectures and films, there is a continual interplay between the student and the materials. Programming does not eliminate the need for the teacher either. The teacher is the key person who arranges the contingencies of reinforcement for the student, but now he or she will make these arrangements pay off in effective learning. In addition, the teacher will still have the tremendous responsibility of weaning the student from the machine and showing him how the facts and principles he has learned can be related to other areas of life.

The teaching machine is programmed in such a way that it ensures the student thoroughly understands a point before he or she can proceed. One of the tragedies of traditional educational practices is that all too often the teacher is faced with the task of educating large numbers of students simultaneously. Under such "massed madness" conditions, it is impossible for even the best teacher to give each student the amount of attention he or she needs to learn the materials well. Still another advantage is that the machine reinforces the student sufficiently for each response and does it immediately (Skinner, 1968, p. 39). Very often the teacher in the traditional setting knows the value of immediate and adequate reinforcement, but cannot provide it. Finally, the programmed learning approach recognizes the importance of individual differences. Skinner (1968, p. 242) maintains that failure to account for these differences is the greatest single inefficiency in education today.

For all these reasons, Skinner strongly advocates the adoption of his programmed learning approach. But although he is hopeful of eventual change in our educational system, his innovations may be resisted by educators:

> Many of those charged with the improvement of education are unaware that . . . technical help is available, and many are afraid of it when it is pointed out. They resist any new practice which does not have the familiar and reassuring character of day-to-day communication. They continue to discuss learning and teaching in the language of the layman. (Skinner, 1968, p. 259)

Skinner is recommending the application of a scientific analysis of behavior to educational practices. It seems that his approach is gaining some support among educators, as evidenced by the large numbers of academic institutions now using the programmed learning format to help educate students.

CRITICAL COMMENTS

An examination and evaluation of the scientific worth of Skinner's theory in terms of our six criteria is now in order.

Comprehensiveness. Skinner has constructed a theory of behavior that, until recently, focused almost exclusively on the functioning of lower animals. His primary concern seems to have been to generate a set of learning principles for certain types of simple, nonsocial performance. From this perspective, the range of topics actually covered by Skinner in his initial theorizing was highly limited. He has been severely criticized for this narrow focus by a variety of investigators. His primary rebuttal has been that, in all sciences, advances occur as investigators focus first on the simple and then progress to the more complex. The focus on simple behaviors allows scientists to control current situational conditions better and to record behavior over longer periods of time. In addition, genetic and environmental history variables can be brought under control (Skinner, 1953, p. 38). Once the basic processes are revealed, this information can be utilized in the study of the more diverse and complicated behavior of human beings.

Such a research strategy is eminently reasonable and, of course, it has had considerable payoff value in terms of the important findings about behavior it has generated. Yet, there is a kind of conservatism about it that may seem unnecessarily stultifying to investigators of human behavior. Science, as mentioned in the opening chapter, is a human enterprise and should, at least occasionally, be fun. Part of the enjoyment is based on taking risks—on testing hunches that are not firmly grounded in data. Of course, it would be unwise to pursue one's research goals by indiscriminately using such a risk-taking approach; and Skinner's allegiance to the strict simple to complex principle is generally cogent.

Recently, Skinner has argued that the imbalance in his work has been corrected since much of the current work in behavior modification focuses exclusively on human behavior. Still, it seems clear that he has not constructed a theory that rivals Freud's in terms of comprehensiveness.

Precision and Testability. The terms of Skinner's theory are precisely defined, and the various relational statements are capable of experimental verification. The concern with rigor and precision in the study of behavioral phenomena is one of the impressive strengths of the work of Skinner and his operant colleagues.

Simplicity. Skinner's theory is relatively parsimonious, especially when compared with some of the psychodynamic positions. It is not burdened by excess concepts and assumptions. In fact, it can be argued that the theory lacks a number of concepts that could help to explain various social learning phenomena. Skinner himself recognizes that there may be a need for additional concepts in a theory that attempts to account for complex and cognitively based human learning.

Empirical Validity. Skinner's position is firmly grounded in laboratory data. This fact places it in sharp contrast to the psychodynamic positions we have considered thus far. Although there is strong empirical support for many aspects of his learning theory, critics have claimed that Skinner often gives the impression that a technology of behavior exists to solve the complex problems that confront us. In fact, they say, this is not the case, and he is making sweeping and unwarranted generalizations on the basis of limited empirical evidence (Black, 1973, p. 129). Skinner attempts to refute this criticism by acknowledging that he is indeed offering interpretations about the functioning of society from limited data, but that this is perfectly legitimate and is done by scientists in other fields without attracting much attention. He maintains further that "[w]hen phenomena are out of reach in time or space, or too large or small to be directly manipulated, we must talk about them with less than a complete account of relevant conditions" (Skinner, 1973, p. 261). This is true, but we should also bear in mind that it is often easy to confuse speculation with fact, and that Skinner's arguments about the efficacy of his approach in solving social problems are as yet unproved.

Heuristic Value. Skinner's theory has had tremendous impact on the thinking and research activities of investigators in many disciplines. He has become a controversial figure whose position has been severely criticized by a variety of critics, including psychologists, psychiatrists, philosophers, theologians, biologists, novelists, and journalists. Some people have taken these attacks as proof that Skinner is a revolutionary thinker whose position will eventually force a major shift in the way we view ourselves and others (Platt, 1973, p. 23). Although it is too early to comment on the validity of such an assertion, it is clear that Skinner's theory ranks high on heuristic value.

Applied Value. Skinner's position has far-reaching implications for the functioning of society. Beginning with experiments on the behavior of lower animals, he has, over approximately a forty-five-year period, derived a set of simple and precise reinforcement principles that have been applied to a number of significant problems faced by human beings. The theory's applied value can perhaps be seen most clearly in the areas of psychopathology and education.

DISCUSSION QUESTIONS

1. Why does Skinner think there is a need for a scientific technology of behavior? Do you agree or disagree with him?

2. Do you ever use "mentalistic" explanations to account for behavior? If so, cite some recent instances and try to reanalyze them in terms of possible environmental variables salient at the time.

3. How might the stereotypic belief that individuals are solely responsible for their behavior result in the continuation of discrimination against minority group members?

4. Is all control of behavior bad? In what ways does control yield positive or negative outcomes for people? Why do many people dislike those who control the outcomes of others?

5. What is operant conditioning? How does it differ from classical conditioning?

6. Do you agree with Skinner that punishment is the most common technique of control in modern life? What are the limitations of punishment as a control technique? Is its use ever effective and desirable? Discuss the implications of the use of failing grades as a punishment technique. Can you propose alternate, more effective, and rewarding ways of evaluating students' performance with accurate feedback to them of their progress or lack of it in a course?

7. What is extinction? Have you ever tried to extinguish someone's obnoxious behavior by ignoring it? What happened? What are some of the limitations of the technique?

8. Describe the various types of reinforcement schedules. Cite some examples in your everyday routine in which your behavior is controlled by the different schedule types.

9. What is behavior modification? What are its strengths and weaknesses? Do you think that token economies are useless, sterile, and unethical ways of changing undesirable behavior? Who decides which behaviors are undesirable? Who should decide?

10.   Do you agree with Skinner's application of behavioral technology to education? What are the strengths and deficiencies of his arguments for reform of the educational system?

NOTES

T. Allyon and N. H. Azrin, "The Measurement and Reinforcement of Behavior of Psychotics," *Journal of the Experimental Analysis of Behavior*, 1965, **8,** 357–383.

M. Black, "Some Aversive Responses to a Would-Be Reinforcer," in H. Wheeler, ed., *Beyond the Punitive Society* (San Francisco: Freeman, 1973).

F. Carpenter, *The Skinner Primer* (New York: Free Press, 1974).

C. B. Ferster and M. C. Perrott, *Behavior Principles* (New York: Appleton-Century-Crofts, 1968).

J. H. Flavell, *The Developmental Psychology of Jean Piaget* (New York: Van Nostrand, 1963).

A. E. Kazdin, *Behavior Modification in Applied Settings* (Homewood, Ill.: Dorsey Press, 1975).

L. Krasner, "Behavior Modification, Token Economies, and Training in Clinical Psychology," in C. Newringer and J. L. Michael, eds., *Behavior Modification in Clinical Psychology* (New York: Appleton-Century-Crofts, 1970).

M. Kushner, "Faradic Aversive Controls in Clinical Practice," in C. Neuringer and J. L. Michael, eds., *Behavior Modification in Clinical Psychology* (New York: Appleton-Century-Crofts, 1970).

J. R. Platt, "The Skinnerian Revolution," in H. Wheeler, ed., *Beyond the Punitive Society* (San Francisco: Freeman, 1973).

B. F. Skinner, *The Behavior of Organisms* (New York: Appleton-Century-Crofts, 1938).

B. F. Skinner, *Science and Human Behavior* (New York: Macmillan, 1953).

B. F. Skinner, *Cumulative Record* (New York: Appleton-Century-Crofts, 1959).

B. F. Skinner, *The Technology of Teaching* (New York: Appleton-Century-Crofts, 1968).

B. F. Skinner, "An Autobiography," in P. B. Dews, ed., *Festschrift for B. F. Skinner* (New York: Appleton-Century-Crofts, 1970).

B. F. Skinner, *Beyond Freedom and Dignity* (New York: Knopf, 1971).

B. F. Skinner, "Answers for My Critics," in H. Wheeler, ed., *Beyond the Punitive Society* (San Fransciso: Freeman, 1973).

B. F. Skinner, *About Behaviorism* (New York: Knopf, 1974).

SUGGESTED READINGS

Skinner, B. F. *Walden Two.* New York: Macmillan, 1948.

Skinner, B. F. *Science and Human Behavior.* New York: Macmillan, 1953.

Skinner, B. F. *Beyond Freedom and Dignity.* New York: Knopf, 1971.

Skinner, B. F. *About Behaviorism.* New York: Knopf, 1974.

GLOSSARY

Behavior Modification. Series of procedures that seek to change behavior through reliance on reinforcement principles.

Conditioning. Establishment of the linkage or association between the behavior and its consequences.

Continuous Reinforcement. Schedule of reinforcement in which each response is followed by a reinforcer.

Discriminative Stimulus. Stimulus whose presence leads an individual to respond because he or she has learned previously that its presence leads to particular reinforcing consequences.

Extinction. Reduction in behavior that eventually occurs as a result of the failure to reinforce the behavior.

Fixed-Interval Schedule. Schedule of reinforcement in which the first response that occurs after an absolute amount of time has elapsed is reinforced.

Fixed-Ratio Schedule. Schedule of reinforcement in which an absolute number of responses is required before a reinforcer is applied.

Functional Analysis. Attempt to understand behavior by identifying the environmental conditions that determine its occurrence or nonoccurrence.

Intermittent Reinforcement. Schedule of reinforcement in which reinforcers are applied to given responses occasionally or intermittently.

Law of Effect. For Thorndike, the principle that behavior is determined by its consequences. In his view, behavior followed by reward was "stamped in," whereas behavior followed by punishment was "stamped out."

Mentalism. Pejorative term used by some learning theorists to indicate their dissatisfaction with the use of concepts that cannot be objectively validated as explanatory devices in attempts to account for behavior.

Negative Reinforcer. Stimulus that maintains or strengthens the occurrence of a response through the removal of aversive stimuli.

Operant Analysis. Study of the ways in which behavior is acquired, maintained, or modified by its reinforcing consequences.

Positive Reinforcer. Stimulus associated with behavior that increases the probability of the occurrence of the behavior.

Punishment. Presentation of aversive stimuli following a behavior that results in a decrease in the performance of that behavior.

Reinforcement. In classical or respondent conditioning, the association formed through the repeated pairing of the conditioned stimulus and the unconditioned stimulus. In operant or instrumental learning, the association that is formed when an operant response is followed by a reinforcing stimulus.

Repertoire. Unique, acquired behavior patterns.

Self-Control Processes. Actions instigated by a person to alter the conditions that influence his or her behavior.

Stimulus. Goad to behavior; a condition that affects behavior.

Stimulus Control. Stimulus to which a person has learned to respond. If a person has been reinforced for a given behavior in the presence of certain stimuli and not in the presence of others, he or she learns to respond only in the presence of those stimuli that provide the opportunity for reinforcement.

Token Economy. A behavior modification procedure in which tokens are earned by patients for performing behaviors the hospital staff judges are necessary if the patients are to live effectively in the outside world. The tokens are conditioned reinforcers which can be exchanged for experiences and/or goods that are desirable to the patients.

Julian Rotter (Courtesy of Julian Rotter and University of Connecticut)

CHAPTER 10

Rotter's Expectancy—
Reinforcement Model

BIOGRAPHICAL SKETCH

Julian Rotter was born in Brooklyn, New York, in 1916. He received his B.A. degree from Brooklyn College in 1937, his M.A. from the University of Iowa in 1938, and his Ph.D. in psychology from Indiana University in 1941. During his undergraduate and graduate days, he was greatly influenced by the neo-analyst Alfred Adler and by Kurt Lewin, a prominent social psychologist. Rotter attended a series of Adler's clinics, demonstrations, and university seminars and also met informally with Adler at his home (Mosher, 1968). He credits Adler with focusing his attention on the goal-directedness of behavior and on the unity of personality. Many of the concepts in Rotter's position can be traced directly to Adler's influence. The similarities between various concepts in the two theories will become apparent later in the chapter.

Rotter was also affected by the field theory approach promulgated by Lewin. Two of the principal attributes of this approach are its emphasis on the interrelatedness of behavior and the premise that multiple factors are responsible for the occurrence of behavior at a given time. Rotter accepted these assumptions, as well as one which maintains that behavior must be described from the perspective of the person whose behavior is under scrutiny, rather than from the viewpoint of the observer (Rotter and Hochreich, 1975, p. 97). In addition to Adler and Lewin, Rotter reports that he was influenced by the writings of a variety of learning theorists including Thorndike, Tolman, and Hull. In general terms, his social learning position is an attempt to integrate two major trends embodied in the work of these theorists—namely, reinforcement approaches and cognitive or *field theories* (Rotter, Chance, and Phares, 1972, p. 1).

After receiving his doctorate, Rotter served during World War II as a psychologist and personnel consultant to the U.S. Army. After the war, he accepted a position at Ohio State University, where he eventually became director of the Psychological Clinic. During his stay at Ohio State, he published a book entitled *Social Learning and Clinical Psychology* (1954), in which for the first time he presented an extended treatment of his social learning theory of personality. His stay at Ohio State was productive in terms of research as well. Rotter attracted a number of capable students who worked with him to test various predictions derived from the theory. Some of these students have since become leading proponents of the social learning view in contemporary psychology.

In 1963, Rotter left Ohio State and accepted a position as a full professor in the department of psychology at the University of Connecticut. He is also director of the Clinical Psychology Training Program and a diplomate in clinical psychology of the American Board of Examiners in Professional Psychology. At the present time, he continues to develop and revise his position and to engage actively in research. The most current statement of his position can be found in his *Applications of a Social Learning Theory of Personality* (1972), a text he co-authored with two former students, J. E. Chance and E. J. Phares. He has also co-authored a text entitled *Personality* (1975) with Dorothy Hochreich.

BASIC CONCEPTS AND PRINCIPLES

Rotter has constructed a theory of personality based on learning concepts and principles. It is an approach that focuses on learned behavior. The assumption is that most of our behavior is learned and that it is acquired through our experiences with other people (Rotter, Chance, and Phares, 1972, p. 4). Such a social learning view also makes use of a historical approach to the study of personality, for it is thought necessary to investigate the antecedent events in a person's life to understand his behavior adequately. Unlike the Freudians, however, Rotter does not believe it is essential to sample the individual's past experiences in great detail in order to predict behavior adequately. Instead, he argues that we should focus on these past events only to the extent that they help us to meet our predictive goals (Rotter, Chance, and Phares, 1972, p. 5). For example, there may be no need to inquire into a student's traumatic experiences during the oral stage of infancy in order to predict his failure to attain a college degree. An examination of his relatively poor high school grades and low college board scores may be sufficent.

In order to understand personality, Rotter also thinks that we must consider it to have unity or interdependence (Rotter, Chance, and Phares, 1972, p. 7). One aspect of this belief is that a person's experiences or interactions influence one another. Past experiences influence current experiences, and current experiences change the things he or she has learned in the past. For example, a student might reject potentially helpful advice from her college counselor because she has consistently been given poor advice by other couselors in the past. If she could be induced to accept the advice of this counselor, however, and it proved helpful, her general attitude toward counselors might become more positive. Thus, personality is seen as involving change, since the individual is continuously exposed to new experiences, and as having stability, since previous experiences affect new learning (Rotter and Hochreich, 1975, p. 94).

The other aspect of the belief that personality has unity concerns the fact that different behaviors may lead to the same outcome for the individual. The behaviors are then said to be *functionally related* (Katkovsky, 1968, p. 215). A student may be successful in registering for a popular course in political science by engaging in such diverse behaviors as getting up earlier than the other students and securing a place in front of the line, asking a friend to register him, speaking directly to the instructor, getting approval from the college dean, and so on. Reinforcements can also become functionally related (Rotter, Chance, and Phares, 1972, p. 19). For instance, a star hockey player may learn that leading his team to the coveted Stanley Cup by scoring more goals than any other player in the league means not only a healthy increase in his annual salary, but praise from teammates, the coach, and members of the media, as well as lucrative advertising contracts with major manufacturers of hockey equipment. He may then come to expect these reinforcements whenever he has such a season.

In Rotter's position there is also the assumption that behavior is goal-directed. This directional aspect is inferred from the effect of reinforcing conditions (Rotter, Chance, and Phares, 1972, p. 8). A simpler way of saying the same thing is that Rotter considers human behavior to be motivated. People strive to maximize rewards and to minimize or avoid punishment. In other words, Rotter, like Skinner, endorses the principle of the empirical law of effect. In Rotter's words, ". . . any stimulus complex has reinforcing properties to the extent that it influences movement toward or away from a goal" (Rotter, Chance, and Phares, 1972, p. 9). Some investigators have objected to this principle because it seems circular and because there is no attempt to define a reinforcer independently of behavior. Rotter maintains that such a view would be correct if we studied only the behavior of people from other cultures and were able to identify reinforcers only *after* they had occurred. In reality, the situation is quite different. We live in a culture where it is possible to identify reinforcing events that have known effects both for groups and individuals (Rotter, Chance, and Phares, 1972, p. 9). Thus, it is possible to use this knowledge to make predictions about behavior.

A few other corollary points about human motivation should be made. First, when investigators using social learning theory focus on the environmental conditions that determine the direction of behavior, they discuss their interests in terms of goals or reinforcements. When they focus on the person determining the direction of behavior, they speak of needs. For Rotter, the distinction between needs and goals is a semantic one used merely for convenience (Rotter, Chance, and Phares, 1972, p. 10). Second, social learning theory assumes that early goals are learned within a family setting. We are born with certain physiological needs which are satisfied by parents and parental surrogates. Their association with the satisfaction or frustration of our basic or unlearned needs provides the basis, in Rotter's judgment, for our later reliance on them and others for affection and love, praise, recognition, status, and dependency (Rotter, Chance, and Phares, 1972, p. 10).

This view, however, creates special theoretical difficulties. It assumes that all reinforcers are reinforcing because they have become associated with drive reduction. For example, a mother's praise of her son's performance in school is positively reinforcing to him because it is associated with earlier feeding experiences that reduced his hunger drive. Such a drive-reduction view of reinforcement may be fine when we are dealing with simple behaviors, but it becomes difficult to defend when we begin to consider complex social behavior (Rotter, Chance, and Phares, 1972, p. 9). For example, how can we show that an athlete with a high need for achievement has experienced reduction of an unlearned drive by winning the mile run in a track meet? There would seem to be no connection between his success and the reduction of his hunger drive, for example. To overcome this difficulty, social learning theory relies instead on an empirical law of effect. It focuses on changes in behavior as a function of the introduction or removal of stimulating events as its criterion for reinforcement (see Chapter 9 on Skinner for a more detailed treatment of this view of reinforcement). In summary, social learning theory assumes that the initial learning of goals occurs within a drive-reduction framework, but that the later acquisition of highly complex behaviors is better explained by using a reinforcement concept based on the empirical law of effect.

Social Learning Concepts

There are four major concepts in the social learning approach: behavior potential, expectancy, reinforcement value, and the psychological situation. In its simplest form, the formula for behavior is that ". . . the potential for a behavior to occur in any specific situation is a function of the expectancy that the behavior will lead to a particular reinforcement in that situation and the value of that reinforcement" (Rotter, 1975). Let us examine each of these concepts in order.

Behavior Potential. For Rotter, *behavior potential* refers to ". . . the potentiality of any behavior's occuring in any situation or situations as calculated in relation to any single reinforcement or set of reinforcements" (Rotter, Chance, and Phares, 1972, p. 12). Like Skinner, Rotter is actually talking about the probability of the individual's responding when certain environmental conditions are present. Rotter's view, however, places more emphasis on the role of cognitive factors in the prediction of behavior than does Skinner's, since Rotter makes active use of the person's subjective interpretation of the events that confront him. For example, he assumes that the person's potential for behavior is affected by his preception of the other behaviors available to him in a given situation, along with the operation of other factors. Thus, a complex set of internal or cognitive factors is typically involved in the prediction of behavior. Finally, it should be noted that Rotter's definition of behavior is quite broad:

> [B]ehavior may be that which is directly observed, but also that which is indirect or implicit. This notion includes a broad spectrum of possibilities— swearing, running, crying, fighting, smiling, choosing, and so on, are all included. These are all observable behaviors, but implicit behavior that can only be measured indirectly, such as rationalizing, repressing, considering alternatives, planning, and reclassifying, would also be included. The objective study of cognitive activity is a difficult but important aspect of social learning theory. Principles governing the occurrence of such cognitive activities are not considered different from those that might apply to any observable behavior. (Rotter, Chance, and Phares, 1972, p. 12)

As we can see, the prediction of behavior is a monumental task.

Expectancy. Rotter defines *expectancy* as "the probability held by the individual that a particular reinforcement will occur as a function of a specific behavior on his part in a specific situation or situations" (Rotter, Chance, and Phares, 1972, p. 12). Each behavior that has been associated with a reinforcement gives rise to an expectancy. Thus, each expectancy is based upon past experience (Rotter and Hochreich, 1975, p. 96). According to Rotter, simply knowing how important a goal or reinforcement is to a person is no guarantee that we can predict his behavior. A student may want to obtain an A in a history course very badly, but if his previous experiences in other courses lead him to believe or expect that he will fail no matter how much effort he expends, it is virtually certain he will not study and will, as a consequence, fail.

Expectancies also vary in terms of their generality; that is, we may acquire generalized expectancies or expectancies specific to a given situation (Rotter and Hochreich, 1975, p. 97). Generalized expectancies operate across a variety of situations. For example, a student may acquire a generalized expectancy for success in her courses. She may have obtained As in a variety of different courses or situations, so that she always expects to do well. Another student may have learned a specific expectancy in her academic career—that she is an excellent student in mathematics, but horribly inept in literature and philosophy. She then expects to do well only in mathematics courses.

Later in the chapter, we will focus on another generalized expectancy called internal-external control of reinforcement, a construct that has generated a considerable amount of interesting research. For now, however, let us continue with our examination of the major terms in the theory.

Reinforcement Value. *Reinforcement value* is defined as "the degree of preference for any one of a group of reinforcements to occur, if the probabilities of all occurring were equal" (Rotter, Chance, and Phares, 1972, p. 21). In simplest terms, reinforcement value refers to the importance we attach to different activities. For some of us, attending a symphony concert is important; others would find it dreadfully dull. Some of us like to play tennis, others do not. In addition to these differences between people, we can arrange our own activities in order of preference. Given the option, we may attach more importance to reading a novel by Dostoevsky than to playing a game of basketball or riding a bicycle. Like expectancies, the values associated with different reinforcers are based on our past experiences.

Psychological Situation. The fourth major concept utilized in the prediction of behavior is the psychological situation—that is, the situation as it is defined from the perspective of the person. In Rotter's view, this concept plays an extremely important part in the determination of behavior. As he points out, traditional theories tend to focus almost exclusively on an "inner core" of personality in which certain motives or traits are considered to control behavior, irrespective of the operation of situational demands (Rotter, Chance, and Phares, 1972, p. 37). For example, a man may be seized periodically by uncontrollable sexual impulses manifested in his spouting of obscenities in a wide variety of situations. In terms of trait theory, a person may be considered to have a strong "need for aggression" which then erupts into fighting, irrespective of the situation. On the other end of the spectrum, approaches such as Skinner's exphasize the importance of situational influences and minimize, at least in research practice, individual differences based on idiosyncratic learning histories. Social learning theory, in contrast, recognizes the importance of *both* dispositional and situational influences. In other words, it pays attention to the ways in which the unique past experiences of the person, as well as current situational cues, affect behavior. Thus, a person may be described as having strong aggressive tendencies based upon a learning experience, but he may not act aggressively in a given situation if such behavior is likely to lead to punishment by others.

Freedom of Movement and Minimal Goal. Two other concepts, freedom of movement and minimal goal, play a lesser, but nevertheless important, role in Rotter's position.

Freedom of movement is defined as "the . . . mean expectancy of obtaining positive satisfactions as a result of a set of related behaviors directed toward obtaining a group of functionally related reinforcements"(Rotter, Chance, and Phares, 1972, p. 34). For example, students usually acquire general expectancies for how well they will do in various academic courses and situations. Some students have high general expectations for success, others have very low ones. Thus, we could say that the former students have high freedom of movement, whereas the latter are hindered by low freedom of movement. The second concept, *minimal goal*, is defined as ". . . the lowest goal in a continuum of potential reinforcements for some life situation or situations which will be perceived as a satisfaction" (Rotter, 1954, p. 213). In other words, a minimal goal is conceptualized as the dividing point between those reinforcements which are positively reinforcing and those which are punishing on some dimension. For instance, if we consider course grades on a continuum, one student may find a grade of B punishing, whereas another would be happy with it. The first student would be said to have a higher minimal goal than the second.

These concepts can be combined and used in the prediction of behavior, as shown in the following example. A student who is adjusted in terms of academic achievement is probably one who has high freedom of movement in his academic expectations and who does not set exceedingly high minimal goals for himself in that area. He is a person who, on the basis of many successful experiences in a variety of courses, comes to expect to succeed. He is also a person who values such success. At the same time, he does not set his goals for positive reinforcement so high that he is bound to experience disappointment. For example, he does not set a minimal goal of A in all his courses. Such indiscriminate goal striving is unrealistic for most people. The parallel between Adler's conception of the neurotic person who sets fictional goals that cannot be attained and Rotter's conception of the maladjusted person who sets unattainable minimal goals is striking. In a related way, a student would be considered maladjusted if he had low freedom of movement in terms of academic achievement, but continued to set high minimal goals for himself. In other words, if on the basis of past experiences he expected to fail in virtually all his courses and yet felt that he must attain all As, he would be considered to be engaging in unproductive behavior. Once again, the similarity between Rotter's low freedom of movement concept and Adler's concept of feelings of inferiority should be apparent.

More will be said about the ways in which the major theoretical concepts can be used to help understand abnormal and maladjusted behavior later in the chapter. First, however, we turn to a consideration of Rotter's views on development.

THE PROCESS OF PERSONALITY DEVELOPMENT

Rotter believes that a person's development hinges largely upon the range, diversity, and quality of his or her experiences with other people. Early in life, these important figures are usually, and quite obviously, one's parents. The individual's early goals arise out of certain physiological needs that are then satisfied by the parents or parental sub-stitutes. As a result of their association with need reduction, parents be-come reinforcing stimuli in their own right. The child comes to rely on them for affection, love, praise, recognition, and other reinforcers. Rot-ter assumes that *stimulus generalization* occurs and that other people who resemble the parents are perceived and evaluated in the same or similar ways. Once the parents and others (teachers, other adults, clergy) ac-quire value as conditioned reinforcers, Rotter assumes the child will work to secure their approval and avoid their disapproval, irrespective of whether or not their behavior toward him or her results in primary drive reduction.

In Rotter's view, language acquisition also plays a critical role in the child's development. Words serve as cues in directing the person's be-havior. Parents issue instructions that often help children to solve prob-lems in a few trials rather than in the hundreds of trials it would take if they had to perform their actions in trial-and-error fashion. The parents thus direct their children to the relevant cues in given situations and show them how to avoid the irrelevant ones. Parents also use words as verbal reinforcers—for example, in statements of recognition, love, re-jection, and shame—to shape their children's behavior (Rotter, 1954, p. 218). Through these procedures, children learn different expectancies for success and failure in many different situations.

These expectancies are also subject to modification through the use of verbalizations. People can build up or tear down children's ex-pectancies, and the value of their reinforcers for that matter, by directing their attention to new and previously neglected consequences of performing given behaviors. Or people can change their expectancies by analyzing children's previous experiences and showing them how they are responding to the wrong cues and how to rectify the situation (Rot-ter, 1954, pp. 219–220). Language can be used not only to help them make appropriate discriminations between events, but to increase generalization:

> Since the effect of language is to classify, to categorize, or to abstract simi-larity in events, it serves, therefore, to determine and enhance the nature of generalization. If an event is symbolized, it will increase generalization to other events that are similarly abstracted. Not only does language de-termine generalization . . . on the basis of the subject's implicit categoriz-ing, . . . the language of others may be used by the observer as a stimulus to determine, control, or enhance generalization. (Rotter, 1954, p. 220)

Thus, the developmental process involves the acquisition and modifi-cation of expectancies and reinforcement values through contact with various socialization agents. These socialization agents include not only adult authority figures, but the person's peers (Rotter, 1954, p. 414). In Rotter's opinion, to a great extent the person's development is contin-gent on the standards, mores, goals, and techniques communicated to him by his classmates, as well as by his parents. Next to the home, he believes that the school has the greatest influence on the child's development (Rotter, 1954, p. 416). The origins of healthy or unhealthy behavior are in the home, according to Rotter, and later transfer to the school situation. Characteristics of the home that promote health include parents who encourage the development and maintenance of behavior that leads to acceptance, love, and identification with others. Such behavior is most likely to occur in homes where the parents themselves show affection and concern for the welfare and development of their offspring. In homes where parents do not provide such reinforcement, the child is unlikely to learn the kinds of behaviors that will permit him or her to adjust to the larger society (Rotter, 1954, pp. 406–407). Such an individual is likely to develop in an antisocial way and to show selfish behaviors that produce hostility in others.

In addition to his speculation that neglect or rejection of the child may result in maladjustment, Rotter feels that overindulgence and overprotection can create problems. Under these circumstances, he thinks school life will be a traumatic experience. In contrast to the home, a child may perceive the school as a place where he is unwanted, unloved, and unprotected (Rotter, 1954, p. 418). Generally speaking, the rejected child is likely to enter school with low expectations for success, whereas the overindulged one will likely have expectations that are too high. Both attitudes are unrealistic. According to Rotter, the main importance of the school is to correct these views and help the child attain a feeling of security and a realistic set of expectations for success that will serve him well when he assumes adult responsibilities (Rotter, 1954, p. 419). To help a child grow into an effective citizen, then, Rotter believes that parents, teachers, and others should be warm, accepting, good-natured, democratic, and consistent in their disciplinary practices.

TECHNIQUES OF ASSESSMENT

Rotter relies on a variety of measurement procedures in his attempts to assess personality. In his early efforts at testing hypotheses derived from social learning theory, he utilized the experimental method to good advantage. His concern centered on determining whether or not people learn tasks and perform differently in situations where they perceive reinforcing outcomes as related or unrelated to their behavior. In other words, he wanted to determine whether or not learning and performance were different for people under skill and chance conditions. After a series of experimental studies, he came to the conclusion that there were significant differences in behavior in the two situations. When people perceived the task as controlled by chance, they relied less on their past experiences in guiding their current behavior, learned less, and performed less well than people who perceived the task as skill-determined (Rotter, 1966).

These results were seen as having important implications for traditional learning theory and research. They suggested that reinforcement effects did not have a direct impact on behavior but were mediated by the person's perception of the relationship (or lack of it) between behavior and application of the reinforcer. Later, Rotter and his colleagues developed a personality measure to assess individual differences in perception. We will discuss research studies done with this internal-external control measure below. For now, though, we simply want to note that many of Rotter's studies have utilized the experimental method to secure data to test the validity of hypotheses based on his theoretical formulations.

In addition to this method, Rotter notes the potential usefulness of five major techniques for the clinical measurement of personality: (1) the interview, (2) projective tests, (3) controlled behavioral tests, (4) behavioral observation methods, and (5) the questionnaire (Rotter, 1954, p. 250). There are limitations as well as strengths associated with each of these techniques, and Rotter insists that investigators attempt to account for and try to minimize the weaknesses before utilizing them. The interview is seen by him as a procedure to be used for the assessment of personality traits and for counseling and therapeutic purposes. In terms of social learning theory, it can be used to assess an individual's need potentials, freedom of movement, and need value (Rotter, 1954, p. 252).

In his view, projective tests like the Rorschach, Thematic Apperception Test (TAT), and his own Incomplete Sentences Blank can be used to advantage in clinical diagnostic work. He finds the Rorschach of relatively little use in measuring social learning concepts (Rotter, 1954, p. 289). But since the social learning position is concerned with the reactions of the person to stimuli such as mother and father, the TAT can be used to advantage. The incomplete sentences method can also be used to measure freedom of movement. In this technique, people are asked to finish a sentence of which the first word or words are given by an investigator. Responses are assumed to give indications of underlying conflicts that determine expectancy levels for failure in given situations. Examples include sentences beginning with the word or words "I like," "I suffer," "I wish," "My father," "Sometimes I feel" (Rotter, 1954, pp. 302–304).

Controlled behavioral tests are assessment procedures in which people are placed in actual situations and their behavior assessed as a reaction to stimulus changes engineered by the investigator (Rotter, 1954, p. 311). For example, if a clinician wanted to know how a client would react to stress, he would not simply ask the person to report how he might behave, but instead would place him under actual conditions of stress and watch his reactions. Such measures have been used to test hypotheses derived from social learning theory, most notably in the area of expectancy changes following the experiencing of success or failure. The behavioral observation technique, in contrast to the controlled behavioral test, involves the relatively informal assessment of behavior by observers in natural settings (Rotter, 1954, p. 326). Rotter believes that such a technique should be employed to assess the generality of experimental findings to real life situations. Rotter also thinks that questionnaires such as his I-E Scale can be employed to test social learning hypotheses. We turn now to a consideration of this test and some of its personality and behavioral correlates.

Internal-External Control of Reinforcement

One of the key constructs in social learning theory is called *internal-external control of reinforcement.* According to Rotter, people acquire generalized expectancies to perceive reinforcing events either as dependent upon their own behavior or as being beyond their control (Rotter, 1966, p. 1). Internally oriented people tend to believe that reinforcers are subject to their own control and occur as a result of displaying their skills. Externals, in contrast, see little or no connection between their behavior and various reinforcers. Instead, they perceive the occurrence of the reinforcers as being determined by fate, luck, or powerful others. Constructs such as competence, powerlessness, helplessness, hopelessness, mastery, and alienation have all been used by other investigators in psychology and sociology to describe the degree to which people can control important events in their lives. They are all related to a belief in internal-external control, but Rotter's construct has the advantage of being an integral part of a formal theory from which relatively precise predictions can be made.

Although there are a great variety of measures of control orientation for use with children and adults, the *I-E Scale* constructed by Rotter has been used most often by investigators in the area. It is a forced-choice scale consisting of twenty-three items (see Table 10.1). Scores are obtained by assigning one point for each external alternative endorsed by the subject and summing across all items. Thus, scores can range from

TABLE 10.1   Examples of Items from Rotter's Internal-External Scale

1. a. I have often found that what is going to happen will happen (E).
    b. Trusting to fate has never turned out as well for me as making a decision to take a definite course of action (I).
2. a. Becoming a success is a matter of hard work; luck has little or nothing to do with it (I).
    b. Getting a good job depends mainly on being in the right place at the right time (E).
3. a. In the long run people get the respect they deserve in this world (I).
    b. Unfortunately, an individual's worth often passes unrecognized no matter how hard the tries (E).

Adapted from Rotter, 1966, p. 11.

zero to twenty-three, with higher scores indicating greater externality. Research using the measure is usually done by dividing the distribution of scores at the median or mean, classifying the subjects as either internals or externals, and then correlating these test responses with other personality variables and behavior. This split into two categories is not meant to imply a typology, but is done for research convenience. Rotter conceptualized people as being more or less internal or external and not as being either internal or external (Rotter, 1975, p. 57). With this preliminary information in mind, let us turn to an examination of research that has utilized this individual difference construct.

Origins and Development of I-E Orientations

The bulk of the research literature indicates that beliefs in internal control are learned initially in families where the parents are warm and supportive of children, praise them for their accomplishments, and do not try to exert authoritarian control over their behavior (Crandall, 1973, p. 2). In addition, these parents are consistent in their disciplining of the children. They do not change the rules continually, or administer punishments that are much more severe than the offense. Under such warm and supportive conditions, the children learn to accept blame for failure as well as credit for success.

In late childhood, however, the family atmosphere tends to change from one of support and involvement to one of more parental detachment. At this stage, both parents, but especially the mothers, encourage their children to be independent. They do not reward dependency behaviors as often. They also show less involvement and less contact with their offspring (Crandall, 1973, p. 12). According to one prominent researcher, this parental "coolness" may force the child ". . . into more active intercourse with his physical and social environment so that there is more opportunity for him to observe the effect of his own behavior [and] the contingency between his own actions and ensuing events (Crandall, 1973, p. 13).

Research has also indicated that children tend to acquire a progressive sense of personal efficacy as they grow older; that is, they become more internal with age (Milgram, 1971). Much research with college students shows that they are generally quite internal in their orientations (Rotter, 1966, p. 15). But what about the *locus of control* orientations of adults and the elderly? Are college students more internal than adults of varying ages? Are the elderly more external than college students? The answer to both questions is a tentative "No." A recent study has shown that there is an increasing sense of personal efficacy from college age to adulthood, a stabilized sense of internal control through middle age, and no decrease in internality among the elderly (Ryckman and Malikiosi, 1975). This last finding runs contrary to popular stereotypes of the elderly as helpless and dependent. The study suggests that many of the elderly believe they are personally competent and not at the mercy of authority figures or a capricious environment.

Locus of Control and Performance Effectiveness. Various studies have shown that internals not only believe they have the power to affect their outcomes, but they actually perform more effectively than their external counterparts. These investigations indicate further that internals are more cognitively active and flexible, and learn the rules necessary to solve problems more quickly. They also gather more information than externals about their situations in an attempt to cope with and control outcomes. In one early study concerned with the relationship between locus of control and information-seeking behavior in tuberculosis patients, for example, investigators found that internal patients knew more about their particular medical problems and sought more information about their situation from their physicians, as reported by their attending doctors and nurses (Seeman and Evans, 1962). A similar study using a different population found essentially the same results. Internal inmates in a federal reformatory knew more about the way in which the institution was run and more about the conditions affecting their possible parole than externals (Seeman, 1963). A recent study has shown that internals even have more information about critical political events that have strong implications for their well-being than do externals (Ryckman and Sherman, 1976).

Locus of Control and Persuasibility. If internals have more information about their situations and greater problem-solving ability than externals, it should not be surprising that they are more resistant to influence from others. In fact, many of the early studies in the I-E literature reported findings consistent with that view. They found that internals tended to make judgments independently of the demands of others, whereas externals were much more compliant in the same situations (Lefcourt, 1971, pp. 3–4). You should not get the impression, however, that internals always act rationally, since recent data indicate that some internals are capable of acting quite irrationally under certain circumstances (Ryckman, Rodda, and Sherman, 1972). In circumstances in which they perceive that others are trying to manipulate their behavior, for example, internals tend to reject the requests of these people out of hand and to act in a strongly oppositional manner. Such behavior, of course, may eventually be detrimental both to themselves and others.

A concrete example may make these points clearer. A professor gives a lecture and the students react in different ways to his message, depending, at least in part, on their own personality characteristics. An external student may react uncritically and accept whatever information is given, regardless of whether or not it is accurate. The external may pay more attention to the source and less to the message. The defensively internal student, on the other hand, may reject the information from the professor uncritically; that is, he may have learned to reject any statements from authority figures. As a consequence, he pays less attention to the message. Thus, both internal and external students in this example pay less attention to the message, but for different reasons. Both kinds of students also fail to acquire potentially useful information. Of course, other students who are nondefensive weigh information critically and act rationally without being unduly swayed by the source of the message. Future research on the relationship between I-E and conformity will probably provide us with more insight concerning the ways in which these individuals react to influence attempts in a variety of situations.

Internals not only tend to resist influence attempts by others, but when given an opportunity, make more efforts to control the behavior of others (Phares, 1965). They also tend to like people they can easily manipulate and dislike those they cannot influence (Silverman and Shrauger, 1970).

Some interesting research has shown that internal and external students differ in the number and kinds of romantic heterosexual experiences they have (Dion and Dion, 1973). Internals were found to have proportionally fewer romantic attachments than externals. They also reported experiencing romantic love as less mysterious and volatile than externals. In addition, internals were more strongly opposed to an idealistic view of romantic love than were externals. In comparison with externals, they disagreed more with these statements: (1) There is only one real love for a person; (2) true love lasts forever; and (3) true love leads to almost perfect happiness. But why do internals and externals differ in their orientations toward romantic love? The investigators who conducted the study suggest a number of reasons, all compatible with previous research findings. First, romantic love implies that both parties "give themselves up" to their partners—that is, that they become vulnerable and pliable to the wishes of the partner. But we have already learned that internals do not like to be influenced by others. In addition, internals are often concerned with manipulating others, so that strong feelings of attraction toward another may not serve their purposes; it is difficult to assume a calculating, manipulative attitude toward someone you love. For these reasons, then, perhaps it was not surprising that many of the internal students did not become as involved in romantic liaisons as externals.

I-E and Attribution of Responsibility

We have painted a general picture of internals as competent, responsible, and independent people who, in comparison to externals, perform more effectively on a variety of skill-determined tasks. It should be clear that a person's willingness to strive for excellence in performance is dependent upon the way in which he or she accounts for success and failure experiences. A great variety of studies, with only one or two exceptions, have shown that internals tend to attribute success to internal factors (ability and effort), rather than to external factors (luck or task difficulty), in comparison to externals. In other words, internals attribute their success to ability and hard work, whereas externals attribute it to good luck or an easy task. Thus, internals experience more pride in their achievements and a greater willingness to persist at tasks than externals.

Research has also shown that internals attribute their failures internally, whereas externals rely on external attributions. That is, internals attribute their failures to a lack of ability and/or little effort, whereas externals blame their failures on bad luck or on the difficulty of the task. Thus, internals experience more shame and guilt than externals when they suffer defeat (Phares, 1976, pp. 113–115). Although extreme and indiscriminate reliance on either internal or external factors to account for one's experiences may be unhealthy, it seems reasonable that an internal factor accounting system would be necessary if individuals are to attain competence, with its attendant feeling of self-worth. Thus, it has been proposed that an internal orientation is necessary for adequate social adjustment and functioning.

Research has indicated that internals not only take responsiblity for their own actions, but assume that others are responsible for theirs. Externals, in contrast, assume that their behavior and the behavior of others is controlled by outside forces (Phares, 1976, pp. 102–104). Internals are thus more likely, when given the opportunity, to mete out more severe punishment to rule violators in a variety of situations than externals. Thus, they may be seen as being more punitive and less sympathetic than externals in their judgments and behavior toward wrongdoers.

This judgment about internals is corroborated indirectly by a recent study in which internal and external college women were asked to evaluate an autobiographical essay allegedly written by a woman applying for admission to a university and then to make a decision about whether to reject her application on the basis of that information (Ryckman and Cannon, 1977). By means of a photo attached to the application form, internal and external subjects were led to believe that the applicant was physically attractive or unattractive. When evaluating an essay of objectively good quality, as determined by ratings from a comparable and independent student sample, it was predicted and found that internal women discriminated more against the unattractive person. They downgraded her essay and indicated a greater willingness to reject her application than one completed by an attractive person.

This prediction was based on a previous finding, which showed that people tend to see attractive people as having good personal qualities, whereas unattractive people are perceived as having negative qualities. Since internals tend to see internal factors such as ability and effort as causing a person's behavior, it was assumed they would see the attractive person as having good ability and strong motivation to do well, whereas the unattractive individual would be seen as lazy and having little ability. Thus, it was assumed that an objectively good performance by an attractive person would be seen by internals as consistent with their expectations of such people. That is, she would be seen as performing well because she had ability and strong motivation, and there would therefore be no need to downgrade her performance. In contrast, it was assumed that a good performance by an unattractive person would be seen as inconsistent with the internals' orientation. How could a lazy person with little ability perform well? The answer is that she could not, and thus it was expected that internals would downgrade her performance in order to make her performance fit their expectations. Externals were not expected to downgrade the work of either the attractive or the unattractive performer, since they were expected to assume that the outcomes were beyond the performer's control.

In order to reduce such discriminatory practices, the authors suggested that employers and admissions personnel in various academic, business, and government institutions make their judgments of the person's qualifications, where possible, without requiring a photo with the application. Where job applicants are interviewed directly by prospective employers, they advocated making the interviewers aware of their own biases in the hope that it might serve to reduce their tendencies to discriminate. This information might be especially enlightening to those internally oriented employers who see themselves as responsible and constructive members of society and who try to act accordingly, but who may be unaware of their prejudice against the unattractive.

As you can see from a consideration of the many research studies with the I-E variable, the composite picture of internals and externals formed by integrating study findings is a complicated and intriguing one. Although internals are more adjusted than externals in some respects, we see that they also have their limitations. Research with the I-E construct has proved very informative, and there is little doubt that it will continue to be a popular area of investigation for personality psychologists in the future.

APPLICATION OF THE THEORY TO THE TREATMENT OF PSYCHOPATHOLOGY

For Rotter, psychotherapy is a learning process, so that the same learning principles applied to change the behavior of people in everyday situations can also be utilized to advantage in a therapeutic setting (Rotter, 1954, p. 335). The problems of maladjusted people are seen as originating not in their heads, but in their relationships with other people (Rotter and Hochreich, 1975, p. 109). In general, adjusted individuals experience satisfactions growing out of the performance of behaviors that are seen as constructive from the standpoint of society. Maladjusted people, in contrast, are perpetually dissatisfied with themselves and behave in ways that precipitate punishing responses from society. Furthermore, Rotter believes that maladjusted people are often characterized by low freedom of movement and high need value (Rotter and Hochreich, 1975, p. 106). In his view, such individuals are convinced that they are unable to obtain the gratifications they desire. As a result, instead of learning how to achieve their goals, they learn how to avoid or defend themselves against actual or anticipated failure.

The defense mechanisms postulated by Freud are accepted by Rotter and other social learning theorists, but are conceptualized as avoidance or escape behaviors. Projection, for example, involves blaming others for one's own mistakes in order to avoid anticipated punishment. Rationalization involves the construction of elaborate excuses for one's own inadequate behavior in an effort to stave off punishment. One of the unfortunate results of such maneuvering is that maladjusted people fail to learn new behaviors. They simply continue to gain temporary relief by avoiding the punishment, criticism, failure, or rejection they believe will follow if they attempt to perform behaviors for which they have low expectations for success. In the long run, however, such defensive maneuvers have maladjustive consequences.

Maladjusted people not only have low expectations for success, but often their expectancies in one area, (for example, in their work situation) generalize inappropriately into other areas (for example, into their home lives), so that they come to perceive themselves as generally worthless. Clinicians have found that maladjusted people also tend to place too much importance on the gratification of one need (Katkovsky, 1968, p. 228). For example, a person may have a strong need to dominate others—that is, he finds it satisfying to be able to influence the behavior of others. Such a person may distort what others say in order to maintain control of the situation, ignore important events unrelated to dominance, and act in an aggressive manner when it is totally inappropriate (Katkovsky, 1968, p. 228). There is little doubt that such an individual will often be dissatisfied, since his need to dominate will bring him into repeated conflicts with others.

Maladjusted individuals tend to engage in behaviors that lead to immediate rewards, but are punishing in the long run (Katkovsky, 1968, pp. 229–230). The compulsive gambler finds gambling exciting, but usually learns that his behavior has severe negative consequences for himself and his family. In order to obtain money to pursue his passion, he may sell household property, reduce expenditures for food drastically, and even steal from other family members. Maladjusted people not only engage in behavior that others consider undesirable, but they often fail to show behaviors that others consider desirable (Katkovsky, 1968, p. 230). Society encourages its members to communicate with one another, for example, and people who fail to do so in a wide variety of situations are considered maladjusted. It is often said that they lack the necessary verbal and social skills.

In order to change the behavior of such individuals, Rotter believes it is nesessary for therapists to be flexible. Since clients come into the therapeutic setting with different problems based on unique life experiences and motives, the environmental conditions that promote optimal change will vary from person to person. Treatment strategies can include recommendations for changes in the client's job, academic situation, home life, and so forth. For other clients, various behavior therapies, direct or indirect suggestions, or support and reassurance may be called for (see the final chapter for a discussion of the behavior therapies). All these procedures and others can be used singly or in combination to help clients (Rotter and Hochreich, 1975, p. 109).

In general, Rotter believes that therapy should be an evolving relationship between client and therapist in which the client is helped to discover how his present needs, attitudes, and behaviors developed, which are appropriate or inappropriate for effective living, and what alternatives are available to him. The therapist emphasizes that the client must take responsibility for change, be motivated to change, and be willing to try out new behaviors (Rotter, 1954, p. 353). Change advocated by the therapist may include teaching the client to discriminate between situations in which behaviors are likely to lead to failure and those likely to produce success, helping him to lower unrealistically high expectations for punishment, and encouraging him to assess the importance of his goals more critically and appropriately.

In order to encourage adjustive discrimination between situations, for instance, the therapist may analyze and contrast the client's past life situation with his present situation and show him that his experiences of previous failure are unlikely to transfer into the present. The therapist might, for example, encourage a freshman to minimize past experiences of failure in elementary school and to believe instead that he can and will be successful in college on the basis of outstanding aptitude and ability test scores. In this case, the therapist's job is one of teaching the person to differentiate between two situations and to raise his expectations for success on the basis of solid evidence. Some clients may have inordinately high expectations for success that need lowering. We all know or have heard of people who brag about abilities they in fact do not possess. The mediocre student who claims to be brilliant is a pertinent example. The bragging done by such an individual may bring temporary gratification and a bolstering of self-esteem, but the long-range consequences of such behavior may be punishing. Therapy in such a case may center around a lowering of the person's expectations.

Therapy may also require changes in the importance a person attaches to certain goals. A person who has learned to value winning above everything else because it brought him acceptance and love from his parents may be encouraged to deemphasize the goal. The therapist might point out to him that his indiscriminate attempts to prove himself better than others, even when competing in a game of ping-pong, serve only to alienate others. He would be shown that his feelings that no one likes him stem from indiscriminate pursuit of his goal and that a change in behavior is therefore necessary.

It should be emphasized that Rotter adovcates a therapy which focuses not only on the elimination of undersirable and inadequate behaviors, but on the acquisition of desirable ones. The person is trained to learn methods of analyzing problems as a means of finding better solutions and to try out new behaviors. It is not enough, in Rotter's view, for therapists to help clients understand the sources of their problems. They must be shown how to perform new behaviors designed to overcome them (Rotter, 1954, p. 398).

CRITICAL COMMENTS

We now examine the scientific worth of Rotter's theory in terms of our six criteria.

Comprehensiveness. Rotter's theory has its roots in both the clinical setting and the experimental laboratory. It covers a wide range of phenomena, including parental attitudes and behaviors, academic achievement, defensive behavior, interpersonal trust, social activism, alcoholism, maladjustment, mental retardation, and a host of psychopathological behaviors. As such, it is a theory that is quite comprehensive in nature.

Precision and Testability. Compared to most of the other theories covered in the text, Rotter's is characterized by concepts that are well-defined and hypotheses that are capable of being tested.

Simplicity. Rotter's position seems fairly parsimonious, at least in terms of its attempts to account for individual performance phenomena. The picture is unsettled, however, when we consider the theory's treatment of abnormal and therapeutic phenomena. Rotter seems undecided about whether to retain, modify, or reject some of the psychoanalytic concepts, for example. As a result, it is difficult to assess the parsimony of the position in accounting for abnormal phenomena.

Empirical Validity. Empirical support for the theory is strong. There have been many tests of hypotheses concerned with an understanding of the conditions that facilitate or hinder learning and performance, but relatively few tests of hypotheses involving clinical phenomena. Many research tests of Rotter's position have centered on his I-E concept, but unfortunately, work with this concept has generally proceeded independently of the rest of the theory.

Heuristic Value. The theory has stimulated research in various areas, including learning theory, psychopathology, psychotherapy, personality development, and social psychology. Thus, it has proved to have good heuristic value.

Applied Value. Thus far Rotter's position has had little direct practical impact on the solution of social problems. It does appear, however, that the knowledge gained about locus of control has potential applied value. It seems clear, for example, that persuasive messages designed to get people to reduce their weight or their smoking behavior should take individual differences in control orientation into account if they are to be effective. Research on locus of control has suggested the kinds of messages that are more likely to persuade internals than externals in a variety of situations. Such knowledge can be put to good use to help people overcome various personal problems.

I-E measures can also be used by clinicians and educators to diagnose locus of control beliefs and to gauge changes in orientation following therapeutic interventions. A therapist, for example, should be able to use the measure to evaluate whether or not the therapy efforts have been able to reduce the client's feelings of powerlessness by noting changes in responses to the I-E test over time.

DISCUSSION QUESTIONS

1. Describe the four basic concepts of Rotter's social learning theory of personality. Give some personal examples of how the concepts could be combined to predict the behavior of one of your friends.

2. What is a minimal goal? What is your minimal goal for academic grades? Do you think it is realistic in terms of your abilities and motivation as a student? What is your minimal goal for establishing a friendship with someone?

3. Describe the behavior of a maladjusted person using terminology of Rotter's social learning position.

4. What is meant by internal-external control of reinforcement? How much of your own behavior is controlled by forces beyond your own control? Are you an internal in every situation? Is it healthy to be externally oriented in some situations? Which ones?

5. What are some of the determinants of a person's locus of control orientation? Are the elderly primarily external in their orientations?

6. Which concepts in Rotter's system bear striking resemblance to ones postulated by Adler?

7. Do you agree with Rotter that it is usually unnecessary to study in great detail the ways in which the person's early childhood experiences are related to his or her current behavior in order to predict such behavior accurately?

8. What is the empirical law of effect? Is a concept of reinforcement always necessary to account for behavior adequately?

9. What are some of the strengths and weaknesses of the social learning approach to the study of maladjusted behavior?

10. What are some of the primary assessment techniques used by Rotter to help him understand human personality?

NOTES

V. C. Crandall, "Differences in Parental Antecedents of Internal-External Control in Children and in Young Adulthood" (unpublished manuscript, Fels Research Institute, 1973).

K. L. Dion and K. K. Dion, "Correlates of Romantic Love," *Journal of Consulting and Clinical Psychology*, 1973, **41,** 51–56.

W. Katkovsky, "Social-Learning Theory and Maladjustment," in L. Gorlow and W. Katkovsky, eds., *Readings in the Psychology of Adjustment*, 2nd ed., (New York: McGraw-Hill, 1968).

H. M. Lefcourt, *Internal versus External Control of Reinforcement Revisited: Recent Developments* (Research Report No. 27, University of Waterloo, Ontario, Canada, 1971).

N. A. Milgram, "Locus of Control in Negro and White Children at Four Age Levels," *Psychological Reports*, 1971, **29,** 459–465.

D. L. Mosher, "The Influence of Adler on Rotter's Social Learning Theory of Personality," *Journal of Individual Psychology*, 1968, **24,** 33–45.

E. J. Phares, "Internal-External Control as a Determinant of Amount of Social Influence Exerted," *Journal of Personality and Social Psychology*, 1965, **2,** 642–647.

E. J. Phares, *Locus of Control in Personality* (Morristown, N.J.: General Learning Press, 1976).

J. B. Rotter, *Social Learning and Clinical Psychology* (Englewood Cliffs, N.J.: Prentice-Hall, 1954).

J. B. Rotter, "Generalized Expectancies for Internal versus External Control of Reinforcement," *Psychological Monographs*, 1966, **80** (Whole No. 609).

J. B. Rotter, "Some Problems and Misconceptions Related to the Construct of Internal versus External Control of Reinforcement," *Journal of Consulting and Clinical Psychology*, 1975, **43,** 56–67.

J. B. Rotter, J. E. Chance, and E. J. Phares, *Applications of a Social Learning Theory of Personality* (New York: Holt, Rinehart and Winston, 1972).

J. B. Rotter and D. J. Hochreich, *Personality* (Glenview, Ill.: Scott, Foresman, 1975).

R. M. Ryckman and D. W. Cannon, "Task Evaluation as a Function of the Performer's Physical Attractiveness, Quality of the Performance, and the Evaluator's Locus of Control Orientation" (Paper presented at the annual meeting of the Eastern Psychological Association, Boston, April 1977).

R. M. Ryckman and M. X. Malikiosi, "Relationship Between Locus of Control and Chronological Age," *Psychological Reports*, 1975, **36,** 655–658.

R. M. Ryckman, W. C. Rodda, and M. F. Sherman, "Locus of Control and Expertise Relevance as Determinants of Changes in Opinion About Student Activism," *The Journal of Social Psychology*, 1972, **88,** 107–114.

R. M. Ryckman and M. F. Sherman, "Locus of Control and Student Reaction to the Watergate Break-in," *The Journal of Social Psychology*, 1976, **99,** 305–306.

M. Seeman, Alienation and Social Learning in a Reformatory," *American Journal of Sociology*, 1963, **69,** 270–284.

M. Seeman and J. W. Evans, "Alienation and Learning in a Hospital Setting," *American Sociological Review*, 1962, **27,** 772–783.

R. E. Silverman and J. S. Shrauger, "Locus of Control and Correlates of Attraction toward Others" (Paper presented at the annual meeting of the Eastern Psychological Association, Atlantic City, April 1970).

SUGGESTED READINGS

Lefcourt, H. M. *Locus of Control: Current Trends in Theory and Research.* Hillsdale, N.J.: Lawrence Erlbaum, 1976.

Phares, E. J. *Locus of Control in Personality.* Morristown, N.J.: General Learning Press, 1976.

Rotter, J. B. *Social Learning and Clinical Psychology.* Englewood Cliffs, N.J.: Prentice-Hall, 1954.

Rotter, J. B. "Generalized Expectancies for Internal versus External Control of Reinforcement, *Psychological Monographs*, 1966, **80** (Whole No. 609).

Rotter, J. B., Chance, J., and Phares, E. J., eds. *Application of a Social Learning Theory of Personality.* New York: Holt, Rinehart and Winston, 1972.

GLOSSARY

Behavior Potential. Possiblity that a particular behavior will occur as a function of the person's unique expectancies and the value of the reinforcer for showing the behavior in a given situation.

Expectancy. Probability held by a person that a particular reinforcer will occur as a function of his or her behavior in a particular kind of situation. Expectancies may be generalized or specific.

Field Theory. Theory which maintains that behavior is determined by the complex interplay between cognitive and environmental variables.

Freedom of Movement. In Rotter's theory, high freedom of movement refers to a person's expectancy that many of his behaviors will lead to success; low freedom of movement refers to his or her expectancy that behavior will be unsuccessful.

I-E Scale. Test designed by Rotter to measure the person's belief that forces are or are not beyond his control. Internals (Is) are people who believe that events are under their own control; externals (Es) are people who believe that outcomes are controlled by outside forces like luck, fate, God, or powerful others.

Locus of Control. Term used by Rotter to refer to people's beliefs about the location of controlling forces in their lives.

Minimal Goal. Dividing point between those reinforcers that produce feelings of satisfaction for a person and those that produce dissatisfaction.

Psychological Situation. In Rotter's theory, the meaning of the situation as it is defined by the person.

Reinforcement Value. Importance of a given reinforcer to an individual in relation to other reinforcers if the possibilities for the attainment of all of them are equal.

Stimulus Generalization. Responses made by a person in the presence of an original stimulus come to be made in the presence of other stimuli that resemble the original one.

Albert Bandura (Courtesy of Albert Bandura)

CHAPTER $\mathcal{II}$

Bandura's Social Learning Theory

BIOGRAPHICAL SKETCH

Albert Bandura was born on December 4, 1925, to a family of wheat farmers of Polish heritage. He grew up in the small town of Mundare in Alberta, Canada, and attended a high school that had only two teachers and twenty students. He received his B.A. degree from the University of British Columbia in Vancouver in 1949 and then earned an M.A. and Ph.D. in psychology from the University of Iowa in 1951 and 1952, respectively. After receiving his doctorate, he served a year's clinical internship at the Wichita Guidance Center and then accepted a position in the department of psychology at Stanford University, where he has remained ever since.

During his tenure at Stanford, Bandura has been actively engaged in the development of a social learning approach to the understanding of human behavior. He has also been a productive scholar, publishing several influential books and countless research articles in scientific journals. His early books, *Adolescent Aggression* (1952) and *Social Learning and Personality Development* (1963), were written in collaboration with Richard H. Walters. More recently, he has published *Principles of Behavior Modification* (1969), an extensive review and summary of the social psychological principles that govern behavior. In 1971, he published a module entitled *Social Learning Theory*, an abbreviated treatment of these principles. In 1973, he published *Aggression*, a review of current theory and research into the determinants of aggressive behavior. The book shows how research on this important topic can help us to understand the origins of behavior that is almost always harmful to ourselves and others, as well as giving an exposition of the kinds of variables responsible for its reduction and elimination. In his most recent book, *Social Learning Theory* (1977), he has presented a concise overview of recent theoretical and research developments in his theory.

279

In recognition of his contributions to psychology, Bandura received the Distinguished Scientist Award in 1972 from the American Psychological Association and the Distinguished Scientific Achievement Award from the California Psychological Association in 1973. He was also elected president of the American Psychological Association in 1974.

BASIC CONCEPTS AND PRINCIPLES

Assumptions of the Social Learning Approach

According to Bandura, behavior is caused solely neither by inner forces nor environmental influences. Instead, he believes, like Rotter, that behavior occurs as a result of a complex interplay between inner processes and environmental influences (Bandura, 1971, p. 2). These internal processes are based largely on the previous experiences of the individual and are conceptualized as measurable and manipulable covert events. As he puts it, "These mediating events are extensively controlled by external stimulus events and in turn regulate overt responsiveness" (Bandura, 1969, p. 10). Unlike Skinner, who acknowledges that stimulus-response covariations are mediated by internal events but proceeds to neglect them in favor of causal explanations couched in terms of external manipulable events, Bandura places special emphasis on the role of the cognitive determinants of behavior (Bandura, 1969, p. 38). He argues that our superior cognitive capacity often determines the direction of our actions. We represent external events symbolically and later use both *verbal* and *imaginal representations* to guide our behavior. We also solve problems symbolically without having to resort to actual, overt trial and error behavior, and we foresee the probable consequences of our behavior and modify our actions accordingly. Thus, our higher mental processes allow us to perform both insightful and foresightful behavior (Bandura, 1971, pp. 2–3).

The fact that Bandura places such emphasis on cognitive processes in his analysis of behavior should not mislead us into thinking he ignores the effects of reinforcement. On the contrary, the reinforcement construct plays a major role in his theory, but one compatible with a cognitive orientation, and one that goes beyond the view offered by many traditional learning theorists. Skinner, for example, focuses on the changes in behavior that occur as a result of our direct experiences with the rewarding and punishing consequences of our actions. Responses that prove successful tend to be repeated; those that are punished tend to be inhibited. Bandura acknowledges the validity of this position, but he maintains that it does not fully account for the ways in which our behavior is acquired, maintained, or altered (Bandura, 1971, p. 3). In his view, most of our behavior is not controlled by immediate external reinforcement. As a result of earlier experiences, we tend to expect that certain kinds of behavior will have effects we desire, that others will produce unwanted outcomes, and that still others will have little significant impact. Our behavior is therefore regulated to a large extent by *anticipated outcomes* (Bandura, 1971, p. 3). For example, we do not wait until we have a car accident to buy insurance. Instead, we rely on information from others about the potentially disastrous consequences of not owning insurance in making our decision to purchase it. We do not wait until we are caught in a blinding snowstorm to decide what to wear on a camping trip. We can imagine the consequences of being poorly prepared and take the proper precautionary steps. In countless ways, we make decisions based on the anticipation of consequences. This notion is similar to one espoused by Rotter, except that Rotter calls it expectancy rather than anticipation.   [P. 38, 1977]

Bandura also maintains that behavior can be acquired without the administration of *external reinforcement.* We learn much of the behavior we eventually display through the influence of example: we simply watch what others do and then repeat their actions. Technically, we are also said to have acquired the behavior through *observational learning.* In Bandura's opinion, modeling figures prominently in our lives for several reasons. First, the environment is loaded with potentially lethal consequences, so that trial and error behavior would be too costly. We do not rely on trial and error or direct experience to teach children to swim, people to drive automobiles, or pilots to fly planes. Furthermore, it would be too cumbersome to try to socialize people by selective reinforcement of their activities. Imagine trying to teach children language and the many rules and customs of the culture this way. The acquisition process can be shortened considerably by providing us with the appropriate models (Bandura, 1971, p. 5). Although early learning theorists tended to neglect the role of observational learning in their attempts to understand human behavior, Bandura and other proponents of the social learning approach have rectified this shortcoming and shed much more light on the ways in which we acquire, maintain, and modify our behavior through emulation of models.

Modeling Theory

At first glance, the modeling process seems simple and straightforward. We have an observer and a model, and the primary question is whether or not the observer will imitate the actions of the model. But the answer is far from simple, since it depends upon the operation of a host of factors, among them the personality characteristics of the observer. For example, the sex of the observer may play a part in determining whether or not the model's behavior will be followed. In addition, the sex of the model may influence the behavior of male and female observers. An early study by Bandura and his colleagues showed, for instance, that boys tended to show more aggressive behavior than girls after watching a male model who was aggressive than after watching a female model, whereas girls tended to imitate the aggressive actions of a female model more often than those of a male model (Bandura, Ross, and Ross, 1968). Whether or not this study could be replicated today because of changes in the status of women during the past decade or so is debatable, but that issue should not obscure the general principle: People do learn sex-linked behaviors that influence the extent to which they will imitate the actions of others. Other research has shown that people who lack self-esteem, or who are incompetent, as well as those who have been rewarded in the past for imitative behavior, are likely to follow the behavior of a successful model (Bandura and Walters, 1963, p. 85).

Although it is true that certain characteristics and prior experiences affect observers' imitative behavior, there is also ample evidence that the characteristics of the model or models play a significant role. Observers imitate the behavior of a competent model more rapidly than the behavior of an incompetent one (Rosenbaum and Tucker, 1952). They tend to be more strongly influenced by models who are similar to themselves in terms of personal background and physical appearance (Rosenkrans, 1967). Observers also tend to learn more of the behaviors of models when the models are highly nurturant or rewarding and when they have control over the future resources of the observers (Grusec and Mischel, 1966). Bandura & Huston (1961)

Research indicates that rewards and punishments associated with the behavior of models, as well as their personal characteristics, can affect the imitative behavior of observers. We learn by observing the behavior of others and the occasions on which they are reinforced for their actions, and alter our behavior accordingly. Such *vicarious reinforcement* has a special impact on our behavior, as the following study suggests. In this investigation, Bandura exposed nursery school children to a five-minute film on a television console showing an adult model behaving aggressively toward a large plastic doll:

> The film began with a scene in which a model walked up to an adult-size plastic Bobo doll and ordered him to clear the way. After glaring for a moment at the noncompliant antagonist the model exhibited four novel aggressive responses each accompanied by a distinctive verbalization.
>
> First, the model laid the Bobo doll on its side, sat on it, and punched it in the nose while remarking, "Pow, right on the nose, boom, boom." The model then raised the doll and pommelled it on the head with a mallet. Each response was followed by the verbalization, "Sockeroo . . . stay down." Following the mallet aggression, the model kicked the doll about the room, and these responses were interspersed with the comment, "Fly away." Finally, the model threw rubber balls at the Bobo doll, each strike punctuated with "Bang." This sequence of physically and verbally aggressive behavior was repeated twice. (Bandura, 1965)

The children in the control condition simply saw this film and observed no consequences to the model for his aggressive actions. Other children, however, saw a film sequence in which the model was rewarded or punished for his behavior. In the reward condition, a second adult praised the aggressive model for his behavior and rewarded him with soda pop and candy. In the punishment condition, the second adult spoke disparagingly to the aggressive model, accusing him of being a coward and a bully. The punishing adult also spanked the model with a rolled-up newspaper and threatened him with a beating if he was caught being aggressive again.

The independent variable in this study was the nature of the reinforcement administered to the model for aggressive actions. The dependent measure was the amount of aggression exhibited by the children in the three conditions when they were given an opportunity to display the behavior they had seen modeled. The children were escorted to a separate room that contained a Bobo doll, three balls, a mallet and pegboard, as well as an assortment of other toys. A wide variety of toys was presented so that the children had full opportunity to engage in either imitative or nonimitative behaviors. The experimenter then left the room, presumably to fetch other toys, and the children were left alone to play. Observers then recorded their responses after watching their behavior through a one-way mirror. As expected, the children exposed to the model who had been punished for his aggression showed significantly less aggression in the free play situation than the children who observed the rewarded model or the one who had incurred no consequences for his behavior. Thus, the first phase of this study showed clearly that the differential reinforcements administered to a model can indeed have a profound impact on the performance of observers.

But a question with practical social implications still remained. Although we know that the children in the various reinforcement conditions *performed* differently, did they all actually *acquire* the model's behavior? In other words, is it possible that all the children learned the model's behavior, but that only those who saw him rewarded or go unpunished decided to imitate him? In the second phase of the study, Bandura showed that this was the case. After their performances in phase one were measured, all the children were offered attractive prizes contingent upon their reproducing the model's aggressive responses. The introduction of these attractive incentives completely washed out the previously observed differences in performance, revealing that an equivalent amount of learning had taken place in the model-rewarded, model-punished, and no-consequences conditions. Thus, the study suggests that people may learn a variety of behaviors but actively decide to perform or not to perform them depending upon their estimates of rewards for performing them. Why is this acquisition-performance distinction so important? Bandura suggests it is because it helps counter the arguments of critics who maintain that showing crime in the mass media is not harmful to young observers, since the criminal is always punished for wrongdoing. These results show that punishment of the model (the criminal) may not prevent the acquisition of immoral and illegal behavior. It may eventually surface under the appropriate circumstances—for example, under conditions where his peers reward a person for such behavior. The conclusion is that such activities should not be presented in the media because they may have potentially harmful effects.

We have seen that both direct, external reinforcement and vicarious reinforcement can affect imitative behavior, but we have not yet discussed the manner in which people come to maintain a variety of behaviors in the absence of external sanctions. This involves the development of self-control processes by the individual and has been a central area of concern for investigators interested in modeling phenomena.

Self-Control Processes [P.133 1977]

Social learning theorists have focused on three subprocesses of self-control and provided empirical support for their existence and operation that goes considerably beyond the description provided initially by Skinner. These three aspects are (1) resistance to temptation; (2) delay of reinforcement; and (3) self-reinforcement and evaluation. Let us consider each of them in turn.

Resistance to Temptation. In the typical resistance-to-temptation paradigm, children are first shown an assortment of attractive toys and then forbidden to play with them. The experimenter then leaves the children alone with the toys and watches to see if they will transgress and play with them. In one early study, this procedure was followed and then different groups of kindergarten children were exposed to a film in which a peer-model was either rewarded or rebuked by a parent for playing with the toys (Walters, Leat, and Mezei, 1963). Children in the control condition, of course, saw no film. The children who saw the rewarded model deviated more quickly and spent more time being deviant than children in the punished-model or control conditions. In fact, the children who saw the model punished deviated hardly at all. These results show that the nature of the reinforcement applied to the model's behavior may have either *inhibitory* or *disinhibitory* effects on the behavior of observers.

Further research suggests that this inhibition or disinhibition may be mediated by two major factors. One is the person's estimate that repeating the behavior of the model will lead to either positive or negative consequences. The second concerns the possibility that the observer will display conditioned fear responses after watching the model being punished for his behavior, or experience a conditioned positive, emotional reaction after seeing the model rewarded (Berger, 1962). Either or both factors may operate to affect the probability of occurrence of imitative behavior. This research suggests that we sometimes consciously weigh the potential consequences of our behavior and inhibit responding if we believe that punishment will follow. We also sometimes actively resist temptation by changing the variables responsible for our punishment.

Delay of Reinforcement. Delay of reinforcement usually refers to a self-imposed postponement of an immediate, smaller reward for a larger reward in the future. An example would be the child who foregoes buying candy in order to save his money for a summer camping trip. Another example might be the newly married couple who postpone taking vacations and buying luxury items in order to acquire a down payment on a house. From a developmental perspective, research studies have shown that people who have a preference for delayed rewards grow up in homes where parents stress the importance of achievement and encourage them to be self-reliant and independent. In addition, evidence indirectly suggests that the parents of such people model high delay of reward behavior for them (Bandura and Mischel, 1965). It should not be surprising to learn that Rotter's internals (see Chapter 10) are more willing and able to delay gratification of their needs than are externals (Strickland, 1972).

In contrast to the social learning approach, which emphasizes the social determinants of delay of reward behavior, the Freudian position focuses on the way in which id impulses press for expression in behavior and are changed into ideational representations (ego thought processes) as a means of exerting control until the appropriate behavior whose expression would gratify the id can be found. Such a position places stress on rather obscure internal factors such as "ego-organizations" and "energy-binding ideations" that do not lend themselves readily to experimental study (Mischel, 1968, p. 153).

[P.128 -133 1977]   [P. 133 - 137 /1977]

Self-Reinforcement and Evaluation. Standards for self-reward and punishment can be learned in a variety of ways. Children may be taught rules of behavior by their parents and others and be rewarded for following them and punished for violating them. Children may also learn these standards through exposure to books, newspapers, films, television, and radio. They may also learn them, as you might expect, through modeling procedures. In one study, two groups of children participated in a miniature bowling game with adult models (Bandura and Kupers, 1964). In one condition, the children watched a model reward himself with candies only for excellent performances. In another condition, they watched a model reward himself for poor performances. After exposure to the models, the children were left alone to play the game with no models present. The results indicated that the children

Bandura , Grusec d Menlove (1967) [1977. p. 135]

tended to match the behavior of the model to which they had been exposed. Although both groups of children had access to a generous supply of candy, those who were exposed to a high performance standard rewarded themselves sparingly and only when they had matched or exceeded the criterion, whereas those who were exposed to the low-standard model rewarded themselves quite often, even for poor performances.

In a recent extension of this work, two investigators sought to determine the effects of *multiple modeling* on imitative behavior (McMains and Liebert, 1968). Using the same bowling game described above, adults in phase one imposed either a stringent criterion for self-reward (that is, they rewarded themselves only for attaining a particular score and told the children to do likewise), or a lenient standard for self-reward (that is, they rewarded themselves for attaining either one of two particular scores). In phase two of the investigation, a second model performed on the bowling game and either adhered to the stringent criterion set by the first model or violated it by rewarding himself for attaining the lenient standard. The results indicated that children trained on the stringent criterion by the first adult and who then saw the second model adhere to that standard deviated very little from the standard; that is, they rewarded themselves only when they met the stringent standard. Children who were first trained on the stringent standard but who saw a second adult violate that standard were least willing to hold to the stringent standard in the absence of the models. They rewarded themselves for attaining a variety of scores. These findings have some interesting implications. They suggest that parents and others who impose severe restrictions on children but do not follow through by example are likely to be quite ineffective in "training" their children to adopt certain social rules. It is not adequate, it seems, to use the old saw, "Do as I say, not as I do" to instill appropriate values in children. Rather, our motto should probably be, "Do as I say *and* do!"

Another implication of this study concerns the relationship between the learning of standards and the person's feelings of well-being. If the standards the individual learns to accept are too high or can be attained only rarely, he or she may experience stress. Under such conditions, the person is said to feel anxious, guilty, and depressed. Part of the tragedy here is that many people who adopt such standards are relatively competent, but live in continual agony since their best efforts are rarely considered by them to be good enough. Approval—that is, the application of rewards and praise—by others may not be acceptable to such people. In such instances, external reinforcement may have little impact on their behavior.

Recall the similarities between Rotter's concept of high minimal goals, Adler's concept of the unrealistic pursuit of fictional goals, and this notion of self-reward contingent upon the attainment of extremely high standards. As Bandura well recognizes, an adequate social learning theory must account for the impact of self-determined reinforcement on behavior as well as for the effects of external reinforcement (Bandura, 1969, p. 39).

At this point in our treatment of modeling influences, we have seen that the process is anything but simple and straightforward. A large number of factors, both personal and situational, determine the extent to which behavior will or will not be imitated. It should also be mentioned in passing that Bandura considers the construct of reinforcement to be relational, and not absolute. In order to understand the modeling process thoroughly, we must treat reinforcement effects as sequential and not as static, one-shot applications. For example, studies have shown that when models are not punished for behavior which has been punished in the past, observers of the history of this reinforcement will increase their own transgressive behavior to the same degree as when they have seen the model rewarded. Bandura argues that "[t]hese findings suggest that nonreaction to formerly prohibited activities may take on, through contrast, positive significance" (Bandura, 1969, p. 195). Similarly, nonreward following a series of rewards may be perceived as a negative reinforcer. The general point is that a full understanding of modeling behavior would be determined not only by the characteristics of observers and models, but by the context or situation in which the events occur and by the history of positive and negative sanctions associated with the modeled behavior (Bandura, 1969, p. 195).

AGGRESSION AND PROBLEM BEHAVIORS

Now let us turn to an examination of some applications of modeling principles and research to two major social problems: violence in the media and problem behaviors.

Violence in the Mass Media and Imitative Behavior

As virtually all of us recognize, violence and aggressive acts permeate our society. We read in the newspapers every day about inhumane actions on the local, national, and international levels. We cannot help but notice the violence in the cartoons children watch on television. In the evenings, we watch the news and listen as commentators document for us the latest "kill counts" of faceless people who live in obscure foreign lands where political factions vie for power. A short time later, we are "treated" to law-and-order shows in which the good guys and bad guys resolve their problems by systematically blowing holes in one another with a wide assortment of weapons. Many of the films we watch provide the same gruesome cataloguing of aggression. The old John Wayne shoot-em-ups, though laden with aggression, are tame fare indeed in comparison to the films shown today.

It may be relatively easy to grant that we are exposed to a steady diet of violence in the media, but many people claim that such exposure does not lead inevitably to aggression. Further, they maintain that when such exposure does have an impact on viewers, the impact is minimal and relatively innocuous. In contrast, Bandura believes that media portrayal of violence can have serious and harmful effects on our behavior and the behavior of others. He acknowledges that the portrayal of violence in the media is neither a sufficient nor a necessary cause of aggression, but argues vigorously that this does not preclude the possibility that such exposure can, under the right circumstances, facilitate aggression (Bandura, 1973, p. 267). In reply to the argument that the general impact of media violence on people is minor, Bandura maintains that such a contention flies in the face of the evidence: "[T]he same stimulus can have weak or powerful effects for different individuals and even for the same individual on different occasions, depending on the presence of other aggression inducements" (Bandura, 1973, p. 267).

Another argument used by critics is that exposure to violence affects only disturbed individuals. Bandura counters by pointing out research which shows that models can get so-called normal people to aggress against others under the right circumstances. The Milgram study cited in Chapter 1 showed quite conclusively that many ordinary people are willing to act in violent ways under strong prompting from authority figures. By countering these and other arguments with an impressive mass of research evidence, Bandura has tried to make all of us aware of the potential danger involved in the unabated portrayal of violence in the media. Let us examine some of these findings to see how both personal and situational variables can act to facilitate or inhibit aggressive behavior.

Research on Modeling and Aggression

We have already learned that observers who watch models being punished for their actions tend not to repeat those actions, whereas observers who see models rewarded for certain behaviors tend to repeat them. We have also seen that, even though observers tend not to perform the actions of punished models, they have still learned the disapproved behaviors. Research has also shown that observers will imitate the aggressive behavior of filmed as well as live models.

Another study has shown that, even though young observers reported they disliked a model who had been rewarded for aggression, they still imitated him and reported wanting to be like him. It seems as though they knew aggression was wrong, but also believed that it was fun. This finding suggested to the investigators an analogous situation in many television programs, where the "bad guy" is rewarded throughout an episode for his wrongdoing and punished only at the very end of the program (Bandura, Ross, and Ross, 1963). The viewers may know he is guilty of wrongdoing and has been punished for it, but they may nevertheless admire him for performing exciting and reward-ing feats they themselves would love to perform. In other words, all the positive reinforcement he has received for his actions may easily over-ride and outweigh the punishment he finally receives. Even if he suffers the ultimate punishment in the end, they may conclude that it was worth it, since he had a "helluva good time along the way." In many programs and films, the "hero" may have only a fine imposed upon him for his crimes. We can readily imagine the lessons being learned by young and naive viewers.

There is also a serious question about the advisability of using vio-lence to punish wrongdoers. Although it is true that witnessing such punishment will indeed, at least temporarily, inhibit imitative behavior, we have already seen that viewers may learn the behavior anyway and show it under more favorable circumstances. More importantly, it gives viewers the impression that the use of violence is both justifiable and a ready solution for problems. It hinders their consideration of alternative nonviolent strategies. An experiment by Berkowitz has indicated that when people view acts of violence that seem justified, their inhibitions are lowered and aggressive responding is facilitated. If, on the other hand, they witness violence they consider inappropriate, their ag-gressive responding is inhibited (Berkowitz, 1962). A more recent study shows that similar results are obtained irrespective of whether the filmed violence represents nonfictional (real) or fictional events (Meyer, 1972).

In that investigation, subjects were individually introduced to an ex-perimenter who informed them that the purpose of the study was to see how students reacted to grading each other's work on the same task by means of electric shocks. Each person was then asked to write an essay on the importance of obtaining a college education. His composition was graded by his partner. The grading scale ranged from 1 to 10, with fewer shocks indicating good performance and many shocks indicating poor performance. All subjects were then angered by being given eight shocks, regardless of what they wrote. Under the pretext of giving their partners enough time to write their essays, all the subjects were asked to participate in a second experiment in which they would see different film segments and then be asked for their reactions in order to learn how people react to news stories. Subjects were randomly assigned to eight different experimental conditions: (1) a real violence segment, (2) an un-justified real violence segment, (3) a justified real violence segment, (4) a fictional violence segment, (5) an unjustified fictional violence segment, (6) a justified fictional violence segment, (7) a nonviolent film, and (8) a control condition in which subjects were not exposed to a film.

The nonfictional or real violence segment was two and a half minutes taken from the "CBS Evening News with Walter Cronkite." It depicted South Vietnamese soldiers on patrol who encounter the enemy and later execute a North Vietnamese prisoner by knifing him in the chest. Some

subjects saw this film and heard a voice track which justified the execu-
tion by saying that the enemy soldier had previously killed innocent
women and children. Other subjects saw the same film but heard a voice
track which said the killing was unjustified because the enemy soldier
was technically a prisoner of war and should have been turned over to
South Vietnamese authorities. The fictional piece was a segment from
the movie *From Here to Eternity* in which two soldiers engage in a knife
fight and one of them stabs the other to death. In one condition, subjects
heard a sound track which said that the victim's punishment was justified; in another, the sound track informed subjects that the attack was
unjustified. Still other subjects saw both films without a voice track.
Other subjects were exposed either to a nonviolent film showing a
cowboy breaking in a wild horse or to no film.

Following this part of the experiment, all subjects were given an opportunity to grade the essays of their partners. The results are depicted
graphically in Figure 11.1. As you can see, subjects who viewed the

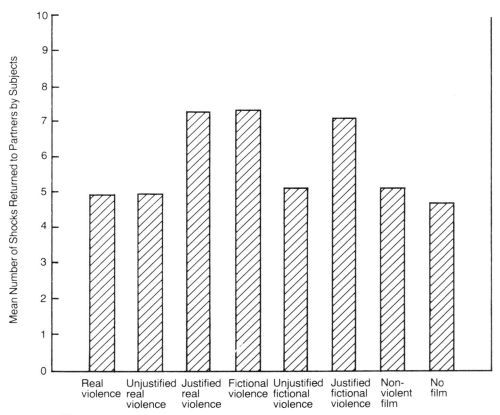

Figure 11.1.
Comparisons of the average number of shocks returned by subjects to partners in
the unjustified and justified real and fictional filmed violence conditions. Adapted
from T. Meyer, 1972, p. 26.

films in which violence was justified showed more aggression toward their partners than those who saw violent actions that were unjustified. You might have also noted that levels of aggression in the control conditions of the real and fictional segments without the soundtracks differed, although such differences were not expected. The author of the study checked and found that these differences were obtained because the subjects seeing the fictional violence perceived the violence as justified despite the lack of a voice track saying that the attack was justified. Subjects who saw the real violence segment without a voice track saying that the attack was unjustified perceived the violence as unjustified. In general, though, the results provided confirmation of the investigator's predictions. These findings suggest that typical film and television presentations in which the hero legitimately annihilates the villain by violent means may actually lead to an increase in aggressive behavior among viewers. The motto of such angry viewers may well be, "Give it to him, he deserves it!" This primitive eye-for-an-eye and tooth-for-a-tooth philosophy, which still governs the behavior of many people, seems unfortunately to add to the problem of aggression in our culture.

Thus, a number of factors, both personal and situational, can serve to instigate and facilitate aggressive effects. In addition to these variables, research has shown that viewers are more apt to behave aggressively if they identify with the victor, as in the case of moviegoers who imagine themselves to be the winners of fights in the films (Turner and Berkowitz, 1972). Observers are also more apt to aggress if they find themselves in the presence of stimuli previously associated with violence—for example, in the presence of guns and knives (Berkowitz and LePage, 1967).

Controlling Media Violence

If we grant the possibility that media violence can have harmful effects on viewers under the appropriate circumstances, what steps can people take to modify and control the showing of aggressive behavior? Bandura (1973, pp. 276–281) suggests a number of possible remedies. One popular but not very effective procedure, according to him, involves appeals by members of the public to government agencies to control the commercial marketing of violence. This procedure is ineffective because the Constitution guarantees free communication and restricts the government's tampering with program content. In addition, Bandura argues that we as a people have a strong tradition of opposing government control over what we watch. Some members of the broadcasting industry cater to our concerns and fears of government regulation and censorship by likening such controls to practices used in military dictatorships. Yet, as Bandura points out, most countries have adopted some regulations without jeopardizing their democratic institutions. He suggests that perhaps eventually the public will gain some control over program content through concerted legal action.

A second step that can and has been taken is to have members of the public protest loudly and strongly to government officials about the amount of violence shown in the media. Officials cannot ignore such protests, but Bandura feels they are relatively ineffective because the congressional committees formed to deal with the protests usually only issue threats to the broadcasting industry to stop their unsavory practices and do not follow through to see that the industry complies. The third procedure is to allow broadcasters to regulate themselves. According to Bandura, this method is unworkable because, no matter how well-intentioned the media people are, content is dictated by profit. A fourth procedure is to create a public violence-monitoring system. It would be funded by private sources and would exercise control by publicized assessment of violence levels in the media. Publication of scientific surveys on this topic could be disseminated in a variety of sources, including TV guides, popular magazines, PTA publications, and newspapers. Bandura feels this approach might be effective because media advertisers are conscious of their public images and would act to change policies detrimental to their companies and stockholders.

In addition to these suggestions, Bandura cites a fifth procedure that might be helpful. It involves rewarding desirable practices by members of the media rather than focusing solely on the curtailment of undesirable practices. Creating shows that are interesting, informative, and non-violent would probably lead to greater progress than simply condemning shows that reek with violence. One successful example is in the area of children's programming. "Sesame Street," which was designed with the help of psychologists, is informative as well as entertaining, and has demonstrated that it can attract large audiences of children. It does not rely on violence, as do many of the morning cartoon shows, and yet it has proved successful.

Bandura also suggests that, on a personal level, parents model nonaggressive behavior for their children and reward nonviolent behavior. In addition, they should try to limit their children's exposure to violence in the media by monitoring the content of programs in advance. Although these efforts may serve to curtail violence to some extent, Bandura does not delude himself that his recommendations would eliminate the problem. Yet, he believes that we must begin:

> Like so many other problems confronting man, there is no single grand design for lowering the level of destructiveness within a society. It requires both individual corrective effort and group action aimed at changing the practices of social systems. Since aggression is not an inevitable or unchangeable aspect of man but a product of aggression-promoting conditions operating within a society, man has the power to reduce his level of aggressiveness. Whether this capability is used wisely or destructively is another matter. (Bandura, 1973, p. 323)

At this juncture, let us consider the ways in which modeling principles have been applied to behavioral problems experienced by individuals.

Modeling as a Therapeutic Technique

Modeling has been used successfully to modify certain problem behaviors. For example, Bandura cites the work of one investigator who
showed that the behavior of domineering and hyperaggressive children
could be changed by presenting models who first demonstrated how aggression in interpersonal disputes leads to painful outcomes and then
how cooperation leads to the solution of their conflicts (Chittenden,
1973, pp. 254–255). In one of the modeled situations, two children were
shown fighting over a toy wagon. It broke, and both children were unhappy. In contrast, the cooperative solution showed the children enjoying themselves as they took turns playing with the wagon. A series of
such modeled demonstrations proved successful in reducing aggression
in the children exposed to them, whereas children in a control group
were unchanged.

Modeling has also been employed successfully in the treatment of language deficiencies in autistic children (Lovaas, 1967, pp. 108–159). Such
children are typically not very responsive to environmental influences;
the therapist must first gain their attention before employing modeling
procedures. He accomplishes this goal by sitting directly in front of them
so that they cannot ignore him. He also rewards them for maintaining
eye contact and physically restrains any effort to move away from him.
Once he has established attentional control, the therapist proceeds to
model sounds, words, and phrases of speech and to administer rewards
for appropriate responding. Under such training procedures, it has been
possible to develop some language skills in autistic children. Studies using modeling have also been utilized to increase communication skills in
asocial psychiatric patients (Gutride, Goldstein, and Hunter, 1973).

Modeling has been used to reduce fears in children. In one particularly interesting study, two investigators showed that modeling
procedures could be used to eliminate avoidance behaviors through
observation of modeled approach responses (Bandura and Menlove,
1968). In more concrete language, the investigators were able to
eliminate a fear of dogs in certain children by having them watch
another person approach, pet, and handle the animals without being
bitten. The study was conducted in the following way. A standardized
test of avoidance behavior was administered to a group of nursery
school children in order to identify those who were fearful of dogs. The
test consisted of a graded series of fourteen tasks in which the children
were required to participate in increasingly intimate interactions with a
dog. Some of these tasks included walking up to a playpen containing a
dog and looking down at her, touching and petting her, opening the en-
closure, walking her, and eventually getting into the playpen with her
and petting her. Following the identification procedure, the dog-phobic
children were assigned randomly to one of three experimental treatment
conditions. In one condition, children observed a single model display
progressively bolder approach responses to a cocker spaniel. In a second
multiple-model condition, other children observed the sequence of

events just described and in addition watched other models of various ages playing with a wide variety of dogs, both small and large. In the control condition, still other children were shown movies of Disneyland and Marineland, but no modeled interactions with dogs. Following the administration of these procedures, all the children were again tested for their fear of dogs via a readministration of the standardized test used initially. They were given the test a third time approximately one month after the posttest in order to determine the stability of the modeling effects. The results showed clearly that the modeling procedures were instrumental in reducing and sustaining a reduction in the children's fears. These findings are shown graphically in Figure 11.2. Similar modeling procedures were used to reduce fear of snakes in adolescents and adults (Bandura, Blanchard, and Ritter, 1969).

Research has shown that high test-anxious college students tend to perform poorly because they spend much of their time paying attention

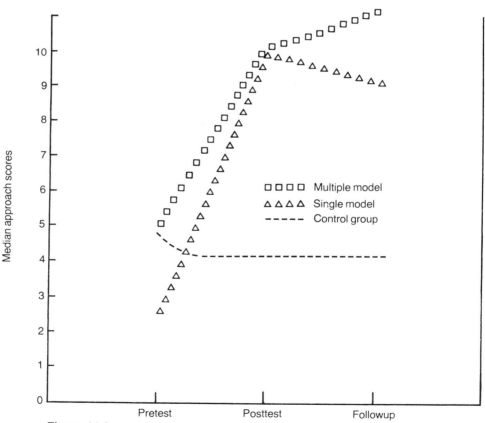

Figure 11.2.
Median approach scores obtained by children under the various conditions of the experiment. Adapted from A. Bandura, and F. L. Menlove, 1968, p. 102.

to irrelevant cues. For example, such students tend to be self-centered and overly concerned with questions about their intellectual competence and the reactions of others to their performances. A recent investigation was conducted to determine whether or not disclosures by models about their own anxieties in evaluation situations and the strategies they had devised to cope with these interfering cues could improve the task performances of the highly anxious students (Sarason, 1975). All study participants filled out a personality questionnaire to determine their characteristic levels of test anxiety. Then groups of subjects who were classified as either high or low test-anxious were exposed to a variety of models. In one condition, they were exposed to an anxious coping model who mentioned that she became anxious during testing situations. She also mentioned that she attempted to cope with her anxiety by (a) reminding herself periodically to stop thinking about herself and to concentrate on the task; (b) thinking about interesting aspects of the task; (c) not allowing herself to get flustered by errors; and (d) forcing herself not to think about the reactions of other people. In a noncoping anxious model condition, the model simply mentioned that she became very anxious during testing, had difficulty in concentrating on the task, and was continually worried about what others would think of her if she failed. In a third condition, a neutral model did not mention testing or grading and talked instead about activities, programs, and issues on the campus.

All subjects then performed a task which involved learning a series of nonsense syllables. As expected, the model who not only mentioned that testing situations made her anxious but provided information on how to cope with it had the greatest positive impact on the high test-anxious students. Apparently, the self-disclosures provided the subjects with modeled information about ways to improve their performances, and they utilized it. Figure 11.3 provides a graphic illustration of these results.

The results of all these studies and countless others demonstrate quite conclusively the impact that modeling can have in changing undesirable behavior. Modeling is thus a viable alternative to traditional psychodynamic approaches that seek to give people insights into their behavior through protracted and costly analysis, but provide little guidance on how they might take specific courses of action to help themselves. Its continued usage as an aid in therapeutic settings seems assured.

THE PROCESS OF PERSONALITY DEVELOPMENT

For Bandura, social learning experiences play a crucial role in the development and modification of each person's behavior. New behaviors are acquired as the individual watches the behavior of his or her caretakers. Imitation of the behaviors of the parents often meets with reward, but sometimes with punishment. Rewarded behavior tends to

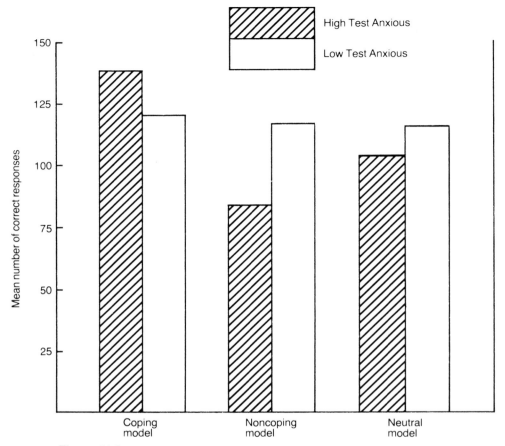

Figure 11.3
Mean number of correct responses on serial learning task for low and high anxious
students under the different modeling conditions. Adapted from I. G. Sarason,
1975, p. 150.

be repeated and, when performed in the presence of other people, is
reinforced positively. As a result, children learn at an early age to match
the behavior of successful models. They also learn to avoid imitating the
behavior of unsuccessful ones. Unfortunately, the acquisition of complex forms of behavior is not always so simple and direct. Children are
often exposed to multiple models who present behaviors that conflict
with one another. One parent might reward them for speaking in the
presence of guests, for example, whereas the other might punish them
for showing the same behavior. Even when both parents are in
agreement, other socializing agents such as teachers may disagree and
communicate that information to the children. Peers might try to indoc-
trinate the children in still other ways. Thus, the reinforcers for given
behaviors are not always applied consistently. Complicating the picture

still more is the fact that behavior is not always imitated accurately or completely and must be shaped by the socializing agents through the application of the successive approximation principles pioneered by Skinner. The establishment of proper table manners in children provides a clear example of the necessity of applying reinforcers in a subtle manner to a variety of behaviors that initially bear little resemblance to the complicated set of behaviors that eventually "emerges."

In addition to imitation and successive approximation, Bandura thinks that the maintenance and extinction of behaviors in the person's repertoire depends on the application of various schedules of reinforcement. In particular, he contends that behavior is maintained through the application of combined schedules. To make his point, he uses the example of attention-seeking in children:

> In the training of children, the use of combined schedules certainly predominates. Let us take the example of attention-seeking behavior. Most young children attempt many times in the day to elicit a nurturant response from their mothers. Sometimes the mother will respond immediately, but more often she is busy. At varying intervals she will reward the child with interest and attention. Many mothers are inclined to ignore mild forms of attention-seeking behavior and to respond only when this behavior is frequent or intense. It can be predicted, on the basis of laboratory studies to which reference was made above, that these mothers should have children who show persistent attention-seeking behavior occurring at the rates and intensities that have previously brought reward. One may suspect that most "troublesome" behavior has been rewarded on a combined schedule by which undesirable responses of high magnitude and frequency are unwittingly reinforced. The behavior is thus persistent, difficult to extinguish, and baffling for the parents. Perhaps the genesis of much aggressive behavior is to be found in the use of schedules which reward *only* responses of high magnitude; these could be attention-seeking, food-seeking, and other so-called "dependency" responses, as well as responses of the kind more usually regarded as "aggressive." (Bandura and Walters, 1963, p. 7)

Thus, reinforcers appear to be administered dispensed in complicated ways by various socializing agents.

Although Bandura places great emphasis on observational and instrumental learning in the development of the individual personality, he does not pay similar attention to the biological determinants of behavior. He does recognize, however, that constitutional factors inevitably influence the nature of the individual's social learning history:

> Social manipulations can have relatively little influence on some biologically determined characteristics, such as the body type or facial features of an individual. Yet within a society that sets high value on the possession of certain physical attributes, the frequency with which social reinforcers are dispensed is partly dependent on the extent to which these cultural ideals are met. In North American society, where prestige and social rewards are bestowed for athletic ability and physique, boys who are small, lack muscular strength or dexterity, or who are obese and possess feminine-like phy-

siques are relatively unsuccessful in obtaining positive reinforcement from peers. Similarly, a female who does not match the standards of beauty within her society evokes far fewer positive responses, especially from males, than one who possesses these socially esteemed characteristics. The slender, petite female has been highly admired in North American culture; she may, however, be the recipient of relatively few positive reinforcers and considerable aversive treatment in cultures lacking in labor-saving devices. (Bandura and Walters, 1963, pp. 26–27)

Not only do constitutional factors exert an indirect influence on development, so do biochemical factors. Despite his recognition of the role of biology in personality development, Bandura deemphasizes it in his theory because he says there is currently little knowledge of the specific ways in which it operates to control behavior. As a consequence, he feels there is more to be gained by studying the role of social learning variables in personality development.

TECHNIQUES OF ASSESSMENT

Bandura does not utilize dream analysis, free association, the method of amplification, or any of the other techniques utilized by practitioners in the psychodynamic tradition. Nor does he seem particularly interested in using personality questionnaires as assessment devices, although his position does not preclude the use of reliable and valid questionnaires such as Rotter's I-E Scale where they are helpful in understanding behavior.

For the most part, Bandura relies on experimental methods to assess personality functioning and behavior. He is concerned with identifying covariations between manipulable, antecedent events and consequent response variables. The modeling research cited in this chapter provides a good illustration of Bandura's assessment orientation. If the problem area is complex and unchartered, however, Bandura thinks it is advantageous to begin by conducting field studies that are essentially correlational in nature (Bandura and Walters, 1963, p. 391).

APPLICATION OF THE THEORY TO THE TREATMENT OF PSYCHOPATHOLOGY

In contrast to the Freudian and neo-Freudian positions, which seek the determinants of deviant behavior in terms of the operation of relatively free internal forces and elaborate and imprecise defensive manuverings, Bandura's social learning position treats internal processes as mediators, and *not* causal agents, between on-going stimulation from the environment and the person's eventual observable responses. These mediators are utilized in the prediction of behavior " . . . only to the extent that they are systematically related to both manipulable stimulus conditions and the observable response variables, a condition that is rarely met in the cases of the constructs employed in psychodynamic theories" (Bandura and Walters, 1963, p. 31).

In addition, whereas the psychodynamic approach assumes that the removal of a behavioral symptom results in the emergence of other symptoms since there is no reduction in underlying energy, the social learning approach advocated by Bandura maintains that the elimination of the undesirable behavior (symptom) does not necessarily result in the appearance of new deviant behaviors. Thus, the focus in Bandura's position is on the behavior itself and not on the underlying dynamics of the problem. To eliminate the undesirable behavior, Bandura has used a variety of techniques based on learning principles. These include modeling procedures, as well as counterconditioning and behavioral training procedures that will be discussed more fully in Chapter 16.

CRITICAL COMMENTS

We now turn to an evaluation of the scientific worth of Bandura's theory in terms of how well it meets our six criteria.

Comprehensiveness. In comparison to Freudian theory, for example, Bandura's position is quite limited in terms of the range and diversity of phenomena it covers. It does, however, provide a relatively thorough analysis of the social learning variables responsible for the acquisition, maintenance, and modification of disordered behavior. These learning principles have been used to help increase our understanding of such disorders as alcoholism, academic anxieties, frigidity, impotence, exhibitionism, insomnia, nightmares, obsessive-compulsive problems, and phobias. In addition, much of Bandura's work and the work of his associates has focused on the illumination of the variables responsible for the acquisition of aggressive behavior and its modification.

Social learning research has increased our knowledge of the ways in which childhood training practices influence personality development, how language is acquired and honed, and how self-reinforcement can be utilized in the acquisition, maintenance, and modification of behavior. This last area seems especially promising and exciting to investigators, as evidenced by the amount of research conducted on such phenomena in recent years.

Precision and Testability. Bandura's theory has some difficulty in meeting the precision criterion. Although there are intensive efforts to define and measure concepts precisely, many of the cognitive variables utilized in the theory are complex and difficult to define. Skinner, for example, maintains that the position invents needless cognitive constructs which are not amenable to study and manipulation. It is also sometimes not at all clear what exactly is going on in the person's "mind" when he is given certain instructions by a model. Is he actively rehearsing the instructions? If so, how many times does he rehearse them? Sometimes the instructions are so complex that one cannot be certain the subject even understands them, let alone acts in terms of them.

For example, in the study we reviewed concerned with the effects of self-discipline by models on the performances of highly anxious students, we know that the model disclosed information about her own anxieties and also about the strategies she used to cope with this problem. We also know that, after receiving this information, the performances of the high test-anxious people improved. But was it because of the instructions? It seems reasonable to assume that the changes were produced by the information, but we do not know that this was the case. Maybe the experimenter (the model) gave the subjects other, perhaps nonverbal, cues which told them that the experimenter expected a change in their behavior. Even if we assume that the subjects did *covertly rehearse* the coping strategies, did they rehearse all the strategies mentioned by the model or just some of them? As you can see, there is some question about the rigor and preciseness of the experimental manipulations in these studies and in others.

Simplicity. Social learning theory is based on relatively few assumptions, but those it does make are broadly stated and designed to encourage investigation of the ways in which biological, social, and cultural phenomena affect behavior and thought. The theory consists not only of the concepts traditionally associated with learning positions (reinforcement, discrimination, generalization, extinction) but of a variety of new and different cognitive concepts. Although Skinner believes Bandura's position invents needless constructs to account for behavior, it is our judgment that these constructs are necessary for the development of an adequate theory of personality and that perhaps those now employed by Bandura are too global to allow for the most accurate prediction of behavior. A more adequate version of social learning theory in the future may involve the utilization of new and specific concepts.

Empirical Validity. The evidence in support of Bandura's position is quite impressive. There have been countless empirical tests of the theory, and the results to date have been encouraging. For example, studies of observational learning have yielded evidence showing the importance of modeling in helping to mold, maintain, and vary behavior. Although much of this research has focused on the use of modeling to eliminate fears, anxieties, and disordered behaviors, modeling principles have also been applied to the study of nonneurotic behaviors as well. In addition to modeling, a variety of other behavioral therapy techniques derived from social learning theory have been successfully utilized in the treatment of an assortment of problems. In general, then, Bandura's position has a high degree of empirical validity.

Heuristic Value. Although Bandura's position has had considerable impact on the work of psychologists, especially in the clinical and social psychology areas, it has not had much influence on the work of professionals in other disciplines. Certainly it has not had the interdisciplinary impact of Freud's theory. Still, its promise remains strong and, in the future, we might see an increase in its heuristic value for professionals in other disciplines.

Applied Value. The applied value of social learning theory is high in the area of psychopathology. As mentioned earlier, social learning principles have been successfully employed in the treatment of a variety of behavioral problems. Two basic problems, however, prevent the theory from having outstanding applied value in this area. One concerns the stability of the behavioral changes following treatment. Most studies have been concerned only with the temporary effects of treatment on behavior. Bandura is acutely aware of this problem, and other investigators have begun to conduct research in an attempt to overcome it.

Another problem is the lack of solid evidence about the generalizability of treatment effects from the laboratory to natural settings. To what extent do the findings in the laboratory hold up in less artificial environments? This question is of the utmost importance in assessing the effectiveness of the various behavioral therapies that are part of the social learning position. If we reduce a person's aggressiveness through the use of modeling procedures in a clinical setting, will he also behave less aggressively in his relationships with the people he meets in his daily routine? Once again, there are smatterings of research addressed to this problem, and it seems clear that greater attention will be paid to it by investigators in the future.

Bandura's research in the area of aggression has increased our understanding of the origins of such behavior and provided insights into the ways it can be modified and controlled. Unfortunately, the implications of these findings have not been utilized fully by government policymakers, despite long and persistent attempts by Bandura and his associates to transmit such information and to effect changes. In general, it seems reasonable to conclude that Bandura's theory has not reached its potential in helping to generate new solutions to problems, but that its applied value should become increasingly apparent in the future.

DISCUSSION QUESTIONS

1. Is it possible for a person to survive in his or her environment by relying solely on the trial-and-error method of learning? Cite reasons for your position.

2. Do you agree with the findings of the study cited in the chapter which suggested that girls will more readily imitate female models, whereas boys will mimic male authority figures? Have there been

any changes in the imitative behavior of boys and girls since the advent of the women's movement? Cite reasons for your answer.

3. Why is the distinction between acquisition and performance such an important one in the argument about the effects of television violence on children's behavior? Do you agree with Bandura on this point?

4. What are some of the major ways in which you exercise control over your study behavior?

5. If positive reinforcers are such a potent determiner of behavior, why don't we praise and reinforce each other more often?

6. Do you believe that violence in the media has had an adverse effect on your behavior and that of your friends and relatives? Why or why not?

7. What are some of the primary personal and situational determinants of aggressive behavior?

8. What suggestions do you have for decreasing aggressive behavior in our culture, assuming you believe it should be brought under control?

9. Design an experiment that would utilize modeling procedures to rid a boy of his fear of bugs.

10. How anxious do you and your friends become before taking an examination? Does this anxiety interfere with your performance and theirs? If your answer is in the affirmative in regard to their behavior or yours, how would you rearrange environmental conditions to minimize it?

NOTES

A. Bandura, "Influence of Models' Reinforcement Contingencies on the Acquisition of Imitative Responses," *Journal of Personality and Social Psychology,* 1965, **1,** 589–595.

A. Bandura, *Principles of Behavior Modification* (New York: Holt, Rinehart and Winston, 1969).

A. Bandura, *Social Learning Theory* (Morristown, N.J.: General Learning Press, 1971).

A. Bandura, *Aggression: A Social Learning Analysis* (Englewood Cliffs, N.J.: Prentice-Hall, 1973).

A. Bandura, B. Blanchard, and B. Ritter, "Relative Efficiency of Desensitization and Modeling Approaches for Inducing Behavioral, Affective, and Attitudinal Changes," *Journal of Personality and Social Psychology,* 1969, **13,** 173–199.

A. Bandura and C. J. Kupers, "The Transmission of Patterns of Self-Reinforcement through Modeling," *Journal of Abnormal and Social Psychology,* 1964, **69,** 1–9.

A. Bandura and F. L. Menlove, "Factors Determining Vicarious Extinction of Avoidance Behavior through Symbolic Modeling," *Journal of Personality and Social Psychology*, 1968, **8**, 99–108.

A. Bandura and W. Mischel, "Modification of Self-Imposed Delay of Reward through Exposure to Live and Symbolic Models," *Journal of Personality and Social Psychology*, 1965, **2**, 698–705.

A. Bandura, D. Ross, and S. A. Ross, "Vicarious Reinforcement and Imitative Learning," *Journal of Abnormal and Social Psychology*, 1963, **67**, 601–607.

A. Bandura, D. Ross, and S. A. Ross, "Imitation of Film-Mediated Aggressive Models," *Journal of Abnormal and Social Psychology*, 1963, **66**, 3–11.

A. Bandura and R. H. Walters, *Social Learning and Personality Development* (New York: Holt, Rinehart and Winston, 1963).

S. M. Berger, "Conditioning through Vicarious Instigation," *Psychological Review*, 1962, **69**, 450–466.

L. Berkowitz, *Aggression: A Social Psychological Analysis* (New York: McGraw-Hill, 1962).

L. Berkowitz and A. LePage, "Weapons as Aggression-Eliciting Stimuli," *Journal of Personality and Social Psychology*, 1967, **7**, 202–207.

G. E. Chittenden, "An Experimental Study in Measuring and Modifying Assertive Behavior in Young Children," *Monographs of the Society for Research in Child Development*, 1973, **7**, 1 (Serial No. 31).

J. Grusec and W. Mischel, "Model's Characteristics as Determinants of Social Learning," *Journal of Personality and Social Psychology*, 1966, **4**, 211–215.

M. E. Gutride, A. P. Goldstein, and G. F. Hunter, "The Use of Modeling to Increase Social Interaction among Asocial Psychiatric Patients," *Journal of Consulting and Clinical Psychology*, 1973, **40**, 408–415.

O. I. Lovaas, "A Behavior Therapy Approach to the Treatment of Childhood Schizophrenia," in J. P. Hill, ed., *Minnesota Symposia on Child Psychology*, Vol. 1 (Minneapolis: University of Minnesota Press, 1967).

M. J. McMains and R. M. Liebert, "The Influence of Discrepancies Between Successively Modeled Self-Reward Criteria on the Adoption of a Self-Imposed Standard," *Journal of Personality and Social Psychology*, 1968, **8**, 166–171.

T. P. Meyer, "Effects of Viewing Justified and Unjustified Real Film Violence on Aggressive Behavior," *Journal of Personality and Social Psychology*, 1972, **23**, 21–29.

W. Mischel, *Personality Assessment* (New York: Wiley, 1968).

M. E. Rosenbaum and I. F. Tucker, "Competence of the Model and the Learning of Imitation and Nonimitation," *Journal of Experimental Psychology*, 1962, **63**, 183–190.

M. A. Rosenkrans, "Imitation in Children as a Function of Perceived Similarity to a Social Model and Vicarious Reinforcement," *Journal of Personality and Social Psychology*, 1967, **7**, 307–315.

I. G. Sarason, "Test Anxiety and the Self-Disclosing Coping Model," *Journal of Consulting and Clinical Psychology*, 1975, **43**, 148–153.

B. R. Strickland, "Delay of Gratification as a Function of Race of the Experimenter," *Journal of Personality and Social Psychology*, 1972, **22**, 108–112.

C. Turner and L. Berkowitz, "Identification with Film Aggression (Covert Role Taking) and Reactions to Film Violence," *Journal of Personality and Social Psychology*, 1972, **21**, 256–264.

R. H. Walters, M. Leat, and L. Mezei, "Response Inhibition and Disinhibition through Empathetic Learning," *Canadian Journal of Psychology*, 1963, **17**, 225–243.

SUGGESTED READINGS

Bandura, A., and R. H. Walters. *Social Learning and Personality Development*. New York: Holt, Rinehart and Winston, 1963.

Bandura, A. *Principles of Behavior Modification*. New York: Holt, Rinehart and Winston, 1969.

Bandura, A. *Aggression: A Social Learning Analysis*. Englewood Cliffs, N.J.: Prentice-Hall, 1973.

Bandura, A. *Social Learning Theory*. Englewood Cliffs, N.J.: Prentice-Hall, 1977.

GLOSSARY

Anticipated Outcome. Person's expectancy that the performance of a given behavior will lead to the attainment of a given reinforcer.

Covert Rehearsal. Private repetition of information that may result in changes in behavior.

Disinhibitory Variable. Condition that serves to facilitate the occurrence of a particular behavior.

External Reinforcement. Reinforcing environmental stimuli that control the occurrence of behavior. External reinforcement can vary in form; money is a reinforcer, but so is praise, approval from others, a pat on the back, and a smile.

Inhibitory Variable. Condition that restrains the behavior of a person.

Imaginal Representation. Image a person has which is similar to the object in the environment. For example, the person can "picture" or imagine his father, and his father is a real object.

Multiple Modeling Effects. Impact on a person's behavior as a result of being exposed to a variety of models.

Observational Learning. Type of learning in which new responses can be made by the person as a result of watching the performance of others; also called imitative learning.

Verbal Representation. Word that signifies an object in the environment. For example, the word "dog" is a verbal representation of a four-legged creature that barks and exists in the environment.

Vicarious Reinforcement. Changes in a person's behavior due to the witnessing of a model being reinforced for the same behavior.

PART 6

HUMANISTIC — EXISTENTIAL PERSPECTIVES

The three forces in contemporary psyc. :
- psychoanalysis
- behaviorism
- humanism /existentialism

T he materials in this section of the text are part of the Third Force movement in contemporary psychology (the other movements are psychoanalysis and behaviorism). The term was coined by Maslow to describe a position that focuses on the creative potentialities inherent in human beings and that seeks ways to help them realize their highest and most important goals. The theories embodied by the movement tend to assume that human beings are basically good and worthy of respect. Virtually all of them also postulate the existence of an innate "growth" mechanism within individuals that will move them toward the realization of their potentialities, if environmental conditions are "right." This growth process has been variously labeled the drive toward self-actualization, self-realization, or selfhood by its numerous proponents.

The roots of the humanistic movement can be found in the writings of Jung, Adler, Fromm, Allport, Maslow, Rogers, May, and others. In each of these perspectives, we find an emphasis on the uniqueness of individuals and a belief that they should be free to make their own choices about the directions they want to take in their own lives. They should be allowed the opportunity to organize and control their own behavior; they should not be controlled by society. In most of these positions, society is generally seen as the "bad guy," as the enforcer of rules and regulations that stifle personal growth. According to the humanists, a benevolent, helpful attitude toward people allow them to grow and prosper. Instead, most societies attempt to coerce individuals into behaving "appropriately," that is, "normally." The result is rather conventional, dull people who usually obey, without much question, the moral prescriptions of the majority. In other words, the result is the average, law-abiding man or woman.

The humanistic psychologists argue instead for allowing individuals to develop to their fullest potential. They see people as naturally striving to be creative and happy rather than mediocre and conventional. Of course, the assumption that what is conventional is very often mediocre is open to question, especially in a society which encourages people to try to attain excellence in their pursuits. There is also another assumption underlying many of the humanist positions—namely, that it is possible to specify a universal set of values which will provide people with a moral anchor so that they will be able to decide what is right or wrong and good or bad. Such a set of values, rooted in the person's biology, would allow people to make moral decisions by looking inside themselves, instead of relying on the judgments of society. What are these universal values? Who decides which ones are to be included in this system of natural ethics? What is the scientific evidence for the existence of an innate mechanism that would allow people to make valid moral judgments?

There has never been clear-cut agreement among philosophers or psychologists on a universal set of values, although numerous attempts to devise such a list have been made. The question of who will decide which are universally valid has never been resolved. Is it the philosophers? the psychologists? the politicians? the artists? the theologians? As we learned in Chapter 9, Skinner thinks that behavioral psychologists can best make this decision, but surely not everyone will agree with him. Finally, as we will see, there is little scientific evidence for the existence of an innate mechanism that would allow us to make morally correct decisions.

Yet, instead of rejecting this aspect of the humanistic psychologists' position, we ought to give it a fair hearing. First, the fact that there is no agreement among scholars and others about the existence of a universal set of values does not mean that such a value system can never be devised. Also, although there is currently no evidence for the existence of an internal biologically based mechanism that would guide moral behavior, it does not mean that such evidence will never be forthcoming. Even if these questions can never be answered, this does not mean there is nothing of merit in the humanistic position. By raising significant questions and challenging the tenets of orthodox psychology, humanistic psychologists have forced psychologists to reconsider the directions and value of their work. The overall impact of humanists has been most beneficial, although some of the more rigorous experimental psychologists would certainly disagree with this judgment. At this point, let us review the two major challenges hurled by the humanists at orthodox psychology and ask you to make your own judgment.

The first challenge involves the claim that contemporary psychologies like psychoanalysis and behaviorism provide only a partial and limited view of human functioning, a view that needs drastic revision. Allport put the matter succinctly and picturesquely:

> It is especially in relation to the formation and development of human *personality* that we need to open doors. For it is precisely here that our ignorance and uncertainty are greatest. Our methods, however well suited to

the study of sensory processes, animal research, and pathology, are not fully adequate; and interpretations arising from the exclusive use of these methods are stultifying. Some theories . . . are based largely upon the behavior of sick and anxious people or upon the antics of captive and desperate rats. Fewer theories have derived from the study of healthy beings, those who strive not so much to preserve life as to make it worth living. Thus we find today many studies of criminals, few of law-abiders; many of fear, few of courage, more on hostility than on affiliation; much on the blindness in man, little on his vision; much on his past, little on his outreaching into the future. (Allport, 1955, p. 18)

In building his theory of self-actualization, Maslow also pointed out the limitations in the Freudian conception. Freud devoted most of his attention to understanding the unconscious forces that determine behavior and neglected the rational, conscious forces. The Freudian world is one in which neurotic people are continually stuggling to adjust to the environment and to gain a feeling of security. Maslow, in contrast, posited a need hierarchy in human beings consisting of basic and growth urges. The need for security is one of the lower basic needs; if gratified, it frees the individual to pursue "higher" goals. Most of Maslow's attention was directed to the establishment of a psychology of personal growth and creative striving, as we will see in Chapter 12. Thus, Maslow set out to study the behavior of psychologically healthy people in order to learn more about the growth process. The materials in Chapter 12 outline his efforts and provide a review of the major characteristics of self-actualizing individuals.

In general terms, Maslow and other humanistic psychologists advocate a drastic revision of contemporary psychology in which primary attention would be paid to topics that have been relatively ignored by existing theories. These topics would include, among others, love, affiliation, creativity, spontaneity, joy, courage, humor, independence, and personal growth. Focusing on them should teach us about the "good" side of human nature and serve as a corrective to the more limited and pessimistic picture projected by the Freudians and the behaviorists.

The second challenge voiced by the humanists centers on the prevailing view in the discipline that psychology is a natural science and must therefore employ methods of study consistent with those used in physics, chemistry, physiology, and biology. The humanists claim this attitude has led to a psychology that does not do justice to the full range of human esperience and behavior. To understand the arguments of the humanists more fully, let us look at the history of psychology and the reasons for its initial alliance with the natural sciences.

As you undoubtedly know, psychology as a science began in 1879, when Wundt established his experimental laboratory in Leipzig, Germany. Psychologists had originally been linked with speculative philosophers, but dissatisfaction with this relationship and the desire to establish an independent discipline led them toward the natural sciences and toward the use of the scientific method in the study of phenomena. The benefits of this move were twofold: First, psychologists would have a ready-made approach to the study of behavior acceptable to members of the scientific community; second, psychology would gain status and respectability. So appealing was this prospect that psychologists adopted in rather uncritical fashion the scientific method used by the natural sciences.

The natural science approach to the study of problems focuses on the accumulation of facts through the employment of objective and reliable measurement procedures. It avoids speculation and deduction in the attempt to understand phenomena and relies instead on induction. This tough-minded empiricism can be seen most clearly in the work of Watson and Skinner. Because of their concern with objective and precise measurement, advocates of this approach have focused on only those problems that can meet their criteria. But many important human problems cannot, so that such phenomena as jealousy, hatred of a parent, and a man's love for a woman have been excluded from consideration.

The natural science approach also insists that investigators be objective in their study of problems. There is a tendency to see the investigator as a potential source of bias whose influence on the inquiry process must be neutralized and controlled. There is also the implication that science is a value-free enterprise and that the investigator should study phenomena dispassionately as well as objectively. It is this depersonalized view of science that has been rejected by the humanistic psychologists. Rogers, for example, argues that:

> Science exists only in people. Each scientific project has its creative inception, its process, and its tentative conclusion, in a person or persons. Knowledge—even scientific knowledge—is that which is subjectively acceptable. Scientific knowledge can be communicated only to those who are subjectively ready to receive its communication. The utilization of science also occurs only through people who are in pursuit of values which have meaning for them. (Rogers, 1965, p. 164)

Rogers would ask psychologists to develop a science and a psychology that has its primary focus within the person. Chapter 13 reviews Rogers' reasons for the establishment of such a science and his theory of personality. It presents the concepts and principles of a position based on personal growth and on respect for the worth of the individual and his or her innate potential.

Rollo May (Chapter 14) has an orientation similar to that of Rogers. For example, he points out that we should consider science a human endeavor and begin our inquiry by asking "What is it in human nature that leads to the emergence of the scientific attitude?" We should not, in other words, begin with an established methodology and try to fit human problems into that mold. Instead, we should start with our own experiences and formulations of problems and use procedures that will allow us to obtain answers. This orientation would mean emphasizing the problem rather than the use of elegant measurement techniques and equipment for the sake of being "scientific." It would make psychology, in other words, a "human" rather than a "natural" science.

The humanists do not think the natural science approach meaningless; their point is that psychology should adopt an expanded set of methods to help us understand reality better. We turn now to a treatment of theories in the humanistic-existential tradition that reflect these hopes for change.

NOTES

G. W. Allport, *Becoming* (New Haven, Conn.: Yale University Press, 1955).

C. R. Rogers, "Persons of Science?" in F. T. Severin, ed., *Humanistic Viewpoints in Psychology* (New York: McGraw-Hill, 1965).

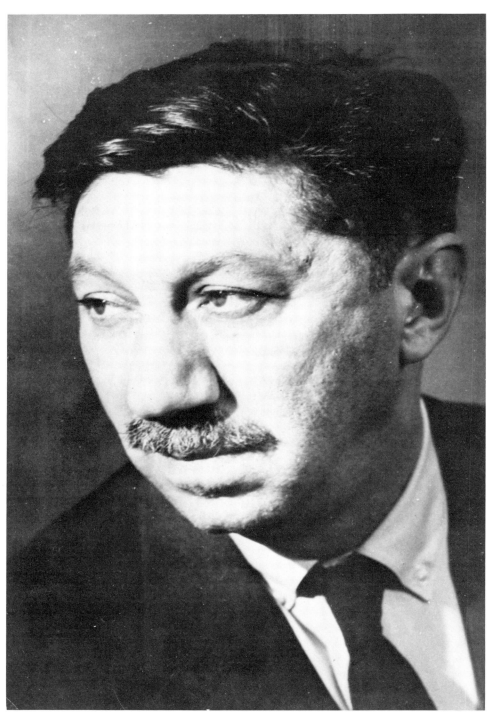

Abraham Maslow (Courtesy of Brandeis University)

CHAPTER 12

Maslow's Self-Actualization Position

BIOGRAPHICAL SKETCH

Abraham Maslow was born in Brooklyn, New York, in 1908. His parents were Russian Jews who had emigrated to the United States, and Maslow was the eldest of seven children. At eighteen, he entered City College of New York to study law. Despite his high IQ, he began to do poorly in some of his courses. He had little interest in becoming a lawyer and had only taken the courses to satisfy his father's wishes.One day during the second semester of his first year, he quit school. Eventually, he matriculated at the University of Wisconsin, where he was first exposed to the scientific psychology of the Wundt-Titchener structuralism school. Advocates of the structuralist position were concerned with demonstrating that "mental life" could be studied in the same way as phenomena in chemistry—that is, by analyzing the various "elements" of sensation and perception and the ways in which they combined to affect behavior. Maslow found this approach boring, but his interest was piqued by the behavioristic approach being promulgated by John B. Watson. It is difficult to imagine Maslow being stimulated by the crude stimulus-response (S-R) treatment of human behavior that Watson was offering and, in fact, later in his career he rejected the position. While he was a student, however, Watson's approach did interest him because it seemed to imply that people could be understood and improved scientifically, a belief directly in line with Maslow's interest in helping people realize their potential.

During his Wisconsin days, Maslow worked with Harry Harlow, who later became famous for his work on curiosity and affectional motives in monkeys. Maslow was interested in the fact that monkeys would work to solve problems for long periods of time, even when they were not hungry. He observed similar behavior in pigs. The stronger and healthier pigs would explore their surroundings much more than the weaker ones. Maslow was also aware of an early experiment which showed that if chickens are allowed to choose their own diets, some of them will select a healthy diet and others will not. These results suggested to Maslow that there is a fundamental drive toward health in animals. Eventually, he came to believe that such a drive toward knowledge, power, and insight also existed in humans. Thus, his initial work in animal biology provided the groundwork for the theory of self-actualization.

Maslow received his doctorate from Wisconsin in 1934 and then worked for eighteen months at Columbia University with the eminent learning theorist E. L. Thorndike. As Thorndike's assistant, Maslow was required to do research to discover the percentage of human behavior determined by genes and the percentage controlled by culture. Maslow found the project "rather silly," since he believed that "everything was determined by both." He made his views known to Thorndike, and much to his surprise, Thorndike gave him permission to pursue his own research on dominance and sexuality in monkeys and humans. Out of this work emerged Maslow's ideas about the existence of a hierarchy of needs in human beings. His classic paper was published in *Psychological Review* in 1943, after he had left Columbia and begun teaching at Brooklyn College. During Maslow's fourteen years at Brooklyn College, he had an opportunity to meet and be exposed to the ideas of such prominent psychologists, psychoanalysts, and cultural anthropologists as Max Wertheimer, Karen Horney, Alfred Adler, Erich Fromm, and Ruth Benedict. The exposure had a considerable influence on his thinking, and it was at this point that he rejected the oversimplified S-R view of human behavior and embraced instead a more holistic and dynamic view of personality functioning.

In 1951, Maslow moved to Brandeis University, where he served as department chairman for many years. While at Brandeis, he produced two of his most creative works, *Motivation and Personality* and *Toward a Psychology of Being*. In 1967, he was elected president of the American Psychological Association. The same year, he accepted a fellowship at the Laughlin Foundation in Menlo Park, California, to devote all his time to writing. Unfortunately. he died of a heart attack one year later at the age of sixty-two (Wilson, 1972, pp. 129–202).

HUMANISTIC BIOLOGY AND SELF-ACTUALIZATION

Maslow laid the groundwork for his theory of self-actualization by making the assumption that each of us has an intrinsic nature which is good or, at the very least, neutral (Maslow, 1962, p. 3). (The experimental evidence offered in support of this contention is not solid, however, as we shall learn in Chapter 13 when we discuss Rogers' "organismic wisdom" hypothesis.) Maslow proceeded to argue that, since this inner nature is good or neutral, it is best to encourage its development. Furthermore, he maintained that healthy development is likely only in a good society. Such a society would be one that ". . . offers all [the] necessary raw materials and then gets out of the way and stands aside to let the . . . organism itself utter its wishes and demands and make its choices" (Maslow, 1970, p. 277). If the environment is restrictive and minimizes personal choice, the individual is likely to develop in neurotic ways, since this inner nature is weak and subject to control by environmental forces. Maslow believed that the tendency, although weak, remains and continuously presses toward actualization (Maslow, 1962, pp. 3–4).

The objective of Maslow's theorizing about human nature was to establish a ". . . scientific ethics, a natural value system, a court of ultimate appeal for the determination of good and bad, of right and wrong" (Maslow, 1962, p. 4). Such an ethic would allow investigators of human personality to overcome the relativism inherent in traditional appeals to moral authority. It would provide a set of ideals that would serve as guides for human conduct. If our inner natures, for example, told us that aggression against others is wrong, then no amount of preaching or exhortation by authorities that it is justified under certain circumstances would dissuade us from our inner conviction. Presumably, we would be able to cast out this evil in ourselves. Unfortunately, since the evidence for a natural ethic is unconvincing, we are left only with the work of a moral authority—Maslow—that such a set of values indeed exists.

BASIC CONCEPTS AND PRINCIPLES

Human Motivation and the Actualization Process

According to Maslow, human beings have two basic sets of needs that are rooted in their biology. These are the basic or *deficiency* needs and the meta or *growth* needs. The basic needs are more urgent than the growth needs and are arranged in a hierarchical order. Maslow acknowledged that there may be exceptions to this hierarchical arrangement. For example, he maintained that there are creative people whose drive to create is more important than any other need. There are also people whose values and ideals are so strong that they will die rather than renounce them. The meta needs, in contrast, are not arranged hierarchically. In general, they are equally powerful and can be easily substituted one for another (Chiang and Maslow, 1969, p. 46). When any of these needs are not fulfilled, the person becomes sick. Just as we need adequate amounts of vitamin C to remain healthy, so we need love from others in sufficient quantities to function properly (Maslow, 1962, p. 21). In order to move toward self-actualization, we must have sufficiently gratified our basic needs so that we are free to pursue fulfillment of the higher, transcending meta needs (Maslow, 1962, p. 23).

The Basic Needs

From most to least powerful, the basic needs include the physiological drives, safety needs, belongingness and love needs, and esteem needs. The preconditions necessary for the satisfaction of these needs include the ". . . freedom to speak, freedom to do what one wishes so long as no harm is done to others, freedom to express oneself, freedom to investigate and seek for information, freedom to defend oneself, justice, fairness, honesty, orderliness in the group" (Maslow, 1970, p. 47). Without these freedoms, basic satisfaction of the needs is virtually impossible.

The physiological needs include, among others, hunger, thirst, and sex. A person deprived of food for long periods of time, for example, would begin to focus more and more of his attention on that deficiency. He would start to think and dream about food in an obsessive way. He would become less and less concerned with other activities such as a desire to buy a car, to fix the roof on his house, and to take his sons on camping and fishing trips. He would also become less interested in what other people might think of him and with trying to help others. In short, the person would be less concerned with safety needs, love and belongingness, esteem needs, and movement toward self-actualization. One of the implications of Maslow's scheme is thus that not many poor people are involved in the quest for self-actualization. They use all their energies in finding enough work to feed themselves and their families.

Once the person's physiological needs are relatively well satisfied, however, a set of safety needs is presumed to emerge. This set includes needs for security, protection, structure, law, order, limits, and freedom from fear, anxiety, and chaos (Maslow, 1970, p. 39). In Maslow's view, the need for security manifests itself in infants and children when there are disturbances in their environments. For example, they may be threatened by loud noises, flashing lights, rough handling, and inadequate support (Maslow, 1970, p. 39). Their needs for safety may also be reflected in their preference for an environment where reinforcers are dispensed in a systematic and consistent manner. Erratic behavior on the part of parents can be especially debilitating. Children also need limits on their behavior, according to Maslow. Without them, they function poorly. Maslow maintained that the typical child will often react with panic in unfamiliar and unmanageable situations. For example, a father may be surprised to find his young son crying and clinging to the handrail of a stairway that leads to his classroom a few minutes after he had received repeated assurances from the boy that he knew how to get there.

Like children, adults also have definite needs for safety, but they are more subtle and difficult to detect. The stable society is one that frees adults from worry about adequate food supplies and housing, about being assaulted on the streets or in their homes, about military coups or civilian takeovers of the government, and the like. In a more moderate way, people act to secure tenure in their jobs, and to receive old age pensions and medical coverage in case of illness or accidents.

The needs for belongingness and love tend to emerge once the physiological and safety needs have been met. Like Fromm in his discussion of the need for rootedness, Maslow argued that all of us need to feel wanted and accepted by others. Some of us find gratification of these needs through our friends, others through family life, and still others through membership in groups and organizations. Without such ties, we would feel rootless and lonely. Of course, loneliness need not always have harmful implications for personal development; it can provide the basis for creativity and self-insight in some people. Often, however, loneliness is an unwanted and painful experience. Maslow believed that the current emphasis on sensitivity and encounter groups in our culture is evidence of our strong need for contact and affection. He felt that increased mobility, the breakdown of the traditional family, and depersonalization resulting from increased urbanization lend themselves to greater personal loneliness and alienation (Maslow, 1970, p. 44).

The need for love Maslow listed with the basic needs is different from Fromm's concept of mature love, as discussed in Chapter 5. Mature love is concern for the welfare of others. Maslow's conceptualization of love as a deficiency need, on the other hand, is a selfish concern with seeking love from others. Maslow termed it *D-love*, or deficiency love. Once this need is relatively gratified, however, we become capable of loving others in the sense that Fromm proposed. Maslow called this type of love *B-love* or Being-love to distinguish it from the lower need to be loved. B-love or mature love becomes possible in Maslow's system only when the basic needs have been sufficiently gratified and the person is moving toward self-actualization.

Esteem needs are the last of the basic urges to emerge. Maslow divided them into two sets: esteem based on respect for our own competence, independence, and accomplishments, and esteem based on evaluation from others. Esteem in this latter sense is best seen in our striving for recognition from others, in attempts to secure status, fame, dominance, importance, and appreciation (Maslow, 1970, p. 45). Maslow maintained that individuals become sick when these needs are thwarted. He also believed that we should base our self-esteem on actual competence and adequacy at the task rather than on praise or criticism from others. Surely there is little question that acceptance of undeserved praise from others may eventually have harmful consequences for our personal development. The young woman who has been continually praised by her high school teachers and her parents for academic prowess that she does not really possess and who is also encouraged to believe she will excel on the college level may have a traumatic experience during her first year at the university. Conversely, undeserved criticism may hinder functioning. A person may be creative and write marvelous poems but never share them with others because of excessive reliance on the opinion of various family members who continually derogate his efforts. Eventually he might even give up poetry completely.

In these extreme cases, it is not difficult to understand why these people should rely on themselves and not others in making their judgments. But other decisions we must make may not be as readily resolved. There may be numerous instances where we do not have the competence to make correct judgments and should rely on the advice of others. For example, a child on a picnic with his family might do well to heed the advice of his parents to avoid swimming in certain areas. In addition, self-diagnosis and treatment for illness has often had serious consequences for people. Listening to the advice of a competent doctor may be the wiser course of action.

The general conclusion to be drawn from these examples is that Maslow's suggestion that we rely on ourselves and not on others in making decisions is questionable. We do not exist in a social vacuum and we do not always know what actions are in our best interest. We simply cannot always rely on that ". . . which comes naturally and easily out of one's own true inner nature, one's constitution, one's biological fate or destiny," as Maslow (1970, p. 46) advocates. There is simply little evidence to support his contention, although on philosophical grounds it is difficult to disagree with a position that places such a high value on individualism. The most unfortunate outcome of such a biologically based individualism is that it sometimes deteriorates into a kind of subjectivism which assumes that each person's comprehension of reality is equally competent to the comprehension possessed by others.

The Meta Needs

Once the basic needs in Maslow's hierarchy have been sufficiently gratified, the needs for self-actualization and cognitive understanding become salient. The person's curiosity about himself and the workings of the environment are aroused. There is a desire to know and understand phenomena that go beyond events associated with the gratification of basic needs. There is the possibility of moving toward the realization of one's own unique potentialities. But movement in this positive direction is not automatic. Maslow believed that we often fear ". . . our best side, . . . our talents, . . . our finest impulses, . . . our creativeness" (Maslow, 1962, p. 58). Discovery of our abilities brings happiness, but it also brings fear of our responsibilities and duties. Sometimes it also brings a fear of the unknown.

Maslow pointed out that many women fear the best in themselves. They do not utilize their intellectual abilities to the fullest because they fear social rejection. Achievement is considered "unfeminine" and hence is avoided. In a recent study, researchers tested this contention by hypothesizing that sex-role training in our culture leads both men and women to value positively achievement by men, but to value negatively similar accomplishments by women (Monahan, Kuhn, and Shaver, 1974). They asked both male and female students to make up stories in response to the statement: "At the end of first term finals, Ann/John finds herself/himself at the top of her/his medical school class." They were also asked to describe Ann and John, to tell about the events leading up to their situation, and to guess what the future would be like for them. Seventy-nine percent of the men and 70 percent of the women "projected" stories that showed little fear of success in regard to the achievement of John, but 68 percent of the men and 51 percent of the women reported negative consequences for Ann because of her accomplishment. The following two excerpts illustrate the point:

> Soon Ann became one of the leading doctors in the world. When she was in France, she met an American man. They both fell in love. Soon they were married. But after they had their first child, Ann turned all her attention to her work. So they got divorced. Ann always was involved in her work. The only people she talked to were fellow doctors and the nurses. Soon she got very ill and died. No one even went to her funeral because she was very mean.

> Ann looks like a telephone pole and has purple eyes. Ann is a person who is a mental case which likes to cut up people. . . . We worry about the unfortunate people who have to have her as their doctor. (Monahan, Kuhn, and Shaver, 1974, pp. 62–63)

These results support Maslow's arguments and suggest that many women will have difficulty moving toward actualization because environmental forces (socialization practices) restrict their options. It is also readily apparent that men may experience similar difficulties as a function of sex-role indoctrination which prevents expression of emotion and feelings of tenderness toward others. Thus, "good" environmental conditions are needed if we are to begin moving toward actualization (Maslow, 1970, p. 99). These conditions involve a socialization process that fosters equality and trust between people, along with respect and support of the individual's right to make her own decisions.

B-Cognition and Actualization

Assuming that these conditions are present and that people are willing and able to take risks, positive growth will occur. Individuals begin more and more to exist in a *B-cognition* state. In sharp contrast to *D-cognition* experiences that involve judging, condemning, and approving and disapproving of ourselves and others, B-cognition experiences are nonjudgmental, self-validating, nonstriving, and temporary (Maslow, 1962, p.68). In such states of *peak experience*, we experience phenomena in their simplicity, "oughtness," beauty, goodness, and completeness. There is a lack of strain, an effortlessness, a spontaneity about the experience that is almost overwhelming (Maslow, 1962, p. 78). Examples include " . . . perceiving the beautiful person or the beautiful painting, experiencing perfect sex and/or perfect love, insight, creativeness" (Maslow, 1962, p. 79).

But there are negative features to experiencing in the B-cognition realm, according to Maslow. It is not a perfect state in which people "live happily forever after." Thus, self-actualizing people are more capable than ordinary people of B-cognizing, but they do not live in this state continuously (Maslow, 1962, pp. 109–110). Continual existence in such a passive and noninterfering state would prove fatal, since action is often demanded for survival. The person who appreciates the beauty of the tiger without taking safety precautions may not survive the experience. As Maslow (1962, p. 111) put it, "The demands of self-actualization may necessitate killing the tiger, even though B-cognition of the tiger is against killing the tiger." As a consequence, self-actualization demands D-cognition or the arousal of safety needs as well as B-cognition. In a broader sense, this means that the actualization process will involve conflict, struggle, uncertainty, guilt, and regret, as well as bliss and pleasure (Maslow, 1962. p. 111).

Another danger associated with B-cognizing is that it often leads to an indiscriminate acceptance of others. According to Maslow, this outcome occurs ". . . because every person, seen from the viewpoint of his own Being exclusively, is seen as perfect in his own kind. Evaluation, condemnation, . . . criticism, comparison [with others] are all then inapplicable and beside the point" (Maslow, 1962, p. 115). Yet there are times when people can be too tolerant of others. Maslow argued that they must also accept the responsibility for fostering growth in others by setting limits for them, by disciplining them, and by deliberately being the frustrater. Parents and teachers are confronted continuously by this dilemma (Maslow, 1962, p. 112).

There is also the danger that people who are B-cognizing will be misunderstood by others, who will interpret the B-cognizer's inactivity as a lack of love, of concern and compassion. As a consequence, their own growth may be retarded because they may come to perceive others as "bad," as less deserving of their trust and respect (Maslow, 1962, p. 113).

Characteristics of Self-Actualizing People.

In order to discover the distinguishing characteristics of actualizers, Maslow reported using the following procedure. He selected the best specimens of humanity he could find from among his friends and acquaintances and from among various public and historical figures. The latter individuals included Abraham Lincoln in his later years, Thomas

Jefferson, Albert Einstein, Eleanor Roosevelt, Jane Addams, William James, Albert Schweitzer, Aldous Huxley, and Spinoza, among others. Individuals were selected for intensive study because, according to Maslow, they all showed an absence of neurosis, psychopathic personality, or psychosis, and the presence of self-actualization tendencies. He admitted that his data were impressionistic and did not meet conventional scientific reliability, validity, and sampling standards. Yet he felt the problem of psychological health was so important that he was compelled to present this "evidence" for its heuristic value (Maslow, 1970, pp. 149–152).

After extensive analysis of these individuals' lives, he found that actualizers have a more efficient perception of reality than nonactualizers. They are more capable than nonactualizers of perceiving the truth in many different situations. They are capable of detecting dishonesty and fakery in others. In addition, they are less guided in their judgments by stereotypes and prejudices (Maslow, 1970, pp. 153–154). Actualizers show a greater acceptance of themselves, others, and nature than nonactualizers. They recognize their own shortcomings and those of others, but they do not feel excessively guilty or anxious about them. Instead, they tend to deal with them stoically in the same way that one accepts the workings of nature. Maslow also found that actualizers tend to be hearty in their appetites and enjoy themselves without regret or shame or apology (Maslow, 1970, p. 156). They sleep well and enjoy sex without unneccessary inhibitions. They are not ashamed of their biological functioning—urination, defecation, menstruation, pregnancy, and growing older. These functions are part of reality and are accepted (Maslow, 1970, p. 156).

Actualizing people are more problem-centered than nonactualizers. Nonactualizers tend to be very concerned with themselves and are characterized by feelings of inferiority. Actualizers, in contrast, are more concerned with undertaking tasks that will benefit others. They are less introspective and more task-oriented (Maslow, 1970, pp. 159-160). Actualizers were also found to show greater resistance to enculturation than their more ordinary counterparts. They tend to be ". . . ruled by the laws of their own character rather than by the rules of society" (Maslow, 1970, p. 174). They show neither excessive rejection nor uncritical acceptance of the rules of society. Instead, they are more detached from the culture. They can yield to folkways perceived by them as harmless and yet react strongly against injustices. In general, though, they ". . . show what might be called a calm, long-time concern with culture improvement that seems . . . to imply an acceptance of slowness of change along with the unquestioned desirability and necessity of such change" (Maslow, 1970, p. 172).

Finally, Maslow claimed that actualizers possess a democratic character structure. In contrast to nonactualizers, they are less likely to focus their attention on race, color, creed, sex, religious affiliation, educational level, or social class. Although they tend to be more creative than their more average counterparts, they do not consider themselves superior in all respects to others. They acknowledge their own limitations and can ask for help in areas where they lack expertise. They honestly respect others and can be genuinely humble before people who can teach them something they do not know. Although they tend to select elite individuals for their friends, Maslow argued that the choice is made on the basis of talent and ability and not birth, race, sex, family, age, fame, or power (Maslow, 1970, pp. 167-168).

After reviewing Maslow's list of characteristics for the actualizer, many students report having uncontrollable impulses to leap to their feet and recite the Boy Scout Oath. When they regain their senses, they say that Maslow's actualizers seem to be caricatures of the good human being. Maslow acknowledged this problem, and said he found evidence in his studies that actualizers had a number of weaknesses. They ". . . can be boring, stubborn, [and] irritating. They are by no means free from . . . superficial vanity, pride, partiality to their own productions, family, friends, and children. Temper outbursts are not rare" (Maslow, 1970, p. 175). They can also show extraordinary ruthlessness. For example, they can reject a friend totally and irrevocably if they discover he has been dishonest with them. At times they can also show behavior and use language that is shocking and insulting. In brief, they are as capable as any other human being of displaying injurious and primitive behavior on occasion.

THE PROCESS OF PERSONALITY DEVELOPMENT

Maslow posited a universal stage-emergent theory of personal development, according to which the individual must, at least to a certain extent, satisfy his lower needs before higher ones can become operative. The emergence or nonemergence of the stages depends to a considerable degree on the kind of environment that confronts the individual. As noted earlier, environments that threaten the individual and do not allow for the satisfaction of basic needs are detrimental to growth, whereas environments that are supportive and provide for the gratification of these needs promote growth toward self-actualization. In Maslow's view, the role of the environment is crucial in the early stages of development, when the person is struggling to gratify basic needs. For example, it is clear that needs for safety, love, and belongingness all depend upon the cooperation of other people for gratification. Later on, as the higher needs emerge, the person becomes less dependent on the environment and relies on his or her inner experiences to guide behavior. That behavior is determined by his or her inner nature, capacities, potentialities, talents, and creative impulses (Maslow, 1962, p. 32). Such an individual is clearly less dependent on rewards or approval from others. Thus, the shift is from the instrumental learning (associative learning) to perceptual learning. Whereas instrumental learning generally involves voluntary responding to secure external rewards, perceptual learning involves an increase in insight and self-understanding. As Maslow put it:

> "[T]he techniques of repeatedly acquiring from the outside world satisfactions of motivational deficiencies are much less needed. Associative learning . . . give[s] way more to perceptual learning, to the increase of insight and understanding, to knowledge of self and to the steady growth of personality . . . change becomes much less an acquisition of habits or associations one by one, and much more a total change of the total person. . . . This kind of character-change learning means changing a very complex, highly integrated, holistic organism, which in turn means that many impacts will make no change at all because more and more such impacts will be rejected as the person becomes more stable and more autonomous. (Maslow, 1962, p. 36)

With the advent of persistent perceptual learning, the person is free to make his or her own spontaneous choices. These choices are made by listening to one's inner nature and not by relying on the values and expectations of others.

TECHNIQUES OF ASSESSMENT

Maslow utilized a variety of research techniques in an attempt to identify self-actualizing individuals. He began by employing a selection technique called *iteration* (Maslow, 1970, p. 151). It consisted of starting with his general belief concerning the meaning of self-actualization and then collating it and other existing definitions, as they were used by people in the culture, in an attempt to discover a common ground. A common definition was made possible by the systematic elimination of logical inconsistencies among the various definitions. Once the term had been refined and redefined, it was used to screen three thousand college students in terms of whether they were high or low in self-actualization. Once the group had been divided into actualizers or nonactualizers, each person was examined in case-study fashion through use of the Rorschach test, Murray's Thematic Apperception Test, free association, and in-depth interviews to determine whether or not they possessed the characteristics of actualizers.

This effort can be thought of as an attempt to validate the concept of self-actualization empirically. The definition of the term was then changed and corrected further, where necessary, in light of the findings. Then the original subject pool was reselected on the basis of the new definition, and the retainees were restudied using the same clinical procedures. On the basis of the new data, the self-actualization definition was again revised, and the new definition used to reselect subjects from the remaining subject pool for further clinical study, and so on, until a precise identification of actualizers and nonactualizers was obtained. Thus, the procedure involves beginning with a vague notion of the meaning of a term and continued, subsequent refinement of it on the basis of the collection of empirical evidence. As you might suspect, the use of such a procedure greatly reduced the number of individuals considered to be self-actualizers. In fact, Maslow found only one student in three thousand who met this stringent criterion. He then argued that perhaps young people had not had sufficient time and experience to develop the characteristics associated with actualization, so that it might be best to study middle-aged and older people. These people where chosen from among his personal acquaintances and friends and from public and historical figues.

The historical and public figures included approximately sixty definite, partial, and potential cases of self-actualization such as Lincoln, Jefferson, Eleanor Roosevelt, Einstein, Schweitzer, Spinoza, G. W. Carver, Eugene V. Debs, Pablo Casals, Adlai Stevenson, George Washington, Robert Benchley, and Camille Pissarro. Maslow employed the historical method because he found that it was possible to secure sufficient information about these individuals' lives from autobiographical sources to draw meaningful conclusions, whereas it was nearly impossible to do the same for living figures. He noted that many of the latter subjects, when informed of the purpose of his research, ". . . became self-consious, froze up, laughed off the whole effort, or broke off the relationship" (Maslow, 1970, p. 151). The results of his investigations revealed that, although more older people than college students were self-actualized, the actual numbers of both were very small.

As noted earlier, Maslow's assessment procedures are fraught with ambiguities and imprecisions. We are not certain, for example, of how the various tests used in the interviews were administered or scored, of what kinds of free associations led Maslow to conclude that his subjects were or were not actualized; of how he decided that some of his historical figures were definitely self-actualized and others were not. Most important, since Maslow chose for study figures he greatly admired, it is distinctly possible that his definition of self-actualization was simply a reflection of his own personal value system. Maslow, in short, may have superimposed his own values on the research process and selectively interpreted his data in line with his own orientation.

Because of these problems, research tests of Maslow's theory have been difficult to carry out. Now, however, research has been growing because of the construction of a more reliable and valid measure of self-actualization called the *Personal Orientation Inventory* (POI) (Shostrom, 1963). The POI is a self-report questionaire consisting of 150 two-choice items that purportedly reflect the values and behavior of major importance in the development of a self-actualizing person. In responding to POI items, the person is asked to select the one statement in each of the 150 pairs that is most true of himself or herself. The subject's responses can then be scored in terms of two major scales, one dealing with the effective use of time (time competence), and one assessing the extent to which the individual depends on himself or herself or on others in making judgements (inner direction), and in terms of ten subscales. The subscales measure values important to the development of the self-actualizing person—namely, self-actualizing value, existentiality, feeling reactivity, spontaneity, self-regard, self-acceptance, nature of man, synergy, acceptance of aggression, and capacity for intimate contact. Sample items and scoring for the two major scales and for some of the subsidiary scales are presented in Table 12.1.

The scores have the following meanings and interpretations: High scores on the time competence scale indicate that the respondents are living in the present. Self-actualizing individuals are considered to live most fully in the here and now and to relate the past and the future to current experiencing in a meaningful way. They do not dwell either on the past or the future, but instead use the past for current reflections about problems and aspirations for the future to help make decisions. In regard to the inner-direction dimension, self-actualizing respondents show that the source of their behavior is essentially inner-directed, but that to a certain degree they recognize they must be sensitive to other people's approval and affection. High scores on the self-actualizing values dimension suggest that respondents hold and practice the values of self-actualizing people. High scores on the existentiality dimension measure respondents' ability to hold and practice self-actualizing values flexibly. Low scores indicate that respondents hold their values rigidly and compulsively. High scores on the remaining dimensions indicate that respondents have a sensitivity to their own needs, act spontaneously, consider themselves worthwhile, accept their weaknesses and like themselves in spite of these deficiencies, believe that human beings are essentially good, can see that the opposites of life are related, can accept their feelings of anger as natural, and have an ability to develop meaningful relationships with other human beings.

Much of the early work with the POI was concerned with establishing its reliability and validity as a research instrument. Test-retest reliabilities for various samples are satisfactory, although the coefficients for certain subscales are low to moderate in certain studies (Ilardi and May, 1968).

In terms of validity, a number of studies show that the measure can be used to distinguish between groups in society that we would ordinarily consider to differ in their actualization levels. For example, two studies have shown that groups of psychiatric patients scored lower (were less self-actualized) on virtually all the POI scales than groups of people judged by experienced clinical psychologists to be self-actualized (Fox, Knapp, and Michael, 1968). Another study has shown that all scales of the POI discriminated among groups of alcoholic wives, nonalcoholic wives, and clinically judged self-actualizers in the expected way. A group of normal subjects also scored higher on many of the POI scales

TABLE 12.1 Sample Items from Shostrom's Personal Orientation Inventory*

Time Competence
1.   a. I strive always to predict what will happen in the future.
     b. I do not feel it necessary always to predict what will happen in the future.
2.   a. I prefer to save good things for future use.
     b. I prefer to use good things now.
3.   a. I worry about the future.
     b. I do not worry about the future.
4.   a. It is important to me how I live in the here and now.
     b. It is of little importance to me how I live in the here and now.

Inner Direction
1.   *a. My moral values are dictated by society.*
     b. My moral values are self-determined.
2.   a. I feel guilty when I am selfish.
     b. I don't feel guilty when I am selfish.
3.   a. I am bound by the principle of fairness.
     b. I am not absolutely bound by the principle of fairness.
4.   a. I feel I must always tell the truth.
     b. I do not always tell the truth.

Self-Actualizing Values
1.   *a.* I often make my decisions spontaneously.
     b. I seldom make my decisions spontaneously.
2.   *a.* It is possible to live life in terms of what I want to do.
     b. It is not possible to live life in terms of what I want to do.

Feeling Reactivity
1.   a. I live by values which are in agreement with others.
     b. I live by values which are primarily based on my own feelings.

Spontaneity
1.   a. I must justify my actions in the pursuit of my own interests.
     b. I need not justify my actions in the pursuit of my own interests.

Self-Regard
1.   a. It is important that others accept my point of view.
     b. It is not necessary for others to accept my point of view.

Self-Acceptance
1.   a. I try to be sincere but I sometimes fail.
     b. I try to be sincere and I am sincere.

Nature of Man Constructive
1.   *a.* I have a problem in fusing sex and love.
     b. I have no problem in fusing sex and love.

Synergy
1.   *a.* People are both good and evil.
     b. People are not both good and evil.

Acceptance of Aggression

1.   *a.*   I find some people who are stupid and uninteresting.
     b.   I never find any people who are stupid and uninteresting.

Capacity for Intimate Contact

1.   a.   I am afraid to be tender.
     b.   I am not afraid to be tender.

Adapted from Shostrom, 1963.

*A person who answers the items by choosing the italicized alternatives is more self-actualizing than one who does not.

than the alcoholic wives (Zaccaria and Weir, 1967). In general, these studies and others indicate that the POI is a valid discriminator between normal and abnormal groups.

A number of studies have indicated that the POI can be utilized effectively to measure changes in self-actualization following encounter group experiences. In one investigation, for example, there were changes in POI scores on most of the subscales as well as on the two major scales in the direction of greater self-actualization following counseling that emphasized expression of feelings and the need to be sensitive to the desires of others, as compared to a variety of control groups who received no counseling (Pearson, 1966).

Despite these generally positive results, we cannot conclude that the scale has no methodological flaws. One primary, recurring problem concerns the fact that subjects can deliberately fake their responses in ways designed to elicit positive impressions from others. It is possible for subjects who are familiar with the humanistic psychology literature deliberately to present themselves as actualized, when in fact they are not. Even though the POI has a built-in lie detection scale to uncover such dissimulation, its usefulness as a research instrument would be weakened if it could be shown that sizable numbers of subjects do indeed fake their responses. The percentage of such subjects in a variety of populations has yet to be determined. At this point, a reasonable conclusion would be that the instrument is usable primarily with naive populations.

A related problem springs from the fact that the POI is constructed so that responding in a self-actualizing manner is directly at variance with responding in a culturally approved way. For example, it would be considered socially desirable to respond to the second item under the inner-direction heading in Table 12.1 by endorsing alternative *a*, I feel guilty when I am selfish, but undesirable to endorse the self-actualization alternative, *b*, I don't feel guilty when I am selfish. Under these conditions, respondents who are antagonistic to the experimenter may choose to respond in socially undesirable ways by endorsing the self-actualization alternatives of various items. For example, they might report that "I don't feel guilty when I am selfish, I am not absolutely bound by the principles of fairness, and I do not always tell the truth." All these responses are socially undesirable, but self-actualizing in terms of scoring using the POI (see Table 12.1). The "screw-you" effect is the term used by researchers to describe the phenomenon in which certain subjects may act in uncooperative and hostile ways during experiments. Thus, it may be that a number of psychopathic individuals (individuals who are not bound by the principles of fair play and truthfulness, who feel no guilt when they are selfish, and who say, in effect, "screw you" indiscriminately to the demands of the experimenter) may be classified as self-actualizing in terms of their total responding on the POI. If this is the case, then the POI is not a very good measure of self-actualization. At the very least, efforts should be made to determine whether the POI is measuring psychopathy or self-actualization.

There are other problems with the measure. For example, subjects generally do not like to respond to forced-choice questionnaires, since they feel that such instruments often do not provide them with an opportunity to present their feelings and opinions on a given topic fully and accurately. There is also the problem, common to most measures of personality, of neglecting to assess the person's traits in interaction with specific situations. How would you feel about being forced to select one of these alternatives for this POI item?

    a. I can cope with the ups and downs of life.
    b. I cannot cope with the ups and downs of life.

Perhaps you can cope with the "downs" or failures in life when they involve school work, but not when they involve the loss of a close friend. Maybe you can cope well with success in school, but react poorly to praise from teachers or friends. Maybe you can cope well with the loss of your transistor radio, but not when you discover the theft of your new stereo set. The point is that a number of questions on the POI do not assess individual reactions in specific situations.

APPLICATION OF THE THEORY TO THE TREATMENT OF PSYCHOPATHOLOGY

For Maslow, neurotics are people who have been prevented and who have prevented themselves from attaining gratification of their basic needs. This fact stops them from moving toward the ultimate goal of self-actualization. They are individuals who feel threatened and insecure and who have little self-respect and esteem. Since the gratification of these basic needs can occur only through contact with other people, it follows that therapy must be interpersonal in nature (Maslow, 1970, p. 242). Maslow likened the psychotherapeutic relationship between therapist and client to a relationship between friends. The therapy situation must involve mutual frankness, trust, honesty, and lack of defensiveness. It should also allow for the expression of a healthy amount of childishness and silliness (Maslow, 1970, p. 249). The expression of these "weaknesses" is possible when the relationship is nonthreatening and supportive. In such a democratic context, the therapist should provide the client with the respect, love, and feelings of belongingness he or she must have in order to grow. In other words, the therapist must act to gratify the client's basic need deficiencies. But effective therapy must go beyond this point. The therapeutic relationship should not only encourage the giving of love by the therapist to the client, but also the expression of love and affection by the client toward the therapist and others (Maslow, 1970, p. 250). The client should, in general, be encouraged to display those values associated with positive growth. He or she should be encouraged to "open up" to the world and to learn to understand more about its complex nature.

Maslow realized that a warm, supportive therapeutic approach was unworkable with some clients, particularly those with chronic, stabilized neuroses involving deep mistrust and hostility toward others (Maslow, 1970, p. 251). Under such conditions, Maslow believed that a depth analysis in the Freudian tradition might be more workable. Such an analysis would involve both a cognitive *and* an emotional "working through" by the person of his or her problems as a means of achieving change and self-improvement.

CRITICAL COMMENTS

We turn now to an evaluation of the scientific worth of Maslow's position in terms of our six criteria.

Comprehensiveness. Maslow's theory is a pioneering and creative effort aimed at pushing personality psychology away from an exclusive concern with psychopathology and toward a more positive and optimistic view of people concerned with their potential creativeness. His theory can be considered quite comprehensive in the sense that it incorporates much of the Freudian model of pathology and, in addition, addresses itself to the issue of positive growth, but technically speaking its focus is primarily and explicitly on the latter rather than the former. In this sense, the theory is not quite as comprehensive as it appears at first. The theory itself does not spell out precisely the variables that control the occurrence, maintenance, and modification of self-actualization phenomena. Under these circumstances, Maslow's theory can be judged as somewhat limited both in the range and diversity of phenomena it explicitly encompasses and in the explanatory system it uses to account for these events.

Precision and Testability. Maslow's theory is not very precise, and as a result is difficult to test properly. For example, his hierarchical scheme of human motivation, which is presumed to involve the emergence of our basic needs from most to least potent following their relative gratification, is marked by deficiencies. There are people who are willing to suffer hunger and thirst and eventually even to die for values Maslow assumed are less potent than the physiological needs. Although he recognized this problem, the theory does not account for the exceptions.

There is also a lack of precision concerning the exact amount of gratification the individual must experience before the next higher need will emerge. Maslow maintained that most people are partially satisfied and partially dissatisfied in their basic needs at the same time, so it is incorrect to assume that a given need must be completely gratified before the next will emerge. Instead, Maslow posited a gradual emergence of a higher need as the lower need becomes increasingly gratified. For example, if a lower need is 10 percent gratified, perhaps there will be no emergence of the next higher need. But if the lower need is 25 percent gratified, then the higher need may emerge at 5 percent of potency; if the lower need is 50 percent gratified, then there may be a 25 percent emergence, and so on (Maslow, 1970, pp. 53–54).

Adequate definition of self-actualization and a number of other terms (purposefulness, inner requiredness, and "good" and "bad" situations) remains a major problem with the theory (see Chapter 16 for a more detailed discussion of these points).

Simplicity. Maslow's theory fails to meet the parsimony criterion. The motivational deficiency scheme he uses to account for various behaviors, although more detailed than that employed by Rogers (see Chapter 13), is still too simplistic to account adequately for the phenomena within its domain.

Empirical Validity. There is little empirical evidence to support Maslow's theory. For example, there is little proof that the various B-values emerge once the basic needs have been gratified. Instead, it appears that Maslow has simply given us a list of the kinds of "higher" needs he assumes would emerge once we have satisfied our more basic urges, a practice reminiscent of the behavior of the instinctivists of the 1920s and 1930s. They also constructed long lists of motives that presumably would help them account for the greater diversity in our behavior. But their efforts failed and so will Maslow's unless further attempts are made to demonstrate empirically how the actualization process works and how knowledge of its operation can aid us in the accurate prediction of behavior. At present, Maslow's scheme is based on a philosophical doctrine that has its roots in naturalism, romaticism, and existentialism, and not in scientific fact.

Heuristic Value. Despite its many limitations, Maslow's theory has been provocative and has stimulated the thinking of many investigators in a variety of disciplines. Not only has he encouraged theorists and researchers to consider the healthy side of human nature, but he has forced some of them to reconsider their own myopic view of science and its limitations for understanding human functioning. Specifically, he castigated them for their "inevitable stress of elegance, polish, technique, and apparatus [which] has, as a frequent consequence, a playing down of meaningfulness, vitality, and significance of a problem and of creativeness in general" (Maslow, 1970, p. 11). As a result, he has gotten some of them to think of science as an enterprise in which people ask significant questions and then adopt techniques to help answer them rather than as a situation in which sophisticated techniques are used to study relatively unimportant problems.

Applied Value. Maslow's theory is also very strong in the applied area. His formulations have had a decided impact on pastoral and educational counseling programs and on various business management programs.

DISCUSSION QUESTIONS

1. What are the implications for the development of an individual's personality of Maslow's equivocal assumption that human nature is good or, at the very least, neutral?
2. Is it possible, in your opinion, to discover a universal set of ethical principles we can use to guide our behavior? What principles guide your life?
3. What are some of the limitations of Maslow's proposed self-actualization hierarchy of needs?
4. Do you agree with Maslow that children need limits on their behavior? Why?
5. Have you experienced B-love? How could you be certain?
7. What is the need for cognitive understanding? In what ways can this need be satisfied?
7. Maslow maintains that we not only fear failure, but that often we are afraid to be successful. Why does he hold such a belief? What great work are you planning in your own life? Are you satisfied with your progress toward your goals?
8. What are some of the dangers associated with B-cognition states?
9. In terms of the self-actualization hierarchy, how would you characterize yourself?
10. List and discuss the strengths and weaknesses of self-actualizing people.

NOTES

H. Chiang and A. H. Maslow, eds., *The Healthy Personality* (New York: Van Nostrand, 1969).

J. Fox, R. R. Knapp, and W. B. Michael, "Assessment of Self-Actualization of Psychiatric Patients: Validity of the Personal Orientation Inventory," *Educational and Psychological Measurement,* 1968, **28,** 565–569.

R. L. Ilardi and W. T. May, "A Reliability Study of Shostram's Personal Orientation Inventory," *Journal of Humanistic Psychology,* 1968, **8,** 68–72.

A. H. Maslow, *Toward a Psychology of Being* (New York: Van Nostrand, 1962).

A. H. Maslow, *Motivation and Personality*, 2nd ed. (New York: Harper & Row, 1970).

L. Monahan, D. Kuhn, and P. Shaver, "Intrapsychic versus Cultural Explanations of the Fear of Success," *Journal of Personality and Social Psychology*, 1974, **29,** 60–64.

O. Pearson, "Effects of Group Guidance upon College Adjustment" (Unpublished doctoral dissertation, University of Kentucky, 1966).

E. L. Shostrom, *Personal Orientation Inventory* (San Diego, Calif.: EdITS/Educational and Industrial Testing Service, 1963).

C. Wilson, *New Pathways in Psychology* (London: Gollancz, 1972).

J. S. Zaccaria and W. R. Weir, "A Comparison of Alcoholics and Selected Samples of Nonalcoholics in Terms of a Positive Concept of Mental Health," *Journal of Social Psychology*, 1967, **71,** 151–157.

SUGGESTED READINGS

Chiang, H., and A. Maslow. *The Healthy Personality*, 2nd ed., New York: Van Nostrand, 1977.

Goble, F. *The Third Force: The Psychology of Abraham Maslow.* New York: Pocket Books, 1970.

Maslow, A. *Toward a Psychology of Being.* New York: Van Nostrand, 1962.

Maslow, A. *Motivation and Personality*, 2nd ed. New York: Harper & Row, 1970.

GLOSSARY

B-Cognition State. State of experiencing that is nonjudgmental and self-validating.

B-Love. Being-love, that is, a mature form of love in which the person is more concerned with giving love to benefit others than in receiving love from others for gratification of his or her needs.

D-Cognition State. State of experiencing that involves judgments of approval and disapproval.

Deficiency Need. Basic need that must be gratified to a large extent before an individual can progress toward self-actualization.

D-Love. Deficiency-love, that is, a selfish love in which the individual is concerned more with receiving love and gratifying his or her needs than with giving love to another.

Growth Need. Higher needs that may emerge once the basic needs have been satisfied (meta needs).

Humanistic Biology. The view that the basic nature of human beings is potentially good and capable of pushing people in the direction of self-realization if the "right" social conditions prevail.

Humanistic Psychology. Type of psychology primarily concerned with helping individuals to reach their maximum. It is also a psychology that emphasizes and tries to foster the dignity and worth of each human being.

Personal Orientation Inventory (POI). Test designed to measure the self-actualizing tendencies of the individual.

Self-Actualization. Process postulated by Maslow in his theory of personality involving the healthy development of the abilities of people so that they can fulfill their own true natures; see also self-realization.

Self-Actualizers. Individuals who have gratified their basic needs and developed their potentialities to the point that they can be considered healthy, fully functioning human beings.

Carl Rogers (The Bettmann Archive, Inc.)

13

Rogers' Self Theory

BIOGRAPHICAL SKETCH

Carl Ransom Rogers was born in 1902 in Oak Park, Illinois, a suburb of Chicago. He was the fourth in a family of six children whose head was a successful civil engineer and contractor. Rogers reports that he was raised in a home marked by close and warm family relationships, but also by strict and uncompromising religious principles. His parents controlled his behavior and would allow no alcoholic beverages, no dancing, no cardplaying or theater-going and very little contact with other people. Instead, they extolled the virtues of the Protestant Ethic—hard work, responsibility for one's actions, and the importance of personal success. Rogers reports that "even carbonated beverages had a faintly sinful aroma, and I remember my slight feeling of wickedness when I had my first bottle of 'pop' " (Rogers, 1961, pp. 3–27). His wife, who was his childhood sweetheart, also remembers him as a "shy, sensitive and unsocial boy, who preferred to live in his books and his dream world rather than encounter the rough [and] tumble of the play yard or enter into competitive sports" (H. E. Rogers, 1965, pp. 93–98). Thus Rogers seems to have been a rather solitary figure who had strong scholarly interests from an early age.

When he was twelve, his parents bought a farm a short distance from Chicago where Rogers spent his adolescence. His father encouraged his sons to raise animals for profit, so Rogers reared chickens, lambs, pigs, and calves. The venture caused him to become interested in scientific agriculture and how scientific methods could be applied to farming. In retrospect, Rogers believes the experience taught him a healthy respect for science and the ways in which it could be used to solve problems. He entered the University of Wisconsin and chose scientific agriculture as his field of study. Shortly afterward, his professional goals shifted dramatically as a result of some emotion-laden experiences at student religious conferences. After graduation, he entered Union Theological Seminary in New York City. There, he and a group of other students decided they were being unilaterally presented with ideas by their instructors, but were not being given an opportunity fully to explore their own personal doubts and questions. Accordingly, they petitioned the administration for a seminar without a formal instructor. To their surprise, the request was granted. Rogers found the seminar most gratifying and reports that, as a result of the experience, he thought himself right out of religious work.

Since he had taken some courses in psychology and enjoyed them, he decided to enter the field, and began his studies at Columbia University, which was located across the street from the seminary. At the end of his clinical internship, even though he had not completed his doctorate, Rogers felt he had to have a job to support a growing family. He took a position as a psychologist in the Child Study Department of the Society for the Prevention of Cruelty to Children in Rochester, New York, and completed his doctorate in 1928. Rogers reports that the twelve years spent at Rochester were valuable ones. During most of these years, he was immersed in practical work, the diagnosis and treatment of delinquent and disadvantaged children. Rogers' unique nondirective or client-centered therapy approach evolved during this period, and culminated in a book entitled *Clinical Treatment of the Child*. In 1940, he accepted an academic position at Ohio State University as a full professor. He began to attract capable students and to conduct research tests of his theory; it was also at this point that he achieved international recognition. *Counseling and Psychotherapy* (1942), a book designed to provide therapists with procedures he felt would engender constructive changes in their clients, was written during this time.

In 1944, Rogers was given an opportunity to establish a counseling center at the University of Chicago. He then wrote *Client-Centered Therapy* (1951), in which he provided readers with the theory that underlies his approach to an understanding of human relationships. Still later he published *On Becoming a Person* (1961), a collection of papers concerned with a variety of issues relating to this basic approach to understanding personality.

In 1957, Rogers returned to the University of Wisconsin. He recalls that his experiences there were generally unpleasant as he became aware of the restrictions under which graduate students were forced to work. Rogers called for massive reform in the graduate program, arguing that students have the potential for learning and development within themselves, but that this potential can be realized only when they are provided with freedom and a supportive environment (Rogers, 1968, pp. 687–703). Shortly after he released the reasons for his disagreement with current educational policies, he resigned from the department and took a position in 1964 as a fellow in residence at the Western Behavioral Sciences Institute in La Jolla, California. In 1969 he wrote a book called *Freedom to Learn,* and in 1970 his *Carl Rogers on Encounter Groups* was published. Rogers followed these publications with

Person to Person: The Problems of Being Human. Most recently, he has been working on problems related to personal growth. He has continued to publish and has also become a leading proponent of the use of encounter groups to promote constructive growth.

AN INDUCTIVE APPROACH TO THEORY CONSTRUCTION

The theory of personality and psychotherapy created by Rogers has its roots in the soil of his personal experience. When he first started practicing psychotherapy with children and adults at the guidance center in Rochester, he reported having very definite preconceptions about the nature of personality functioning. His ideas were based on an acceptance of Freudian thinking, since such thinking was an important part of the guidance center orientation. In practice, however, Rogers found that the Freudian formulations were unworkable. All too often, constructive changes in his clients were not forthcoming. As a consequence, he abandoned the Freudian view and adopted instead a more expedient orientation toward therapy. That is, the only criterion he used to judge the validity of his work with his patients was "Does it work? Is it effective?" (Rogers, 1961, p. 10). Out of this inductive approach, Rogers began to fashion his own concepts, theory, and principles of personality functioning.

BASIC CONCEPTS AND PRINCIPLES

Therapeutic Conditions That Facilitate Growth

In order to identify the conditions that promote growth, Rogers focused not only on his direct experiences with clients, but on the history of attempts by counselors and others to change behavior. He notes that four major techniques have been used: ordering and forbidding, exhortation, suggestion (which includes reassurance and encouragement), and advice (Rogers, 1942, pp. 20–27). Since none of these techniques have been successful, Rogers thinks it is time they were abandoned. But what is wrong with reassuring someone who is experiencing doubts about his personal worth, for example? Rogers maintains that there is a tendency for counselors to use the technique indiscriminately. Telling the client repeatedly that he is improving leads to a denial of the problem and no exploration of the client's feelings about it. Under these conditions, Rogers maintains it is impossible for the client to improve.

In a broader sense, he holds that all these techniques have directive aspects. That is, one person (the therapist) thinks of himself as an authority figure who understands the nature of the other person's problems and the best way or ways to solve them. In terms of the therapeutic process, the counselor perceives himself as an expert who discovers, diagnoses, and treats the person's problems. In Rogers' nondirective approach, on the other hand, the focus is primarily on the client himself. Instead of asking "How can I treat and cure this person?" Rogers asks: "How can I provide a relationship which this person may use for his own personal growth?" (Rogers, 1961, p. 32).

Rogers believes the person has the capacity for change within himself and will change in constructive ways if the therapist creates the appropriate conditions. Specifically, the therapist must be "genuine in the relationship," meaning that he needs to be fully aware of his own feelings and willing to express them (Rogers, 1961, p. 33). The therapist must also accept the client unconditionally as a person of worth and dignity in his own right. Acceptance means understanding the feelings of the person, no matter how positive or negative they are or how much they contradict your own attitudes. In Rogers' opinion, acceptance and empathy provide the basis for a relationship of warmth and safety in which the person can feel he is liked and respected.

How does Rogers know that constructive change or growth will occur if these conditions are met? He came to this conclusion on the basis of experience with many troubled individuals (Rogers, 1961, p. 35). He noticed in them

> . . . a growth tendency, a drive toward self-actualization. . . . It is the urge which is evident in all organic and human life—to expand, extend, become autonomous, develop, mature. . . . This tendency may become deeply buried under layer after layer of encrusted psychological defenses . . but it is my belief that it exists in every individual, and awaits only the proper conditions to be released and expressed. (Rogers, 1961, p. 35)

Rogers also believes this self-actualization tendency is positive in nature. Under the proper conditions, then, each of us moves toward maturity. As our "false fronts" drop and we become more genuine, we inevitably experience growth. Rogers claims his view of human nature is not unrealistic, since he does recognize that we can be incredibly cruel and hurtful to one another (Rogers, 1961, pp. 26–27). Nevertheless, Rogers is so persistently optimistic about the possibility of personal growth that many investigators discount his disclaimer.

The Nature of Client Growth

When the proper conditions prevail, Rogers believes that people feel increasingly free to express their own feelings and that these expressions lead to an increasingly differentiated and sensitive understanding of themselves and others. In brief, their experiences become accurately symbolized. The expression of feelings also make them aware of certain incongruities or discrepancies between some of their experiences and their concepts of self. Thus they are threatened, because for the first time they experience fully feelings that were either denied or distorted in awareness. Out of such incongruity comes the reorganization of the self structure as it assimilates the previously denied experiences. As a result, fewer experiences can be threatening, and defensiveness is decreased. They feel an unconditional positive regard for themselves and react to subsequent experiences less in terms of what others think and more in terms of what they feel innately to be valid (Rogers, 1959, p. 216). They also may feel more accepting of others (Rogers, 1959, p. 218). Other important concepts in the theory will be covered in the following section on the developmental process.

THE PROCESS OF PERSONALITY DEVELOPMENT

Rogers maintains that during infancy the person perceives his experience as reality. He operates from an internal frame of reference and is unencumbered by the evaluations of others. Rogers also believes that the person "interacts with his reality in terms of his basic actualizing tendency" (Rogers, 1959, p. 222)—that is, his behavior is directed toward the goal of satisfying his need for actualization as he perceives it. As a result, the person engages in an organismic valuing process in which he uses the actualization tendency as a criterion in making judgments about the worth of a given experience. Experiences that help to promote actualization are "good" or positively valued; experiences that hinder actualization are "bad" or negatively valued. In support of his argument, Rogers cites the example of an infant who values food positively when he is hungry, but who is disgusted with it when satiated. He maintains further that an infant has a built-in mechanism which leads him to select the diet that, in the long run, enhances his development (Rogers, 1959, p. 210). Thus, Rogers contends that an infant "knows" which foods and experiences are good for him and which are bad. Yet the scientific evidence in support of Rogers' "organismic wisdom" hypothesis is virtually nonexistent.

The Davis Infant Study

Let us examine the study most cited by Rogers, Maslow, and others who have attempted to build a psychology on the notion that people not only know what foods are best for them, but know the answers to their problems instinctively (Davis, 1928). In that study, three infants ranging in age from eight to ten months were given thorough physical examinations by a medical doctor. These examinations included a blood count, urinalysis, and X rays of the bones. Following the examinations, the infants were given an opportunity to select their own diets from saucers holding a variety of foods and from glasses of liquids. A list of a typical meal is shown in Table 13.1. Nurses were also present at each feeding but did not offer any food to the infants. If the infants reached or pointed to a food, they were allowed by the experimenter to offer them a

TABLE 13.1 Typical Meal Served to Test for Adequacy of Self-selection Diet

Milk, grade A	Beets, cooked
Milk, lactic	Carrots, raw
Seasalt (Seisal)	Carrots, cooked
Rye-Krisp	Turnips, cooked
Bone marrow, raw	Cauliflower, cooked
Bone marrow, cooked	Cabbage, raw
Beef, raw	Cabbage, cooked
Lamb, cooked	Spinach, cooked
Beef, cooked	Peas, cooked
Chicken, cooked	Peas, raw
Lettuce, raw	Cornmeal, cooked
Potatoes, cooked	

Adapted from C. M. Davis, 1928, p. 659.

spoonful. Two infants were on such a diet for six months and one for a period of a year. At the end of this period, the infants were again given complete physical examinations. The results showed that, in general, the diets selected were optimal and the infants were healthy.

What is wrong with this study? With acumen born of hindsight, we could point to literally dozens of methodological flaws. First, only three infants participated in the study, so that it is preposterous to generalize the results to all the infants in the culture, not to mention to the entire population of adults! Another serious deficiency includes the fact that none of the foods was lacking in nutritive value, so that the choices available to the infants could only promote health. Even if "control" foods with little or no nutritive value had been used, a rigorous scientist would insist on controlling for differences in food color and odor, among other factors. The role of the nurses introduces another possible source of error, since they could have misjudged random arm-waving and reaching as signs of the infants' wanting a particular food. Also, since the experiment lasted a relatively short period of time, it is impossible to assess the impact of the diet on development. Harmful effects could surface after much longer periods of time had elapsed. In fairness to the author, she pointed out this fact, along with other problems such as accounting for spillage in assessing the amounts of food consumed.

The detailed criticism of this experiment is included to make you more aware of the fact that the organismic wisdom notion advocated by Rogers and others is open to serious question. Of course, numerous studies done with lower animals support the notion of specific hungers (Krieckhaus, 1970), but still other studies in the same research literature show that these innate propensities in lower animals can be rather easily overriden by learning experiences (Garcia, Kimeldurf, and Hunt, 1961).

Thus, if we could generalize the results of studies conducted on rats to the behavior of human beings, we might conclude that humans would have an extremely difficult time "getting in touch" with their organismic wisdom mechanism in order to make good decisions, since their learning experiences would interfere with the search process. Rogers hints at this problem when he states that the drive toward self-actualization may be ". . . deeply buried under layer after layer of encrusted psychological defenses." At the very least, then, the process of getting in touch with our innermost feelings will be difficult.

Finally, even if we grant the validity of the organismic wisdom hypothesis in regard to the selection of food, it does not follow that we can now make the right decisions about complex social issues and problems. How does the innate mechanism responsible for guiding us to make the proper decisions about our diets operate to lead us to make the right decisions about career selection, mate selection, and so forth? The conceptual gap between food decisions and value decisions is tremendous. Also, there is no scientific evidence for the existence of an innate mechanism to guide us in making complex ethical decisions.

Congruence and Incongruence

Rogers believes that, as the person interacts with the environment and particularly with significant others like parents, brothers, sisters, and various relatives, he begins to develop a concept of self that is largely based on the evaluations of others. He also develops a *need for positive regard*. According to Rogers, this need is either learned or innate. The person then becomes aware of the fact that when he satisfies another individual's need for positive regard, he necessarily experiences satisfaction of his own need for such regard (Rogers, 1959, p. 223). As a consequence, the desire for positive regard from others may become more compelling than the individual's organismic valuing process (Rogers, 1959, p. 224). If, for example, the person feels that aggression against others is wrong but significant others place a positive value on it, the person may ignore the validity of his feelings, and act in terms of their expectations.

This need to seek approval or positive regard from people and to avoid disapproval also has a definite impact on self-concept. When experiences are discriminated by the person only if they meet with the approval of others or are not discriminated because they meet with disapproval, his own self-regard becomes similarly selective. When this happens, the person is said to have acquired a *condition of worth* or the feeling that acceptance of him by others is conditional upon performance of given kinds of behavior (Rogers, 1959, p. 209). If, on the other hand, the person experienced only unconditional positive regard from others, then no conditions of worth would be present and the needs for self-regard and positive regard would never be at variance with an organismic evaluation of experiences. In such a case, there would be *congruence* between self and experience and the person would be psychologically healthy.

This state of affairs, however, is an ideal. We all have conditions of worth placed on our behavior. We all learn in the course of socialization that some of our feelings and behaviors are "appropriate" and others are "inappropriate." When these normative rules are congruent or in line with our organismic evaluations, we continue our movement toward self-actualization. When the expectations run counter to our innate evaluations, however, problems occur and movement toward actualization is hindered. Congruence between self and organismic experiencing leads to accurate symbolization of experiences and positive growth. Incongruence leads to inaccurate or distorted symbolization and psychological maladjustment and vulnerability. If, under incongruent conditions, the unpleasant experience is accurately symbolized in awareness, a state of anxiety exists. This anxiety then leads to the use of elaborate defense mechanisms for coping with the threat. If the incongruence between self and experience is too large or significant, defense may be unsuccessful and a state of profound disorganization occurs. Such a person may be labeled psychotic.

Empirical Support for the Theory

There have been many research tests of Rogers' original formulations, but there are problems in interpreting the data as supportive (Rogers, 1959). For example, a study by Chodorkoff (1954) is cited by Rogers as illustrating the manner in which the theory can be tested. Chodorkoff was interested in testing Rogers' ideas about the relationship between personal defensiveness and adjustment. This investigator hypothesized that the greater the agreement between a person's self-description and a description of him provided by others, the less perceptual defense he will show. This hypothesis was based on the assumption that the nondefensive person is open to all his experiences, threatening or otherwise. He should be able to assimilate them into his self-concept, providing they are organismically valid. Of course, it is assumed that the "objective" description by the judges mirrors the individual's own assessment on an organismic level. (This is a questionable assumption in view of Roger's repeated warnings that judgments based on diagnostic tests violate the individual's integrity and are, at best, only crude approximations of the person's experiencing.)

In the study, clinical judges provided descriptions based on biographical information and the results of two projective tests, the

Rorschach and the Thematic Apperception Test (TAT). Scores based on the degree of agreement between the two sets of ratings were then correlated with the person's perceptual defense score, as measured by the time it took the subject to react to tachistoscopic presentations of threatening words (for example, "bitch" and "whore") compared with time latencies for nonthreatening words (for example "chair" and "table"). As mentioned initially, the prediction was confirmed.

Another hypothesis tested was that the greater the agreement between the personal and objective descriptions of the person, the more adequate would be his personal adjustment. Adjustment was measured by having the judges check on a list any number of adjectives they thought described the subject, such as kind, confident, and well-liked. The more checks the person received, the greater his personal adjustment. This hypothesis was also confirmed.

It should be clear at this point that there is a considerable gap between Rogers' original theorizing and the measurement procedures used to assess its validity. In addition, the reliability and validity of the projective techniques can be questioned (Mischel, 1968, pp. 118–123). Despite the fact that the predictions were confirmed, we should be cautious in drawing conclusions about the validity of this part of the theory.

The Chodorkoff study is, however, only one example of early attempts to test parts of Rogers' theory. Since that investigation, there have been numerous attempts to put the theory to a more complete test, and to revise and elaborate on the original formulations.

Carkhuff's Helper-Helpee Therapeutic Model

Carkhuff (1969), for example, has presented an interesting and more differentiated view of the therapist-client variables that are an important part of any therapeutic relationship. He takes issue with the one-sided nature of the original client-centered therapy proposed by Rogers. In Rogers' original view, the therapist is discouraged from actively participating in the relationship and from discussing his own personal concerns and experiences. Carkhuff believes that such a view is artificial and can be harmful to the relationship. He proposes an interactional model in which both therapist and client take an active part in the process and have the opportunity to experience growth. In addition to active involvement, Carkhuff's model of facilitative growth processes consists of a variety of other factors:

> The therapist's personal characteristics, such as age, sex, and socioeconomic status, as well as specialized techniques and other specific influences upon his role concept are relevant. The therapist variables, in turn, may be meaningful insofar as they interact with client characteristics, including especially population types in addition to other personal characteristics. Situation

variables, such as the environmental setting and "atmosphere" in which therapy takes place as well as the "set" which the client has or has not been given . . . might also become extremely important considerations. (Carkhuff, 1963)

The success of therapy rests on the therapist's level of psychological health as he or she relates to the client. Carkhuff has utilized some of the same dimensions proposed by Rogers as an integral part of the effective therapist's personality. He also believes that the effective therapist is empathic, genuine, congruent, and has positive regard for the client. The effective therapist must be able to express his own feelings and experiences directly and completely, irrespective of their emotional content. This dimension, which Carkhuff calls *concreteness*, has been found in one study to be the most significant contributing factor in effective therapy, far exceeding the contributions of empathy, genuineness, and positive regard (Carkhuff and Berenson, 1967). Other variables involved in effective counseling include confrontation, respect, warmth, and self-disclosure.

Unlike Rogers, who believes people have an innate tendency for positive growth that can be facilitated by the understanding therapist, Carkhuff maintains that people have neither a disposition for constructive growth nor one for destructiveness. He thinks that growth, either positive or negative, is largely under the control of the important figures in a person's life, such as parents, teachers, and clergy (Carkhuff and Berenson, 1967, pp. 47–48). Improvement in therapy rests on the behavior of the therapist, as well as on the creative efforts of the client. Thus, the client who finds himself in a relationship with a facilitative helper may experience positive growth. If, on the other hand, he finds himself confronted by a helper who lacks empathy, genuineness, and positive regard, the outcome is likely to be disastrous. Thus, Carkhuff focuses more clearly than Rogers on the possible destructive consequences to a client of participating in a relationship with a low-level (nonfacilitative) therapist. There is also scientific evidence to support Carkhuff's contention.

Not only does Carkhuff present a more differentiated view of the therapist, he also sees the client in more complex terms. Like the therapist, the client has personality characteristics that can facilitate or hinder growth. If the client is worried about physical survival matters, for example, it is doubtful that he or she is in a position to profit from the therapy experience. By implication, then, the client must come into the relationship free from worries about money, food, clothing, and shelter, if he or she is to be in a position to benefit from treatment. Such a position is quite similar to that proposed by Maslow (see Chapter 12 for a more detailed exploration of the conditions that hinder movement toward self-actualization).

It should be clear from this discussion that helpers may function at different levels. Thus, in Carkhuff's view, they should be given forms of treatment suitable to their level of functioning. Client-centered therapy may work well with certain kinds of neurotics, but be unsuited for use with psychotics who have little contact with external reality. With this sketchy outline of Carkhuff's position in mind, let us turn now to a general assessment of the research evidence for his model.

Research Support for the Neo-Rogerian Model

The measurement and research problems confronting the researcher concerned with the process and outcomes of therapy are formidable. To his credit, Carkhuff has not evaded these problems, but has instead engaged in an active program designed to overcome them. He has constructed scales that purport to measure the primary personality dimensions therapists need to engage in effective therapy. These scales are based on judgments by independent raters of the counselor's possession of these qualities after listening to taperecordings of therapy sessions. At present, these scaling procedures are full of ambiguities. For example, there are problems in securing and training raters who are able to make discriminating and accurate judgments of therapist and client qualities and the effectiveness of the treatment. Other major problems include the focus in outcome studies on measuring personality change only in terms of client or therapist verbalizations or self-reports, but *not* in terms of changes in the client's behavior. There is also a lack of long-term followup studies. That is, most studies of treatment effectiveness assess only immediate changes in client functioning and do not make any attempt to assess the permanence of the change.

Despite these difficulties, a variety of studies lend support to Carkhuff's formulations and, by implication, to certain aspects of Rogers' theory. For example, some investigations have shown that therapists high on facilitative conditions (high on empathy, genuineness, and positive regard) are more effective in bringing about constructive growth in clients than therapists low on these conditions (Carkhuff and Berenson, 1967, p. 4). In a crucial study of the long-range effects of client-centered therapy, psychologist Truax showed that the clients of high-facilitative therapists showed lower recidivism rates than clients of low-facilitative therapists. Analyses also showed that the clients of high-facilitative helpers tended to show improvement over time, whereas the clients of nonfacilitative therapists deteriorated.

Although these studies and others provide support for the *neo-Rogerian model*, others yield nonconfirmatory or inconsistent results. Possible reasons include ambiguities in the measures of the primary dimensions and differences in the severity of the pathology in patients. It may be that therapists who are warm and accepting produce better results with certain kinds of patients—for example, schizophrenics—whereas other patients—for example, neurotics—may respond more favorably to therapists who are empathetic; that is, to therapists who show a more differentiated understanding of the client.

All in all, the research support for the neo-Rogerian model at the present time is sufficiently positive to warrant further exploration and testing. Given the complexity of the therapeutic process and the difficulty in measuring its various concepts, enormous strides have been made in the direction of understanding the variables that facilitate or hinder personality change.

TECHNIQUES OF ASSESSMENT

Rogers believes that assessment of the individual's personality must be based on an exploration of the person's feelings and attitudes toward himself or herself and others. It is the client who subjectively interprets experiences and who provides the therapist with valid information about his or her functioning. Rogers recognizes that this phenomenolgical extremism has its limitations. For example, the therapist can gain only that experiential information about the client that he or she is able or willing to articulate. In addition, the client may purposely distort reports to the therapist and reveal information he or she believes will win approval. Despite these limitations, Rogers believes that his client-centered approach provides a meaningful way to understand the individual's personality. The therapist provides a supportive and nonthreatening milieu for the client so that distortions and evasions are minimized. He or she also tries actively not to prejudge the client by fitting him or her into a preconceived theoretical structure. Under these conditions, the therapist may gain an increased and accurate understanding of the unique strengths and weaknesses of the person and the client will probably move toward self-realization.

Although Rogers argues against the use of formal assessment techniques in the study of the client's personality, he is forced to rely on measurement procedures to test his theory. In the Chodorkoff study, for example, judges' ratings were used to assess the person's organismic experiencing. Rogers has also been a pioneer in developing a technique for assessing the nature of the interactions between client and therapist and in showing how these data are related to the therapeutic outcome. The technique involves the use of video and audio taperecordings of the therapeutic process. These tapes provide a more comprehensive and available set of data for analysis and interpretation than has ever been possible, for earlier assessment procedures relied on written records of therapy sessions made by the therapist from memory.

Rogers has also conducted research concerned with the impact of client-centered therapy on personality functioning using an assessment procedure pioneered by Stephenson (1953) and labeled the *Q-sort*. The Q-sort is a technique designed to measure a person's self-concept. Rogers maintains that a self-concept should change over the course of therapy. He believes the initial discrepancies between the way in which clients actually view themselves and the way in which they like to view themselves are reduced by effective counseling. The Q-sort technique enables investigators to measure these discrepancies between actual and ideal selves. Upon entering therapy, clients are asked to sort a large number of self-referent statements on a continuum ranging from "not like me" to "like me." The list might include statements such as "I am a submissive person," "I am really disturbed," and "I am confident." After sorting the statements in terms of their actual selves, clients are asked to sort the same set of statements in terms of their views of their ideal selves on a continuum ranging from "like ideal" to "unlike ideal." The two sets of scores are then correlated. Correlations between sorts for clients entering therapy are generally low, suggesting large discrepancies between their actual and ideal selves whereas correlations for normals tends to be high and positive, suggesting few discrepancies in their views of themselves.

If therapy is effective, correlations should change from low to high and positive. Correlations for normal control subjects who do not receive client-centered therapy, on the other hand, should be high initially and remain so over time. In an early study designed to test the Rogerian approach, the results were supportive (Rogers and Dymond, 1954). The mean Pearson r for a precounseling group of clients was $-.01$. Following therapy, the correlation was .34. The controls showed an actual-ideal self correlation of .58 in precounseling and an r of .59 when they were tested in the follow-up. Unfortunately, this study has a number of methodological flaws, as noted by Eysenck (1960). One is that Rogers and his associates failed to equate their control and treatment groups in terms of initial psychological adjustment, so that it is impossible to assess the effectiveness of the client-centered therapy in producing changes in self-concept among the clients. (The reader interested in further elaboration of these criticisms is referred to the original Eysenck study, listed in the Suggested Readings at the end of the chapter.)

Rogers utilizes a variety of assessment procedures to ascertain the validity of his theory and the efficacy of his approach to therapy. Although this fact may seem to be in direct contradiction to his statements about the necessity for avoiding the use of techniques in therapy, a more reasonable interpretation might be that assessment procedures, although an inevitable and necessary part of the therapeutic process, should be deemphasized. They should not be allowed to become so important that they prevent the therapist from understanding the experiencing of clients.

APPLICATION OF THE THEORY TO THE TREATMENT OF PSYCHOPATHOLOGY

Neurotic and psychotic individuals are seen by Rogers as people who lack congruence between their self-concepts and their experiences. They are individuals who are afraid to accept their experiences as valid in their own right and who consequently distort them in order to protect themselves or to win positive regard from others. To overcome these problems, therapists must create the appropriate conditions for change and growth, as mentioned earlier. They must respect their clients, be warm and empathic, think and feel kind thoughts about them, be genuine and authentic in the relationship, and be concerned about their welfare. Under these conditions, Rogers theorizes that clients will be more willing and able to cope with their problems and anxieties. They will become aware of their own thought patterns and feelings and the kinds of relationships with others that are threatening. As a result of accurate symbolization, Rogers assumes that clients will be able to understand the sources and consequences of their difficulties and be in a position to modify them. They will then be on their way toward self-realization. In Rogers' terminology, the clients have an opportunity to become *full functioning persons.*

What are the characteristics of such healthy people? Rogers theorizes that they are people who "move away from facades." They become more real and genuine in their experiencing and more able to identify and to reject the false selves they have acquired. They are people in transition, moving away from the roles and expectations others have imposed on them. They are also people who are learning to trust themselves and to be open to their experiences. Finally, as they become more trusting of themselves, they move toward greater acceptance of others. In all this movement toward self-realization, Rogers wants it clearly understood that it is the client, not the therapist, who is responsible for growth. The therapist does indeed establish the conditions for progress, but it is the client who is the real agent of change.

Other Practical Applications

Rogers believes his theory has applicability in areas besides therapy, including family life, group leadership, and education (Rogers, 1959, pp. 241–242). As mentioned in the biographical summary, Rogers has passionate feelings about the harmful impact of graduate training on student development. Since this topic is of special importance to all of us, let us review Rogers' arguments in detail as well as attempt to rebut his contentions by two other psychologists, Brown and Tedeschi (1972).

Rogers begins his argument by stating that faculty members are doing an unintelligent and ineffectual job in preparing psychologists for their roles in society. The faculty is doing a poor job, according to Rogers, because it bases its programs on the following kinds of assumptions (Rogers, 1968, pp. 689–697).

1. *The student cannot be trusted to pursue his own scientific and professional learning.* In Rogers' view, the fact that faculty assign work to students, supervise their behavior, and then evaluate the product of their efforts is proof they do not trust students. He feels that a program in which the student is set free to pursue goals important to him would have greater educational benefit. It seems clear that Rogers is basing his judgments on his limited personal experience and that many faculty members would contend that they do trust their students. These faculty, like Brown and Tedeschi, would argue further that there is nothing really contradictory between having confidence and trust in a student and requiring him to accept certain responsibilities (Brown and Tedeschi, 1972, p. 8). For them, trust is based on mutual expectations or promises, and these promises can be fulfilled or violated.

When a faculty member makes an assignment, he has confidence that the student will accept the responsibility and fulfill it. If he did not trust the student, why make the assignment in the first place? Trust would also imply that the faculty member does not check continuously to see what the student is or is not doing, but this should not mean that he never makes an attempt to evaluate the end result of the student's efforts. Why? Because the student may have failed to fulfill his responsibilities. Two admittedly exaggerated cases will serve to make the point. What would you think of a pilot instructor who gave his pupils assignments concerning the workings of an aircraft and never checked to see what they were doing or never evaluated their progress by testing them? Would you conclude he was a good man, a person who was worthy of your respect, and one who trusted his students? Or would you call him a fool and an incompetent? For a second example, imagine a medical school faculty member who gave assignments to his students, never monitored their behavior, and never evaluated their performance. Would you trust his students after graduation to operate on you or members of your family?

In fairness to Rogers, he does see the necessity of some ability testing for students, and is really arguing that students should simply have more time to pursue their own goals (Rogers, 1968, p. 691). His argument, however, assumes that students themselves know what their goals in education are, a dubious assumption in view of the continual shifting of goals by many students throughout their undergraduate and even graduate school careers. In addition, goals important to students may be of little or no value to others. Obviously, people should have the right to pursue whatever goals they wish, and it is true that others may be wrong in assessing their potential usefulness to society. But the members of the established order also have the right to express their views and to act in terms of them.

2. *Creative scientists develop from passive learners.* Rogers objects strongly to what he considers the primary emphasis in graduate educational—that students are passive learners. Students are given information and expected to regurgitate that information on examinations. Rogers believes that such an emphasis stifles the production of original and creative ideals. Students are taught to conform, to defer coming to grips with their own ideas, and to accept unquestioningly the ideas of their professors. He argues further that, in an atmosphere of trust and mutual respect and freedom from constraints, students would be free to test their own ideas and to become creative individuals. Thus, according to Rogers, graduate students should be selected on three criteria: originality, intelligence, and independence of thought. If students who meet these criteria are educated in the atmosphere described above, both students and society will benefit.

Brown and Tedeschi argue that, in fact, many creative individuals throughout history have been impatient with the constraints of institutions. But these complaints "are interesting not because they tell us anything about the development of genius but because they tell us of their reactions to the formalities of the learning environment" (Brown and Tedeschi, 1972, p. 5). They maintain further that child prodigies such as John Stuart Mill, Charles Sanders Pierce, and Ludwig van Beethoven all learned under demanding circumstances and their creative impulses were not stifled. In addition, Brown and Tedeschi state:

> It is clear both from the evidence and from history that the mere absence of constraint or evaluation is not a necessary condition for the development of creative persons. Great ideas are not gathered while sitting under the banyan tree waiting for them to drop. Edison once said that creativity was 99% perspiration and 1% inspiration. What was meant is that the individual must gather a great deal of information that may be relevant for solving a problem. This assimilation process can be quite tedious and tests the motivational intensity of the individual's interest in the problem. Hence, there are times when the work takes on the form of sheer drudgery and there are times when the work is intensely exciting and exhilarating. (Brown and Tedeschi, 1972, p. 6)

Rogers' rebuttal is that Brown and Tedeschi ignore the fact that self-discipline is one of the most demanding and fruitful of all constraints, one that is present in almost every creative experience. But conformity does not breed this self-discipline. To the contrary, it breeds undisciplined people dependent on the evaluations of others (Rogers, 1972, pp. 17–18).

3. *Evaluation is education: Education is evaluation.* Rogers argues that "examinations have become the beginning and the end of education" (Rogers, 1968, p. 691). They are, in Rogers' view, stultifying the student.

He points out further that the graduate student at one university faces the following major evaluation obstacles (Rogers, 1968, p. 692):

1. Examination in first foreign language
2. Examination in second foreign language
3. First six-hour qualifying examination
4. Second six-hour qualifying examination (both of these in the first graduate year)
5. Three-hour examination in methodology and statistics
6. Four-hour examination in a chosen major field of psychology
7. Two-hour examination in a minor field
8. Oral examination on master's thesis
9. Committee evaluation of Ph.D. proposal
10. Committee evaluation of Ph.D. thesis
11. Oral examination on Ph.D. thesis

In addition to these hurdles, the student faces endless quizzes and final examinations in his courses. Such obstacles prevent the student from doing the real independent learning necessary to a creative life. I agree with Rogers on this point. Recent data indicate that many graduate departments in psychology still require examinations of the graduate student similar to those listed above (Merenda, 1974). It is doubtful that the student has sufficient time to pursue his own interests under such a grueling schedule. It would seem more reasonable to first ensure that the student has the basic concepts which are a prerequisite of creative activity by testing him early in graduate career and then to provide her or him with the latitude Rogers advocates.

CRITICAL COMMENTS

Let us examine Rogers' theory in terms of how well it meets the criteria outlined in Chapter 1 for acceptance of scientific theories.

Comprehensiveness. Although Rogers believes his principles involving facilitative growth in clients are also applicable to normal human beings, it seems apparent that most of his theorizing is concerned with the prediction of changes in self-concept on the part of troubled individuals. The focus of the theory is thus primarily on changes within the person that occur as a result of lowering defenses and coping with incompatibilities between the person's self-concepts and his experiences. Changes in self-concept are then presumed to be positively related to changes in actual behavior, although often no evidence is presented to support such an assumption. Rogers' theory could be said to account for diverse phenomena in the sense that changes in self-concept will have an impact on many different behaviors, but he makes little attempt to spell out precisely the implications of changes in self-concept for behavior.

Neither does he pay much attention to the variables that control the occurrence of diverse phenomena. For example, he has no theory of learning and has little to say about the developmental process. For these reasons, then, it can be argued that Rogers' theory is currently only moderately comprehensive.

Precision and Testability. To Rogers' credit, he has made a tremendous effort to construct a precise and testable theory. Yet, some of the concepts that he utilizes are vague and poorly defined. What are the specific dimensions subsumed under the self-actualization drive, for example? How is the self-concept defined? Is it possible to measure therapist genuineness and empathy in a reliable and valid way? We have already reviewed a number of measurement difficulties associated with the study of these concepts. Despite these criticisms, Rogers has made significant strides toward the creation of a theory with explicitly stated concepts and relational statements that are capable of being tested. Thus, it would seem that Rogers has created a theory which has attempted to account for a complex set of phenomena in an area where such creative efforts have been traditionally lacking.

Simplicity. Rogers' theory fails to meet the parsimony criterion. Although the data he chooses to examine are complex, he relies upon only a few concepts and assumptions in his explanatory system. He assumes, for example, that human beings are basically good and rational and that given the opportunity, they will make the right decisions. He recognizes human irrationality, but he does not devote sufficient attention to it in his account of personality functioning. His treatment of the ways in which defense mechanisms operate to control behavior is rather undifferentiated, especially when compared to the treatment accorded the subject by Freud, for example.

Empirical Validity. The judgment of how well Rogers' theory meets the validity criterion is a difficult one to make. Although there have been a number of tests of the theory, the results have been mixed. Generally, though, they provide some encouragement for investigators to continue their explorations and testing, especially when we realize that Rogers accepts many of the modifications of his original theory made by Carkhuff, and that this revised model has some empirical support and promise.

Heuristic Value. Rogers' views have been controversial in some quarters of psychology, and have provoked continued, vigorous debate. The neo-Rogerian model devised by Carkhuff and his associates provides a fine example of the stimulating nature of Rogers' position. Rogers' strong stand on the sanctity of the person is also a strength. His humanistic concern for the integrity and uniqueness of the individual has led many investigators to question views of men and women that picture them as automatons who simply react uncritically to environmental forces. His thinking has forced people to reconsider the importance of the self-concept in their theorizing.

Applied Value. Rogers' theory is very strong in the applied area. Aspects of it have been fruitfully applied to such diverse areas as education, family life, leadership, and therapy.

DISCUSSION QUESTIONS

1. Why did Rogers abandon the Freudian view of personality functioning?
2. In what ways is Rogers' position different from the one offered by Freud?
3. Discuss Rogers' concept of the "organismic valuing process" and how it is related to the development of the person. What scientific evidence is there to support the "organismic wisdom" hypothesis?
4. What are the consequences of an individual's need for positive regard?
5. What are some of the "conditions of worth" that you have placed upon your parents? What "conditions of worth" have they attached to your behavior?
6. In what ways does the neo-Rogerian model of therapeutic growth espoused by Carkhuff differ from the one offered originally by Rogers?
7. Why does Rogers feel that many educators are doing an ineffectual job in educating people? Do you agree with him? Can you cite additional problems with the current educational system? What are some of its strengths?
8. Do you believe it is possible to be creative without learning the basic concepts in a discipline first? Why?
9. What are some of the major problems of the Chodorkoff study cited in this chapter?
10. What are some of the possible consequences to a person holding the Rogerian belief that "evaluation by others is no guide for me"?

NOTES

R. C. Brown and J. T. Tedeschi, "Graduate Education and Psychology: A Comment on Rogers' Passionate Statement," *Journal of Humanistic Psychology,* 1972, **12,** 1–15.

R. R. Carkhuff, "On the Necessary Conditions of Therapeutic Personality Change," *Discussion Papers, Wisconsin Psychiatric Institute* (University of Wisconsin, 1963).

R. R. Carkhuff, *Helping and Human Relations,* Vols. I and II (New York: Holt, Rinehart and Winston, 1969).

R. R. Carkhuff and B. G. Berenson, *Beyond Counseling and Therapy* (New York: Holt, Rinehart and Winston, 1967).

B. Chodorkoff, "Self-Perception, Perceptual Defense, and Adjustment," *Journal of Abnormal and Social Psychology*, 1954, **49,** 508–512.

C. M. Davis, "Self-Selection of Diet by Newly Weaned Infants," *American Journal of Diseases of Children*, 1928, **36,** 651–679.

H. J. Eysenck, "The Effects of Psychotherapy," in H. J. Eysenck, ed., *Handbook of Abnormal Psychology: An Experimental Approach* (London: Pitman Medical Publishing, 1960).

J. Garcia, D. J. Kimeldurf, and E. L. Hunt, "The Use of Ionizing Radiation as a Motivating Stimulus," *Psychological Review*, 1961, **68,** 383–395.

E. E. Krieckhaus, "Innate Recognition Aids Rate in Sodium Regulation," *I.C.C.P.*, 1970, **73,** 117–122.

P. F. Merenda, "Current Status of Graduate Education in Psychology," *American Psychologist*, 1974, **29,** 627–631.

W. Mischel, *Personality and Assessment* (New York: Wiley, 1968).

C. R. Rogers, "A Theory of Therapy, Personality, and Interpersonal Relationships, as Developed in the Client-Centered Framework," in S. Koch, ed., *Psychology: A Study of a Science*, Vol. 3 (New York: McGraw-Hill, 1959).

C. R. Rogers, *On Becoming a Person* (Boston: Houghton Mifflin, 1961).

C. R. Rogers, "Graduate Education in Psychology: A Passionate Statement," in W. G. Bennis, E. H. Schein, F. I. Steele, and D. E. Berlew, eds., *Interpersonal Dynamics*, 2nd ed. (Homewood, Ill.: Dorsey Press, 1968).

C. R. Rogers, "Comment on Brown and Tedeschi's Article," *Journal of Humanistic Psychology*, 1972, **12,** 16–21.

C. R. Rogers and R. F. Dymond, *Psychotherapy and Personality Change* (Chicago: University of Chicago Press, 1954).

H. E. Rogers, "A Wife's View of Carl Rogers," *Voices*, 1965, **1,** 93–98.

W. Stephenson, *The Study of Behavior* (Chicago: University of Chicago Press, 1953).

SUGGESTED READINGS

Eysenck, H. J. "The Effects of Psychotherapy," In H. J. Eysenck, ed., *Handbook of Abnormal Psychology: An Experimental Approach.* London: Pitman Medical Publishing, 1960, pp. 697–725.

Rogers, C. R. *Counseling and Psychotherapy: Newer Concepts in Practice.* Boston: Houghton Mifflin, 1942.

Rogers, C. R. *Client-Centered Therapy: Its Current Practice, Implications, and Theory.* Boston: Houghton Mifflin, 1951.

Rogers, C. R. "A Theory of Therapy, Personality, and Interpersonal Relationships, as Developed in the Client-Centered Framework," in S. Koch, ed., *Psychology: A Study of a Science*, Vol. 3. New York: McGraw-Hill, 1959, pp. 184–256.

Rogers, C. R. *On Becoming a Person.* Boston: Houghton Mifflin, 1961.

Rogers, C. R. "In Retrospect: Forty-six Years," *American Psychologist*, 1974, **29**, 115–123.

Rogers, C. R. and B. Stevens. *Person to Person: The Problems of Being Human.* New York: Simon and Schuster, 1971.

GLOSSARY

Condition of Worth. People's beliefs that they are worthwhile only if they perform behaviors that others think are good and refrain from performing those actions others think are bad.

Congruity. State of harmony that occurs when there is no discrepancy between the person's experiencing and his or her self-concept.

Fully Functioning Person. Individual who is utilizing his or her potentials to the maximum degree.

Need for Positive Regard. Learned or innate tendency on the part of individuals to seek the approval of others.

Neo-Rogerian Model. Theory of personality functioning developed by Carkhuff that modifies and extends Rogers' original theorizing.

Organismic Wisdom. The hypothesis that a person will innately choose what is "best" for him, will direct his behavior toward satisfying his need for self-actualization.

Q-Sort. Self-report assessment procedure designed to measure the discrepancy between the person's actual and ideal selves.

Rollo May (Courtesy of Mark Kaufman)

CHAPTER 14

May's Existential– Analytic Position

BIOGRAPHICAL SKETCH

Rollo May was born in a small town in Ohio in 1909. He received a bachelor of arts degree from Oberlin College in 1930, a bachelor of divinity degree from Columbia in 1938, and a Ph.D. in clinical psychology from that institution in 1949. During the thirties and forties he worked as a counselor to students at both Michigan State University and City College of New York. In addition to his private practice as a psychotherapist, he has served as a faculty member at a variety of institutions, including New York University, Harvard, Yale, and Princeton. He has also published a number of texts, including *The Art of Counseling* (1939), *The Meaning of Anxiety* (1950), *Man's Search for Himself* (1953), *Psychology and the Human Dilemma* (1967), *Love and Will* (1969), the *Courage to Create* (1975), and an edited volume with E. Angel and H. F. Ellenberger of articles by leading advocates of the existential view entitled *Existence: A New Dimension in Psychiatry and Psychology* (1958).

May is currently a supervisory and training analyst at the William Alanson White Institute of Psychiatry, Psychology, and Psychoanalysis in New York City.

BASIC CONCEPTS AND PRINCIPLES

What Is Existentialism?

The term *existentialism* has become popular in academic and literary circles and is used in so many different ways by philosophers, psychologists, theologians, novelists, actors, and others that it has almost lost its meaning. In the popular mind, it is a term equated with things like gloom and despair, not to mention suicide and death. For some, it suggests that the world is an absurd place with no meaning and is invoked self-righteously when any misfortune befalls them. Since the concept is so central to an understanding of May's position, it might be wise to trace its use historically by leading philosophers and exponents.

Existentialism has its roots in the nineteenth-century writings of the Danish philosopher Soren Kierkegaard. Kierkegaard's attempts to understand human functioning were based to a large degree on his rejection of Hegel's monumental effort to understand reality by identifying it with abstract thought and logic (May, 1973, p. 200). Kierkegaard, and later Nietzsche, sought to correct the one-sidedness of Hegel's arguments by starting the analysis with a focus on the basic realities of people's existence or *Dasein*. Thus, existentialism is concerned with *ontology* or the study of the core of one's being. It focuses directly on personal experiences and tries to avoid analyzing the lives of people by means of logical systems that treat human beings as abstracted, impersonal objects.

Proponents of this philosophy, and especially Kierkegaard, argued that we must not treat truth as something detached from human experience. Truth can only be known, according to Kierkegaard, by starting with the person's perception of it as it relates to natural phenomena. According to Rollo May, Kierkegaard's insight changed our way of thinking about truth, and his radical stance has had tremendous implications for all scientific endeavors, including psychology. Kierkegaard has given us the concept of relational truth, an idea that was the forerunner of the notion of relativity. In other words, May (1958b, p. 26) believes Kierkegaard has shown us that ". . . the *subject*, man, can never be separated from the *object* which he observes." Thus existentialism can be defined as ". . . the endeavor to understand man by cutting below the cleavage between subject and object which has bedeviled Western thought and science since shortly after the Renaissance" (May, 1958b, p. 11).

What exactly are some of the major problems with Western science as seen by existentialists? One is that the traditional approach to the study of human beings uses scientific methods which treat people as *objects*. Orthodox scientists have tended to view us in an impersonal way and to restrict themselves to detached and objective measurement of our behavior. According to the existentialists, this value-free approach is incorrect. In their view, we are human beings, first and foremost, and the scientific approach should emerge from that fundamental fact. As one prominent existentialist puts it

> Man may seek the meaning of science by approaching it as a typically human endeavor and asking: What is it in human nature that leads to the emergence of the scientific attitude? . . . Once I have the answer to this question . . . I may begin to grasp what science really means. From that moment on, I may be able to trace back to man's existence all forms, aims, and methods of science and to demonstrate that they are manifestations of his nature. (Van Kaam, 1969, p. 15)

What the existentialists are maintaining, in effect, is that we bring the *subject*—that is, our own "inner world" of experiences—into our view of science. This does not imply that they think the object side of the reality equation should be dismissed. Rather, they believe we should focus first on our own subjective experiences in the formulation of problems to be studied, and then proceed to study them in as objective a way as possible. By proceeding in this manner, the horse is put before the cart, and not the cart before the horse. Scientists should also try to adapt their methods of study to meaningful human problems, and not tailor their problems to a restricted methodology borrowed from physics or physiology (Van Kaam, 1969, p. 26). May tells us an amusing story of what might eventually happen to psychologists who avoid studying the complexities of human experience and focus solely on behavior that can be precisely and objectively quantified:

> A psychologist—any psychologist, or all of us—arrives at the heavenly gates at the end of his long and productive life. He is brought up before St. Peter for the customary accounting. . . . An angel assistant in a white jacket drops a manila folder on the table which St. Peter opens and looks at, frowning. St. Peter's frown deepens. He drums with his fingers on the table and grunts a few nondirective "uhm-uhms" as he fixes the candidate with his Mosaic eyes.
>
> The silence is discomfiting. Finally, the psychologist opens his briefcase and cries, "Here! The reprints of my hundred and thirty-two papers."
>
> St. Peter slowly shakes his head. . . . At last [he] speaks, "I'm aware, my good man, [of] how industrious you were. It's not sloth you're accused of. . . . [Then he] slaps his hand resoundingly down on the table, and his tone is like Moses breaking the news of the ten commandments. "You are charged with *Nimis simplicandum!* [Oversimplifying]. You have spent your life making molehills out of mountains—that's what you're guilty of. When man was tragic, you made him trivial. . . . When he suffered passively, you described him as simpering; and when he drummed up enough courage to act, you called it stimulus and response. . . . You made man over into the image of your childhood Erector Set or Sunday School maxims—both equally horrendous. (May, 1967, pp. 3–4)

In May's story, there is no ending. There is only the implication that eternal damnation is waiting for psychologists and other investigators in the sciences who study human beings, who continue to dissect the human experience, and who, by so doing, tend to trivialize it. May also takes issue with proponents who utilize only the subjective or objective views of reality in their formulations (May, 1967, pp. 15–20). As examples, he mentions the positions of Rogers and Skinner. He maintains that Rogers overemphasizes the subjective side of our natures. Rogers is also guilty, in May's view, of assuming that we are "exquisitely rational" and will always make the "right" choices if we are given an opportunity. In May's opinion, Rogers is wrong because he ignores the irrational side of our natures. Skinner, in contrast, places too much emphasis on the objective side of human behavior. He is concerned almost exclusively with the ways in which the manipulation of precisely defined, environmental variables determine behavior and ignores the subjective side of human functioning.

May believes both views of human nature are necessary for a science of psychology and for meaningful living. He maintains that we are all faced with the dilemma of living in both modes or "worlds" at once. In his words, "[t]he human dilemma is that which arises out of a man's capacity to experience himself as both subject and object at the same time" (May, 1967, p. 8). A major aspect of the dilemma is that we know we are subject to illness, death, and the limitations of intelligence and experience, and other deterministic forces. At the same time we realize we have the subjective freedom to choose to relate to these objective and deterministic forces. We alone can assign meaning to them. We are responsible for our own destinies. Of course, strict determinists like Skinner (see Chapter 9) would say that all our behavior is determined, including our belief that we are free to make our own decisions. They would maintain further that we consider only those options determined by our past experiences and by current stimulation from the external environment.

Besides the compelling points made by early existentialists concerning the subject-object dichotomy, a number of other interesting ideas put forth by prominent figures in the movement have contributed to existentialism's growth in popularity since World War II. These contributors include the philosophers Heidegger, Jaspers, Merleau-Ponty, Tillich, Camus, and Sartre, among others, and the psychotherapists Binswanger, Boss, Frankl, and May. Although existentialism cannot be called a systematic and unified philosophy, these positions do have certain features in common.

One such commonality concerns the fact that all take the *person* as the starting point in their analyses of human existence. They all ask fundamental questions about existence. Who am I? What is the meaning of life? Is there a meaning to life? Is life worth living? How do I realize my potentialities? How do I become an individual?

Another similiarity is that, in order to move toward answers the existentialists focus on the immediate experience of the person as he exists in the world. The person views the world of natural phenomena from a subjective perspective. He faces a world filled with the uncertainties, a world which, in many respects, is absurd. The greatest absurdity from their viewpoint is that the person realizes he is finite and must die. Death is the great equalizer. All his accomplishments, all his hopes and dreams, will inevitably be blasted into oblivion at some point in time. The key question for the person under these circumstances is: What should I do? Should I retreat into nothingness or should I, in Tillich's words, have the courage to be? It is up to the person to make a choice and take action. As Kierkegaard said, "Truth exists only as the individual himself produces it in action" (May, 1958b, p. 12). The individual must also be committed to the goals he chooses to pursue.

Thus, it is clear that the person assumes almost godlike status in the existential design. He must assign meaning to his existence and act in terms of it. He must exercise his freedom and act authentically. To be authentic, the person must be who he is. He acts inauthentically when he lets other people define his goals and tell him how he should behave.

The fundamental choice certainly seems obvious if we assume that nothingness and suicide are synonymous. But how many people choose suicide, the ultimate form of nothingness? Nothingness can be seen in less extreme terms as well. A person may choose not to exercise his freedom to be. He may avoid commitment to goals and responsibilities. He may decide to follow the moral dictates of the crowd. These are all forms of nonbeing or nothingness. He may make these decisions because it is easier than facing his responsibilities. The exercise of freedom is costly. In many instances it creates severe anxiety, and an immediate and easier way of coping with it is to lose oneself by accepting the moral values dictated by society. Such acceptance of values at variance with one's being leads to self-alienation, apathy, and despair. We can see clearly here the similarity between the existentialists and Rogers and Maslow. Human existence is seen as a continuous struggle for the person as he tries to deal with the problems of life and to move toward the realization of his potentialities.

Existentialism and Psychoanalysis

The major applications of existentialism to personality and psychotherapy have come from the work of people trained in classical psychoanalysis. In order to better understand May's position, which is, in general, an integration of the Freudian and existentialist positions, let us look at some of the similarities and differences between the two approaches to the study of human behavior.

First, both psychoanalysis and existentialism ask fundamental questions about human existence. Although Freud was distrustful of philosophy and mere speculation, he nevertheless frankly acknowledged at an early point in his career that he was vitally concerned with the great problems of human existence and with understanding human nature (see Chapter 2). Both positions also focus on the irrational as well as the rational side of our natures. The existentialists talk about the inevitability of death and nothingness and the varied ways in which we try to cope with it. Freud too recognized the overwhelming importance of death in the psyche of the individual and incorporated it into his theory in terms of a self-destructive urge he called the Death Instinct. Freud was also quite pessimistic about our long-range chances for survival as a species because he believed that we have within us the seeds for our own destruction.

Although the existentialists have generally been labeled by critics as unduly concerned with death and highly pessimistic, a careful reading of their work suggests that this opinion is not entirely correct. It is true death is given a high priority in their formulations, but they would argue that their stance is quite reasonable since death "touches" us all. They would maintain further that their focus may be seen as morbid because many of us have an unrealistic view of death and have been taught from a very early age to avoid thinking about it. Accordingly, they would argue that we are the ones with the unhealthy attitude, not they:

> Throughout the ages men have shunned the sight of death and the mention of death, and they have devised innumerable ways of assuring themselves, when the reality of death inevitably confronts them, that death does not really change anything and that after death it will be business as usual. In contemporary America the attempts to deprive death of its reality are just as frantic as they ever were in any culture—the embalming of bodies, the expensive caskets designed to delay as long as possible decay and decomposition, soft music piped into the tombs. Then there is the deep-freezing of bodies, in the hope that one day medicine will have discovered a cure for the victim's disease, and there can take place a joyous (?) resurrection.

> It is, of course, natural to fear death or to be anxious in the face of death. But this is very different from constructing a vast cultural illusion (to say nothing of a highly profitable industry) to help us forget about death or to persuade ourselves that it is unreal. (Macquarrie, 1972, pp. 154–155)

In addition, not all existentialists treat death in the same way. Some are more optimistic than others. For example, Sartre sees death as the final absurdity, but Heidegger maintains that an honest acceptance of death can help us to live more authentically and happily (Macquarrie, 1972, p. 155). Thus, the existentialists disagree among themselves as to the meaning of death for human existence.

The next point of agreement between advocates of the two positions lies in their concern with the alleviation of human suffering. Both Freudians and existentialists discuss the ways in which conflict and anxiety disrupt functioning. Some existentialists focus on the positive features of anxiety, on anxiety as a prerequisite of self-affirmation. Both groups also assume that people often deal with severe anxiety by avoiding responsibilities. For the existentialists, people deny what they really *are* (Boss, 1963, p. 68). Freudians talk about the avoidance of responsibility through the repression of impulses that are an integral part of human nature.

Both positions blame society to a large extent for not allowing people to be true to their natures. In the Freudian scheme, society works through superego mechanisms to restrain the expression of "uncivilized" impulses. In the existential design, society often waylays individuals by inducing them to behave in inauthentic and self-alienating ways. Finally, advocates of both positions are deeply concerned with understanding human nature. Freud, like the existentialists, sought to free people from illusions about themselves and to get them to recognize who they really are (Boss, 1963, p. 62).

Despite these commonalities, there are a number of interesting and provocative differences between the two positions. As you probably guessed from our discussion of the subject-object dichotomy, the existentialists disapprove strongly of Freud's attempts to fashion a science of human nature by relying on an abstract and logical system of thought. The existentialists want to avoid creating "lofty" theories removed from human experience. As Kierkegaard proclaimed, "away from Speculation, away from the System, and back to reality" (May, 1958b, p. 25). By reality, he meant experience as it is immediately given to us. This phenomenological stance, which is so characteristic of existential thought, is quite different from Freud's attempts to objectify experience, to measure and calculate it precisely.

In the existential view, Freudian theorizing also led to a reductionism that violates the unity of experience. Reductionism means lessening an entity by changing it from one state to another. For example, the existentialists accuse Freud of changing complex human experience into a few hypothetical components which he called id, ego, and superego. They accuse him of intellectualizing and analyzing the interplay of these three components in a structure he called the psyche. Such a reductionism destroyed his primary understanding of our "being-in-the-world," according to them.

One further result of Freud's emphasis on the use of objective techniques to study behavior, according to the existentialists, was that it limited his sphere of investigation. Existentialists contend that the stress on technique dictated the kinds of problems Freud considered worthy of investigation. They maintain that these techniques led Freud to investigate problems in the *Umwelt* or the world of man in his biological environment, but prevented him from dealing with or comprehending the problems faced by people in their *Mitwelt*, their sphere of personal relations with their fellow men and women, or their *Eigenwelt*, the world of their relationships with themselves (May, 1958b, p. 34). Existentialists take a much more interactionist stance in their inquiries and stress problems and issues that involve not only the biology of the person, but his attempts to relate to others and to himself. They want to develop a science that aims to understand the unique problems of men and women, but not by fragmentizing their humanity (May, 1958b, p. 36).

With these distinctions firmly in mind, we turn now to an examination of May's position.

The Disintegration of Values in Modern Society

May begins his theory by pointing out that we live in an age of transition in which our values and goals are continually being called into question. According to him, one central value that did have a positive impact on our society in some respects in the nineteenth century was individual competitiveness. It was necessary for people to utilize a philosophy of "each man for himself" to ensure the clearing of the frontier and economic growth and to secure benefits for the community. Fromm and others might argue that the barons of industry who operated in the last century continually exploited the members of society as they sought to maximize their own gains (see Chapter 5). May, however, is not talking about the unbridled capitalism of the nineteenth century but about the competitiveness that emphasized social welfare during frontier times (May, 1953, p. 48). He argues that today we have lost the notion of individual competition designed to maximize the prosperity of all. Instead, we have adopted an unhealthy, exploitative competitiveness that ". . . makes every [person] the potential enemy of his neighbor, . . . generates much interpersonal hostility and resentment and increases our anxiety and isolation from each other" (May, 1953, p. 48). To hide our feelings of hostility, May contends we have become a nation of joiners. As adolescents, we give allegiance to peer groups. As adults, we belong to civic organizations and social clubs. We develop strong needs to be accepted and well-liked, according to May, and this orientation has led to a deepening self-alienation and dissatisfaction.

Another central value we have lost is a belief in the efficacy of reason in solving problems (May, 1953, pp. 49–50). May maintains that during the Enlightenment in the eighteenth century this belief led to magnificent advances in science and education. In the nineteenth century, the belief became corrupted. People began to split reason from emotion. To reason was rational and good; to feel was irrational and bad. In this century, reason was supposed to provide the answers to our problems, but obviously it has not. This fragmentation of reason and emotion is also seen in the Freudian scheme of human nature, in which unacceptable instincts and emotions are repressed by ego and superego functions based, in part at least, on rational input from others in the environment. Such compartmentalization has led, in May's view, to a splitting of the personality and of the person so that we act inappropriately—that is, in terms of either reason or emotion—in situations which call for unity in our experiencing.

The third value we have lost is our sense of worth and dignity (May, 1953, p. 55). In May's view, this loss of sense of self grows partially out of the fact that people feel they are powerless to change the operations of government and business. Government and business are seen as huge, impersonal enterprises unresponsive to the needs of society. In the recent past, for example, government leaders arbitrarily committed us and our resources to an undeclared war that did untold damage to the national psyche. Feelings of powerlessness also accrue in a worsening economy where inflation and recession operate simultaneously to raise the cost of living almost beyond the capacity of its citizens to pay and to terminate the jobs of millions of workers with little or no warning. In such a threatening and uncertain world, people feel the situation is beyond their control. They come to feel they are pawns in a terrifying game in which a few mediocre men make moves that affect their destinies. Of course, the situation is not quite as simplistic and one-sided as May would have us believe, but he has pointed out an orientation that characterizes some people in our culture. (See the material on internal and external individuals in Chapter 10 for a review of the characteristics and behavior of people who feel powerless and how they differ from those of individuals who feel they are in control of their destinies.)

Next, May maintains that many of us have lost not only our sense of identity, but our sense of relatedness to nature (May, 1953, p. 68). In his opinion, we have been too concerned in Western society with the development of techniques to master nature and not concerned enough with understanding our relationship to it. Perhaps the romantic, back-to-earth movement in this country can be seen as a reaction to an indiscriminate emphasis on technology. Because of our anxiety and emptiness, we have lost our feelings for and sense of awe about nature (May, 1953, p. 69). Our task, as May sees it, is to fill the impersonality of nature with our own aliveness and awareness. We must confront the power and vastness of nature and relate to nature creatively (May, 1953, p. 75) (note the similarity between May's ideas and those presented by Fromm in Chapter 5).

May argues that our sense of worthlessness leads to a loss of the sense of the tragic significance of human life (May, 1953, p. 75). For May, tragedy is an integral part of the human experience. It implies the fall of someone who believes strongly in his own dignity and worth. It also implies a final optimism, because it suggests that we take our freedom seriously and continue to struggle to achieve our potentialities.

Emptiness and Loneliness

The primary result of the confusion that comes from the disintegration of values is that we feel "empty" inside and isolated from other men and women. The vastness and complexity of the problems that confront us contribute to these feelings. For May, however, feelings of emptiness should not be taken to mean that we are literally empty or without potential for feeling (May, 1953, p. 24). Instead, the experience of emptiness comes from feelings of powerlessness in which events seem beyond our control. We do not seem to be able to direct our own lives, to influence others, or to change the world around us. As a result, we tend to feel a deep sense of despair and futility. Eventually, if we see that our actions make no difference, we give up wanting and feeling. We become apathetic. In May's opinion, the greatest danger at this point is that the attempt to defend ourselves against despair will lead to painful anxiety. At that point, if the situation goes uncorrected, the result is the restriction of our potential to grow as human beings or our surrender to some destructive form of authoritarianism (May, 1953, pp. 25–26).

May also believes there is a close association between emptiness and loneliness. He contends that when we do not know what we want or feel and when we stand in the midst of a general upheaval and confusion about values in our society, we sense danger and turn to the people around us for answers (May, 1953, p. 27). We may turn to them because we have been taught by society to rely on others in times of crisis. Yet, paradoxically, the more we attempt to reach out to others to ease our feelings of loneliness, the more lonely and desperate we become. Many of us need to be "going with someone" all the time in order to feel safe and secure. We tend to cling to partners we really do not like or respect. We are afraid that others will think less of us if we do not have a "steady." As a result, we suffer in silence and try to make the best of a bad situation. We learn to "adjust" to the person, to stifle our own individuality in order to protect the status quo. We yearn for security and yet are stifled by it.

Part of the syndrome also involves seeking invitations to parties or dinners or other outings with people. Often we do not especially want to go, but feel compelled to as a means of proving to ourselves that we are not alone and that we are acceptable to others. We know we have "made it" if we are continually sought after and if we are never alone. We do not even see the positive value of solitude (May, 1953, p. 26). We must be accepted in order to consider ourselves alive. This compulsive need for acceptance may not manifest itself among college students in some of the ways described, but consider the frantic search for acceptance among some students in the form of the same clothes and the same opinions. The search for acceptance is also seen in attempts to be as average academically as possible. There is an effort not to be different. There is ridicule of academic excellence and an extolling of mediocrity. There is safety in being average and anti-intellectual. There is also security. But May maintains that such pursuits are illusory and, in the final analysis, harmful to human growth. They are temporarily comforting, but the eventual price is that we give up our existences as identities in our own right. We avoid relying on ourselves and renounce the one thing that would help us overcome our loneliness in the long run—the development of our inner resources and values (May, 1953, p. 33).

The Emergence of Anxiety

According to May, feelings of anxiety stem from loneliness and emptiness. Like Freud, he believes that anxiety signals a conflict within us. Their theorizing about the nature and source of the conflict, however, differs. For Freud, the conflict was nearly always sexual in nature. It generated anxiety, and the person reduced these unpleasant feelings by banning the conflict from consciousness. For May, anxiety is not simply an unpleasant feeling; it is ". . . the human being's basic reaction to a danger to his existence, or to some value he identifies with his anxiety" (May, 1953, p. 40). It is "the experience of the threat of imminent nonbeing" (May, 1958b, p. 50). An example might be the rejection of friendship overtures. In such a case, the threat or anxiety may strike at the core of the individual's being. Another example might be the student who flunks out of the university. Such an outcome may strike at the very center of the person's sense of self. As May puts it, ". . . anxiety can be understood only as a threat to *Dasein*" (May, 1958a, p. 51). Thus anxiety, in May's theory, is to be understood in ontological terms.

In May's position, the conflict that generates ontological anxiety is between being and nonbeing. Anxiety occurs as the individual attempts to realize his potentialities. In the example above about an attempt to be friendly, the individual who has been rejected faces a fundamental conflict between being and nonbeing: He can try to understand the reasons for the rejection by questioning the other person or he can avoid asking questions that may prove embarrassing. The person is thus faced with a fundamental choice, but a choice that generates anxiety. He has the freedom to move forward or backward, and it makes him anxious. Kierkegaard describes this feeling of anxiety as the "dizziness of freedom" (May, 1958a, p. 52). If the person decides to assume responsibility and questions the person, he is using the experience of anxiety constructively. If he fails to ask the pertinent questions he is denying his responsibility and blocking the realization of his potentialities. In this case, May would say he is guilty. Like anxiety, then, guilt is also an ontological characteristic of human existence (May, 1957, p. 52). But ontological guilt does not occur because the person fails to act in terms of cultural prohibitions, as Freud thought. It occurs because an individual who can choose fails to do so (May, 1958a, p. 55). Such a person fails to act in terms of his central need in life—the fulfillment of his potentialities (May, 1953, p. 93).

Coping with Anxiety and the Expansion of Consciousness

In May's theory, individuals fulfill their potentialities only to the extent that they, in their own consciousness, plan and choose their goals (May, 1953, p. 94). Furthermore, he believes that the more conscious of ourselves we are, the more spontaneous and creative we will be at the same time (May, 1953, p. 104). Our objective, then, would clearly be an increase in consciousness. Severe anxiety tends to restrict our consciousness, according to May, and we try to defend ourselves from pain through a variety of defense mechanisms, including those first postulated by Freud. These defenses help us avoid coping with our own being and are thus detrimental to growth.

In May's view, the sense of being that needs to be uncovered refers to our capability of seeing ourselves as beings-in-the world, who are capable of dealing with the problems of our existence. It is fundamental, and not identical with the ego. The Freudian ego, according to May, was conceived of as weak and passive and as being buffeted by id impulses and admonishments from the superego. It has little of the vitality and aliveness associated with a sense of being. Movement toward realization begins with awareness of our potentialities as we journey toward becoming fully human (May, 1958a, pp. 46–47). In such a state, there is a gradual unfolding of our potentialities.

THE PROCESS OF PERSONALITY DEVELOPMENT

May's discussion of the developmental process centers on the physical and psychological ties between us and our parents and their substitutes—teachers, friends, clergy. He begins by noting our physical dependence on our mothers because we are all fed as fetuses through the umbilical cord. This tie is severed at birth, but physical dependency remains. As we grow older, physical dependence tends to subside, but psychological dependence often does not. This to May is a major problem, and the way in which we handle it will determine in large degree whether or not we will move toward maturity and personal growth. We must make a decision to assume responsibility for our actions or to let others make our decisions for us. In May's words, ". . . the conflict is between every human being's need to struggle toward enlarged self-awareness, maturity, freedom and responsibility, and his tendency to remain a child and cling to the protection of parents or parental substitutes" (May, 1953, p. 193).

The classic Oedipal conflict postulated by Freud is reinterpreted by May in terms of this dependency struggle. Whereas Freud believed the conflict was sexual in nature, May sees it in terms of a power confrontation. The struggle focuses on our attempts to establish autonomy and identity in our relationships with people who are very powerful. This battle for freedom also involves our going through several stages of consciousness (May, 1953, pp. 138–139). The first stage is simply our innocence as infants before a consciousness of self is created. The second stage is one of rebellion in which we seek to establish our inner strength. This struggle typically takes place, in May's view, at age two or three and during adolescence. Although rebellion is seen as a necessary step in the evolution of consciousness, it should not be confused with freedom. Rebellion involves defiance and an active rejection of parental and societal rules. Such behavior is automatic, rigid, and reflexive. True freedom, in contrast, involves ". . . *openness*, a readiness to grow; it means being flexible, ready to change for the sake of greater human values" (May, 1953, p. 159).

The third stage involves the ordinary consciousness of self. At this point we are capable of understanding some of our errors and of recognizing some of our prejudices. We are also capable of learning from our mistakes and assuming responsibility for our actions. May maintains that many people identify such a state of consciousness with being, maturity, and health. But, he argues, there is still another stage, a fourth stage of consciousness, which if attained actually signifies maturity. He calls this stage the creative consciousness of self. It is a stage that transcends the usual limits of consciousness. We are able to see the truth without distortion. These moments of insight are joyous ones and occur only occasionally. Note the similarity between May's ideas of the various levels of consciousness and Maslow's argument about the self-actualization process. Peak experiences and creative consciousness appear to be interchangeable terms.

We attain maturity and move close to self-realization when we experience these joyous moments. We are able to make choices, confront our problems, and take responsibility for our actions. We are not pushed along by deterministic forces. We are not bound by the past, by our role training, by the standards we have been taught by others. We are conscious of these forces, but are capable of coping with them and freely choosing to act in terms of them or not. As May puts it, ". . . consciousness of self gives us the power to stand outside the rigid chain of stimulus and response, to pause, and by this pause to throw some weight on either side, to cast some decision about what the response will be" (May, 1953, p. 161). Opponents might argue that this view is nonsensical and that our behavior is not really determined by some incredibly vague term called "consiousness of self." "How can a phantom make a decision for us?" they might ask.

May might counter this criticism with the argument that, although behavior is often determined by other events, we still have the freedom to make choices. May maintains that we move away from self-realization and maturity when our consciousness is restricted or stifled. Such a lessening of consciousness results from threats to our sense of being or existence. Neurosis and psychosis are seen by him as attempts to adjust to these threats. They are ways of accepting nonbeing so that some aspect of being can be preserved (May, 1967, p. 117). To cope with the threats to our being, we repress or distort our experiences through defensive manuevers. The overwhelming threats then recede into unconsciousness. But through these manuevers we deny our own freedom to make choices. We shrink from our responsibilities, and reject our own potentialities (May, Angel, and Ellenberger, 1958).

TECHNIQUES OF ASSESSMENT

Like Rogers, May is not primarily concerned with the use of a variety of techniques in his attempts to understand human functioning. Instead, his primary focus in the therapeutic relationship is on the dynamic encounter between the two participants. In fact, May believes that a premature emphasis on technique may actually hinder understanding:

> Existential analysis is a way of understanding human existence, and its representatives believe that one of the chief (if not *the* chief) blocks to the understanding of human beings in Western culture is precisely the overemphasis on technique, an overemphasis which goes along with the tendency to see the human being as an object to be calculated, managed, "analyzed." Our Western tendency has been to believe that *understanding follows technique;* if we get the right technique, then we can penetrate the riddle of the

patient. . . . The existential approach holds the exact opposite; namely, that *technique follows understanding*. (May, 1958a, pp. 76–77)

May maintains that existential analysis is an *attitude* rather than a set of psychotherapeutic techniques. It involves a stress on understanding the special meanings of the person's existence. In the pursuit of this understanding, the therapist may derive new techniques or utilize existing ones. Thus, the therapist may employ dream analysis, free association, and transference, as do the Freudians, or personality measures, as do the Rogerians. But he would also seek to interpret the patient's dreams and symbols in terms of their meaning for his existence now and their implications for his future (May, 1958a, p. 77).

May's approach to the understanding of his patients is also characterized by flexibility and versatility, so that the techniques will vary from patient to patient and from time to time during the therapeutic process (May, 1958, p. 78). This implies an eclectic orientation, but one that systematically uses each selected procedure to shed light on the person's unique potentialities and existence.

APPLICATION OF THE THEORY TO THE TREATMENT OF PSYCHOPATHOLOGY

The primary task of the therapist, according to May, is to make empty and lonely people more aware of themselves and their potential for growth through the expansion of their consciousness and experience (May, 1967, p. 126). To accomplish these goals, the therapist must seek to understand patients as human beings and as beings-in-the-world (May, 1958, p. 77). The focus is not on a detailed analysis of the patient's problems, but on how past experiences and aspirations shed light on where they are at the moment and where they are headed. In May's words, "the context is the patient not as a set of psychic dynamisms or mechanisms but as a human being who is choosing, committing, and pointing himself toward something right now; the context is dynamic, immediately real, and present" (May, 1958a, p. 77). In short, the focus is on the ontological basis of the person's problem. These problems can be understood only in a therapeutic situation where the relationship between patient and therapist is a real one. The therapist, if he is to be successful, must relate to the person as "one existence communicating with another" (May, 1958a, p. 81).

Under such conditions, May believes the patient can experience his existence as real. Under these conditions, the patient also becomes aware of his potentialities and develops the courage to act on the basis of them (May, 1958, p. 45). The patient is "cured," according to May, not when he comes to accept the standards of the culture, but when he becomes oriented toward the fulfillment of his unique existence (May, 1958a, p. 87).

CRITICAL COMMENTS

We turn now to an evaluation of May's theory in terms of our six criteria.

Comprehensiveness. Like the other humanistic psychologists, May seems most concerned with the development of a model of positive growth as a means of alleviating human suffering. Thus, his focus seems to be more on understanding abnormal behavior and experience. Yet his position seems more comprehensive than those of Rogers and Maslow because he does a more thorough job of integrating psychoanalytic and existential principles into his theory. Maslow focuses more on the growth aspects of his model and Rogers presents a more global and undifferentiated view of the defense process. May's treatment of the developmental process is also more detailed than the views presented by these other two theorists.

In addition to his efforts at incorporating existential and psychoanalytic principles into his theory, May also attempts a compromise with American behaviorism and its assumptions. In some of his earlier work, for example, he attempted to utilize learning principles and experiments to increase our understanding of the meaning of anxiety, although he did see this approach as limited. In general, then, May's system seems comprehensive, especially when compared with the other major humanistic positions.

Precision and Testability. May's theory is quite imprecise and difficult to test. Numerous terms like "demonic," "being," "potentiality," and "ontological guilt" are vague and nearly impossible to define accurately. In addition, the theory consists of a series of disjointed and unconnected propositions that do not lend themselves readily to scientific inquiry. Instead, his position appears to retain close ties to philosophy. This, of course, is not a weakness in itself, as some psychologists seem to think, but it does become a liability if May hopes to convince investigators of his theory's scientific status. In such a case, his theory would have to meet the precision and testability standards ordinarily applied to such efforts by members of the scientific community. But at this point, its deficiencies in this sense are painfully apparent. One of the unfortunate implications of this state of affairs is that May will probably not even get a fair hearing from the members of the scientific establishment. It is unfortunate because there are many interesting and provocative ideas in his position, especially in his arguments about the need for the change in our ideas about science, which will not have the impact on investigators that they merit. At best, he will be seen as a gadfly to be endured. Some constructive changes may eventually be forthcoming, but the full impact of his message about the need for a humanistic science of psychology will go unheeded. It is a message that deserves a better fate.

Simplicity. In terms of its present state of development, it is difficult to make a judgment about how well May's position meets the parsimony criterion. A tentative judgment might be that it has an excess of concepts. And as we have seen, the scientific utility of many of the terms in the system is doubtful.

Empirical Validity. Empirical support for the theory is limited. Much of the evidence for the position is based on clinical observation in therapy sessions and is largely unsystematic and retrospective. Thus, research on May's position is still in an exploratory stage.

Heuristic Value. May's position has proved stimulating to investigators in the humanistic psychology movement and to members of the public, but for the most part, his efforts have been ignored by traditional investigators within psychology.

Applied Value. May's theory has been fruitfully applied to problems in areas such as education, pastoral counseling, and family life.

DISCUSSION QUESTIONS

1. How would you define existentialism?
2. Do you agree with May that many psychologists tend to study human behavior and experience in abstract and oversimplified terms? Give reasons for your judgment.
3. What does it mean to "act authentically"? Would you ever be willing to let others define your goals for you?
4. Compare and contrast psychoanalysis and existentialism.
5. Do you agree with May that we have lost our sense of values? Do you feel powerless to control your own destiny?
6. Has there been too much emphasis in our society on the development of new technology to help us master the environment? Do we have a good understanding of our relationship to the environment? Have you seen any progress in our attempts to preserve the environment in recent years?
7. How often do you feel "empty," in the sense of being powerless to control your own outcomes? What are the causes of such feelings in yourself and others?
8. Do you agree with May that many people continue to endure basically unsatisfying relationships because they want to alleviate feelings of loneliness?
9. Do you think that many students yearn for uncritical acceptance from others? Do you believe that some students are anti-intellectual because it makes them more acceptable to others?
10. Do you think that many students are struggling to become independent of parental control? Do you agree with May that one of the basic struggles in life involves our attempts to accept ultimate responsibility for our actions? Is dependency always harmful to the person?

NOTES

M. Boss, *Psychoanalysis and Daseinsanalysis* (New York: Basic Books, 1963).

J. Macquarrie, *Existentialism* (Baltimore: Penguin Books, 1972).

R. May, *Man's Search for Himself* (New York: Norton, 1953).

R. May, "Contributions of Existential Psychotherapy," in R. May, E. Angel, and H. F. Ellenberger, eds., *Existence: A New Dimension in Psychiatry and Psychology* (New York: Basic Books, 1958a).

R. May, "The Origins and Significance of the Existential Movement in Psychology," in R. May, E. Angel, and H. F. Ellenberger, eds., *Existence: A New Dimension in Psychiatry and Psychology* (New York: Basic Books, 1958b).

R. May, *Psychology and the Human Dilemma* (New York: Van Nostrand, 1967).

R. May, "Existential Psychology," in T. Millon, ed., *Theories of Psychopathology and Personality* (Philadelphia: Saunders, 1973).

R. May, E. Angel, and H. F. Ellenberger, eds., *Existence: A New Dimension in Psychiatry and Psychology* (New York: Basic Books, 1958).

A. Van Kaam, *Existential Foundations of Psychology* (Garden City, N. Y.: Image Books, 1969).

SUGGESTED READINGS

Macquarrie, J. *Existentialism.* Baltimore: Penguin Books, 1972.

May, R. *Love and Will.* New York: Norton, 1969.

May, R. *Man's Search for Himself.* New York: Norton, 1953.

May, R. *Psychology and the Human Dilemma.* New York: Van Nostrand, 1967.

May, R., E. Angel, and H. F. Ellenberger, eds. *Existence: A New Dimension in Psychiatry and Psychology.* New York: Basic Books, 1958.

GLOSSARY

Dasein. Term existentialists use to describe the unique character of human existence. Each of us can become aware of the fact that we exist in a particular place at a particular time. We can then make our own decisions in a responsible way.

Existential-Analytic Perspectives. Theoretical positions that combine elements of existential philosophy with Freudian concepts as a means of furthering understanding of human personality. Both positions, for example, focus on the ways in which human beings try to cope with the anxieties that result from the inability to love others and from the inevitability of death.

Existentialism. Philosophy that focuses on a person's attempts to make sense out of his existence by assigning meaning to it and then taking responsibility for his own actions as he tries to live in accordance with his values and principles.

Ontology. Branch of philosophy which examines the nature of being or reality.

PART 7

CONSTITUTIONAL PERSPECTIVES

T he view that differences in behavior are produced by differences in our biological functioning is an ancient one. Historically, efforts to understand the nature of this relationship have included emphases on the ways in which behavior is determined by the operation of certain fluids in the body and on the role played by body shape and size. There have also been numerous attempts to understand how differences in skull shape and facial features produce variations in behavior. More recently, scientific investigations have focused on temperament differences in children, on individual differences in physiological reactivity patterns as a result of stress, and on showing how chromosomal abnormalities lead to Mongolism and other forms of mental retardation.

It is popularly believed that the Greek physician Hippocrates first undertook to study the nature of the relationship between body type and individual differences in behavior. He was an advocate of the position that changes in the amount of internal fluids or "humors" in the body produced distinctive temperaments and behaviors. He maintained that there were four distinctive kinds of personalities: A predominance of black bile caused a person to be melancholic and depressed, whereas an excess of yellow bile made one irritable and short tempered. Too much phlegm, on the other hand, caused a person to be slow and lethargic, whereas disproportionate amounts of blood caused an individual to be hopeful and sanguine. Hippocrates also believed that body type was related to physical disease. On the basis of his many observations of patients, he concluded that people with short and thick bodies were prone to stroke (*habitus apoplecticus*); people who were tall and thin were susceptible to tuberculosis (*habitus phthisicus*).

The inadequacies of such typologies are painfully clear. They involve unsophisticated and oversimplified theoretical and empirical treatments of individual differences in behavior, along with medical "explanations" that are obsolete in light of current knowledge. But useful vestiges of Hippocrates' legacy to the medical profession and to behavioral science can still be seen in research on hormonal therapy and on the effects of various hormones on performance in lower animals and people.

The assessment of personality from the study of facial features also had its origins in antiquity and has throughout history commanded the attention of a variety of theologians, poets, philosophers, artists, writers, and scientists. Interest in the subject seems to have reached a peak in the late nineteenth century, but even today there are occasional books and studies on the topic. Before the beginning of the nineteenth century, devotees of physiognomy tended to make their judgments about personality on artistic grounds. They offered lyrical descriptions of the beauties of the various aspects of the face and sometimes presented their version of truth in aphorisms like the following:

> A beard on a woman is a sign of little honesty.
> Bright eyes are the sign of wantonness.
> The smallness of the forehead indicates a choleric man.
> Men with curved noses are magnanimous. (Mantegazza, 1899, p. 13)

The primary orientation in the nineteenth century was scientific, with attempts to measure the various features of the face and to relate these measurements to psychological characteristics. Unfortunately, virtually all these findings are meaningless in a scientific sense because they are based upon the biased and subjective impressions of the investigators and the use of woefully inadequate methodologies.

Scientific research that examines the effects of physical attractiveness on behavior is extremely popular today. Most contemporary researchers in this area assume that standards of beauty are learned and not biologically based, however. Their judgment is based on cross-cultural evidence which shows that standards of beauty vary from country to country. Their work shows that physically attractive people are better liked by their peers and by adults than are people who are unattractive. There is the assumption on the part of teachers, for example, that socially undesirable acts committed by attractive children are less reprehensible than those committed by unattractive children (Dion, 1972). For college students, physically attractive people are seen as possessing more socially desirable traits than unattractive people. For example, beautiful people are seen as more altruistic, genuine, sensitive, sincere, modest, poised, and sophisticated than their less physically attractive counterparts. Attractive men and women are also expected to attain more prestigious occupations and to have better prospects for happy social and professional lives. It does seem, then, that people who are seen as beautiful are also seen as good, a finding which was, incidentally, accurately predicted by a number of the early physiognomists (Dion, Berscheid, and Walster, 1972).

Phrenology was still another attempt to relate constitutional factors and individual differences in behavior. This system purports to assess personality from a knowledge of skull shape and contours. Popularly known as the study of bumps on the head, phrenology originated in the nineteenth century as a serious attempt to relate knowledge about brain structure and function to behavior (Davies, 1955, p. 3). Its foremost proponent was Franz Gall (1758–1828), a German anatomist and physician who believed that the mind was composed of approximately forty independent faculties, variously catalogued by him and later by other disciples under such headings as combativeness, benevolence, amativeness, language, secretiveness, self-esteem, destructiveness, and hope (Davies, 1955, p. 6). Gall claimed that these faculties were located in various "organs" or regions of the brain and that the development or lack of development of these organs affected the size and shape of the skull. In order to judge a person's so-called character or personality, therefore, he believed it was only necessary to study these contours. A person with a well-developed benevolence region, for example, would be judged as having a kindly character; one with an underdeveloped region would be characterized as cruel.

Gall had a single-minded passion for scientific inquiry about brain structure and function. His pupil and colleague, Johann Spurzheim, did not. Spurzheim's view of phrenology was based on religious and philosophical speculations, as well as scientific research. He sought to popularize phrenology and to discuss, in public lectures, its applications to education, medicine, mental health, and penology (Davies, 1955, p. 8). These efforts, and efforts by other disciples, proved very successful, and phrenology flourished. During the last half of the nineteenth century, however, phrenology was attacked by numerous critics on religious and philosophical as well as scientific grounds (Davies, 1955, pp. 65–75).

Opponents argued that phrenology was atheistic and immoral because it held that behavior had natural and not divine causes and that acceptance of it necessarily meant an endorsement of fatalism. This latter argument was not consistent with the aims of the movement, however, since phrenology was directly linked with social reform by its proponents. For example, people who were judged insane were considered by phrenologists to have diseased brains that resulted from violations of "natural laws." To overcome these deficiencies, these people should once again follow these natural laws. This meant that they should get plenty of fresh air and physical exercise, eat bland foods, and avoid liquor and tobacco. In the crudest sense, the phrenologists were arguing that the establishment of a warm, supportive environment for the insane was therapeutic, an idea still acceptable to those in the contemporary mental health movement.

Despite the irrational nature of the attacks on phrenology, its critics were effective in damaging the movement. Scientific evidence also took its toll. Flourens demonstrated in his experiments with pigeon brains in 1845 that large portions of the brain could be destroyed without impairment of any of the functions. In 1861, Broca showed conclusively that the faculty of speech was not located near the eyeballs, as Gall maintained, but in the temporal region (Davies, 1955, p. 142). Despite these overwhelming criticisms, phrenology is credited with having an important impact on the field of neurology in the sense that it directed the attention of researchers to the problem of cerebral structure and function. There is still sporadic interest in the topic, not within the scientific community, but within certain segments of the public who also embrace pseudosciences like astrology and palmistry.

Although there have been numerous other investigators of the relationship between body build and behavior since Hippocrates, the leading researcher in this area in modern times is William Sheldon. The materials in Chapter 15 will focus primarily on his theory, since it is the most comprehensive and systematic statement of the constitutional position and the most thoroughly researched.

The basic concepts and principles of the theory are reviewed first. This review includes a discussion of the measurement procedures used by Sheldon to establish the primary and secondary components of physique. Then there is a presentation of the manner in which Sheldon proceeded to search for the basic components of temperament. Next, data supporting Sheldon's hypothesis concerning the relationship between morphology and temperament are presented. Included in this review is a discussion of a social learning hypothesis as a possible alternative explanation of the data, in preference to the constitutional view.

Sheldon's theory of personality development is outlined next, along with the implications of his position for child-rearing and parental use of discipline. Inferences are also drawn concerning the relationships between morphology and abnormality. There is also a brief treatment of Sheldon's techniques of assessment and of the kinds of therapy that should be employed in the treatment of pathology. Finally, the theory itself is assessed in terms of how well it meets the six criteria for providing the worth of scientific theories.

NOTES

J. D. Davies, *Phrenology: Fad and Science* (New Haven, Conn.: Yale University Press, 1955).

K. Dion, "Physical Attractiveness and Evaluations of Children's Transgressions," *Journal of Personality and Social Psychology,* 1972, **24,** 207–213.

K. Dion, E. Berscheid, and E. Walster, "What Is Beautiful Is Good," *Journal of Personality and Social Psychology,* 1972, **24,** 285–290.

P. Mantegazza, *Physiognomy and Expression* (New York: Scribner's, 1899).

William Sheldon (Courtesy of Dorothy Paschal)

CHAPTER 15

Sheldon's Somatotyping Position

BIOGRAPHICAL SKETCH

William Sheldon was born in 1899 in Warwick, Rhode Island. His father was a naturalist and animal breeder, and Sheldon reports that, as a boy, he was trained to judge the quality of poultry and dogs. Sheldon attended many livestock exhibits by the time he reached fifteen, and says he was a competent judge of livestock. Quantitative scales were used by the judges at such exhibits and agreement on ratings was uniformly high. Sheldon clearly remembers the keen disappointment on his father's face when the boy gave a rooster a score of 83 on a 100-point scale after the other officials had rated the bird at 80 (Sheldon, Hartl, and McDermott, 1949, pp. 20–21). It seems likely that these early experiences had a lasting effect on his view of human behavior and his advocacy of a biologically based psychology.

As a young man, Sheldon attended Brown University and received a B.A. in 1919. Later he earned a master's degree from the University of Colorado and a Ph.D. in psychology from the University of Chicago in 1926. In 1933, he added an M.D. from the University of Chicago to his credentials.

After brief academic stints at Wisconsin and Chicago, he moved to Harvard, where he continued to write and conduct research. At this time he also began a collaboration with the eminent experimental psychologist S. S. Stevens. Stevens seems to have heightened Sheldon's interest and concern with the need for precise measuring instruments to assess physique and temperament. The result was the construction of a measurement system of the human body decidedly superior in most respects to any of the systems devised by his predecessors.

Until recently, Sheldon has been an active researcher and a productive writer. Some of his more notable books include *The Varieties of Human Physique* (1940), *The Varieties of Temperament* (1942), *Varieties of Delinquent Youth* (1949), written in collaboration with E. M. Hartl and E.

McDermott, and the *Atlas of Men* (1954). In 1947, Sheldon accepted an appointment as director of the Constitution Laboratory at Columbia University, where he remained until his death.

THE RADICAL PREMISE OF SHELDON'S PSYCHOLOGY

It should be clear at the onset that although Sheldon's position is firmly rooted in human biology, he is not simple-mindedly arguing that environmental forces such as our past experiences with other people have no impact on our behavior. He recognizes the importance of our social experiences, but has decided quite consciously and deliberately to adopt the radical premise that biological structure determines our behavior because of his belief that such an orientation has been largely ignored by American psychologists and that this unbalance must be rectified (Sheldon, Hartl, and McDermott, 1949, pp. 3–6). The value orientation of many American psychologists stresses the importance of equality among people and the goodness of self-improvement and social progress. A frequently accompanying belief is that endorsement of a strong hereditarian position precludes the attainment of these social goals. Although the constitutional position does stress innate differences between people, it does not necessarily follow that proponents of the position are incapable of endorsing and supporting a social philosophy which emphasizes equality of opportunity under the law. Biological superiority does not necessarily imply social superiority, but the strong liberal bias of psychologists leads them to fear, perhaps rightly, that such a distinction is often difficult ot maintain. The specter of Hitler and his Aryan race is not easily forgotten, nor should it be.

BASIC CONCEPTS AND PRINCIPLES

The Primary Components of Body Build

Sheldon and his associates set out to examine the physiques of thousands of college students in an attempt to determine whether or not there were any basic regularities among them. He first photographed them in the nude from the front, side, and rear. After careful examination, he concluded that there were three extreme variations. Repeated efforts to find a fourth major type failed. These three basic types correspond approximately to the pyknic (plump), athletic (muscular), and leptosomatic or asthenic (thin and frail) types identified by Sheldon's historical predecessor and acquaintance, Ernest Kretschmer (1856–1926). Sheldon insists, however, that he did not simply borrow Kretschmer's classification scheme and add new labels to the various types. He maintains that the three types were determined solely by empirical investigation—that is, they were found by examining the photographs. Whether this was actually the case is debatable.

The first component identified by Sheldon is labeled *endomorphy*, the second *mesomorphy*, and the third *ectomorphy*. According to Sheldon,

> *Endomorphy* means relative predominance of soft roundness throughout the various regions of the body. When endomorphy is dominant the digestive viscera are massive and tend relatively to dominate the bodily economy. The digestive viscera are derived principally from the *endodermal* embryonic layer.

> *Mesomorphy* means relative predominence of muscle, bone, and connective tissue. The mesomorphic physique is normally heavy, hard, and rectangular in outline. Bone and muscle are prominent and the skin is made thick by a heavy underlying connective tissue. The entire bodily economy is dominated, relatively, by tissues derived from the *mesodermal* embryonic layer.

> *Ectomorphy* means relative predominance of linearity and fragility. In proportion to his mass, the ectomorph has the greatest surface area and hence relatively the greatest sensory exposure to the outside world. Relative to his mass he also has the largest brain and central nervous system. In a sense, therefore, his bodily economy is relatively dominated by tissues derived from the *ectodermal* layer. (Sheldon, 1940, pp. 5–6)

Each of these dimensions was considered to be a continuous variable that varied along a seven-point scale. Each person was assigned a set of three numerals from 1 to 7. The patterning of these nonpsychological components yielded a *somatotype*. For example, a 711 is an extreme endomorph, a 171 an extreme mesomorph, and a 117 an extreme ectomorph. Note that the order of the primary components is always endomorphy, mesomorphy, and ectomorphy (Sheldon, Hartl, and McDermott, 1949, p. 14). The advantage of such a measuring system is that it is possible to obtain a much more reliable, complex, and differentiated picture of an individual's morphology than with any of the systems constructed previously. Theoretically, the system yields 343 different somatotypes, although Sheldon has focused his attention on only 76 (Sheldon, Hartl, and McDermott, 1949, pp. 62–63). The system also avoids extreme types like the 777 or the 111 by stipulating that the sum of the ratings cannot be less than 9 or more than 12.

Sheldon treats extreme types as ideals. He labels God as a 777, for example. God is a projection of our wish for perfection, in Sheldon's view. In other words, God is a reflection of our deepest needs to attain maximum ratings on the three components, that is, to be all-loving, all powerful, and all-knowing. The Devil, in contrast, is labeled a 177. Such a projection would be devoid of compassion and feelings of affection for others, as reflected in the low rating on the first component, but would be rated extremely high on the second and third components, reflecting extreme aggressiveness and hyperawareness (Sheldon, 1940, p. 61). Why the highest ratings on the second and third components can indicate positive characteristics in the case of God and negative characteristics in the case of the Devil is unclear and not explained by Sheldon.

Sheldon maintains that the somatotype is genetically determined and does not change despite advances in age and changes in diet or the environment (Sheldon 1940, pp. 221–226). He distinguishes between the phenotype or physical appearance and the genotype or what the person actually is morphologically. Changes in diet, for example, may change a person's phenotype, but not his genotype. Although it is rather easy to mistake the two, Sheldon maintains that the error can be avoided by keeping careful case history records and taking a series of photographs over the years. In this way, the somatotype can be accurately identified. If the investigator is not careful in his determination of the somatotype, errors can occur. One striking instance of such an error, according to Sheldon, is the *pyknic practical joke* (PPJ). Somatotyped typically as a 443, 442, or 452, this person appears

> stocky but not fat, sturdy but not blocky, and all his features tend to be blunt or rubbery. There are no sharp corners and there is nothing about [him] . . . that appears easy to break. He can be picked up and dropped. . . . In youth he generally has and expresses tremendous energy, but if too well fed or too successful in the middle decades he is prone to grow fat and sodden. The female . . . PPJ . . . is highly active, and is generally a "pep" girl [cheerleader]. Before marriage she remains extraordinarily slender, like the bud of a late-blossoming tree. The unpracticed eye does not perceive the latent first component. After marriage the joke is sprung. (Sheldon, 1940, pp. 198–199)

The Secondary Components of Physique

As a result of further examination of the photographs, Sheldon was able to isolate a number of secondary dimensions. These he labeled *dysplasia, gynandromorphy, texture,* and *hirsutism.* Sheldon defines dysplasia as the aspect of disharmony between different regions of the same body. Gynandromorphy refers to the bisexuality of the body. For example, a man may have large, soft breasts and wide hips like a woman; a woman may have a hard body with little or no breast development and narrow hips. Texture refers to the person's aesthetic attractiveness. Some people are strikingly handsome or beautiful and have fine features; others are physically unattractive and have coarse features. Sheldon likens those who are aesthetically pleasing to the thoroughbreds of the animal world. Hirsutism refers to the general hairiness of the body (Sheldon, 1940, pp. 68–79).

The Primary Components and Temperament

After establishing the primary and secondary aspects of physique at the morphological level, Sheldon proceeded to search for the basic components of temperament. Drawing on the personality trait literature, he eventually decided to use a list of fifty traits in his investigation. He then rated approximately thirty graduate students and instructors on these characteristics on the basis of observations made over a one-year period during weekly clinical interviews. He then intercorrelated the ratings, looking for basic clusters or dimensions. The basic clusters included ratings on traits that correlated positively with each other and negatively with the traits of other clusters. He eventually decided there were three basic dimensions, which he labeled *viscerotonia, somatotonia,* and *cerebrotonia.* The various traits associated with each temperament type are listed in Table 15.1. In general, viscerotones have a love of comfort, and need approval and affection from people; somatotones like action, and are assertive and vigorous. Cerebrotones tend to be tense and withdrawn.

TABLE 15.1   The Scale for Temperament

Viscerotonia	*Somatotonia*	*Cerebrotonia*
1. Relaxation in posture and movement	1. Assertiveness of posture and movement	1. Restraint in posture and movement, tightness
2. Love of physical comfort	2. Love of physical adventure	2. Physiological overresponse
3. Slow reaction	3. Energetic characteristic	3. Overly fast reactions
4. Love of eating	4. Need and enjoyment of exercise	4. Love of privacy
5. Socialization of eating	5. Love of dominating and lust for power	5. Mental over-intensity, hyper-attentionality, apprehensiveness
6. Pleasure in digestion	6. Love of risk and chance	6. Secretiveness of feeling, emotional restraint
7. Love of polite ceremony	7. Bold directness of manner	7. Self-conscious motility of the eyes and face
8. Sociophilia	8. Physical courage for combat	8. Sociophobia
9. Indiscriminate amiability	9. Competitive aggressiveness	9. Inhibited social address
10. Greed for affection and approval	10. Psychological callousness	10. Resistance to habit, and poor routinizing

TABLE 15.1 The Scale for Temperament (cont.)

Viscerotonia	*Somatotonia*	*Cerebrotonia*
11. Orientation to people	11. Claustrophobia	11. Agoraphobia
12. Evenness of emotional flow	12. Ruthlessness, freedom from squeamishness	12. Unpredictability of attitude
13. Tolerance	13. The unrestrained voice	13. Vocal restraint, and general restraint of noise
14. Complacency	14. Spartan indifference to pain	14. Hypersensitivity to pain
15. Deep sleep	15. General noisiness	15. Poor sleep habits, chronic fatigue
16. The untempered characteristic	16. Overmaturity of appearance	16. Youthful intentness of manner and appearance
17. Smooth, easy communication of feeling, extraversion of viscerotonia	17. Horizontal mental cleavage, extraversion of somatotonia	17. Vertical Mental cleavage, introversion
18. Relaxation and sociophilia under alcohol	18. Assertiveness and aggression under alcohol	18. Resistance to alcohol and to other depressant drugs
19. Need of people when troubled	19. Need of action when troubled	19. Need of solitude when troubled
20. Orientation toward childhood and family relationships	20. Orientation toward goals and activities of youth	20. Orientation toward the later periods of life

Adapted from Sheldon, Hartl, and McDermott, 1949, pp. 26–27.

If Sheldon's radical premise has any validity, there should be a reliable relationship between temperament and morphology. In fact, Sheldon has reported very high correlations between the three morphological and the three temperament dimensions. He found correlations of .79 between endormorphy and viscerotonia, .82 between mesomorphy and somatotonia, and .83 between ectomorphy and cerebrotonia (Sheldon and Stevens, 1942, p. 400). Unfortunately, other investigators have failed to replicate his findings. Furthermore, Sheldon himself made both sets of ratings, so that investigator bias may have affected the judgments and produced the very high correlational outcomes. In short, Sheldon may have found what he was looking for.

In a methodologically sounder study by Child, however, in which investigator bias was minimized by having one investigator rate the somatotypes and having the subjects independently rate their own personality characteristics (temperament), the results yielded much lower correlations, but ones that were still consistent with Sheldon's theorizing (Child, 1950) (see Table 15.2). The findings were reliable enough to compel Child to conclude that somatotypes are an important determinant of personality. In addition to the studies by Sheldon and Child, a recent investigation by Lerner showed that 50 children and adolescents ranging in age from ten to twenty assigned behavioral descriptions to adult endomorphs, mesomorphs, and ectomorphs similar to those that would be expected if Sheldon's ideas about the nature of the association between morphology and temperament were correct (Lerner, 1969). Table 15.3 gives a listing of the results. As would be predicted by Sheldon's theory, an endomorphic adult figure was seen as eating and drinking the most. The mesomorphic figure was seen as being most aggressive, most athletic, able to endure the most pain, and the best soldier. Also in accordance with the theory, the ectomorphic adult was seen as having the fewest friends, eating the least, and being most susceptible to having a nervous breakdown. Other research with children six to ten years of age is also consistent with these findings.

TABLE 15.2   Correlations between the Dimensions of Physique and Sets of College Student Self-Ratings

| | DIMENSIONS OF PHYSIQUE | | |
Self-Rating	Endomorphy	Mesomorphy	Ectomorphy
Viscerotonia	+.13	+.13	−.15
Somatotonia	+.03	+.38	−.37
Cerebrotonia	−.03	−.38	+.27

Adapted from Child, 1950, p. 447.

Before we conclude that a wealth of data supports Sheldon's theorizing, however, we might pause to entertain another hypothesis that is also consistent with the bulk of the data in this area. As an alternative to his constitutional position, social learning theorists argue that the relationship between body build and temperament and behavior is determined *not* by biological factors but by learning factors. That is, from a very early age, people are taught to apply certain traits to themselves and to others, depending upon the body type that is being assessed. We learn positive stereotypes about mesomorphs and negative ones about endomorphs and ectomorphs. This theory would also lead to the research outcome cited above. Thus, a reasonable conclusion would be that at the present time, it has not been determined conclusively whether the behaviors associated with the major body types are determined by biological or learning factors. We cannot, in other words, rule that Sheldon's theory is valid or invalid at this point. What we can conclude is that people seem to agree in their behavioral descriptions of various body builds. *Why* they do is still unknown.

At this point, we turn to a consideration of some of the implications of Sheldon's writings for a theory of personality development.

TABLE 15.3 Frequency of Assignment of Each Phrase to Each Somatotype by Subjects in Each of the Three Age Levels Combined

PHRASE	SOMATOTYPE		
The Man Who Would:	Endomorph	Mesomorph	Ectomorph
1. assume leadership	5	42	3
2. eat the least	4	4	42
3. have many friends	16	30	4
4. be the poorest athlete	37	0	13
5. drink the most	33	8	9
6. not smoke at all*	3	24	23
7. need friends the most	27	2	21
8. eat the most often	45	1	4
9. not smoke at all*	10	24	16
10. have the fewest friends	24	4	22
11. eat the most	46	2	2
12. be the most aggressive	7	39	4
13. be least preferred as a personal friend	22	9	19
14. have fewest friends	25	4	21
15. put his own interests before others	18	28	4
16. endure pain the best	10	30	10
17. eat the least often	5	4	41
18. make the poorest doctor	19	9	22
19. make the best athlete	2	43	5
20. make a poor father	19	7	24
21. be least likely to be chosen leader	25	10	15
22. make the best soldier	1	44	5
23. smoke three packs of cigarettes a day	28	7	15
24. be elected leader	3	44	3

PHRASE	SOMATOTYPE		
The Man Who Would:	Endomorph	Mesomorph	Ectomorph
25. be the least aggressive	22	4	24
26. never have a nervous breakdown	11	35	4
27. endure pain the least	16	8	26
28. make the worst soldier	31	1	18
29. be most wanted as a friend	5	36	9
30. be most likely to have a nervous breakdown	16	4	30

*Items 6 and 9 are the same in the original study.
Adapted from Lerner, 1972, p. 140.

THE PROCESS OF PERSONALITY DEVELOPMENT

The Somatotypes and Movement toward Self-Actualization

From Sheldon's theorizing, it seems reasonable to assume that he believes the socialization process should be geared to the child's unique constitutional background if he or she is to develop his potentialities to the maximum. On this point, Sheldon is curiously aligned with Maslow, Rogers, and other proponents of the human potential movement. He also thinks discipline should be tailored to the child's biology:

> It is possible that some children need rigid discipline for their best develop-ment. This may be true in general of somatotonic children—those given to vigorous assertive characteristics. It may well be that a premature attempt at "reasoning" with somatotonic children is even more baffling and frustrat-ing, and it may in the end be more devastating to character, than is the ruth-less whipping of a sensitive cerebrotonic child—one marked by sharp in-hibition and hyperattentionality. Perhaps viscerotonic children—those characterized by emotional and social warmth, relaxation, gluttony—need to be handled in groups and "socialized" early in their development, whereas the cerebrotonics may need above everything else to be protected from this influence.
>
> Watch young children in a nursery school. There are often a few vigorous-bodied somatotonics who take the lead in all enterprises, a few round, healthy-looking viscertonics who join in with excellent fellowship, and a few little pinch-faced cerebrotonics who constitute a watchful and unso-cialized periphery. These little cerebrotonics seem to want to stay on the side lines and watch. Their eyes are sharp as needlepoints and nothing seems to escape their quick attention, but they do not want to be pushed into the swim. They are under stern internal check, and they seem to want to see without being seen. Should these children be sent to nursery schools and forced into the social press with a score of other children? Should they be sent to boys' camps and girls' camps? We do not know about these things. Modern educators might want to ponder this problem. It may be

that late maturing personalities need a high degree of privacy and seclusion and protection during the formative years. It is possible that loneliness is as essential to the full development of a creature "mentally inclined" as sociability is essential to a viscerotonic or aggressive self-expression to a somatotonic youth. (Sheldon, 1940, pp. 260–261)

Modern child psychologists decry the use of "rigid" discipline, which presumably involves the use of physical punishment. Sheldon, however, seems to imply that such punishment may be entirely appropriate for children with mesomorphic builds and somatotonic temperaments. Sheldon goes even further by arguing that perhaps enforced loneliness and isolation are virtues under some circumstances. In fairness to Sheldon, however, he does state that he is only offering hypotheses. It may turn out that environmental influences are even more important in determining the course of development. The crux of his argument seems to be that adequate development will take place if parents use disciplinary practices consistent with the child's basic nature and that abnormal behavior may be the result of the application of discipline incongruent with this nature. If discipline is consistent with constitution type, the person will develop along viscerotone, somatotone, or cerebrotone lines, with the temperament and personality characteristics peculiar to these types.

Somatotyping and the Normal—Abnormal Continuum

Sheldon rejects the traditional view in psychiatry that mental disorders are diseases to be cured. In such a view, a person is thought either to have a disease or not to have it. He either has the measles or he does not. Similarly, he either suffers or does not suffer from manic-depressive psychosis, paranoid schizophrenia, or hebephrenic schizophrenia. Such a scheme posits qualitative differences in the behavior of people: Normals, neurotics, and psychotics are different kinds of people (Sheldon, Hartl, and McDermott, 1949, p. 43).

Sheldon's view, in contrast, treats normal and abnormal behavior as different points on the same continuum. Normals, neurotics, and psychotics are not characterized by different kinds of behavior, but by differences in the extremity of particular behaviors. These differences in the degree of behavior are then linked with the primary and secondary components of the body, which also vary along continuua. Sheldon's scheme is thus much more complicated and allows for the assessment of subtle differences in both temperament and body build.

The Association between Normality and Balance
in the Primary Components

The relationship Sheldon postulates between the primary components and normal behavior is difficult to express accurately. In general terms, he seems to be arguing that the normal person is one who has a somatotype which is moderate on all three components. For example, the healthy man or woman would be classified as a 444. Since endomorphy is strongly associated with viscerotonia, mesomorphy with somatotonia, and ectomorphy with cerebrotonia, it follows that the 444 somatotype implies well-balanced and moderate temperaments on the three primary components. Such a person, according to Sheldon, would be characterized as humorous. Sheldon defines "humorous" in an unusual way, however:

> Whatever else humor may be it certainly is characterized by two qualities: (1) An inclination toward detachment—the quality of regarding life and self lightly; (2) An inclination to tolerate and to enjoy incompatibilities at a high level of awareness. This second quality may contain the essence of humor, and if it does it may contain the essence of human salvation. (Sheldon, Hartl, and McDermott, 1949, p. 93)

Thus, the humorous person is one who has probably achieved high status in life and who can easily tolerate conflict and uncertainty. He possesses all three temperaments to a moderate degree, and they serve to regulate one another. For example, the person's cerebral cortex serves to inhibit his visceral and muscular energies (Sheldon, Hartl, and Mc-Dermott, 1949, p. 94). Otherwise, the individual would be given to outbursts of emotion and aggressiveness.

The Association between Abnormality and the Primary Components

Somatotypes that suggest abnormality seem to be characterized by excesses or deficiencies in the primary body components (Sheldon, Hartl, and McDermott, 1949, p. 90). For example, a delinquent characterized by loudness, restlessness, directness, and bluntness, as well as by amiability and a love of food, might have the somatotype 731 (Sheldon, Hartl, and McDermott, 1949, p. 414). In such a person, the cerebrotonic component is lacking, so that there are few restraints on his behavior.

In regard to the severe behavior disorders, Sheldon presents scientific evidence that particular body types are associated with different psychotic reactions. Manic-depressives are characterized by continual shifts in moods, ranging from extreme elation and euphoria to utter sorrow, dejection, and self-deprecation. Sheldon found that their somatotypes are high on the first two primary components (endomorphy and mesomorphy), but low on the third (ectomorphy). The primary problem with such people is that there is a pathological absence of inhibition (Sheldon, Hartl, and McDermott, 1949, p. 46). In other words, manic-depressives are characterized by extreme deficiencies in cerebrotonia. There are, as a consequence, few restraints on their tendencies to be expansive and energetic. According to Sheldon, it is pyknic individuals with 551 body types who most often and most easily become manic-depressives (Sheldon, Hartl, and McDermott, 1949, p. 62).

People labeled as paranoid schizophrenics tend to be hostile and suspicious of the intentions of others. They are also egocentric, conceited, condescending, and sarcastic (Sheldon, Hartl, and McDermott, 1949, p. 83). Sheldon discovered that their somatotypes are high on the last two components, but very low on the first. They tend to be aggressive and have a hyperawareness of their surroundings, but they lack compassion and feeling toward other human beings. They tend to overreact and to be indiscriminate in their judgments. Paranoid schizophrenics are especially high on mesomorphy and have somatotypes that approximate 253½ (Sheldon, Hartl, and McDermott, 1949, p. 82).

Individuals labeled as hebephrenic schizophrenics tend to be withdrawn, inadequate, and helpless (Sheldon, Hartl, and McDermott, 1949, p. 90). They are also characterized by bizzare and irrelevant feelings toward others (Sheldon, Hartl, and McDermott, 1949, p. 67). Hebephrenic schizophrenics have somatotypes that are high on the first and third components, but low on the second. Although they are high on endomorphy, they are even higher on ectomorphy. Their somatotypes approximate 316 (Sheldon, Hartl, and McDermott, 1949, pp. 70–71).

TECHNIQUES OF ASSESSMENT

Sheldon's theory is an attempt to provide a basic taxonomy of human beings through the use of somatotyping procedures. The taxonomy focuses on the identification of morphological characteristics in the hope of providing a conceptual scheme that can be used as a framework for the analysis of other related variables, such as physiological function, susceptibility to disease, temperament, and social adjustment.

The identification and measurement of the three primary and several secondary components of the person's physique were accomplished through the use of a photographic technique and several other anthropometric procedures. Photos were taken of the individual from the side, front, and back using a special long-focus lens to ensure that the length and breadth dimensions of the individual's body were not distorted in any way and, in fact, matched the measurements taken of the living body (Sheldon, 1940, p. 30). Observers of the photos then proceeded to identify three extreme types—the endomorph, mesomorph, and ectomorph—as well as several minor components.

The next step in the somatotyping procedure involved an empirical determination of the physical characteristics associated with each major type. In general, endomorphs were found to have round and soft bodies, whereas mesomorphs had a relative predominance of muscle, bone, and connective tissue. Ectomorphs were characterized by large brains and nervous systems. Part of the identification process involved the examination and measurement of the principal internal organs of cadavers during autopsy work. This latter procedure showed that endomorphs were endowed with relatively large intestines, livers, and other digestive viscera in comparison to the other two major types. Very large hearts and arteries were found in mesomorphs as compared to endomorphs and ectomorphs (Sheldon, 1940, pp. 32–35). Sheldon and his associates then developed seven-point rating scales for the three types that allowed for the assessment of variations in the characteristics associated with each component. This measurement procedure made possible the precise delineation and identification of a large number of body types.

Once proper somatotyping procedures were established, Sheldon developed scales for the assessment of the different kinds of temperaments. He collected a list of 650 traits of temperament by combing the research literature. These traits were rated by observers in terms of their similarity of meaning, and then the list was reduced to 50. These 50 traits were then incorporated into five-point and later seven-point rating scales. Subjects could then be rated in terms of the degree to which they possessed the characteristic (Sheldon and Stevens, 1942, p. 13). These assessments were made by interviewing subjects and making judgments concerning their temperament dispositions. The interviews were repeated throughout an entire year and provided Sheldon with a reliable assessment of the kinds of traits possessed by his subjects. In addition to the interviewing, Sheldon had observers watch the subjects during their daily routines over the year period and make assessments on the basis of their observations.

Later, Sheldon computed the degree of association between the individual's physical type and his temperament type (these results were reported earlier in the chapter). Sheldon relied on correlational procedures to assess the relationship between these two sets of variables. Such measurements yield noncausal data that are open to various interpretations. The reliance on correlational procedures by Sheldon was appropriate, however, since he was conducting work in an unexplored area where even the basic relationships between events were unclear. It would have been premature and inappropriate to attempt experimental analyses under such conditions.

APPLICATION OF THE THEORY TO THE TREATMENT OF PSYCHOPATHOLOGY

Sheldon has not been able to develop a systematic position concerning the kinds of treatment that should be used to help alleviate the suffering of troubled individuals. He readily admits that the constitutional approach has little or nothing to offer in these areas. Instead, he suggests that investigators focus most of their attention on diagnosis and ". . . postpone the thought of treatment just as long as postponement can reasonably be tolerated" (Sheldon, 1940, p. 257). Constitutional psychology is in a primitive state and there is little basic information about the ways in which heredity influences our somatotypes and temperament (Sheldon, 1940, p. 227). How can the therapist recommend specific kinds of treatment if he is ignorant of the constitutional processes that underlie behavior? Sheldon maintains that investigators must be able to describe and measure accurately the ways in which our genes exert influence indirectly through the physiology and chemistry of our bodies or directly on our behavior before they attempt to prescribe treatment.

Despite this advocacy of a focus on diagnosis at this stage of our knowledge, Sheldon does make some suggestions concerning treatment. In our previous discussion on the socialization process, we noted that Sheldon strongly believes disciplinary practices should be consistent with the person's basic nature if the person is to develop his potentialities. Discipline that is inconsistent with the person's basic nature, on the other hand, leads to the development of abnormal behavior. Accordingly, the person who is characterized by conflicts is one who exists in an environment that restricts his growth. An example might be the young person who represses his aggressive tendencies (his somatotonia) because they are severely punished by his parents. Such a person can be helped via psychoanalysis since his ability to think and analyze—that is, his cerebrotonic tendencies—are intact. He can also be helped by sympathetic discussion and explanation and thus be freed to express his aggressive tendencies under appropriate circumstances.

A person who has become abnormally dominant and aggressive and represses his cerebrotonia will not be able to resolve his conflicts through psychoanalysis. According to Sheldon, Freudian analysis can reach the person only through the cerebrotonic aspects of his personality, and this component is unavailable. One solution is to confront the person with strict disciplinary measures, including physical punishment, in order to bring his aggressiveness under control so that he can be trained to live effectively in society. Accordingly, the therapist might suggest to the parents that they establish a "benevolent dictatorship" over the child and teach him habits that allow him to function effectively (Sheldon, 1940, pp. 262–263).

On a more general level, Sheldon advocates an eugenics program in which officials would discover the people who would produce the "best stock" of children. Such parents would then be "encouraged" by state authorities to breed, and people with "inferior" constitutions would be discouraged from breeding. Sheldon believes that in this way the number of people who are potentially dangerous to society could be drastically reduced. He offers this plan as an alternative to suppressing the unfit and eliminating or sterilizing people with the "wrong" body types. He does not want the state to subject people to such extreme and harsh treatment (Sheldon, 1940, pp. 229–230). Yet, for all his humanitarian concern, in a later publication Sheldon does advocate a position that is clearly antihumanistic in nature. He proposes that war may be the "solution" to the problem of a society populated with a certain percentage of misfits

> We are . . . scheduled for such inconveniences as social chaos, wars of increasing and crescendic violence, general frustration, and the confusion necessarily attendant upon the pathology of increasing urbanization and loss of zest in human life. All of this we have already earned by irresponsible reproduction in the recent past. No amount of regret or prayer or pacifism can cancel that debt, and nature generally collects her debts. Pacifism might be defined as the expression of a hebophrenic wish to escape the consequences of delinquent reproduction already committed. This delinquency is everybody's for since we all participate in the future unless we die out, the one thing that is everybody's responsibility is guardianship of the quality of the reproduction of his own time. If that responsibility is shirked, war is perhaps the least ungentle of natural punishments.
> We cannot by now declaring how much we would like to have peace escape the devastating wars of the next few generations, nor do I think that a morally responsible person should want to escape them. *That* punishment is needed for without it the delinquency would continue. (Sheldon, Hartl, and McDermott, 1949, pp. 837–838)

We can now perhaps understand the liberal's concern with the potential for a totalitarian state based on a position like Sheldon's. Although the constitutional position does not necessarily imply that its proponents are incapable of supporting a democratic philosophy, the fact is that such a position, which maintains that biological superiority and inferiority is a reality, lends itself quite readily to the establishment of an antidemocratic philosophy. Fortunately for us, Sheldon's social philosophizing and moralizing about the "treatment" have been largely ignored.

CRITICAL COMMENTS

We turn now to an assessment of the scientific worth of Sheldon's position in terms of our six criteria.

Comprehensiveness. The theory Sheldon offers is grossly inadequate in terms of its comprehensiveness and its ability to generate testable hypotheses outside its narrow province. Sheldon seems more interested in the classification of physique and related behaviors than in constructing an internally consistent conceptual system capable of generating testable hypotheses. The attractiveness of his position for many people, however, lies in this very simplicity. They find it easy to understand and easy to apply to people in their everyday encounters. If they meet a fat man who turns out to be jolly and sociable, they consider it a confirmation of their view of the "basic nature" of human beings. If they meet a thin man who is also jolly and sociable, they tend to ignore it, or to judge it as an exceptional case, thus leaving their views intact. Even if knowledge of body type allowed us to predict the sociability of people perfectly, there are still countless other behaviors left untouched and unassessed by the system Sheldon presents. In particular, he has ignored the impact of social learning phenomena on behavior (see Chapter 16 for an assessment of the various theories we have reviewed).

Precision and Testability. In his favor, Sheldon has constructed a somatotyping scheme that is more sophisticated and precise than any devised by his predecessors. By using a seven-point rating scale instead of simple dichotomies, Sheldon has made it possible for other investigators to gauge more precisely the somatotypes and temperaments of people and to assess more accurately the relationship between the two factors. Despite his painstaking attention to measurement procedures, we should not come to the conclusion that the concepts and relational statements in Sheldon's theorizing are clear and lead to precise hypothesizing and rigorous research. Many of the terms are global and ambiguous in nature (for example, viscerotonia and somatotonia) and do not have clear and unequivocal operational referents. The relational statements of the theory are also in a rudimentary stage of development. In spite of these limitations, however, Sheldon deserves credit for attempting needed research in a largely unexplored and undefined area. Under these conditions, he has done a tremendous job in trying to assess precisely the relationships between physique and temperament.

Simplicity. Sheldon's theory fails to meet the parsimony criterion. It has too few concepts and too few assumptions to account adequately for the range and diversity of phenomena involved in a theory of personality. Sheldon recognized that the environment has a tremendous impact on the acquisition, maintenance, and modification of behavior, but his theory virtually ignores social learning phenomena and concepts. The theory, in brief, is too simple and does not do justice to the full range of variables that determine behavioral outcomes.

Empirical Validity. There have been a number of tests of Sheldon's theory, and the results have been mixed. In general, his position has not generated enough research to make a definitive statement about its empirical validity. At the moment, we can say that research support for the position is weak.

Heuristic Value. Sheldon's theory has had little impact on the thinking and research efforts of other investigators. Most are trained in an environmentalist orientation and are convinced that learning phenomena play the major role in determining behavior. As a consequence, they usually pay lip service to the importance of the biological determinants of behavior, but proceed to study problems from an environmentalist perspective. Where investigators have displayed an interest in assessing the role of biology in determining behavior, most efforts have been directed at an examination of the behavior of lower animals in an attempt to generate principles also applicable to human behavior.

Applied Value. Sheldon's theory has had little, if any, practical value. As mentioned previously, most investigators have ignored Sheldon. It is not uncommon to hear students exclaim that they ". . . thought Sheldon was a dead issue!" This chapter should have convinced you that the issues raised by Sheldon have not yet been resolved, and that they are worth further investigation. His position has considerable strengths. He has succeeded, for example, in calling our attention to the importance of the bodily determinants of behavior. He has also studied these problems empirically and helped to generate some interest in the area among investigators. His measuring system is superior to any constructed by his predecessors and provides a much more objective way of assessing physique.

Despite the empirical orientation of his efforts, however, it should be recognized that research in this area is still exploratory. Sheldon himself points out that body build and structure are direct results of heredity and of the way in which the development of the genes influences the physiology and chemistry of the body. Our knowledge of these influences is scant at the present time. There can be little question that heredity sets limits on our activities and influences our behavior in conjunction with our environmental experiences. If he has done nothing else, Sheldon has succeeded in informing us of the need for redress of the imbalance in our theoretical and research work on human behavior.

DISCUSSION QUESTIONS

1. Describe Hippocrates' typology linking the activity of humors to behavior. What are some of the inadequacies of such a typology?

2. What is phrenology? In what ways was it a serious scientific endeavor? What were some of the criticisms leveled at it by critics in a variety of disciplines?

3. Are physiognomy and phrenology completely outdated? If not, how can you explain their continued popularity in certain quarters?

4. List the three basic body types postulated by Sheldon and describe the ways in which each was related to human behavior.

5. Discuss Sheldon's theory in relation to the socialization of children. Do you believe in the use of physical punishment to discipline certain types of children? Why?

6. Discuss the implications of Sheldon's position for the treatment of individuals with behavioral problems.

7. Do constitutional positions necessarily imply the endorsement of an anti-egalitarian philosophy? What are some of the possible dangers of such positions for democratically oriented societies?

8. Why is Sheldon's position so attractive to many people?

9. Can an adequate theory of personality exist without accounting for the operation of genetic variables? Give your reasons.

10. Why do many academics continue to ignore biologically based theories of personality?

NOTES

I. L. Child, "The Relation of Somatotype to Self-Ratings on Sheldon's Temperamental Traits," *Journal of Personality*, 1950, **18**, 440–453.

R. M. Lerner, "The Development of Stereotyped Expectancies of Body Build-Behavior Relations," *Child Development*, 1969, **40**, 137–141.

W. H. Sheldon, *The Varieties of Human Physique* (New York: Harper, 1940).

W. H. Sheldon, E. M. Hartl, and E. McDermott, *Varieties of Delinquent Youth* (New York: Harper, 1949).

W. H. Sheldon and S. S. Stevens, *The Varieties of Temperament* (New York: Harper, 1942).

SUGGESTED READINGS

Sheldon, W. H. *The Varieties of Human Physique.* New York: Harper, 1940.

Sheldon, W. H., E. M. Hartl, and E. McDermott. *Varieties of Delinquent Youth.* New York: Harper, 1949.

Sheldon, W. H., and S. S. Stevens. *The Varieties of Temperament.* New York: Harper, 1942.

GLOSSARY

Cerebrotonia. Temperament type attributed by Sheldon to the ectomorphic individual. The cerebrotone is characterized by emotional restraint, tenseness, and withdrawal from others.

Constitutional Perspective. Theoretical position that emphasizes the biological and genetic determinants of behavior.

Dysplasia. Secondary body component identified by Sheldon. It refers to disharmony between different regions of the same body.

Ectomorphy. One of three basic body dimensions studied by Sheldon. The ectomorph is characterized by thinness and a large skin area and nervous system in proportion to his or her size.

Endomorphy. One of three basic body dimensions studied by Sheldon. The endomorph is characterized by softness, roundness, and a large digestive system.

Gynandromorphy. Secondary body component identified by Sheldon. It refers to the bisexual nature of the body.

Hirsutism. Secondary body component identified by Sheldon. It refers to the general hairiness of the person's body.

Mesomorphy. One of three basic body dimensions studied by Sheldon. The mesomorph is characterized by strong bones and muscles.

Morphology. Body structure of the individual.

Pyknic Practical Joke. Person who appears to have a relatively normal physique but who later in life changes dramatically in appearance and becomes obese.

Somatotonia. Temperament type attributed by Sheldon to the mesomorphic individual. The somatotone is characterized by boldness, aggressiveness, and love of physical danger and risk.

Somatotype. Establishment of a person's general body type or pattern through the assignment of a set of ratings on the three primary components. For example, an extreme mesomorph would have a somatotype of 171.

Texture. Secondary body component identified by Sheldon. It refers to the attractiveness of the person's physique.

Viscerotonia. Temperament type attributed by Sheldon to the endomorphic individual. The viscertone is characterized by relaxed posture, love of comfort, and a need for approval and affection from others.

PART 8

THE FUTURE OF PERSONALITY PSYCHOLOGY

The materials in the final chapter are designed to introduce you to some of the issues currently confronting personality psychologists as they attempt to develop new approaches. These issues are presented within an interactional model of personality format that emphasizes the joint contributions of person and situation variables to an increased understanding of human functioning. This model is actually an exploratory outline that might be utilized eventually in the development of a more adequate personality theory, and it should be seen in that light. It appears to be offered by its creator, Walter Mischel, with the aim of generating discussion of basic issues in the discipline. The major concepts and principles of the position are reviewed first, and then criticisms of it by leading personality psychologists are presented.

Walter Mischel (Courtesy of Walter Mischel)

CHAPTER 16

New Directions in the Discipline: Mischel's Proposal

We have now completed a long and complicated, yet perhaps interesting and enlightening, journey through a variety of the major perspectives on human personality. It should be apparent to you at this point that none of the theoretical systems we have reviewed meet all the criteria used by investigators in judging the scientific worth of a theory. For example, some of the theories are more capable than others of organizing a mass of unrelated facts into a coherent framework. A few are clearly superior in terms of parsimony, internal logic and consistency, and precision, as well as in terms of ability to generate testable predictions that have empirical validity. Some are comprehensive in terms of the number and variety of phenomena they treat; others are much more limited in scope. Some are stimulating and provocative; others are less influential. Some of the theories have greater applied value than others; that is, they allow investigators to create new approaches to the solution of social problems.

All, however, have made major contributions to our understanding of personality functioning. Yet there is clearly a need to develop new approaches to the study of individual differences, along with more adequate theory. What are some of the basic issues that must be addressed if progress is to be made toward that goal? What are some of the possible new directions in personality psychology? Psychologist Walter Mischel has offered us a tentative model of personality aimed at overcoming some of the difficulties in the discipline. We will first describe his model and its strengths and then present criticisms of it by some leading investigators.

AN INTERACTIONAL MODEL OF PERSONALITY

Mischel has proposed that personality psychology should adopt an interactional model which focuses on the contributions of both person and situation variables to understand personality functioning (Mischel, 1973). He believes that such a model would provide the best means for capitalizing upon the strengths of the various theoretical positions and for eliminating many of their weaknesses.

Personality is seen in this framework as a hypothetical construct that " . . . refers to the distinctive patterns of behavior (including thoughts and emotions) that characterize each individual's adaptation to the situations of his or her life" (Mischel, 1976, p. 2). In this definition, the person variables are those past experiences recorded in the nervous system and conceptualized as cognitive structures which help the individual to adapt behavior to the demands of the current situation. Situational variables are the environmental conditions or eliciting stimuli that confront the individual and affect him or her in some way. The response may be a thought or emotional reaction or an overt behavior of some kind. Within this framework, the individual is not an "empty organism" buffeted by external stimuli. Instead, he or she is conceptualized as a potentially active, thinking human being who can reinterpret incoming stimuli in light of his or her past experiences. The person is seen as actively transacting with the environment. That is, he or she is influenced by the environment, but also influences it.

General Limitations of the Person-Oriented View. Although the interactionist position just cited may seem reasonable, and perhaps even obvious, to you, Mischel notes that personality psychologists have traditionally ignored the situation side of the equation. That is, they acknowledge theoretically the interaction between person and situation, but in practice most of their attention has been focused on person variables (Mischel, 1968, p. 281). This one-sided emphasis can be seen clearly in the Freudian position and in the work of trait theorists and humanistic psychologists. It also characterizes much of the work of Adler and Jung, but is somewhat less apparent in Fromm's theory. Sheldon's position too focuses almost exclusively on person variables, since he is mostly concerned with understanding how biology determines behavior and pays little attention to the role of the environment. Finally, Kelly's position is strongly cognitive and focuses almost exclusively on the ways in which the person's unique construct system influences behavior.

The person approach to the study of personality postulates the existence of broad and stable characteristics that operate regularly across virtually all situations, according to Mischel. The assumption is that the situation plays only a minor role in the modification of behavior. Yet we know that people change their behavior in response to environmental influences throughout their lives. The person who marries changes in many ways as a result of that new status. Entrance into careers and the playing of new roles—for example, athlete, lover, and student—also change behavior. We are changed as a result of births in the family, by the deaths of loved ones, by educational experiences, and by increases in taxes and unemployment. The point should be clear. Yet many of the current positions in personality psychology deemphasize the situational determinants of behavior. This practice has tremendous implications for personality assessment and change, as will become apparent when we examine some major theories that utilize the approach later in this chapter. For now, remember that Mischel believes these psychologies present an oversimplified and inaccurate view of the means by which behavior is acquired, maintained, and modified.

General Limitations of the Situation-Oriented View. In contrast to one-sided, person-oriented psychologies that typically have their roots in the clinical tradition, there are positions commonly assumed to rely almost exclusively on the role of environmental or situational factors in their treatment of human behavior. In these positions, personality variables are treated as "error variance" which the theorist needs to minimize, typically by strengthening his environmental manipulations. This view maintains that situations or environmental conditions are the primary causes of behavior. Skinner's position could reasonably be characterized as situationist, despite his recent acknowledgment of the importance of cognitive mediating processes.

The general point to be made is that the construction of theories focused primarily on either person or situation variables has hindered the development of an adequate theory of personality. The interactionist model, in contrast, provides an avenue for rectifying this deficiency. Recent research has also shown that behavior is best understood by accounting for the contributions of both person and situation variables (Endler and Magnusson, 1976).

We now turn to a review of some of the limitations Mischel sees in the various person-oriented theories.

Imprecise Concepts

Mischel argues that the person-oriented perspectives—the psychodynamic, trait, and humanistic views, among others—have limited scientific utility because the constructs they use to describe underlying dispositions that direct behavior are too global in nature and ill-defined. Examples might include Freud's id, ego, and superego; Jung's anima and animus; Adler's striving for superiority; Fromm's need for transcendence; Allport's central traits; Cattell's ego-strength, dominance, venturesome (parmia) and imaginative (autia) traits; Maslow's security needs; Rogers' drive for self-actualization; and May's concept of anxiety, which he defines as a threat to Dasein. To illustrate Mischel's point further, let us examine the measurement and definitional problems associated with three other constructs, namely, Freud's death instinct, Jung's shadow, and Maslow's peak experience.

Freud's Death Instinct. Freud first postulated the existence of a death instinct to "explain" the eruption of aggressive impulses that resulted in destructive behavior toward others or oneself. He based his concept on the idea in biology that all human beings are composed of organic materials which eventually decompose and return to an inanimate state. He then gave this simple description explanatory power. Thus, he saw the death instinct as an agency within the individual causing the person to be aggressive and destructive.

What were the parameters of the death instinct? Freud himself acknowledged that they were not easy to specify. He thought that it was a " . . . special physiological process . . ." that eventually directed behavior (Freud, 1960, p. 30). He then talked about this process in terms of a blending of life forces (Eros) and death forces (Thanatos), because for him, every action was the result of the combined forces of life and death. In his view, the death instinct operated in the following way:

> It *appears* that, as a result of the combination of unicellular organisms into multicellular forms of life, the death instinct of the single cell can successfully be neutralized and the destructive impulses be diverted on to the external world through the instrumentality of a special organ. This special organ would *seem* to be the muscular apparatus; and the death instinct would thus *seem* to express itself—though *probably* only in part—as an instinct of destruction directed against the external world and other organisms. (Freud, 1960, p. 31. Italics added)

As you can see, this description is speculative. The referents in the example are vague, and Freud begs the question by assuming there is a "death instinct" in every single cell. It is clear that cells die, but not that a death instinct causes them to die. Furthermore, even if we grant the validity of his argument, why should a death instinct cell that is successfully neutralized by a life instinct cell have any energy or impulses left to divert into muscular channels? How are they diverted into muscular channels?

In fairness to Freud, he did recognize that the physiological process underlying the death instinct was vague, but the more general point is that he then proceeded to talk about the instinct as though it existed and controlled much of human behavior. He used it as a post hoc device to explain a variety of behaviors he observed among his patients and believed it was a scientifically useful tool. The problems with both its measurement and explanatory status should be evident.

Jung's Shadow. In regard to Jung's shadow construct, we can also ask: What exactly are its referents? That is, what are the publicly observable and agreed-upon indicators of the shadow? If we know what they were, and if we could establish a reliable means of measuring them, then perhaps the construct would have potential scientific utility. Under these conditions, investigators could incorporate it into their hypothesizing and use it to make differential predictions about behavior. If we examine Jung's definition of the term, however, we begin to see the extreme difficulty in establishing such a measure. For him, the shadow

> . . . is a *moral problem* that challenges the *whole ego personality*, for no one can become conscious of the shadow without considerable effort. To become conscious of it involves recognizing the *dark aspects* of the personality as present and real. . . . Closer examination of the dark characteristics—that is, the *inferiorities* constituting the shadow—reveals that they have an emotional nature, a kind of *autonomy*, and accordingly an *obsessive* or, better, *possessive* quality. Emotion, incidentally, is not an activity of the individual but something that happens to him. Affects occur usually where adaptation is weakest, and at the same time they reveal the reason for its weakness, namely, a certain degree of inferiority and the existence of a lower level of personality. (Jung, 1958, p. 7. Italics added, first sentence)

What does Jung mean by *moral problem*? What are the *dark aspects* of personality? Although we may have some intuitive understanding of these terms and others in his definition, it is clear that to define these referents of the shadow would be difficult, if not impossible. In addition, Jung's attempts to have us understand the meaning of the shadow construct hinge upon an exploration of the psyche. In short, we would have to plunge even further into the "depths" of the psyche if we were ever to attain even an approximation of its meaning. Such a procedure takes us further from the observables of external reality and leaves us tangled in a web of mystery that may be interesting and entertaining, but is scientifically not very useful. To highlight these points, it should be mentioned that Jung believed the shadow was easier to define than his anima and animus archetypes, so you can imagine the efforts required to begin to make scientific sense of these constructs, if indeed it is possible at all.

Maslow's Peak Experience. Maslow, like Freud and Jung, recognized the ambiguities of his peak experience construct and the difficulties in defining and measuring it. Yet he persisted in trying to refine the concept, which is perfectly legitimate and to his credit. He believed that the construct was an important one and would have to be incorporated into any adequate theory of personality. The problem is not that he decided to include it in his initial theorizing despite its imprecision, but whether or not it can, in the context of an evolving theory, be refined so that it becomes scientifically useful. With Maslow's peak experience concept, perhaps it is premature to call for a scientific verdict. This is less true for some of the Freudian and Jungian concepts, since they have been in existence so much longer and have undergone little, if any, positive change. It seems reasonable to assume, though, that Maslow's construct is so broad and poorly defined that it will probably eventually suffer the same fate.

What are the distinguishing characteristics of peak experiences, according to Maslow? First, they are good and desirable experiences and never experienced as evil or undesirable. What does Maslow mean by "good" and "evil"? We are not told exactly, but are informed that they are perfect and intrinsically valid experiences. They are, in his words,

> . . . as good as [they] *should* be. [They are] reacted to with awe, wonder, amazement, humility, and even reverence, exaltation and piety. The word sacred is occasionally used to describe the person's reaction to [them]. [They are] delightful and "amusing" in a Being sense. (Maslow, 1962, p. 76)

What does Maslow mean by ". . . as good as [they] *should* be?" If the word "sacred" is used only occasionally to describe the experiences, why is it not used on all occasions? On what occasions would the word not describe the experiences? What is a sense of Being?

Peak experiences have other characteristics as well. They include a sense of wholeness, perfection, completion, justice, aliveness, richness, simplicity, beauty, goodness, uniqueness, effortlessness, playfulness, truth, and self-sufficiency. What do these terms mean? See Table 16.1 for some of their meanings. As you can see from an examination of the

TABLE 16.1   Characteristics of Peak Experiences

A person would have a sense of
  (1) wholeness; (unity; integration; tendency to one-ness; interconnectedness; simplicity; organization; structure; dichotomy-transcendence; order);
  (2) perfection; (necessity; just-right-ness; just-so-ness; inevitability; suitability; justice; completeness; "ought-ness");
  (3) completion; (ending; finality; justice; "it's finished"; fulfillment; finis and telos; destiny; fact);
  (4) justice; (fairness; orderliness; lawfulness; "oughtness");
  (5) aliveness; (process; non-deadness; spontaneity; self-regulation; full-functioning);
  (6) richness; (differentiation, complexity; intricacy);
  (7) simplicity; (honesty; nakedness; essentiality; abstract, essential, skeletal structure);
  (8) beauty; (rightness; form; aliveness; simplicity; richness; wholeness; perfection; completion; uniqueness; honesty);
  (9) goodness; (rightness; desirability; oughtness; justice; benevolence; honesty);
 (10) uniqueness; (idiosyncrasy; individuality; non-comparability; novelty);
 (11) effortlessness; (ease; lack of strain, striving or difficulty; grace; perfect, beautiful functioning);
 (12) playfulness; (fun; joy; amusement; gaiety; humor; exuberance; effortlessness);
 (13) truth; honesty; reality; (nakedness; simplicity; richness; oughtness; beauty; pure, clean and unadulterated completeness; essentiality);
 (14) self-sufficiency; (autonomy; independence; not-needing-other-than-itself-in-order-to-be-itself; self-determining environment-transcendence; separateness; living by its own laws).

Adapted from A. Maslow, *Toward a Psychology of Being*, 1962, p. 78.

table, the problems of precise definition and measurement are stagger-ing.

This discussion was meant only to provide you with a concrete illus-tration of the use of global and imprecisely defined constructs by many theorists who focus on person variables. Similar arguments could be mustered in regard to the ambiguity of many other constructs. Recall the ambiguities in Fromm's definition of conscience as the "reaction of ourselves to ourselves," Freud's concept of the life instincts, and the construct of potentiality that is utilized by the humanistic psychologists.

Interpretational Difficulties

Mischel maintains that in the person-oriented theories there is an added problem of confusion and lack of precision because of the assumption that the various dispositions (traits, id impulses, strivings for supe-riority, needs for self-actualization) are not observed directly, but are in-ferred from various behavioral signs. In short, overt behavior is merely an indicator of the operation of underlying causal factors. The investiga-tor's job, then, is to try to understand the underlying meaning of the overt behavior. To accomplish this goal, he or she must plunge into the "depths" of the person's psyche and untangle the complex interweav-ings of underlying motives that produce the surface behavior. The investigator's primary focus, in other words, is on understanding the "dynamics" of the behavior in question.

In the Freudian scheme, for example, there is the continual attempt by the ego and superego to distort or deny the expression of id impulses in surface behavior. If the behavior ever does reach the surface, it is usually disguised. Dancing, for instance, may be seen as a kind of sublimated activity in which undesirable impulses are converted into socially ac-ceptable forms of behavior. Creative painting can also be thought of in similar terms. Harmless "slips of the tongue" are seen as indicators of underlying conflicts, as you know. Even healthy statements like "I love my mother" may be taken by Freudian therapists under certain circum-stances to be a distortion of one's "true" feelings. As you can imagine, it is extremely difficult to determine the precise meaning of overt behavior in such a theoretical framework.

Although the concepts and propositions in Kelly's theory are clearly defined, it too assumes that overt behavior is merely a sign of underly-ing causal factors. For him, the underlying dispositions are personal constructs. To understand the meaning of overt actions, we must under-stand the underlying personal constructs that cause them. Thus, his Role Construct Repertory Test is conceptualized as a rough indicator of the kinds of personal constructs that guide the person's behavior in certain channels (Kelly, 1955, pp. 204–205). Like Cattell, he thinks that the raw data provided by the test can be factor analyzed to reveal the un-derlying sources of the person's behavior. Once again, precision in interpreting the meaning (or even meanings) of overt behavior becomes difficult.

Finally, Mischel maintains that clinicians guided by concepts about underlying causal factors have not been able to predict behavior better than investigators using the person's self-reports (Mischel, 1973, p. 254). For Mischel, then, it might be best to consider discarding the indirect approach to the assessment of personality. At the very least, Mischel thinks that investigators using the indirect approach will have to demonstrate its usefulness empirically.

Lack of Utility in Making Accurate Predictions

As we have seen, an adequate theory should lead eventually to the testing of hypotheses and the collection of data that are supportive of it. Mischel thinks that the person-oriented theories generally lack predictive utility. He argues, for example, that a knowledge of the person's underlying traits does not allow us to predict current behavior very well. In order to predict accurately, he thinks we must also take into account the specific kinds of situational factors that help to modify the behavior.

That exclusive reliance on person variables can lead to poor predictive validity outcomes can be seen clearly in Sheldon's work. The correlations between the various physique dimensions and behavior ratings in the study designed to test the validity of Sheldon's theorizing were low, as you may recall. The relationship between endomorphy and viscerotonia was only +.13. Between mesomorphy and somatotonia, it was +.38; and between ectomorphy and cerebretotonia, it was only +.27. Again, poor predictive validity outcomes could be expected, since the role of situational parameters has been ignored. Part of the definition of viscerotonia, for example, is *indiscriminate* amiability. It implies that endomorphs will be friendly and happy in all situations, a rarity for virtually all of us regardless of body type. Consider our behavior at family funerals, boxing matches, bankruptcy proceedings, during lover's quarrels, divorce proceedings, academic suspensions, and so forth.

Low correlations would also be expected, according to Mischel, because most of the traditional, person-oriented theories utilize constructs such as viscerotonia, somatotonia, and cerebrotonia, which are so global and contain so many ambiguous and diverse dimensions (Mischel, 1968, p. 60). For example, somatotonia is measured by rating people on dimensions like lust for power, claustrophobia, love of risk and chance, overmaturity of appearance, orientation toward goals and activities of youth, competitive aggressiveness, and so forth. Is it any wonder that accuracy of prediction suffers when an investigator utilizes such an unreliable and crude measure in the prediction equation?

Cattell should be given tremendous credit for trying to establish the empirical validity of some of his major ideas, but his reliance on trait predictors still leads, in general, to only a limited understanding of the variables that control behavior. In the study cited in Chapter 7 in which the 16 PF test was used as a predictor of marital satisfaction, for example, only two of the sixteen factors, ego strength and guilt-prone-ness, correlated significantly with sexual gratification. That is, subjects who reported being emotionally stable (high ego-strength) and secure and untroubled (low on guilt-proneness) also reported high sexual gratification in their marriages. In addition to the fact that only two of the factors were significantly associated with sexual gratification, the correlation between ego-strength and sexual gratification was only + .20. In fairness, it should be noted that the correlation between guilt-proneness and sexual gratification was high, − .73. There were also several other high correlations between various factors and other aspects of marital satisfaction. In general, however, most of the correlations were low or nonexistent.

Even if all the correlations had been high, Mischel might still maintain that the results could have been due to the fact that all the variables were measured through the use of questionnaires. A great deal of research has shown that various personality measures correlate very well with reported behaviors, if both factors have been assessed by use of questionnaires, but that the magnitude of the relationships between these variables are low if one variable was assessed via questionnaire and the other by another method. Thus, questionnaire-questionnaire correlations, such as those utilized in Cattell's study, should be interpreted with caution (Mischel, 1968, p. 77). As you can see, this methodological artifact can create special problems in trying to assess the validity of many of the person-oriented theories, since they tend to rely heavily on the use of paper-and-pencil tests to measure hypothesized underlying traits and dispositions.

In summary, the person-oriented theories reviewed here have limited scientific utility, according to Mischel. This does not mean, that there are no aspects of these theories which are worthwhile. It seems clear, for example, that an adequate conceptualization of personality must account for the ways in which unconscious factors influence behavior, so that Freud's seminal insights in these areas cannot be disregarded. Such a theory must also be comprehensive enough to incorporate the kinds of phenomena (love, hate, passion, creativity, courage, and altruism) that have been largely ignored by the social learning theorists, in line with the cogent recommendations of humanistic psychologists like Maslow, Rogers, and May. It must also deal with the complexity, richness, and organization of inner experience, as advocated by the humanists and by theorists such as Allport and Kelly. The contributions of biology to an understanding of personality, as emphasized by Sheldon and others, also cannot be ignored. These and numerous other positive contributions made by person-oriented theorists need to be incorporated into the new model, if it is to account for personality functioning adequately.

As this point, let us turn to an examination of the basic concepts and principles of Mischel's model.

BASIC CONCEPTS AND PRINCIPLES OF THE INTERACTIONAL MODEL

Basic Unit of Analysis

Mischel's proposed *cognitive social learning model* shifts the focus from global traits and motives that underlie and guide behavior to the individual's idiosyncratic cognitions and behavior patterns. These distinctive cognitive and behavioral activities are studied in relation to the specific conditions that evoke, maintain, and modify them. The ways in which the individual's unique cognitive and behavioral activities effect changes in these conditions is also a topic of major interest and study (Mischel, 1968, p. 265).

Mischel believes that the study of cognitive and behavioral activities will involve an examination of the unique reinforcement histories of individuals and the particular situations which evoked these activities. In order to predict cognitive and behavioral actions accurately, then, analysis must center on the unique meanings that stimuli and reinforcers have for individuals. This is a sentiment echoed loudly by Allport in his arguments favoring the development of an idiographic approach to the study of personality. In Mischel's view,

> . . . behavioral assessment involves an exploration of the unique or idiographic aspects of the single case, perhaps to a greater extent than any other approach. Social behavior theory (or cognitive social learning theory) recognizes the individuality of each person and of each unique situation. This is a curious feature when one considers the "mechanistic S-R" stereotypes not infrequently attached by critics to behavioral analyses. Assessing the acquired meaning of stimuli is the core of social behavior assessment. (Mischel, 1968, p. 190)

Thus, Mischel's approach leads to a focus on the unique aspects of individual behavior and thereby attempts to overcome a criticism long voiced by Allport and many of the humanistic psychologists. Furthermore, to understand the acquired meanings of reinforcers and situational stimuli, it is often necessary to focus on the person's own subjective interpretation of events and not primarily upon assessment by outside observers. The focus is on the person and his or her phenomenological understanding of the meaning of events, a position consistent with one long championed by the humanists. This does not mean, of course, that research focused on "average" differences between people is completely worthless. There may be many instances in which individuals subjectively agree on the meaning of events and in which knowledge about these cultural and experiential equivalences can be utilized to good advantage in the prediction of behavior. It simply means we must try to be aware of the fact that often ". . . idiosyncratic histories produce idiosyncratic stimulus meanings" and that it may be futile to seek common dimensions in such cases (Mischel, 1973, p. 259).

The point can be demonstrated by discussing a hypothetical case in which a student who experiences anxiety in speaking in public is treated with a behavior therapy technique called "systematic desensitization." To help the student overcome his problem, the therapist would first ask him to report the specific conditions that generate anxiety on a gradient of severity from least to most severe. For this person, the situational gradient might include self-report statements such as "I feel slightly anxious in the morning when I first get out of bed and think of having to give the speech"; "I feel more anxious when I see the classroom where I will give the speech"; "I feel even more anxiety when the instructor introduces me to the class"; and "I feel overwhelmed by anxiety when I first begin to speak." Once this anxiety hierarchy had been created, the student would be given deep muscle relaxation training.

Once these two steps had been accomplished, it would be possible for the systematic desensitization process to begin. Using the individually generated anxiety hierarchy, the therapist would present the client with the least severe anxiety-provoking stimuli, either pictorially or verbally, and actually encourage him to make incompatible relaxation responses in their presence. Once the person had learned to relax in their presence and not to feel anxious, the therapist would present the anxiety-provoking stimuli that were next in the hierarchy, and the relaxation procedures would be reinstituted until the person reported feeling no anxiety in their presence. The process would be repeated until the person was able to cope with all the stimuli in his anxiety hierarchy.

It is apparent, however, that this student's hierarchy cannot be utilized in the treatment of all individuals who fear speaking in public. Some individuals, for example, may feel most anxious on arising in the morning on the day of the speech and feel very little anxiety on being introduced by the instructor. The construction of anxiety hierarchies based on the assumption that all individuals experience the same amounts of anxiety in the presence of identical stimuli would lead to ineffective treatment. If, on the other hand, empirical investigation revealed that most students reported similar anxiety hierarchies in these areas, it might be possible to utilize that information in the treatment of comparable groups of students if it were impossible to secure the information from the students individually. In such an instance, it would be predicted that treatment would still be effective.

A New Look at Person Variables

Mischel notes that social learning theory has concerned itself in recent years primarily with the discovery of the various conditions that control the acquisition, maintenance and modification of behavior. This emphasis can perhaps be seen most clearly in the work of Skinner and Bandura, reviewed in Chapters 9 and 11. Yet he feels that not enough attention has been paid to the role played by person variables which are the product of the individual's prior history in mediating the ways in which new experiences affect behavior. As a result, he proposes the incorporation of several cognitive constructs into the current social learning model as a means of improving its scientific usefulness. These variables include the person's competencies to generate diverse behaviors under appropriate conditions and his unique ways of encoding and organizing events. They also include attention to the person's expectancies about outcomes, the subjective value of such outcomes, and his self-regulatory systems and plans. The astute reader of the text will note the similarity between the use of the expectancy and subjective value of outcomes concepts and Rotter's concepts of expectancy and reinforcement value. The general point is that the proposed model attempts to incorporate many of the elements of the theories of Skinner, Rotter, and Bandura, and introduces some new factors as well. At this juncture, let us review each of the five constructs in turn.

Competency Constructs. After reviewing the research literature, Mischel comes to the conclusion that certain cognitive and intellectual abilities are fairly stable and influence a person's behavior in many, but not all, situations. These factors or "competencies" refer to the person's abilities to ". . . transform and use information actively and to create thoughts and actions (as in problem-solving), rather than to a store of static cognitions and responses that one 'has' in some mechanical storehouse (Mischel, 1976, p. 501). These skills include intelligence, task accomplishments, and cognitive style. There are great differences in intellectual abilities among people, vast differences in actual task accomplishments, and marked differences in cognitive structures. In regard to cognitive style, for example, some people are more analytical and differentiated in their views of the world than others, as work by Kelly and others has shown us. These ability differences are important and must be accounted for in an adequate theory of personality. Their inclusion suggests a conception of human beings as active and discriminating in their judgments of the world, not simply possessed of global traits or motives that force them to act in indiscriminate fashion.

Encoding Strategies. Cognitive social learning theory also considers the way in which people with different skills actively represent and symbolize or encode information from the environment. Often people modify the impact of a given stimulus by cognitively transforming it and by assigning it a special meaning. Failure on an examination, for example, will be seen as an opportunity for new learning and self-improvement by one student and as evidence of worthlessness by another. As a result, we might predict that the two students will show different behaviors following failure. One student might seek out the professor and discuss her errors on the examination and improve her knowledge of the materials as a result. The other, convinced that the failure means he is worthless and incompetent, will avoid discussion of his performance with the professor and will, as a consequence, continue to perform incompetently.

People not only assign different meanings to the same stimuli, but select different aspects of the same stimuli for encoding and interpretation (Mischel, 1973, p. 267). These differences in attentional focus have strong implications for performance effectiveness. Research has shown, for example, that high test-anxious students perform more poorly on examinations than low test-anxious students because the two types tend to focus on different aspects of the test (Wine, 1971). While low test-anxious students focus on task-relevant variables during examinations, high test-anxious students focus on irrelevant cues. More specifically, it has been found that while low test-anxious students concern themselves with answering the test items, highly anxious students worry instead about the consequences of failure, about how well others are doing, about their own worthlessness and stupidity in not being able to answer the questions quickly enough, and about how their worrying is affecting them physically. It is no wonder they perform so poorly. It is also clear that an adequate theory of personality must account for individual encoding strategies.

Expectancies and Subjective Values. Not only does Mischel's theory address itself to what the person *can* do and to how he or she categorizes events, it also pays primary attention to the ways in which the person's expectancies and values determine behavior. As you already know from reading the chapter materials on Rotter, the expectancies of the individual refer to his or her hypotheses about the consequences of utilizing different behaviors in given situations. In Mischel's theory, expectancies are classified in terms of *behavior-outcomes* and *stimulus-outcomes*. The first type of expectancy involves the person's hypotheses about the consequences or reinforcement outcomes likely to occur if he or she chooses to perform a given behavior. The second type of expectancy involves the person's hypotheses about the kinds of outcomes that will occur if certain stimuli are present. These stimuli or "signs" help the person predict the kinds of events that are likely to occur (Mischel, 1976, pp. 503–504).

It is clear from our discussions of the expectancy concept in the Rotter chapter that differences in expectancies between people often lead to differences in behavior. But the fact that two people have identical expectancies in a given situation does not necessarily mean they will behave in the same way. Their behavior depends not only upon their expectancies, but upon the subjective value of the outcomes for them. For example, two students may have the same expectancies for success in school—that is, they may be equally confident that the use of their abilities will lead to successful performances on examinations—but they may behave quite differently because one of them feels securing A grades is important, whereas the other feels it is unimportant. Thus, a knowledge of the person's particular likes and dislikes, as well as his expectancies, is critical if we are to account adequately for personality functioning.

Self-Regulatory Systems and Plans. Mischel attempts to account as well for the effects of externally administered and self-administered reinforcers on behavior. That is, the theory addresses itself to an understanding of the various ways in which we regulate our own behavior by imposing goals or standards on ourselves and then by reacting to our performances with self-praise or self-criticism depending upon how well they meet our expectations. In attempting to conceptualize the organization of complex self-regulatory behavior, Mischel believes it will be necessary to consider the kinds of "priority rules" the person uses to select behaviors that will lead him or her to a final goal. In short, it will be necessary to account for the kinds of "plans" the individual makes to control the complicated sequence of steps that will eventually facilitate movement toward the attainment of a long-range goal. Mischel feels personality investigators have not paid enough attention to the planning behavior of people (Mischel, 1973, pp. 274–275).

We have already seen in the chapter material on Skinner and Bandura that the study of self-control processes is a new and exciting one and that there are a variety of techniques we can use to control our behavior. At this point, let us turn to a consideration of the ways in which the social learning principles and techniques that have emerged from the study of self-regulatory processes might be utilized in the development of a personality psychology compatible with the major goals and values of the humanistic psychologists.

A Humanist-Behaviorist Compromise

You will recall from Part 6 on the humanistic existential perspectives that the humanistic psychologists have often accused the behaviorists of creating a picture of human beings as automatons buffeted and controlled by environmental forces. This view has some elements of truth in it. It is true, for example, that the emphasis in many of the early brands of behaviorism was on the environmental determinants of behavior, and that only those behaviors which could be measured precisely and reliably were considered worthy of study. The humanists, in contrast, have consistently opted for the creation of a psychology in which human beings are free to make their own choices and to control their own destinies. They also insist on the study of problems that have meaning for the individual.

A recent article by psychologist Carl Thoresen suggests that the behaviorists and humanists may be able to reconcile their differences in these areas. Behavioral research results on self-control processes suggest that individual freedoms can be maximized when people become aware of the kinds of environmental events that control their behavior and when they use this information actively to change their environments. In so doing, they act as creative human beings capable of fashioning their own destinies in line with their own desires. Thoresen points out further that many of the goals of the humanists can be translated into terms that are objectively researchable. For example, the humanistic statements "Increase self-knowledge; know what is going on within; be really aware of self," and "Accept yourself as worthy; experience yourself as positive; think positively about self and others," can be translated to read "Increase the frequency, variety, and accuracy of self-observation of internal responses such as thoughts, images, and physiological responses," and "Decrease the frequency and variety of self-critical, negative responses," respectively. Once these statements have been translated, it would be possible to conduct research that would eventually result in the identification of techniques to allow the person to increase his self-awareness and reduce self-critical remarks. In brief, behavioral research on various aspects of self-control could thus lead to the development of methods that enable people to act in more humanistic ways (Thoresen, 1974). At the very least, some of the current research in self-control processes offers the exciting possibility of an eventual synthesis between the behavioral and humanistic perspectives.

We have now considered the basic elements and principles in the proposed cognitive social learning model. We have also learned how it incorporates many of the strengths in current personality theorizing and also some of the ways in which it makes unique contributions to the discipline. At this juncture, we turn to an examination of the theory's applied value by focusing on current research in the area of behavioral disorders.

APPLICATION OF THE MODEL TO BEHAVIORAL DISORDER TREATMENT

Traditional Treatment Approaches and the Newer Cognitive-Behavioral Therapies

The traditional approaches to the treatment of "mentally ill" people focus on attempts by the therapist to understand the underlying traits, motives, and dispositions that create problems for individuals. The behaviors these "patients" show are seen merely as "symptoms" of underlying "pathology." Thus, the therapist's job is to unravel the underlying "dynamics" of the problem and "cure" the patient by helping him to understand why he is behaving in ways that cause him pain. The emphasis in these "talk" therapies, constructed by theorists such as Freud, Jung, Adler, Rogers, Maslow, and May, is on personality change through insight, self-awareness, and acceptance of feelings.

The newer behavior therapies, in contrast, involve the application of cognitive social learning principles derived from experimental research to problem behaviors. The assumption in these therapies is that, since behavior is regulated by highly specific stimulus variables and rein-forcers, the focus should be on precise identification of the factors that produce the problem behavior. Once these conditions have been identified, it is assumed that they can be altered in ways advantageous to the person (Mischel, 1968, p. 193). Thus, the emphasis is more on the behavior itself and on the identification of controlling variables rather than on the assessment of global traits and motives. Behavior is seen not as symptomatic of "deep conflicts," but as the focus of interest.

This shift in emphasis from an analysis of the dynamics of a problem to the behavior itself has occurred for a number of reasons. First, at-tempts to categorize people as schizophrenic, manic-depressive, and obsessive-compulsive, for example, have been largely unsuccessful. There is considerable overlap between the behavior subsumed by the different categories and little agreement among raters on how to classify a given behavior. Even if problem behavior could be classified reliably, the underlying dynamics are so poorly specified and related to the sur-face behavior that it is unclear what kinds of treatment should be used to "cure" the person. Second, labeling people with the names of diseases whose referents are largely unknown also prevents the behavior changer (the therapist) from concentrating on the psychological condi-tions that control behavior. Third, and finally, there is little scientific evi-dence that the traditional psychotherapies work. Major research studies have shown, for example, that untreated patients seem to fare as well as patients who have been treated by the traditional insight therapies. Al-though this research has been legitimately criticized on methodological grounds, the lack of significant results in so many of these studies raises serious doubts about their effectiveness (Mischel, 1968, pp. 194–197).

The evidence supporting the effectiveness of the behavior therapies, on the other hand, is stronger. Research has shown that improvement rates in patients treated with behavior therapy range from well over 50 percent to 90 percent. Not only are these therapies generally more effec-tive in helping people, but they are considerably less expensive and time-consuming than many of the more traditional therapies. For these and other reasons, the behavioral therapies have become increasingly popular with clinical psychologists in the last decade. At this point, let us consider some research examples of the treatment of different prob-lems with some of the behavioral therapies.

Systematic Desensitization

As you have already learned, systematic desensitization procedures in-volve a form of counterconditioning in which a person is trained to respond to anxiety-eliciting stimuli with incompatible responses. Eventually, his anxiety in the presence of these stimuli is either greatly reduced or eliminated. Systematic desensitization has proved to be ef-fective in the treatment of public-speaking anxieties, animal phobias, test anxiety in students, acrophobia (fear of high places), claustrophobia (fear of enclosed places), sexual impotence in men and women, fearful avoidance of cars and planes, persistent fears about physical injury, illness, and dying, compulsiveness, insomnia, alcoholism, and so forth.

In one study designed to test the efficacy of systematic desensitization for modifying different kinds of phobic behavior, people who were acrophobic, claustrophobic, or sexually impotent responded to items on their individually created anxiety hierarchies with deep muscle relaxation responses until they reported feeling no anxiety in the presence of the various stimuli. The therapeutic outcomes for the acrophobics and claustrophobics were then objectively assessed by situational tests. That is, the acrophobics were required to climb a fire escape to a height of 50 feet and then to accompany the experimenter in an elevator to the roof of an eight-story building, where they were required to look down for two minutes at the street and to count passing cars. The claustrophobics were required to remain in a small vehicle for five minutes without physical disturbance. For obvious ethical reasons, the behavior of the sexually impotent people was not monitored directly. Instead, the investigator relied on self-report data. The results showed that phobic behavior was completely extinguished in 72 percent of the cases and remained so for a considerable time period (Lazarus, 1969).

More recent studies show that the desensitization procedure does not necessarily need to be administered by a trained therapist. The client can desensitze himself by making taperecordings under the direction of a therapist and then utilizing them in private to overcome his fears. One man who was unable to participate in staff meetings because of intense speaking anxieties successfully desensitized himself at home by using specially constructed tapes (Migler and Wolpe, 1967). Although this procedure has some limitations, it also seems to have considerable clinical promise, since there are many clients and relatively few therapists. The use of such procedures would greatly increase the number of clients who could receive treatment.

Covert Sensitization

In the covert sensitization procedure, undesirable approach behaviors such as overeating, smoking, or excessive drinking are reduced or eliminated by associating them with aversive stimuli. The person is asked to imagine both the desired behavior and the punishing consequences of engaging in it. As a result, he or she can build up an aversion to stimuli that were highly gratifying. Since both the behavior and the punishing consequences are imagined and not actually performed, the technique is called covert sensitization. In the case of an alcoholic, for example, the person is asked to imagine he has entered a bar, ordered a drink and that, after drinking it, aversive consequences follow. The following is a scene actually used in the treatment of an alcoholic:

> You are walking into a bar. You decide to have a glass of beer. You are now walking toward the bar. As you are approaching the bar you have a funny feeling in the pit of your stomach. Your stomach feels all queasy and nauseous. Some liquid comes up your throat and it is very sour. You try to swallow it back down, but as you do this food particles start coming up your throat to your mouth. You are now reaching the bar and you order a beer. As the bartender is pouring the beer, puke comes into your mouth. You try to keep your mouth closed and swallow it back down. You reach for the glass of beer to wash it down. As soon as your hand touches the glass, you can't hold it down any longer. You have to open your mouth and you puke. It goes all over your hand, all over the glass and the beer. You can see it floating around in the beer. Snot and mucous come out of your nose. Your shirt and pants are all full of vomit. The bartender has some on his shirt. You notice people looking at you. You get sick again and you vomit some more and more. You turn away from the beer and immediately you start to feel better. As you run out of the bar room, you start to feel better and better. When you get out into the clean fresh air you feel wonderful. You go home and clean yourself up. (Cautela, 1967)

This vivid scene will probably, and unfortunately, affect your text reading behavior for years to come, but some investigators have pointed out that clients sometimes feel the scenes are not aversive enough to force them to stop their gratifying but maladjustive behavior. In addition, some clients report that they cannot adequately imagine such scenes. Some investigators have modified the procedure by introducing various vomit-inducing drugs or other aversive stimuli. In one recent study, for example, a malodorous substance, valeric acid, was presented at critical times during scene presentations and had excellent results (Maletzky, 1974). Exhibitionist subjects first worked with a therapist to create scenes that varied in their levels of sexual pleasure as well as to create a list of noxious images that varied in their intensity. Such images included scenes of vomiting, contact with urine and feces, and scenes of embarrassment or ridicule on being arrested or being laughed at by the victim. Following the construction of these hierarchies, the subjects were asked to imagine themselves engaging in the desired behavior and then experiencing the aversive consequences. As they proceeded through the hierarchies and reached the scenes that gave them maximum sexual pleasure—for example, driving to a laundry at night, approaching a pretty blonde, and exposing themselves—and they imagined getting nauseous and vomiting all over themselves, they were given a whiff of the highly noxious substance. After this experience, all the scenes were repeated. Subjects went through the series twice during one session. In all, there were five such sessions. Between sessions, scenes were taperecorded and listened to at home. Subjects also administered the valeric acid fumes to themselves in the home situation at the appropriate times.

Self-support data and an objective test of exhibitionistic activity were obtained to measure the effectiveness of the sensitization procedure.

The self-report data consisted of a frequency account of subjects' statements concerning their urges to expose themselves and their fantasies and dreams about exposing themselves. The objective test consisted of having a comely actress try to tempt the subjects by acting seductively and by placing herself in situations in which the subjects had previously acknowledged showing exposure behavior. For example, the actress walked by a subject's car as he drove by a local high school where he had a record of exposing himself. These two tests were conducted shortly after the covert sensitization treatment had been completed and then once again a year later. Both overt and covert exhibitionism ceased completely in all cases but one. In this particular case, the subject called the actress over to the porch where he was sitting and engaged her in conversation by asking her the time. He was then noted stimulating his genitals and finally exposing himself. The experimenter reports that the actress walked away briskly.

Despite the excellent results, you might ask yourself about the ethics of hiring an actress to entice these men. The experimenter was aware of the possible ethical implications of his study and reported that he had informed all the subjects in advance that "experimental and unusual procedures" would be employed, and they all agreed to participate. In addition, the experimenter argued that he had to know whether the treatment he had used was indeed effective, so that he would know whether there was justification in continuing to use it to help other people suffering from the same problem. Finally, he maintained that the two widely spaced and unrewarded temptations would not affect the subjects adversely. You will have to make your own judgment on whether you agree or disagree with the experimenter's contentions. Comments about the ethics of using certain behavior modification procedures have already been made in the Skinner chapter (see Chapter 9); additional comments will be made at the end of this chapter.

Behavioral Training

Behavioral training is the generic term for a multitreatment therapeutic approach that defines behavioral problems as the result of specific skill deficits and that seeks to overcome these deficits by giving the person training to increase skills in deficient areas. Such training has been utilized and proved effective in increasing interpersonal communication skills in psychiatric patients and students, in rehabilitating juvenile offenders, in reducing parent-child conflicts, and in increasing assertive behavior in submissive women (Twentyman and McFall, 1973).

In regard to assertiveness training, the women's movement has made many professional men and women aware of the need to help women overcome some of the debilitating effects of their sex-role indoctrination. Research into this area has mushroomed recently, as have workshops that actively seek to instill confidence in timid and nonassertive women through the utilization of techniques perfected in the laboratory. Before describing the results of a typical experimental study in this area however, it is instructive to note the theoretical differences among psychoanalysts, Rogerians, and behavior therapists in their views of the origins and treatment of these skill deficits in women. The psychoanalysts, for example, view the timid behavior and the accompanying anxiety as an outgrowth of repressed traumatic learning experiences in early childhood. They might then try to give the person an understanding of the origins of the problem. By so doing, they hope that a reliving of the painful experiences will result in a person with a strengthened ego who is more assertive in dialogues with others. The Rogerian, in contrast, would probably view the timid behavior as largely resulting from conditional parental regard. His or her treatment orientation would focus on the creation of a nonthreatening environment in which the person would be able to overcome her nonassertiveness and become more fully functioning.

The behavior therapist would regard the nonassertive behavior as the product of a faulty learning experience. He would maintain that she has learned maladaptive habits which can be changed through the new learning procedures. In one recent study, for example, an experimenter-therapist constructed an elaborate assertiveness training procedure designed to help nonassertive undergraduate women become more assertive (Rathus, 1973). All the women were volunteers who had expressed a desire to be more assertive and outgoing. The experimenter met with the women and proceeded to show them videotapes of assertive models demonstrating the appropriate way to respond in various situations. There were seven videotapes, and they saw one each week. In addition, the women were required to practice twenty types of assertive behaviors in their daily contacts with people and to record for each assertive response practiced the date, the situation, what was done or said, and the outcome of the event or the result of using the particular type of assertion. Table 16.2 provides a list of some of the assertive responses the women were told to use. In contrast to a control group of women who received no training, the results showed that the women who received training showed less fear of disagreement with others and much more assertive behavior.

This study used videotape modeling and practice of assertive responses in actual situations; other studies have used procedures involving covert modeling—that is, procedures where nonassertive women imagine watching an assertive model, covert and overt rehearsal of appropriate behaviors in which women practice assertive arguments by repeating them privately or aloud, and role playing in which women act assertively in situations similar to those they face in real life. Research shows that the use of these techniques is typically quite effective

TABLE 16.2 Nine Types of Assertive Responses

1. Assertive Talk. Do not let others take advantage of you. Demand your right. Insist upon being treated with fairness and justice. Examples: "I was here first," "I'd like more coffee, please," "Excuse me, but I have another appointment," "Please turn down the radio," "This place is a pigsty," "You have kept me waiting here for half an hour," "This steak is well-done and I ordered it medium rare."

2. Feeling Talk. Express your likes and dislikes spontaneously. Be open and frank about your feelings. Do not bottle up emotions. Answer questions honestly. Examples: "What a marvelous shirt," "I am so sick of that man," "How great you look!" "I hate this cold," "I'm tired as hell," "Since you ask, I much prefer you in another type of outfit!"

3. Greeting Talk. Be outgoing and friendly with people you would like to know better. Do not avoid people because of shyness, because you do not know what to say. Smile brightly at people. Look and sound pleased to see them. Examples: "Hi, how are you?" "Hello, I haven't seen you in months," "What are you doing with yourself these days?" "How do you like working at————?" "Taking any good courses?" "What's been happening with so and so?"

4. Disagreeing Passively and Actively. When you disagree with someone, do not feign agreement for the sake of "keeping the peace" by smiling, nodding, or paying close attention. Change the topic. Look away. Disagree actively and emotionally when you are sure of your ground.

5. Asking Why. When you are asked to do something that does not sound reasonable or enjoyable by a person in power or authority, ask WHY you should do it. You are an adult and should not accept authority alone. Insist upon explanations from teachers, relatives and other authority figures that are convincing. Have it understood that you will live up to voluntary commitments and be open to reasonable suggestions, but that you are not to be ordered about at anyone's whim.

6. Talking about Oneself. When you have done something worthwhile or interesting, let others know about it. Let people know how you feel about things. Relate your experiences. Do not monopolize conversations, but do not be afraid to bring them around to yourself when it is appropriate.

7. Agreeing with Compliments. Do not depreciate yourself or become flustered when someone compliments you with sincerity. At the very least, offer an equally sincere "Thank You." Or reward the complimenter by saying, "That's an awfully nice thing to say. I appreciate it." In other words, reward rather than punish others for complimenting you. When appropriate, extend compliments. For example, if someone says, "What a beautiful sweater!" respond, "Isn't it a lovely color? I had a hard time finding it."

8. Avoiding Trying to Justify Opinions. Be reasonable in discussions, but when someone goes out of his way to dominate a social interaction by taking issue with any comments you offer, say something like, "Are you always so disagreeable?" or "I have no time to waste arguing with you," or "You seem to have a great deal invested in being right regardless of what you say, don't you?"

9. Looking People in the Eye. Do not avoid the gaze of others. When you argue, express an opinion, or greet a person, look him directly in the eye.

Adapted from S. A. Rathus, "Instigation of Assertive Behavior through Videotape—Mediated Assertive Models and Directed Practice," 1973, p. 59.

in producing positive changes in performances. The same kinds of procedures have also proved effective in helping shy college men overcome their inhibitions and learn more appropriate ways of relating to women (Twentyman and McFall, 1975).

Behavior Modification Through Self-Control Manipulations

Self-control involves the active manipulation of internal and external variables by individuals to achieve desired outcomes. In order to accomplish their goals, people must be able to identify the variables that control or determine their behavior and know how to change these variables to achieve the desired outcomes. This may sound like a simple process, but it is not. Most of us are not very systematic about observing our own actions, probably because it is a time-consuming and tedious business and we are usually too busy behaving to detach ourselves and make the necessary observations. Yet, successful self-management requires that we observe our actions systematically. We must not only identify the behavior we want to maintain or change in some way, but we must record its occurrence in our lives for purposes of feedback and evaluation. Successful self-control requires that we also change the environment so that the stimuli which control the behavior or the consequences which follow it are changed. Altering the consequences generally involves the administration of self-rewards and self-punishments following the behavior in question. These reinforcers can be either internal or external. Internal reinforcers include self-praise, self-criticism, and rewarding or aversive mental images. External reinforcers include money or some other tangible rewarding objects (an extra piece of cake or a desired vacation), or taking away some desired objects (forgoing a vacation or a movie, giving up some money, or adding four extra miles to a jogging routine) (Mahoney and Thoresen, 1975, pp. 22–25).

Self-management procedures have been utilized successfully in the treatment of such diverse problems as alcoholism, ineffective study habits, smoking, insomnia, obsessions, fetishisms, and obesity. Since a detailed examination of the ways in which these various problems were reduced or eliminated via self-control procedures is beyond the scope of this text, we will consider only the manner in which these procedures have been used to help obese people lose weight.

Rather than attribute the origins of eating problems to unresolved conflicts centering around feeding in the oral stage, as Freudians might, behavior therapists have conducted a number of experimental studies which show that eating behavior is tremendously influenced by a variety of environmental cues. For example, it has been found that, in comparison to normal-weight individuals, obese people are less responsive to internal hunger cues but more responsive to a wide range of food-related cues in the external environment (Schachter, 1967). Obese individuals are more susceptible than normal-weight people to attractive food displays, clocks indicating "mealtime," and to seeing other people eating (Mahoney and Thoresen, 1974, p. 40). Obese people are also found to eat in a wide variety of settings. For example, in the home situation, they may eat while watching television, while reading, while on the phone, at bedtime, and so forth. They may also eat at athletic contests, at business meetings, at the movies, and in a number of other settings outside the home.

To help them reduce, therapists typically require them to follow these procedures (Penick et al., 1974). First, they are asked to keep daily records of the amount, time, and situational circumstances of their eating. For most people, this is an aversive practice and there is much grumbling and complaining about it. Nevertheless, therapists find that the clients eventually acknowledge that keeping the records was very helpful, since it increased their awareness of what and how much they ate, the speed with which they ate, and the large variety of environmental and psychological situations associated with eating. For example, one woman reported that she became aware for the first time that anger stimulated her eating. Thereafter, when she began to feel angry, she left the kitchen, went into another room, and wrote down how she felt, thereby bringing her anger under control.

Once the clients have identified the parameters of their eating behavior, the next step usually involves the modification and control of the various stimuli that govern eating. Clients are taught to eat only in one place (the dining room) and not in others. By gradually narrowing the various situational stimuli, clients can bring their eating behavior under the control of a specific and appropriate set of cues. Other alterations of environmental variables might include bringing only low-calorie foods into the home and making fattening foods less available; learning to eat in the company of people who eat in moderation and not, if possible, in the presence of people who model inappropriate eating behavior; and posting a weight chart on a "pig poster" on the refrigerator (Mahoney and Thoresen, 1974, pp. 41–42). A more extended list of stimulus-control techniques is provided in Table 16.3.

Although therapists generally agree that these procedures may help to institute self-controlling behavior, they also insist that the maintenance of these behaviors will depend upon the clients' ability to prearrange the consequences of violating or adhering to preestablished goals through the application of self-reward and punishment.

One strategy of self-reward and punishment utilized by therapists to help their clients control their weight involves having clients deposit money with them at the outset of treatment and then allowing those who have lost weight to take back some of the money. If they have not lost weight, on the other hand, they punish themselves by giving up some of the money permanently (Mahoney, Moura, and Wade, 1973). Another self-punishment technique involves training clients to imagine the aversive consequences of overeating. First clients are asked to

TABLE 16.3　Stimulus-Control Techniques for Obesity

1. Limit the Cues You Associate with Eating. Eat in one specific room and preferably at one place in that room. This means that eating should become a "pure-experience," that is, it must be separate from other activities that might gain stimulus control over it and/or reinforce it. When you eat, eat—but avoid other simultaneous activities (such as television viewing, phone conversations, pleasure reading, and studying). This means that an ongoing activity (for example, watching a football game) must be interrupted while you eat.

2. Do Not Eat to Avoid Waste. Childhood training and the desire not to waste money have resulted in countless extra calories for people who can't stand seeing food thrown out. A woman who consumes her children's unfinished meals is one example. Another is the individual who stuffs himself at a restaurant in order to consume everything that has been included in an entree. Get in the habit of leaving small portions of food on your plate so that the cue for meal termination will not be an empty bowl or a clean plate.

3. Restrict Your Food Intake Ahead of Time. Bountiful bowls of food on the table are powerful cues for eating (and overeating). Prepare your plate ahead of time, put the foods away (or place them in another room), and then sit down to your meal. Arrange food portions so that they look larger by spreading them out over a plate or by using small or shallow dishes. When you are eating at a restaurant, restrict tempting cues ahead of time. For example, request that the potato or bread be omitted from your plate.

4. Make Fattening Foods Less Available and Nonfattening Foods More Available. You are much more likely to eat fattening snacks if they are stored in your own kitchen instead of at the local store. Don't buy high-calories snacks. It's easier to avoid them if you always shop for groceries after a full meal (never on an empty stomach). If you must keep sweets in the house (for example, for children's lunches), buy brands that you dislike, store them in an inconspicuous place (the back of a cabinet rather than the cookie jar), and instruct your children to get them for themselves. Keep a large supply of safe snacks on hand at all times (for example, popcorn, raw vegetables, diet soda).

5. Alter the Eating Process. Eating slowly reduces the quantity of food consumed. Swallow one bite of food before putting the next bite on your fork. (This may entail actually putting the fork down between bites.) Toward the end of a meal, get in the habit of interrupting your eating for two to five minutes to gain control over the behavior (and to dissociate it with such stimuli as a clean plate or an empty bowl).

6. Modify the Physiological Cues for Eating. Many people eat in response to internal sensations of "emptiness" or "hunger pangs." Eat high-bulk, low-calorie foods (such as celery, carrot sticks, and popcorn) or drink a large amount of liquid before or during the meal to produce a sensation of "fullness." Moreover, to maintain an appropriate blood-sugar level and to avoid cravings for sweets, eat high-protein foods (particularly early in the day) and use sugar substitutes extensively (not only in coffee but also in baking and meal preparation). Reduce intake of nu-

trients that produce large blood-sugar swings (for example, caffeine, processed sugar, white bread, and noodle products).

7. Arrange Social Cues That Encourage Appropriate Eating. Many people find the presence of certain other people a cue for more moderate and adaptive eating patterns. If this is the case, arrange to eat only in the presence of those people. On the other hand, if some persons model inappropriate eating habits, arrange to eat separately from them.

8. Develop Nonfattening Responses to Emotional Upset. Many people report very strong eating temptations when they are anxious, frustrated, or depressed. The association between these emotions and eating has two possible bases: (1) many children grow up learning that foods (particularly sweets) are used to soothe them and to lift their spirits, and (2) emotional upsets actually represent mild physiological arousal that under certain conditions may lead to low blood sugar and cravings for food. To modify the association between emotions and food, develop alternative reactions that are incompatible with eating. For example, you can learn to relax in emotion-provoking situations by engaging in certain breathing exercises.

From Michael J. Mahoney and Carl E. Thoresen, eds., *Self-Control: Power to the Person*, 1974, pp. 41–42.

construct a list of especially noxious consequences of overeating. These consequences might include fear of being rejected socially, incurring physical diseases, overhearing others ridicule their obesity, and the like. These aversive stimuli are then used to suppress eating behavior by applying them just before eating (Kazdin, 1975, pp. 201–202).

One experimenter had clients purchase a pound of suet, which was cut into 16 one-ounce pieces and placed in a plastic bag in the refrigerator. Clients were required to visualize this fat on their bodies. Then for every pound they lost, they were allowed to remove one ounce of fat from the bag and to imagine its removal from their bodies. For every pound gained, they had to get extra suet from the meat market and add it to their fat bag. When clients lost the entire fat bag, they were given prizes (a book or different kinds of cosmetics) and praised lavishly by the group members. These various treatments proved quite effective in helping clients to reduce, in comparison to control subjects who did not undergo any treatment. In addition, weight loss was maintained over a six-month period (Penick et al., 1974, pp. 291–299).

The four major cognitive-behavior modification techniques we have just reviewed provide only a sample of the methods in the arsenal of the behavior therapists. We have seen in previous chapters, for example, the ways in which modeling, token economies, and shock therapies can be utilized to help people overcome crippling problems. Not all these techniques, however, are effective. In some instances they do not bring about significant changes. In addition, some techniques work better than others with particular kinds of problems. Some of the techniques also work better if used in various combinations, whereas others tend to be more effective if utilized singly. Finally, there have been occasional abuses of client rights by some behavior modification therapists. These abuses seem, to me at least, to be less a consequence of deliberate Machiavellian intent and more one of ignorance and insensitivity on the part of investigators to the ethical implications of their research. Clearly, too, investigators differ in their ideas of morally correct behavior. Some investigators have few, if any, qualms about using electric shock to modify certain behaviors; others recoil from the mere thought. Whatever the differences in the value systems of experimenters and therapists, the focus must be on the safeguarding and protection of clients' rights. The struggle to maintain these safeguards and to enlighten investigators about pertinent ethical issues is a unending one. Although it is often painful, it is a task no responsible investigator in the profession will try to avoid.

CRITICISMS OF MISCHEL'S POSITION

It should be noted at the outset that Mischel's position does not as yet have the status of a fully developed theory. Rather, it is a framework for reconceptualizing personality which he hopes will be developed more completely in the future. At this stage, Mischel seems to be content to provoke discussion of various issues in personality psychology that have been largely ignored by investigators in the discipline. What, then, are some of the criticisms of his position that have been voiced by personality psychologists?

First, critics have implied that the new theory treats the study of individual differences as unimportant, that it views situations as the primary determinants of behavior, and that it holds that people show no consistencies in behavior. Mischel says this accusation is untrue. He thinks person variables are very important and must be considered in theorizing. He also maintains that he has purposely refrained from becoming embroiled in an argument over the relative importance of person versus situation variables because there is no satisfactory answer to the question when it is posed in this form. In other words, the question of whether situations *or* persons are the more important determiners of behavior is unanswerable:

> . . . while some situations may be powerful determinants of behavior, others are likely to be exceedingly trival. The relative importance of individual differences (person variables) will depend upon the situation selected, the type of behavior assessed, the particular individual differences sampled, and the purpose of the assessment. (Mischel, 1973, p. 255)

Thus, his theory attempts to account for the contributions of both person and situational variables.

Next, Mischel maintains that there are obviously consistencies in human behavior. If there were not, memory would be a useless construct. It is apparent that we often rely on past experiences to guide our behavior in given situations. If we have voted for Democratic candidates in the past and they have been successful in implementing social programs we strongly support, we might continue to vote for such candidates if they chose to campaign for reelection. If we adopt a particular study pattern in preparing for an important exam and it proves successful, we may be more likely to rely on it again in preparing for other important examinations. If we find that the food offered in the university dining halls tastes bad and that there is a fine restaurant near the campus, we may find ourselves canceling our university dining contracts and eating at the off-campus restaurant.

Yet, although we may show consistency in behavior, especially in situations which are similar in meaning to us, we may change our behavior dramatically in response to even slight alterations in the features of the immediate situation. Long-standing and satisfactory relationships between marriage partners have ended because one of the spouses engaged in a mild flirtation; a minor malfunction in a traffic signal can mean life or death to motorists, depending upon their awareness of the problem. Thus, Mischel maintains the model recognizes both the consistencies and diversities in behavior and seeks to understand the cognitive and social learning conditions that foster or hinder their occurrence in human behavior. In other words, the model seeks to understand the conditions controlling the occurrence of generalization and discrimination processes in behavior (Mischel, 1973, pp. 258–259).

In response to Mischel's criticism that traditional person-oriented approaches have utilized concepts that are too globally defined and poorly measured, critics have argued that the fact that many assessment procedures are unreliable does not mean that the approach has no merit. It just means that we have to refine the measurement procedures. The criticism of concept ambiguity leveled by Mischel at the person-oriented theorists can also be made against Mischel's own position. The terms in his cognitive social learning position are generally more precisely defined and measured than those utilized by person-oriented theorists, but they are certainly not devoid of ambiguity. In particular, there has been controversy recently in the social learning camp concerning the proper definition and measurement of self-reinforcement (Bandura, 1977).

Perhaps Mischel's most controversial contention is that the person-oriented approach has little empirical utility. In support of his argument, Mischel cites evidence that the correlations between the person's responses in different situations are typically between .20 and .30. That is, Mischel maintains that we cannot predict accurately how a person will behave without taking into account the moderating influences of situational factors.

Critics have attacked Mischel on this point in several ways. First, one prominent researcher has maintained that there is empirical evidence which shows that the correlations are much higher than .20 to .30. He cites studies in which correlations range from .40 to .73, suggesting that Mischel's contention is erroneous (Hogan, DeSoto, and Solano, 1977). Even where the correlations are low, critics maintain that there are a number of valid reasons for these outcomes. One investigator has argued that the correlations would be higher if investigators would rely on *several* personality variables for the same individual in making predictions about his behavior (Alker, 1972). That is, it would be possible to increase the magnitude of predictions about individuals by using several personality variables in combination. If we wanted, for example, to predict the test performance of students, we might compare not only students with low and high test anxiety, but those with high test anxiety, low intelligence, low self-esteem, and an external orientation against those with low test anxiety, high intelligence, high self-esteem, and an internal control orientation.

The same critic also maintains that person variables may yield higher correlations with behavior if investigators use a "moderator variable" approach. That is, investigators should assess the ways in which the person's behavior is affected or *moderated* by the situation in which it is made and by the personality characteristics of the people in the situation with the person. This argument appears to be consistent with Mischel's own argument that the person's behavior is shaped or moderated by situational influences. In fact, Mischel's supporters maintain that he is cognizant of and generally sympathetic to the moderator variable approach (Bem, 1972).

A final criticism is that, although Mischel has generally catalogued quite well some of the problems with a strictly person- or situation-oriented approach, this does not necessarily mean that the interactional approach is superior to the other viewpoints. As mentioned earlier, the model he proposes is still in a formative stage. There is much conceptual and empirical work to be done before the scientific worth of the position can be clearly established.

A FINAL SUMMING UP

We have now reviewed the basic concepts and principles of many of the major personality theories. You should now have a better understanding of and appreciation for their unique strengths and weaknesses. You should also have been making an active attempt to evaluate the scientific worth of these positions by noting how well they meet or fail to meet the criteria outlined in Chapter 1. If you have, you now know how difficult a task it is and why more people have not undertaken it. You should also be cognizant of the fact that the judgments I have made in this regard will strike some professionals as presumptuous and premature. They will undoubtedly argue, and correctly so, that there is no agreement among scientists regarding the criteria to be used in evaluating theories. Even if there were, it could be argued that there is little agreement on which criteria are most and which are least important. Yet, as mentioned earlier, I believe that such tentative judgments are necessary if we are to continue to make progress in this discipline.

The materials in this chapter were designed primarily to provide you with an introduction to some of the controversial issues currently being debated in personality psychology. This debate is a healthy sign of interest on the part of investigators in the resolution of some of the problems that have plagued personality psychology. Out of it, we hope, will come a new, revitalized conception of personality that will result in an even better understanding of the functioning of the person.

DISCUSSION QUESTIONS

1. Define personality from a cognitive social learning perspective. How does this definition differ from those offered by the Freudians?

2. What are some of the limitations of the person-oriented view? What are some of the major problems with the situation-oriented view?

3. Do you think it is necessary to retain concepts like the shadow and peak experience in order to explain human behavior adequately? Give reasons for your answer.

4. Why would you expect the correlation between somatotonia and mesomorphy to be low?

5. In your opinion, what are some of the primary personal and situational determinants of a happy marriage? Define a "happy" marriage before proceeding with your analysis.

6. What is self-control? How would you proceed to change a habit— for example, overeating, smoking, drinking too much—that you consider undesirable? How would you change your environment to ensure that you will be prepared fully for your next examination?

7. In what ways is the study of self-control processes compatible with a person's attempt to self-actualize?

8. What are some of the major differences between the traditional psychodynamic approaches and the new behavioral approaches to therapy?

9. What is systematic desensitization, and how does it differ from covert sensitization?

10. Do you agree that the proposed cognitive social learning approach to the study of personality has greater scientific utility than the more traditional positions? Why or why not?

NOTES

H. A. Alker, "Is Personality Situationally Specific or Intrapsychically Consistent?" *Journal of Personality*, 1972, **40**, 1–16.

A. Bandura, "Self-Reinforcement: Theoretical and Methodological Considerations," *Behaviorism*, 1977, **4**, 135–155.

D. J. Bem, "Constructing Cross-Situational Consistencies in Behavior: Some Thoughts on Alker's Critique of Mischel," *Journal of Personality*, 1972, **40**, 17–26.

J. R. Cautela, "Covert Sensitization," *Psychological Reports*, 1967, **20**, 459–468.

 N. S. Endler and D. Magnusson, "Toward an Interactional Psychology of Personality," *Psychological Bulletin*, 1976, **83**, 956–974.

S. Freud, *The Ego and the Id*, trans. J. Riviere, rev. and ed. J. Strachey (New York: Norton, 1960).

R. Hogan, C. B. DeSoto, and C. Solano, "Traits, Tests, and Personality Research," *American Psychologist*, 1977, **32**, 255–264.

C. G. Jung, "Aion," in V. S. de Laszlo, ed., *Psyche and Symbol* (Garden City, N.Y.: Doubleday Anchor, 1958).

A. E. Kazdin, *Behavior Modification in Applied Settings* (Homewood, Ill.: Dorsey, 1975).

G. A. Kelly, *The Psychology of Personal Constructs*, Vol. 1 (New York: Norton, 1955).

A. A. Lazarus, "Group Therapy of Phobic Disorders by Systematic Desensitization," *Journal of Abnormal and Social Psychology*, 1961, **63**, 504–510. Abstracted from A. Bandura, *Principles of Behavior Modification* (New York: Holt, Rinehart and Winston, 1969), pp. 455–456.

M.J. Mahoney, N. G. M. Moura, and T. C. Wade, "Relative Efficacy of Self-Reward, Self-Punishment, and Self-Monitoring Techniques for Weight Loss," *Journal of Consulting and Clinical Psychology*, 1973, **40**, 404–407.

M. J. Mahoney and C. E. Thoresen, eds., *Self-Control: Power to the Person* (Monterey, Calif.: Brooks/Cole, 1974).

B. M. Maletzky, "'Assisted' Covert Sensitization in the Treatment of Exhibitionism," *Journal of Consulting and Clinical Psychology*, 1974, **42**, 34–40.

A. Maslow, *Toward a Psychology of Being* (New York: Van Nostrand, 1962).

B. Migler and J. Wolpe, "Automated Self-Desensitization: A Case Report," *Behavior Research and Therapy*, 1967, **5**, 133–135. Abstracted from A. Bandura, *Principles of Behavior Modification* (New York: Holt, Rinehart, and Winston, 1969), p. 435.

W. Mischel, *Personality and Assessment* (New York: Wiley, 1968).

W. Mischel, "Toward a Cognitive Social Learning Reconceptualization of Personality," *Psychological Review*, 1973, **80**, 252–283.

W. Mischel, *Introduction to Personality*, 2nd ed. (New York: Holt, Rinehart and Winston, 1976).

S. B. Penick, R. Filion, S. Fox, and A. J. Stunkard, "Behavior Modification in the Treatment of Obesity," in M. J. Mahoney and C. E. Thoresen, eds., *Self-Control: Power to the Person* (Monterey, Calif.: Brooks/Cole, 1974), pp. 291–299.

S. A. Rathus, "Instigation of Assertive Behavior through Videotape-Mediated Assertive Models and Directed Practice," *Behavior Research and Therapy*, 1973, **11**, 57–65.

S. Schachter, "Cognitive Effects on Bodily Funtioning: Studies of Obesity and Eating," in D. C. Glass, ed., *Neurophysiology and Emotion* (New York: Rockefeller University Press and Russell Sage, 1967), pp. 117–174.

C. E. Thoresen, "Behavioral Means and Humanistic Ends," in M. J. Mahoney and C. E. Thoresen, eds., *Self-Control: Power to the Person* (Monterey, Calif.: Brooks/Cole, 1974), pp. 308–322.

C. T. Twentyman and R. M. McFall, "Behavioral Training of Social Skills in Shy Males," *Journal of Consulting and Clinical Psychology*, 1975, **43**, 384–395.

J. Wine, "Test Anxiety and Direction of Attention," *Psychological Bulletin*, 1971, **76**, 92–104.

SUGGESTED READINGS

Alker, H. A. "Is Personality Situationally Specific or Intrapsychically Consistent?" *Journal of Personality*, 1972, **40**, 1–16.

Bem, D. J. "Constructing Cross-Situational Consistencies in Behavior: Some Thoughts on Alker's Critique of Mischel," *Journal of Personality*, 1972, **40**, 17–26.

Endler, N. S., and Magnusson, D. "Toward an Interactional Psychology of Personality," *Psychological Bulletin*, 1976, **83**, 956–974.

Hogan, R., DeSoto, C. B., and Solano, C. "Traits, Tests, and Personality Research," *American Psychologist*, 1977, **32**, 255–264.

Mahoney, M. J. Reflections on the Cognitive-Learning Trend in Psychotherapy, *American Psychologist*, 1977, **32**, 5–13.

Mischel, W. *Personality and Assessment*. New York: Wiley, 1968.

Mischel, W. "Toward a Cognitive Social Learning Reconceptualization of Personality," *Psychological Review*, 1973, **80**, 252–283.

GLOSSARY

Cognitive Social Learning Model. Theoretical position that attempts to account for individual differences in thought and behavior by examining the unique ways in which people actively utilize cognitive strategies based on prior learning experiences in reacting to and coping with demands posed by the environment.

Interactional Model of Personality. Position that attempts to account for personality functioning by examining the joint effects of person and situation variables on behavior.

Person—Oriented Theories. Positions that focus almost exclusively on the ways in which underlying, internal characteristics (person variables) control behavior.

Situationist. Investigator who believes that behavior is primarily controlled by situational variables.

Situation-Oriented Theories. Positions that focus almost exclusively on the ways in which situational parameters control behavior.

Name Index

Subject Index

reaction–formation, 33, 51; repression, 31, 51, 240; sublimation, 33, 51, 240; suppression, 32, 51; undoing, 34, 51

Ego-ideal, 31, 50

Electra complex, 37

Empirical law of effect, 188

Entropy, principle of, 57–58, 82

Environmental–mold traits, 168–185

Equivalence, principle of, 57, 82

Ergs, 154, 168, 185

Evaluation of theories: Adler's 99–101; Allport's, 147–149; Bandura's, 299–301; Cattell's, 180–183; Freud's, 46–48; Fromm's, 118–119; Jung's, 77–79; Kelly's, 212–213; Maslow's, 327–329; May's, 369–370; Rogers', 349–351; Sheldon's, 393–395; Skinner's, 249–251; Rotter's, 273–274

Exhortation, 206

Existential-Analytic Perspectives, defined, 371

Existentialism, 355–356, 371; origins of, 356; and psychoanalysis, 359–361; and Western science, 356–357

Expectancy, 259–260, 276

Experimental analysis of behavior, 240–241

Experimental method, 9, 19

Extinction, 235–236, 253

Extraversion, 61, 66–67, 82

Extraverted feeling type, 69, 82

Extraverted intuitive type, 71, 82

Extraverted sensing type, 70, 82

Extraverted thinking type, 68, 82

F

Factor analysis, 156–158, 185

Factor loadings, 157, 185

Fictional finalism, 88–89, 103

Field theory, 276

Fixation, 34, 50

Fixed-role sketch, 211

Fixed-role therapy, 215; example of, 210–211

Frame of orientation and devotion, 111, 120

Free association, 26, 50, 321

Freedom of movement, 260–261, 276

Free will, 230–232

Freud, S., biographical sketch, 25–29

Fromm, E., biographical sketch, 105–108

Fully functioning persons, 246, 353. *See also* Actualization processes

Functional analysis, 230–253

Functional autonomy, 141–142, 150

G

Genital character, 40

Genotype, 132, 150

Gray-Wheelwright test, 71

Growth; nature of, 336–337; therapeutic conditions fostering, 335–336

H

Human dilemma, 358

Humanistic biology, 312–313, 330

Humanistic communitarian socialism, 115–117, 120

Humanistic psychoanalysis, defined, 120

Humanistic psychology, 330; arguments for 306, 309

Hypothesis, 19

Hypothetical construct, 4, 19; differences between intervening variable and, 220–221

Hysteria, 26

I

Id, 30, 50

Idiographic approach, 150

Imitation learning, 222. *See also* Observational learning

Independent variable, 9, 19

Individual Psychology, defined, 86, 103

Individuation, 73–74

Inductive-hypothetico-deductive spiral, 155–156, 185